"Out of the 1960 election, a drama unprecedented in modern times for the new forces and techniques it introduced, the shadowy imponderables it left in its wake, he has fashioned a narrative as coolly reasoned as an honest pollster's judgment, as hotly exciting as the roar of a crowd that smells victory in the air around its candidate." —John K. Hutchens, *N. Y. Herald Tribune*

"A masterpiece of contemporary history full of deep insights into political power in America and how our democracy works in choosing the President. It gripped me from beginning to end as very few books have in recent years." —William L. Shirer

"More than a fascinating account of how one man succeeded in reaching the White House, while others failed; it is a graduate lesson in the rough, relentless, subtle and devious working of American politics. It is a magnificent job of reporting, but it is also history—and there is a Pulitzer Prize for history."

—Ben Ray Redman, *The Saturday Review*

"To crowd into a story, of which, after all, we have known the outcome for some time, so much suspense is a masterly achievement: but his book is more than a cliff-hanger . . . he produces one of the most exciting and significant pieces of socio-political analysis for years. . . . As journalism [it] is unsurpassed; as a record and textbook it is invaluable; but as a tribute to the sagacity of the American people and, above all, the shrewd, lasting excellence of their political system, it is a book to hearten all of us who must live our lives in its shadow—or its sunlight." —Bernard Levin, *The Spectator* (London)

Other SIGNET Books of Special Interest

THE
MAKING
OF
THE
PRESIDENT
1960

Theodore H. White

A SIGNET BOOK

Published by THE NEW AMERICAN LIBRARY

SIGNET TRADEMARK REG. U.S. PAT. OFF. AND FOREIGN COUNTRIES
REGISTERED TRADEMARK—MARCA REGISTRADA
HECHO EN CHICAGO, U.S.A.

*SIGNET BOOKS are published by
The New American Library, Inc.,
1301 Avenue of the Americas, New York, New York 10019*

PRINTED IN THE UNITED STATES OF AMERICA

For Heyden and David

AUTHOR'S NOTE

THIS BOOK is an attempt to tell part of the story of how the Americans chose their President in 1960.

For no man can tell it all—either now or much later. The transaction in power by which a President is chosen is so vastly complicated that even those most intimately involved in it, even those who seek the office, can never know more than a fragment of it. For it is the nature of politics that men must always act on the basis of uncertain fact, must make their judgments in haste on the basis of today's report by instinct and experience shaped years before in other circumstances. Were it otherwise, then politics would not be what they are now—the art of government and leadership; politics would be an exact science in which our purposes and destiny could be left to great impersonal computers.

It was my thought that though later historians would tell the story of the quest for power in 1960 in more precise terms with greater wealth of established fact, there might, nonetheless, be some permanent value in the effort of a contemporary reporter to catch the mood and the strains, the weariness, elation and uncertainties of the men who sought to lead America in the decade of the sixties. For, to me, the central fact of politics has always been the quality of leadership under the pressure of great forces.

The reading I have made here of the seven men who in 1960 aspired to govern the American people is an entirely personal one, and many will disagree. Yet it is the best that this citizen could make. I began this book in the fall of 1959 and tried to follow as many of the men involved as I could, both in travel and in thought, from then until November 8th, 1960. I have spent the months since putting on paper what I saw and learned in these travels.

There are all too many people who helped me to list them all by name. And there is a further complication in contemporary political reporting. A historian must list his sources and attribute fact to exact reference. But a reporter's obligation is to protect the privacy of those who have befriended him with information. Therefore, since I wrote this book as a reporter, rather than giving an unbalanced table of acknowledgments, I prefer to leave all my kind and generous friends unmentioned except as text and footnote make specific reference.

I cannot, however, fail to invite the reader's attention to two of my associates who have been absolutely essential in giving this story whatever readable merit it may have. They are Chouteau Dyer, whose reportorial skills and even greater skill in the rhythm of our language, have contributed so much; and Shirley Farmer, whose judgment, grace and encouragement have stimulated and sustained so large a part of this effort.

Beyond that, I owe two general acknowledgments:

First, to the politicians of America—men whom I have found over the long years the pleasantest, shrewdest and generally the most honorable of companions. Their counsel, Republican and Democrat alike in state after state, has shaped every page of this book.

Second, I must thank my comrades of the press—whose reporting at every level of American politics purifies, protects and refreshes our system from year to year. Without their shared confidences and magnificent public dispatches the writing of this book would have been entirely impossible.

CONTENTS

PART ONE

PART TWO

PART

ONE

Chapter 1

WAITING

IT WAS invisible, as always.

They had begun to vote in the villages of New Hampshire at midnight, as they always do, seven and a half hours before the candidate rose. His men had canvassed Hart's Location in New Hampshire days before, sending his autographed picture to each of the twelve registered voters in the village. They knew that they had five votes certain there, that Nixon had five votes certain—and that two were still undecided. Yet it was worth the effort, for Hart's Location's results would be the first flash of news on the wires to greet millions of voters as they opened their morning papers over coffee. But from there on it was unpredictable—invisible.

By the time the candidate left his Boston hotel at 8:30, several million had already voted across the country—in schools, libraries, churches, stores, post offices. These, too, were invisible, but it was certain that at this hour the vote was overwhelmingly Republican. On election day America is Republican until five or six in the evening. It is in the last few hours of the day that working people and their families vote, on their way home from work or after supper; it is then, at evening, that America goes Democratic if it goes Democratic at all. All of this is invisible, for it is the essence of the act that as it happens it is a mystery in which millions of people each fit one fragment of a total secret together, none of them knowing the shape of the whole.

What results from the fitting together of these secrets is, of course, the most awesome transfer of power in the world—the power to marshal and mobilize, the power to send men to kill or be killed, the power to tax and destroy, the power to create and the responsibility to do so, the power to guide and the responsibility to heal—all committed into the hands of one man. Heroes and philosophers, brave men and vile, have since Rome and Athens tried to make this particular manner of transfer of power work effectively; no people has succeeded at it better, or over a longer period of time, than the Americans. Yet as the transfer of this power takes place, there is

13

nothing to be seen except an occasional line outside a church or school, or a file of people fidgeting in the rain, waiting to enter the booths. No bands play on election day, no troops march, no guns are readied, no conspirators gather in secret headquarters. The noise and the blare, the bands and the screaming, the pageantry and oratory of the long fall campaign, fade on election day. All the planning is over, all effort spent. Now the candidates must wait.

The candidate drove from his hotel at the head of his cavalcade to the old abandoned West End branch of the Boston Public Library. Here in these reading rooms, the countless immigrants and their children of Boston's West End for two generations had, until a year ago, first set their feet on the ladder that was to take them up and out of the slums. Now, deserted and desolate, the empty library was the balloting place of the Third Precinct, Sixth Ward, and here at 8:43 he voted, signing the register as John F. Kennedy of 122 Bowdoin Street, Boston.

He was tense, it seemed, as he voted, thronged and jostled by the same adhesive train of reporters who had followed him, thronging and jostling, for three months across the country; only now his wife was with him in the press, and he was uncomfortable at how the pushing might affect her, she being eight months pregnant. He let himself be photographed as he came from the booth, and then the last cavalcade began, in familiar campaign order—photographers' car first, candidate's car second (the top of the convertible shut, for he did not want his wife to catch cold), security car next, three press buses following. It moved swiftly out of the West End, down through the grimy blight of Scollay Square, under the tunnel to East Boston and the airport. This had been his first political conquest—the Eleventh Congressional District of Massachusetts, immigrants' land, full of Irish, Italians, Jews, some Negroes, few Yankees.

For a full year of journeys he had bounded up the steps of this same airplane in a grace act that had become familiar to all his trailing entourage—a last handshake to dignitaries, an abrupt turning away and quickstep run up the stairs, a last easy fling of the hand in farewell to the crowd cheering his departure, and then into the cozy homelike Mother Ship and security.

This morning he walked up the stairs slowly, a dark-blue mohair overcoat over his gray suit, bareheaded, slightly stooped. He was very tired. He paused at the top of the stairs and, still stooped, turned away. Then he slowly turned back to the door but made no gesture. Then he disappeared. He was off to Hyannisport: a quick flight of twenty-five minutes; no disturbance; the plane full of messages of congratulation; the welcoming group at the Cape shrunk to a few score—and no more speeches to make.

As he arrived at Hyannisport, accompanied by more than a hundred correspondents and more than eighty staff members from the other planes, the tension broke ridiculously for a moment. Many of this group had followed him now for some 44,000 miles of campaigning since Labor Day, and one of the reporters, strained, caught him, insisting she was being prevented from observing him closely, deprived of her proper rotation in the "pool" choice of reporters who are closest to him. Gravely, and because he was fond of her and knew her to be devoted to him, and because, moreover, this is a man who never forgets either friend or enemy, he turned and said, "You and I will never be apart, Mary." And yet he knew, and everyone knew, that if his hope, which she shared, came true, he would be apart, unreachably, from these people who had been his friends.

A honking cavalcade of local politicians had gathered to lead him through the town. But he could not face one more campaign trip and, turning to a car driven by his cousin, Anne Gargan, he asked her to drive him to his family's summer cottages, already surrounded and barricaded by police. On the way orders were given to the police escort to separate the huge press train from his own car as he drove home. It was the first time anyone could remember that he had sought such isolation this year.

When he came again to greet the press and people, he would be the next President, close to no one. Or else he would be an also-ran, a footnote in the history books. Now there was nothing to do but wait.

Hyannisport sparkled in the sun that day, as did all New England. Hyannisport is the name of a hundred-odd cottages and summer homes that sprawl along the edges of Nantucket Sound just west and adjacent to the village of Hyannis (population not quite 6,000), which is part of Barnstable Township, county seat of Barnstable County, and summer center of the most fashionable area of Cape Cod's summer season. The houses are large and roomy, clapboard and shingle, white and brown, separated from one another across well-tended lawns by hedges or New England stone walls. Hyannisport was molded in the best and simplest of the old New England manner, its homes less ostentatious and snugger in style than the summer homes of the Long Island Hamptons that catch the overflow of New York's wealthy. For generations the good families of Boston had built these homes for solid comfort; the Kennedys, thirty-two years ago, were the first of the Irish to invade its quiet. A large compound encloses a number of homes at the end of Scudder Avenue where it reaches to the water; there Joseph P. Kennedy had bought a seventeen-room house to shelter his amazing brood of children. As the years passed, his son Jack had bought another house within the same compound, a few hundred feet away; and a few years later another son, Bobby, had acquired a third. Together the three houses form a triangle on a smooth green lawn that runs off into the dune grass before plunging to the sands of the beach. (Today the father's home flew the American flag at full mast.)

The local community had never been too happy about the Kennedys, aliens and intruders, and though some, particularly those who lived close, had become friends, most of the neighbors had been upset during the summer of 1960 when, after the nomination, the horde of newspapermen, staff, and curiosity-driven sight-seers that always surrounds a candidate boil'-' up in their quiet streets. The Civic Committee had met informally to control this development after the Los Angeles Convention; indeed, they suggested to the police that Hyannisport be totally sealed off from the public; the police had said that was impossible. Some members threatened to hold a protest meeting. To appease their resentment, Jacqueline Kennedy had begun the construction of a wooden palisade on Irving Avenue, where her front door is exactly thirteen feet from the road. But when her husband returned from the nomination, he ordered that the building of the palisade be stopped. He would do anything he could to cooperate with the Committee short of leaving Hyannisport; but this had been his home; he had spent his boyhood summers there; he planned to keep it as his home. So only a half-finished wooden palisade, a white-picket fence and a dozen local policemen separated the three cottages from the cars that carried the gawkers and peerers. The police were polite, efficient and cooperative; Barnstable Township was doing its best—even though that day it was voting Nixon over Kennedy by 4,515 to 2,783.

Now in November, the New England hardwoods—oak, elm and maple—had given up their color with their leaves, and the scrub pine of the Cape were beginning to show branch tips wind-burned and hurricane-scorched to a rust brown. A slight offshore breeze blew off the surfless waters; the dune grass and the feather-gray tufts of beach rushes bent gently to the breeze. A single gull wheeled over the house and the beach most of the morning, dipping toward the water when a glint suggested food. The sky was pure, the weather still a comfortable few degrees above freezing; the scudding white clouds were to break up by evening as the breeze freshened.

The weather was clear all across Massachusetts and New England, perfect for voting as far as the crest of the Alleghenies. But from Michigan through Illinois and the Northern Plains states it was cloudy: rain in Detroit and Chicago, light snow falling in some states on the approaches of the Rockies. The South was enjoying magnificently balmy weather which ran north as far as the Ohio River; so, too, was the entire Pacific Coast. The weather and the year's efforts were to call out the greatest free vote in the history of this or any other country—68,832,818 in all, 11 per cent more than was called out in 1956.

But there was nothing to do about it now. The people were already voting, their myriad impulses, intuitions, educations, heritages, fears and hopes creating the answer at the moment.

And so the candidate was restless.

He breakfasted at his father's house (across the lawn from his own), where nine of the Kennedy clan had already gathered at the board: he and his wife; his father and mother; brother Robert and sister-in-law Ethel; brother Edward and sister-in-law Joan; and brother-in-law Peter Lawford. In the next few hours of the morning all the rest were to arrive—sister Eunice Shriver and brother-in-law Sargent Shriver; sister Pat Lawford; sister Jean and brother-in-law Stephen Smith.

The candidate finished quickly, and trying to find a place where he might be alone to unwind, he went back to his own cottage and sat briefly on the porch in the sun, huddled under his overcoat against the chill, exhausted from the months that had passed. An aide approached him and chatted—they talked about D-Day; and the aide remembers his talking about the quality of waiting on that longest day, and Rommel. A newspaper plane flicked down over the house as they talked, slipping within 200 feet of the porch to get his photograph—if he were President-elect tomorrow, no plane would be allowed within thousands of feet of him. Some of his neighbors sent through the guards a horseshoe of red roses ten feet high for luck; it was passed on to him without inspection—no such gift would reach his hands again if he were elected, unless the Secret Service unwired and searched it for explosives. He remembered something he had forgotten, and sent a messenger to the plane to fetch it. It was an enormous sack of toys he was bringing back from his year-long journeyings for Caroline, his three-year-old daughter; the teddy bear, wrapped in a cellophane sack, was almost as big as Caroline herself. The returning messenger remembers the warm aroma of Brown Betty baking in the kitchen when he arrived. Briefly his father, Joseph P. Kennedy, came across the lawn to visit; someone observed the father's cupping grip on his son's clenched fist, but no one caught what they said.

At noon a troop of photographers arrived to photograph him ceremonially, and he gave them, as they described it, a taut, tense ten minutes. He emerged minutes later from his cottage, leading Caroline by the hand, and found his younger brothers, Bobby and Teddy, two activists, throwing a football back and forth on the lawn. He beckoned for the football and tossed it back and forth with them for a few minutes, Caroline watching; then he disappeared again into his own house to lunch alone with his wife. He was restless still, and after lunch he came across the lawn, dressed in a heavy sweater over a sports shirt and tan slacks (of his two shoes, one was glossily polished as usual—the other scuffed and dirty), to visit the command post set up in brother Bobby's cottage where an electronic tangle of thirty telephones, four wire-service teletype machines, and direct wires across the country had been established for the evening's vigil. Then, at 3:30 in the afternoon, he went back to his own cottage to try to nap.

It was fifteen minutes later by Pacific Coast Time, or 3:45, when Richard Nixon went back to his hotel room in Los Angeles to try to nap, too. The returns were beginning to come in; they were unreadable for both—yet disturbing. Nothing would be clear until early evening, if then.

A mile and a half away, at Hyannis' National Guard Armory, some 250 men and women of the local, national and international press had assembled—as had a similar group in Los Angeles, at the Ambassador Hotel—to prepare to report the reception of the night's tidings by the possible next President.

Two advance men of the Kennedy staff had appeared in Hyannis only a week before to convert this summer resort of the Cape, now largely shuttered and closed for the winter, into one of the two election capitals upon which the world would wait for news of the next American President. They had worked not only diligently but brilliantly, for the Democratic National Committee was at this point insolvent, and the total sum that could be allowed for operations in Hyannis was $800.00. If the Democrats lost, even this was too much, adding to a hopeless deficit.

The two advance men had persuaded the Massachusetts

National Guard to make available the Armory as press and communications center. A local television dealer was persuaded to contribute a dozen TV sets for use in the Armory and the Kennedy cottages. Western Union and American Telephone and Telegraph Company installed the hundred-odd special long-distance lines and fifty-odd teletypewriters; the news-gathering organizations would pay for those. The two advance men commandeered the ample housing space of the deserted summer resort and arbitrarily assigned the available rooms to the 250 correspondents expected, the eighty-plus staff personnel and their wives. The local lumber company contributed lumber; a local carpenter was persuaded it was an honor to build press-room partitions and platforms free. A local Ford dealer lent a number of new Fords, including ten Thunderbirds, for the use of the candidate's staff. Seats and benches were contributed by the local Protestant churches (the local Catholic church, for some delicate reason, was unwilling to do so). And then, early on the morning of voting day, the antiaircraft gun on which the National Guard unit of Barnstable County trains was removed from the main Armory hall; the benches were installed; seats were assigned alphabetically to all the 250 correspondents; the monk's cloth for the platform arrived from New York and was hung; and the news center was ready to report.

There is a traditional profile to the outline of news on election nights in America that is exciting and instructive, although it is also artificial, deceitful and imposed by the mechanics of counting. Voting in America is a simultaneous act of many citizens; by the time counting has begun, the act is over; only the sequence of tally makes it seem like a narrative drama; yet the drama, though false, is illuminating.

Returns usually start in upper New England, as the clean white hamlets of the northern hills, largely Protestant and overwhelmingly Republican, race each other to hit the news wires first and enjoy a fleeting midmorning fame as their names flash in early newspaper editions. By late afternoon returns from rural and mountain counties across the land begin to trickle in. Tennessee's rural areas close their polls at four in the afternoon; an hour later, eastern (or mountain) Kentucky begins to close its country polls, as does rural Alabama; so do Maine precincts with fewer than 300 voters. By this time substantial returns are in from Kansas (again, heavily Republican) where this year separate tally sheets and separate ballots permitted some Kansas communities to count the vote as it proceeded throughout the day. The early news reports that late afternoon papers show as people come home from work always bear tidings of a Republican lead.

Then, between six and seven, the tide changes. At six the polls close in urban Alabama, rural Illinois, Indiana, Mississippi, rural Oklahoma, South Carolina, urban Tennessee and Vermont. At 6:30 Arkansas, North Carolina and Ohio close their polls and begin to check in. And at seven comes the deluge: the Democrats from the big-city states.

A few minutes after seven the political silhouette of the industrial Northeast first becomes apparent—for Connecticut, a state that closes its polls at seven, votes on machines and counts quickly. At 7:15 the returns from Bridgeport, New Haven, Hartford—Democratic-industrial bastions all—are pouring in. Fifteen minutes later the slightly slower returns are totaled from the suburban towns of Fairfield County, the bedroom of New York's Republican executive class. Connecticut is a switch-voting state, and when Fairfield County's gut-Republicans balance out against the gut-Democrats of the factory towns, the first real clue to the nation's decision shows. At 7:30 on voting day of 1956, when Bridgeport repudiated Adlai E. Stevenson, it was instantly clear that this repudiation in a factory town meant that Eisenhower was to sweep the country nationwide.

By the time the news systems and the commentators on TV and radio have digested Connecticut, the other big Democratic cities of the East are beginning to flood the wires. First Philadelphia (where polls close at 7:30), then Pittsburgh, then Chicago, then, at nine o'clock, New York City. From nine o'clock, when New York closes its polls, to midnight the Democratic tide reaches its peak as the big cities of Michigan, Illinois, Pennsylvania, Ohio, New Jersey, swamp the vote-gathering facilities of the news networks.

Between ten and midnight the United States is politically leaderless—there is no center of information anywhere in the nation except in the New York headquarters of the great broadcasting companies and the two great wire services. No candidate and no party can afford the investment on election night to match the news-gathering resources of the mass media; and so, as every citizen sits in his home watching his TV set or listening to his radio, he is the equal of any other in knowledge. There is nothing that can be done in these hours, for no one can any longer direct the great strike for America's power; the polls have closed. Good or bad, whatever the decision, America will accept the decision—and cut down any man who goes against it, even though for millions the decision runs contrary to their own votes. The general vote is an expression of national will, the only substitute for violence and blood. Its verdict is to be defended as one defends civilization itself.

There is nothing like this American expression of will in England or France, India or Russia or China. Only one other major nation in modern history has ever tried to elect its leader directly by mass, free, popular vote. This was the Weimar Republic of Germany, which modeled its unitary vote for national leader on American practice. Out of its experiment with the system it got Hitler. Americans have had Lincoln, Wilson, two Roosevelts. Nothing can be done when the voting returns are flooding in; the White House and its power will move to one or another of the two candidates, and all will know about it in the morning. But for these hours history stops.

If the Democrats are going to win, they must have a healthy margin of several million votes by midnight. After midnight the tide reverses itself as the farm states, the mountain states, the Pacific Coast, all begin to check in with their traditionally Republican tallies. Thus the profile that repeats itself every four years and creates the arbitrary drama of election night: the afternoon and early-evening trickle of Republican votes, the Democratic tide from the big cities between eight and midnight and then, after midnight, the Republican counter-assault.

There is little that can be done by either political leadership about these tides—except for the opportunity of a grace note that television and radio have recently given them. This last grace note of the campaign hinges on Connecticut. Connecticut, which closes its polls by seven and knows its results by 7:30, has a three-hour advantage over California, whose rhythm of the day is measured by Pacific Time. When it is eight in Connecticut, it is only five in the afternoon in California. If, as in 1956, the early returns from Connecticut show a Republican landslide, it makes the efforts of the Democratic poll workers in California seem hopeless, and they fade for their homes and their headquarters to nurse their wounds among friends. If, on the contrary, Connecticut shows a strong Democratic lead, it inspires the Democratic workers in California—or so the theory runs—to redouble their efforts to bring the last registrants, the laggard voters, to the polls before seven o'clock Pacific Time. The psychology of the bandwagon, of being with the victor, may affect ten, twenty or fifty thousand California votes; conversely, the psychology of emergency may, if there seems the slightest hope, rush sluggards out of their homes to vote their convictions. Both parties focus down tightly on Connecticut on election evening to transmit early results in order to influence the California vote. (The results, historically, in 1960 were open to two contradictory interpretations. California went for Nixon by 35,623 votes out of 6,507,000, or one tenth of one per cent. It was won, one may argue, because Eisenhower took to the air waves at eight o'clock Eastern Standard Time—five o'clock Pacific Time—to counteract the Connecticut influence in California; or it was close, one may argue, because the Democrats had so effectively prepared to get the results there that fast.)

This is the profile, known to all.

Thus it had been an easy and leisurely afternoon in the big Armory hall, as it slowly filled with cigarette smoke while John F. Kennedy and Richard M. Nixon took their naps and the nation waited for the Armory in Hyannis and the Ambassador Hotel in Los Angeles to report what was happening. It was true that early reports showed the New England, Appalachian and Kansas villages going solidly Republican—but that was the normal trickle. On the other hand an early-morning phone call from Sid Holtzman of Chicago's Board of Elections to a Kennedy staff member reported Holtzman's estimate that 93 per cent of Chicago's registered voters would vote that day —an extraordinarily heavy vote, and thus a big-city bonus for Kennedy.

At 6:25 the Kennedy control room in the family compound fed out to the Armory its first shred of hard news. Early returns from Campbell County, Kentucky, which had always voted with the winner since time out of mind, had been telephoned to the control switchboard; with half the returns in, Campbell County counted 56 per cent for Kennedy (5,300 votes) to Nixon's 44 per cent (4,100 votes). In 1956 Republicans had carried Campbell County by 64 per cent to the Democrats' 36 per cent! Did this forecast a national switch?

No one could be certain at the moment, and the news sped over the wires. (Later, when Campbell County brought in its late returns, it was Nixon by 54.2 per cent to Kennedy's 45.8 per cent, the first time in history that Campbell County voted with the loser.)

Quickly after this news came a second item, at 6:30: the Kennedy control room had received the returns of the first complete precinct from Cleveland: Kennedy, 158; Nixon, 121. (In 1956 the same precinct had read Eisenhower, 186, to Adlai Stevenson's 86.) Good.

The Armory was gay now. In Hyannis, as in Los Angeles, the correspondents itched to be with the winner. Closeness to power heightens the dignity of all men. The men in the Hyannis Armory felt close now. The gaiety lasted for almost half an hour.

It stumbled over the first summary total of voting figures transmitted by the AP shortly after seven o'clock: 203,628 for Nixon and only 166,963 for Kennedy. The AP could be ignored by the clattering typewriters, for these returns were probably the usual early Republican trickle. What could not be discounted was the 7:15 flash from the Columbia Broadcasting System over TV. CBS had taken as its partner on election night the brains and resources of International Business Machines. IBM, in turn, had engaged social scientists, mathematicians, analysts, to make a computional model of national voting habits, based on analysis of previous results in 500 key precincts across the nation. Their theory was that politics was an affair of random human particles subject, like other universes of random particles, to statistical analysis and mathematical projection. The IBM-CBS team had made what was, perhaps, the finest survey ever done of a scientifically selected sample of American communities and had coded each of its 500 key precincts on a notched red card to be fed into IBM's 7090 Computer. Each notch in a card indicated a characteristic of the community: white collar, blue collar, rural, urban, Anglo-Saxon, Irish, German, Italian, Jewish, Negro, Scandinavian. All data had been cross-slotted and cross-indexed so that the big computer might scan results in an instant, compare past data with the evening's new reports, and come up instantly with a national projection for the evening. The computer had been fed all necessary facts and figures—but no emotions. Now, at 7:15, as the big machine digested the first cards and first results, it hummed its first prediction: odds on Nixon to win, 100 to 1! And by a margin of 459 Nixon electoral votes to Kennedy's 78.

Gloom lasted no more than twenty minutes, for by 7:35 Connecticut had begun to feed into the TV computers the first strength of the big-city industrial tide. From Hartford, Connecticut, where Governor Abraham Ribicoff and State Boss John Bailey directed the most efficient Democratic machine of the Atlantic Coast, the first returns were now coming in from Hartford, Bridgeport, New Haven—working-class towns all— and they were overwhelmingly Democratic. TV and wire services began to report Boss Bailey's prediction that Connecticut would go for Kennedy by a margin of 100,000 votes. In 1956 Eisenhower had carried Connecticut by a margin of 306,000 Republican votes!

For a few minutes more now, the Kennedy control room

competed with the national TV flow in defining the Kennedy crest. Indicator precinct from Chittenden County, Vermont— Kennedy running 50 per cent ahead of Stevenson in 1956! Indicator precinct from Ward One, Burlington, Vermont— Kennedy, 20 per cent ahead of Stevenson in 1956; Nixon, 40 per cent behind Ike's mark there. Indicator from Fountain Hill, Pennsylvania—Kennedy, 61 per cent of the vote (Stevenson had racked up only 25 per cent in 1956); Nixon, 39 per cent (Ike had had 75 per cent).

And then the control room stopped feeding returns, for by now the TV nets and wire services were in full flow—and every report showed a Kennedy sweep. No one in the press room noticed for quite a while that the report of indicator precincts from the Kennedy control room had stopped.

By eight o'clock the IBM console at CBS had switched sides and now predicted Kennedy by 51 per cent of the popular vote. By nine o'clock it had raised this forecast to a 52-to-48 split. A few minutes after nine Chicago's first precincts came through, staggeringly Democratic—Holtzman had been right, Chicago was going to be good. (As a matter of fact, only Chicago, Philadelphia and New York were really good for Kennedy that evening, getting out the total vote that had been expected of them; most other big cities, except Los Angeles, polled fewer voters in 1960 than in 1956, thus chipping the Democrats' big-city margin.)

Shortly after eight, struggling to keep up morale on the West Coast against what now seemed a Democratic flood, the President of the United States, Dwight D. Eisenhower, appeared on the TV screen, exhorting the workers of his party to keep fighting, reminding them of his battle record and career as a soldier, insisting they "keep fighting right to the last minute." (Dwight D. Eisenhower was angry that evening, disturbed by what he felt was a certain Nixon loss, upset by Nixon's behavior throughout the campaign, bitter against Kennedy.)

By now in the Armory the press feeding Kennedy reports to the nation was almost jubilant—they, not the reporters in Los Angeles, were with the winner. The margin for Kennedy was moving from 800,000 on the totalizers up to 1,100,000. Watching the TV sets, then again watching the platform for new announcements, reporters saw a burly man with the sour face, brown fedora and suspicious manner of a detective mount the platform. He jounced heavily to see whether it would bear the weight of the full Presidential party; all eyes observed him; one could see other plain-clothes men examining the curtains, the pennants, the drapes behind the platform, as if they concealed hidden threats. This was a good sign.

It could not be long now. By 10:30 men began arranging seats on the platform. The margin on the TV totalizers showed a 1,500,000 plurality for Kennedy, and projecting this blindly against the total vote, some guessed that Kennedy might win by a margin of 4,000,000 or 5,000,000.

On the teletypes and on the TV screen the totals mounted. Kennedy was now 1,600,000 ahead. The RCA-501 Computer of the National Broadcasting Company was now predicting 401 electoral votes for Kennedy. Simultaneously the IBM Computer of CBS was predicting a Kennedy electoral total of 311. By midnight the Kennedy margin had swept to 2,000,000 popular votes and now, with the first returns from California showing out of Los Angeles County, it seemed obvious that California was going for Kennedy, too. If Kennedy could carry Nixon's homeland, Los Angeles County, as decisively as he appeared to be doing, then surely in the Great Central Valley of California, full of Okies and gut-Democrats, where even Stevenson had outrun Eisenhower in 1956, the margin would grow and be capped by San Francisco's traditional Democratic plurality. On the TV screen the Governor of California, Pat Brown, was quoted as guessing that California might be carried by a Kennedy margin as high as 800,000. (Unlike John Bailey, Pat Brown was wrong; he did not understand his state.)

It appeared then, in the Hyannis Armory, as the clock hovered at midnight, only a question of when Mr. Nixon would concede. At the buffet in the back of the Armory the Cokes, orange drinks and coffee were replaced by hard liquor; serious celebration was now in order. The hall stank of sweat and stale tobacco; the pecking of typewriters sagged as fingers muttered and minds groped for a new lead on a new President who would soon be here. On the platform photographers were gathering, measuring the light with their photometers, pacing off distances from the place where the new President would soon stand. The "advance men" of the Kennedy party slipped away to organize the motor cavalcade that would leave the Armory immediately to pick up the candidate at the Kennedy cottages and bring him back as the next President. Correspondents filled their glasses at the bar for the last time and filtered back to their assigned seats to wait for his appearance. "He's coming now, he's coming now," ran the word. "The state cops told me that the motor cavalcade is forming up outside his house already," said a local reporter. But no one came.

At the Kennedy compound the mood read otherwise.

For by midnight the shape of the election as they, who understood, read it was not as they had planned. It was not only badly shaped and perilously thin, the margin shrinking as their private analysis screened the mounting results, but shaped so that no one could tell its meaning or tell whether it reflected the past of America's prejudices or the impulse of America's future concerns. All that afternoon and evening the Kennedy control system had been several hours ahead of the press and television in analysis; it was still far ahead in reading the portents. So was the candidate.

The candidate had risen, still restless, from his nap at about five in the afternoon, visited the communications center in the sunroom of his brother Bobby's home, then telephoned John Bailey in Connecticut to see whether any early clues were available. In Hartford, at the Connecticut State House, Boss Bailey gasped as he answered the phone. Turning to Abe Ribicoff, he said, "It's Himself calling," falling back on the homely Irish phrase in excitement. "Himself?" said Ribicoff, unfamiliar with Gaelic idiom. "Who's himself?" "Jack," said Bailey and, turning back to the phone, proceeded to tell the candidate all he could at that early hour of the afternoon: that the high-school straw polls (in which Bailey is a great believer) showed a solid Kennedy margin, that the absentee ballots showed a slimmer margin, but that the first totals from voting machines which had broken down in the afternoon—and thus had been opened for repair and inspection—indicated a sweep.

Kennedy had then gone back to his own home across the lawn; then, once again, impatient, had come back to the communications control center in his brother Bobby's home a few minutes after seven.

He came at seven, of course, to hear the official Connecticut returns, an expected victory; but when he climbed the stairs he arrived on a scene of gloom. The pink-and-white children's bedroom on the second floor had been cleared that evening as a data-analysis section, the beds removed, the baby chairs thrust to the side, a long table set up with mounds of voting statistics; there public-opinion analyst Louis Harris was codifying reports received from the communications center downstairs and from the four teletypewriters of the wire agencies installed in the adjacent bedroom.

From four o'clock on Harris had been growing more and more discouraged. At four he had received and analyzed some 15 per cent of Kansas returns; Nixon, he concluded, was abreast or ahead of Eisenhower's race in 1956; the farmers in this key farm state were, it appeared, not going to vote against Ezra Benson and Republican farm policy, but against the Democrats and the alien culture of the East. By six it was obvious that Kansas was going to give Nixon a margin of 60 to 40—and the other states of the farm belt would probably follow suit. While downstairs in the communications center the happy reports from good indicator precincts were still being fed to the press and public to influence the voters in California, upstairs Harris was reading other indicator reports —not to be released. The first report from the border states had been from Columbia Precinct of Lexington County, Kentucky. And though Kennedy was running slightly *ahead* of the Stevenson record of 1956, he was running *behind* Stevenson's record of 1952 and heavily behind that of Truman in 1948. Early Louisville results came in shortly thereafter; and it was obvious that Kentucky, which Harris had expected to go for Kennedy by 55 to 45, was going to be a hair-thin victory—or a defeat.

"We're being clobbered," said Bobby Kennedy, fresh in from an afternoon of touch football and ready for the long night's vigil. And thereupon, at 7:15, as if to confirm Bobby's first reaction, came the report from the downstairs television monitors—IBM had just quoted odds on Nixon's victory at 100 to 1!

It was at this point that the candidate himself had arrived, to catch the first tide of Connecticut returns. He absorbed the news of IBM's prediction and declared flatly that the machine was crazy. Harris, almost despairing, fearing that IBM had already fed into its calculations returns not yet available in Hyannisport, somberly agreed that of course the machines were crazy—they were projecting only Kansas and Kentucky returns; the polls in the big industrial states had not even closed yet. The candidate grinned, unflustered as ever, and remarked to his statistician that from now on it was he, Lou, against the machine.

Only minutes later, it is described, Bobby Kennedy came whooping up the stairs to the children's bedroom to see his brother: Bailey had just telephoned through with the first Connecticut results! They were being counted now, and in Hartford Kennedy was running 18 percentage points ahead of Stevenson in 1956—Kennedy, said Bailey, would sweep Connecticut by 60,000 votes. Within three minutes Bobby dashed upstairs again—a second call from Bailey in Hartford, as the returns piled up: Bailey was now estimating a 100,000 margin. Three minutes later Bailey had called a third time—

it was going to be solid now, at 90,000. And with this Connecticut disappeared from center stage.

Now the first returns from Pennsylvania were coming in and they were excellent, topped by spectacular figures out of Philadelphia. The mood in the cottage changed. The candidate lit a small cigar, a Havana Royal panatela. The Kennedy girls, dressed in slacks, pranced about the house as if they were at a party. Peter Lawford, fresh from Hollywood and bemused, ran up and down stairs in his stocking feet, tearing off sheets of news from the teletype as returns came in from the wire services. Singer Morton Downey, a guest of Joseph Kennedy, had wandered over from the father's house and was serving as waiter, offering sandwiches and pastries to anyone hungry. It was better now; the early rural vote was beginning to be blanketed by the thundering industrial vote; and the candidate decided to leave the elated communications center and stroll back across the lawn to his own house for dinner.

It was very quiet there. Caroline, a scratch on her nose, was waiting to say goodnight to her father, and he bounced her on his knee several times, then sent her upstairs to bed and settled down to his first drink of the day, a Daiquiri, with his wife, Jacqueline, and his friend, William Walton. Walton is a sturdy sun-faced man of charm and toughness, a distinguished artist, a gay warrior. A friend of Kennedy's over many Washington years, Walton had volunteered early in the spring to serve for the duration of the campaign; for six months, giving up brush and canvas, he had performed through Wisconsin, West Virginia, California and New York as a political coordinator of increasing responsibility. The range of his many moods matched almost any Kennedy mood, and now, as they relaxed in the sitting room (a large white room furnished to Mrs. Kennedy's taste in antiques), they talked of painting, not politics. Did Walton like the painting of the sailing ship over the mantelpiece, which Jacqueline Kennedy had bought her husband as a welcome-home gift after the Los Angeles Convention? Did Walton like the landscape that the candidate had painted himself? (Like Churchill, Montgomery, Eisenhower and countless other men who live under strain, Kennedy had begun to paint a few years before, and in Hyannisport now he had hung his favorite—a Riviera scene, warm with the honey colors of the sun-bleached Mediterranean coast where Kennedy had vacationed shortly after the 1956 Convention.) Walton thought it a fine primitive, and they chatted idly with no interruption from radio, TV or the communications center until dinner was ready promptly at eight in the dining room—an all-white room with red carpeting, elegantly different from the rooms in the other Kennedy cottages in the compound.

At dinner, while totals rolled up in the communications center across the lawn, the candidate talked of politics again, yet at another level. Perhaps because they had been discussing painting before dinner, he was now remembering visual vignettes of the campaign. It was as if, out of the tumult and storm and noise of the campaign, he was fixing, in the hush now growing around him, scenes for later memory. He remembered arriving in Lewiston, Maine, forty hours before, at two in the morning of Monday, and driving through the cold of the airport, through the empty streets with their lights blue in the dark, until suddenly arriving at the park, he found fifteen thousand people waiting for him in the cold, in a burst of light, their torchlights flaring about him. He remembered out of his triumphal tour in Pennsylvania a month before a family group, dressed in black clothes, on a deserted country road—the father with a clothespin on his nose and the mother, as the candidate's eye rested on her, suddenly sticking out her tongue at him. The memory carried him to another: how, wherever he had traveled in the big cities and the crowds had lined the sidewalks and overspilled into the roads, he could look up to the windows of the office buildings and there, above the cheering street mobs, see the white-collared executives staring down at him. And in city after city, as if by common instinct, they were all giving him the universal bent-arm, clenched-fist gesture of contempt and occasionally forming on the lips a curse that he could read above the shouting. The others reminisced, too, but dinner was quick and by 8:45 they were back in the living room, watching a small leather-covered portable TV set that his wife manipulated to bring into focus.

Shortly after dinner Ted Sorensen arrived to watch with them, and thereafter, one by one, in and out, there filtered other members of staff and family from the communications center across the lawn. Pierre Salinger, the Kennedy press chief, came to report; Bobby was back and forth several times; occasionally the telephone rang and the candidate would rise to answer it briefly. His sisters came across the lawn once, giggly and happy, and the candidate scolded them for telling the press (for TV had already reported it) that he was "smoking a big, black cigar" and "jumping up and down for joy."

Between visits the group of four was quiet in the living room. Self-possessed, apparently almost emotionless, the candidate watched the TV screen as the returns from the industrial states poured on. At one point, about 10:30, as a landslide seemed inevitable, his wife said quietly, "Oh, Bunny, you're President now!" and he said to her, equally quietly, "No . . . no . . . it's too early yet."

However possessed he appeared, the candidate felt the tension. Between nine o'clock and midnight he had crossed the lawn to the communications center several times, but always returned to his home to be close to his wife in the sitting room, while concealing his concern at the tidings he read so clearly. At about 11:30, because she was now three weeks from giving birth, she was sent upstairs to bed; and afterward the candidate decided to cross the lawn and wait at the communications center itself. The TV cameras had long since been posted outside his own home, but the cameramen had agreed not to transmit any pictures of him walking back and forth between the cottages until they should get permission. Nevertheless, lights were needed, for this was a mobile TV unit and required forty minutes to warm up. So the lights were left on continuously, and their blinding glare continuously outlined the night—stark white, stark black. In this light the candidate felt his way across the grass at about midnight to his brother's house and the control center, where he was to remain for the rest of the evening.

There, while the public TV report was one of landslide and victory, the mood of the command staff was deep disturbance and unease. The sunporch of the Robert Kennedy home had been cleared of all its furniture, and a telephone central had been established there. One long table ran down its length, another shorter table crossed it in a T-bar. Fourteen telephones, staffed by fourteen girls, rested on the long table. Ten were for use by the scores of Democratic headquarters and chieftains across the country who had been given the special number of the Hyannisport switchboard; two were for use by the ninety poll watchers at the ninety indicator precincts across the country; two were for overflow and emergency messages. Several telephone directors sat at the crossbar tables, switching the calls as they came to the proper recipient. They faced a large Elgin clock whose red sweep hand traced the minutes and the hours as they passed west across the country; in a corner below the clock a TV set showed them what the nation was seeing. As the phones rang and reports came in, the girls filled out mimeographed blanks with individual precinct returns, which were rushed upstairs to Harris' data-analysis room where their meaning could be read.

Behind the sunporch, in Ethel Kennedy's dining room, the Steuben crystal had been cleared away and a huge coffee urn substituted. Two electric typewriters and a tabulating machine rested on the sideboard, and several more direct telephone lines created a tangle of telephone cables over the floor. On the landward side of the house, in Ethel Kennedy's sitting room, a buffet of sandwiches had been established. Around the room were easy chairs, lounge chairs, several more telephones, several more typewriters, a large TV set.

Now, at midnight, as the candidate entered, it was clear here at the command post that the campaign was tracing a course he had not designed.

Elation had swollen here from shortly after eight until 10:30, an elation that had all but erased the early-evening gloom. Hard on the heels of the Connecticut sweep had come the first news from Philadelphia, promising a margin of 300,000 votes in that city alone. ("Too good to be true," said Bobby Kennedy. But it was to be even better than that in the end—a 331,000 margin, a Kennedy victory by 68.1 per cent.) After Philadelphia there came, forty minutes later, the first indicators from Pittsburgh, Wilkes-Barre, Scranton where slack in coal and steel had together created unemployment and discontent. It had been clear very early that nothing the rural or suburban Republican vote might amass would overtake this strength in Pennsylvania. Between nine and ten the first private Texas reports had also come in; and as soon as Laredo had reported, it had been obvious that the Mexican-Americans of South Texas were delivering their vote to Kennedy with such force that the Southern Republican vote of Dallas and Houston could be matched.

As if to confirm Texas, had come the drama of South Carolina, telephoning in at ten-minute intervals. The South Carolina cities had been in first, with their expected Republican pluralities. But as the South Carolina countryside reported, the Republican margin had shrunk from 54 per cent to 53 per cent to 52 per cent to 51 per cent until, with a whoop, the Republican percentages became 49 per cent, and it was certain that South Carolina and the Confederacy would remain basically Democratic. New Jersey was looking good, too, as in suburban Bergen, Mercer and Middlesex counties Kennedy was far outdistancing the Stevenson score in 1956 in these Republican bedrooms; Harris had at this point predicted carrying all of New Jersey by 53 or 54 per cent. As New York, Rhode Island, Massachusetts, Maryland all followed with their heavy pluralities, victory had seemed certain.

It was then, at 10:30, that the tide of voting had moved

from the Atlantic seaboard across the Appalachians into the
Midwest, and the trouble began. Wayne County in Michigan
showed the first break in the parade. Wayne County is the
City of Detroit; here the Kennedy campaign had expected a
vote of 800,000. Only 745,000 voted in Detroit that day (it
rained); the plurality of that big city (311,721), so necessary
to carry Michigan, had thus been shaved to the danger point.
Cleveland came next. Cleveland had been expected to give 60
to 65 per cent of its vote to Kennedy. It had, indeed, done
better than this *percentage* of its vote (70.9 per cent), but the
total of the vote (338,000) was so far below expectation
(measuring out to a Kennedy plurality of 141,000 as against
an expected 200,000) that Ohio was clearly in danger. And
then had followed the rest of the Middle West: Iowa, a landslide for Nixon, as expected; Indiana, another Nixon sweep;
but then came Wisconsin, which Kennedy had stumped so
furiously in March and now expected with certainty to carry
—and Wisconsin was lost. By eleven o'clock, when the electronic indicators read that Kennedy had 241 electoral votes
out of the necessary 269 to elect, the Kennedy thrust had
amassed almost all that it was going to have with certainty—
the industrial Northeast and the Old South. Now from somewhere must come the last thirty electoral votes to make the
victory a reality. And though it was close enough to taste, the
surge of Republican countervotes from the Midwest and
the Rocky Mountain areas denied the victory still.

While such reports had been coming to the center, the
candidate had been absorbing them privately in his own home.
Only once had he shown emotion. It was Ohio that had caused
him bitterness. He had moved through Ohio six times in the
course of the campaign. On his last trip on October 17th,
campaigning from Middletown through Dayton through
Springfield through Columbus, it had been such a day of
marvel and splendor as is reserved only for heroes and gods.
The Ohioans had lined 113 miles of highway almost solidly,
holding their children up to watch him, clutching at him,
tearing at him, waving at him, shrieking at him, until his staff
had feared for his safety. Yet now along this route, precisely
in these cities, from Franklin County through Hamilton County, the Ohioans of the southern tier were showing that their
hearts still belonged to Robert A. Taft and Richard M. Nixon.
The candidate had listened as the profile of Ohio's preference
traced the biggest disappointment of his campaign, and slowly
he rolled back his sleeve. His right hand, by the end of the
campaign, had swollen with the handshaking of the months
to grossly disproportionate size and he displayed it now—

calloused, red, the scratches reaching as far as his elbow. He
held up the inflamed hand, bare to the elbow, and said "Ohio
did that to me—they did it there." Then he had rolled down
the sleeve, had shaken his head, not understanding, and had
become cool again, as ever.

Now as the candidate arrived at the command post shortly
after midnight, a quiet tension had become general in his
brother's house. Earlier, a split mood had unreally divided the
Bobby Kennedy cottage. In the living room about the TV set,
where sandwiches and light drinks were being offered, the
candidate's sisters and a few family friends had jubilantly and
vociferously begun to celebrate. But in the adjacent sunporch,
where the communications center had been established, and
upstairs in the data analysis center, where reports were being
studied, the mood had been, since ten o'clock, one of quiet
and growing concern. Upstairs Lou Harris worked his slide
rule and attempted to sustain optimism by reading the totals in
contrast to the Stevenson race of 1956; but downstairs, where
the operational political chieftains—O'Brien, O'Donnell, Donahue and Dungan—received the reports, they contrasted them
with the Truman scores of 1948, and worried.

By midnight the tension in the sunporch communication
center and the upstairs data-analysis center had communicated itself to everyone in the house and celebration was over.
A waitress of the Mayfair Catering Service wandered back
and forth asking, "Are we doing all right? Are we all right?"
but no one answered her. Actor Peter Lawford sat on the
stairs leading to Harris' data room, worrying about his baggage, which had disappeared that morning somewhere between
Boston and Hyannis. Singer Morton Downey rested quietly
in the living room, munching on the sandwiches he had been
serving. Author Cornelius Ryan (*The Longest Day*), serving
as advance man for the logistics of the Hyannisport operation,
had been summoned earlier in the evening by press-chief
Salinger to marshal the motorcade that would bring the candidate victoriously to the Armory; now he tiptoed quietly
about, measuring the balance of concern and confidence.

No one had to explain to the candidate what was happening
as he entered the command post. He was to stay there for
three long hours. He had mastered politics on so many different levels that no other contemporary American could match
him. He had nursed ward politics with his mother's milk;
heard it from his grandfathers, politicians both, in boyhood;
seen it practiced from his father's embassy in London at the
supreme level of world events in 1939, as war and peace hung
in the balance. He had first sweated out such election nights

in his own polyglot Eleventh Congressional District of Boston, gauging the reaction of his Irish-Italian-Jewish-Yankee-colored voters; he had later sweated out such nights statewide in Massachusetts, measuring the returns from the Berkshires against those of Suffolk County; he had this year sweated them out in Wisconsin, West Virginia, Maryland, Oregon. On nights like these, all that could be done was already done, and there was nothing more to do except wait, and watch, and learn whether power was there or not.

The candidate posed himself in the corner of the room where sunporch, dining room and sitting room join, and watched the TV set in the far corner of the sunporch; too tense to sit; pacing occasionally; clutching back to back two paperback books he had been reading; visiting the upstairs data center now and then. The room was by now quite warm, and he took off his Scotch tweed jacket, stood there in white shirt, tan twill trousers, green necktie, white wool socks and watched. These men at this table were his; they would all be important tomorrow if he won, and some would enter history; or they would leave here nameless and forgotten. The men at the table were quiet now, easy, working hard, thinking, talking with no exuberance yet no alarm; they were practiced in such evenings; no one here was an amateur.

(A grotesquerie worth only a passing note here intervened. From the Armory, Western Union had strung two direct telegraph lines connecting directly with Republican National Headquarters in Washington and with the Ambassador Hotel in Los Angeles. These lines were reserved for the one message of defeat and congratulation that would, that night, have to go either from Hyannisport to Los Angeles and Washington or from Washington and Los Angeles to Hyannisport. At about one A.M., the monitored wire in the Armory clacked—a message of congratulation from President Eisenhower to President-Elect Kennedy! Press Secretary Salinger immediately double-checked by telephone to Washington and James Hagerty, Eisenhower's press secretary, before releasing it. Hagerty, desperate, asked that the wire not be released—he had had two messages in his pocket, one of victory, one of defeat, and had inadvertently let one get away from him too early. Salinger, in the brotherhood of press agentry, understood and held back the news from the press; but for a moment the jubilation at the cottage had boiled; then faded; and now it was tense again.)

Now and then, as the telephones rang from across the country, the candidate would take a call himself; more often he declined. Lyndon Johnson telephoned from Texas; the candidate went upstairs to answer this one. He came down in a few minutes, saw the faces watching him and reported that Lyndon had said, "I hear you're losing Ohio, but we're doing fine in Pennsylvania." He stressed the *you* of defeat in Ohio and the *we* of victory in Pennsylvania just enough to make everyone laugh. But it was laughter without rancor, for they knew that Johnson, in Texas, was sweating it out as much as they were here. From New York, the State Democratic Committee (Tammany controlled), telephoned urging that the candidate send them a telegram of congratulations on their landslide in New York—but the candidate dodged it, knowing this was no moment to enter into the Byzantine Democratic politics of New York State and decide which of the many forces there had truly won the victory.

More generally Bobby Kennedy took or made the calls, and Bobby's calls now reflected the narrowing center of attention: calls to Dick Daley in Chicago (who said not to worry—Daley knew which of *his* precincts were out and which of *theirs* were out, and it was going to be all right); calls to Sid Woolner in Michigan, who claimed nothing yet in Michigan nor conceded anything; calls to Jesse Unruh in Southern California, who could not say which precincts were out, which in—a bad sign.

There was, then, as the hours wore on to three in the morning a general shape to the election. Four states held center stage: Michigan, Minnesota, Illinois, California—three in the Midwest, one in the Far West. And in each, the same pattern of voting rose from the same style of life and the same prejudices—city against countryside, old stock against new. Los Angeles and San Francisco had voted Republican in 1956; now they were giving Kennedy a lead. But in the Central Valley, where Stevenson had led Eisenhower in 1956, Kennedy was barely abreast—the Central Valley is inhabited by Oklahomans and transplants from the Southern Bible Belt. In Los Angeles' suburbs Kennedy was being overwhelmed. In the three Midwestern states, the big cities had all given him the expected plurality; but in the farms and in the suburbs and the small towns it was going abruptly against him.

Two of these four states—any two—would give the candidate the election with certainty. But if he won only one of these four, then the Presidency of the United States would depend on the ballots of fourteen or fifteen unpledged and unbranded segregationist Electors from the Deep South; the election would, by the Constitution, be thrown to the House of Representatives, for the third time in 170 years of American history. Only if Kennedy lost all four, which was unlikely, could Richard Nixon win. So that, though Nixon had almost certainly lost, Kennedy had not yet definitely won.

Shortly after three, as the TV screen showed him hanging at 261 or 262 electoral votes, as it had shown him so hanging for hours, there came a commotion over the video screen; a bustle and turbulence was shown in the clamor of the press room at the Ambassador Hotel in Los Angeles where, said the announcer, Nixon would soon be arriving to make a statement to the nation. Kennedy looked at the scene for a minute and then said to his press secretary, Pierre Salinger, who had been urging him to soothe the press mob in the Hyannis Armory by just such a personal appearance as this: "And you want me to go down into that?"

The candidate stood there, a sandwich in one hand, trailing on the floor his jacket, its yellow silk lining turned out, showing its gold-printed horses.

"Is there any milk in the house?" asked the candidate, munching his sandwich. But his staff was too busy watching the TV screen for the appearance of Nixon. Their faces softened now, with the melancholy of men purchasing victory too dearly, yet sympathizing with the effort of the man who was about to acknowledge defeat, thinking, as one of them remembers now, how close all this had been and there, but for the Grace of God, go we.

They waited silently, intent on the screen; and the candidate had left the room and now returned from the kitchen icebox before Nixon had reached the TV camera. "There wasn't any milk," he remarked irritably, "only beer."

He said nothing as Nixon spoke, watching closely, his expression showing faint distaste. He himself, elegant and correct in all public appearances, had never permitted his wife to be exposed to this sort of thing; the heroic effort to smile by Nixon, the twisted, barely controlled sorrow of Mrs. Nixon, twinged him, almost as if he were embarrassed. It was not, could not be, the sort of thing he himself might do, for Kennedy likes matters clean-cut, correct. Yet when Nixon had finished and the Kennedy staff around the table had swept in an instant from sympathy to a growling anger at the man who would not concede when the stage was set for concession, the candidate calmed their combat anger.

"Why should he concede? I wouldn't," he said curtly.

Salinger, under pressure from the press and the TV cameramen, urged again that Kennedy go down to the Armory and make an appearance before the Eastern cameras to match the one that Nixon had just given in the West. The candidate refused. He would have nothing to say until Nixon spoke

again. He was going home to bed. They should all go home to
bed.

The candidate left the house of his brother by the parlor,
passing through the door to the front porch and then to his
own home.

It was in this same room, with these same people, that a
year before he had reviewed the entire country, state by state,
approved the final plans and set in motion the machinery that
was to bring him to this election night. No press had been
aware then of that meeting; no TV cameras had stalked him
as did the TV cameras now, their blinding light making the
velvet autumnal grass on which he walked a pale, luminous
spring green.

He and his men had planned then a campaign that seemed
utterly preposterous—to take the youngest Democratic candidate to offer himself in this century, of the minority Catholic
faith, a man burdened by wealth and controversial family, relying on lieutenants scarcely more than boys, and make him
President. They had planned shrewdly and skillfully in this
room on that long-ago October day of 1959 to direct a campaign that would sweep out of the decade of the sixties America's past prejudices, the sediment of yesterday's politics, and
make a new politics of the future.

Now, at this hour of twenty minutes to four in the morning,
as he crossed the lawn to his own home, he could not tell
whether he had won or lost—and, if he won or lost, whether
this election spoke America's past or its future.

It had been a long road since that early October meeting,
229,000 miles or more, back and forth across the country, in
a disturbed year. Where the road had finally brought him he
could not yet tell. But along the road, over the past year and
to this point, he had somehow stirred every nerve end of the
American political system, and that system would never be
the same.

This much, at least, he had accomplished.

Chapter 2

THE DEMOCRATS:
FIRST STIRRINGS

THERE is no one way of becoming President of the United States—no avenue as clear as the classic parliamentary ladder that takes men to leadership in Western Europe, or as naked as the tyrant's strike for power in antique and modern despotisms.

Over almost two centuries of national life, as technologies have changed and our way of life with them; as literacy and learning have spread and our culture patterns have been refashioned; as communications have reached their numbing roar; as our population has washed in waves from country to city and from coast to coast—the avenues of Presidential politics have changed with all these changes, to wind in new turnings about the contours of the ever-new nation.

Only the paradoxes of Presidential politics have remained permanent: the paradoxes of the open forum and the closed room, of conspiracy and inevitability, of cynicism and nobility.

Yet of all the paradoxes, the one that summons attention most sharply is that which most distinctively sets American politics off from that of other nations—that so few men can set in motion so vast a mass of freely participating citizens.

Nowhere in the world are more people more freely engaged in active, responsible participation in the choice of national leadership than in the United States during the fall season of any American Presidential campaign. Yet neither in the parliamentary democracies of Europe nor in the dictatorships of the East can so small a group of men mount the reach for power or galvanize so countless a mass to action. The web of American communications, influence and politics is so sensitive that when touched in the right way by men who know how, it clangs with instant response. Nowhere can men gather together on their own initiative and self-election, from distances more apparently remote—and then rush the bridge of state with greater chance of success. It is their fewness that raps at the historian's attention.

On Tuesday, November 8, 1960, 68,832,818 Americans voted. Of these sixty-eight million, between 3,500,000 and

4,000,000 *actively* (according to the combined estimates of
Republican and Democratic party leaders) participated in the
campaign, contributing money, licking envelopes, ringing
doorbells, pasting stamps, organizing rallies, exciting their
neighbors. Yet of all these active citizens, fewer perhaps than
a thousand had been aware a year earlier that the germinal
decisions that would govern their actions were then being
taken or had already been taken. And of this thousand alert
and sensitive enough to know what was happening, fewer than
fifty were present at those initial meetings of three or five or
twelve, far below the level of press notice and public attention, when the seven principal candidates of 1960 coldly
surveyed the awesome problem of acquisition of power in
America.

The meetings took place, variously, in Massachusetts and
Florida, in Minnesota and Texas, in Washington, D.C., and
New York. All were concerned with surveying the country's
then-blurred moods and measuring against these moods the
resources of money, friendship, loyalty and influence that
must be mobilized to ride these moods to power at the White
House. These meetings were obscure indeed, to be touched
with fame and history only if the plots and plans then laid
were to succeed a year or a year and a half later. But the
diversity and commonplace character of the settings—an
ordinary hotel in Duluth, Minnesota, a simple New England
cottage in Hyannisport, a triplex apartment overlooking Central Park in New York, the palm-fringed house of "Beebee"
Rebozo in Key Biscayne, Florida, the white frame home of
Clark Clifford in the Maryland meadows, the spacious offices
of the Majority Leader of the Senate—the simplicity of such
settings, as contrasted with the august or clandestine headquarters of other adventures in power in other lands, all reflect the great fact that in America power is open to all who
have the will and imagination simply to try. For none of those
early meetings in 1958 and 1959 gathered unreasonable men
or nursed unreasonable fantasy.

The attention of Americans was, as always, diffused in the
last six months of 1959 over a variety of matters: the international circus of diplomacy was, after Mr. Khrushchev's first
visit to the United States, approaching a dismal climax; across
the farmlands, a splendid harvest had just moved into the bins
of surplus (3,909,000,000 bushels of corn, 1,126,000,000
bushels of wheat); in the industrial Northeast a seemingly endless steel strike (519,000 steel workers off payroll for a total of
174 days) posed again the apparently insoluble problem of
industrial jurisprudence; the sudden puncturing of a brilliant

young man's career and the nation's juvenile trust in TV quiz shows had made the parochial Broadway expression "payola" into national slang, and the country wallowed in the pleasure of self-humiliation.

Yet these were headline stories; and beneath the headline stories in the fall weeks of 1959, as the candidates conspired with their friends, there swelled other, more complicated concerns. At home the children had just been sent back to school. The schools were better than ever before, but men and women who thirty years earlier had studied in classrooms of forty or fifty in crowded city schools were now upset at a teaching system that packed their children in the suburbs more than thirty to a class. There were not enough schools, nor the right kind of schools, nor was there any clear, agreed-on answer on how to build more. Abroad, Africa was a distant, sputtering rumble of hope and discontent. M. Pierre Wigny, the Foreign Minister of Belgium, was a visitor to New York in the fall of 1959, insisting privately to influential publicists and important state department officers with vehemence, violence and total indignation that never, never, never would Belgium evacuate the Congo at any time in any circumstances; he insisted that it was Belgium's Christian duty to remain and civilize the Congo, to keep it from dissolving into barbarism. But no one paid him heed.

The men who gathered in the closed rooms at this season of 1959 were, of course, vaguely or acutely aware of all these things, for, politicians all, they knew such matters would create the atmospherics of the election year; these atmospherics would be almost as important as their own strivings. Once elected—if one of them were—their own handling of such matters would create the atmospherics of future elections; these matters, a year or eighteen months hence, would be their stubborn, unyielding administrative worries. But not at the moment.

At this moment they were interested not in what they could do with the power of America, but how it might be seized—a completely different problem.

Indeed, in the case of all of them, their concerns were focused far more on the first climax of the electoral process, the nominations, than on the second climax, the November elections of 1960, for the two are entirely different political exercises. The planning of a Presidential nomination is infinitely more calculated than the planning of an election; but capture of the nomination, however complicated, is a process in which the elements are subject to rational analysis and control. An election is something else again. Success or failure in the nomination can always, later, be plausibly rooted in some blunder, decision, deal, coup or treachery. With the nomination, a man is plunged into the wild, uncontrollable electoral half of the Presidential exercise; but with it, he captures control, too, of a political establishment that puts him halfway home to the White House; the nomination must be first target always.

Thus in the spring, summer and fall of 1959, the rivulets of hope and ambition began to descend from their secret places, like tributaries ambling, rushing and twisting toward the two great political streams, Republican and Democratic, that would make in their meeting a year later the campaign of 1960. Some tumbled forward almost by accident; some were to take swift, sharp unplanned turnings; some (like the Stevensonian campaign) were to be drawn down to the valley of contention only by the force of political gravity. In either stream, the names that bobbed to the attention of the nation and the lucky candidate would be touched with recognition that might include them in American history.

First, then, the Democrats.

It is best to begin with Hubert Horatio Humphrey, for, weak and isolated though he was, the earliest tactical decision lay in his hands; it was he who would first have to test, as a patrol in the night tests the main force of the enemy, the strength of John F. Kennedy; all other Democrats would have to react to his initiatives as they made their plans.

When or how the Presidency first glimmered on the horizon of Humphrey's ambition no one, not even his closest friends, can say. It had been apparent to these inner friends perhaps from his first explosive entry into Minneapolis politics in 1945, long before the connoisseurs of national politics noticed him, as Minneapolis' Mayor, leading the civil rights floor fight at the Democratic Convention of 1948. He had been more sharply conspicuous at the Convention of 1952 when, leading the fight for Adlai Stevenson's nomination, he had half hankered after the Vice-Presidency and seen it pass him by. In 1956 he had become an open declared candidate for the Vice-Presidency; indeed, he had been found weeping by one of his friends the evening after Stevenson's second nomination, when he discovered that Stevenson, his idol, had decided to toss the choice of Vice-President to the Convention itself, where Humphrey must certainly lose to either Kefauver or Kennedy. Now, as the Presidential year approached again, he was at that age of life, and the stars of politics so fixed, when he must reach for the Presidency in this season and on his own or not at all.

Humphrey had grown in public measure in the years between 1956 and 1960. Largely ignored by the national press in the years of his growth, or else portrayed as a Midwestern crank, he was now treated more and more as an eminently respectable force. His fall visit to Khrushchev in 1958 had won international attention. His portrait had graced the cover of *Time* magazine after the Democratic Congressional sweep of 1958. He could sense his own increasing weight. In the early winter months of 1959 Humphrey had sounded out Adlai Stevenson, and Stevenson had told him he was the kind of man the country needed. He had sounded out Lyndon Johnson, and Johnson gave Humphrey to understand he had no conflicting ambitions of his own. Beyond that was the cascade of letters pouring into his office after his Khrushchev meeting, asking him to speak here, there, in the Far West, in New York, across the country—sometimes as many as 100 such invitations a week.

As early as the summer of 1958, Humphrey had begun to permit himself to discuss the long reach for the Presidency with a few of his closest friends in Washington. By the summer of 1959, at a June meeting of the leadership of the Minnesota State Democrats at the Leamington Hotel in Minneapolis, the Humphrey candidacy had become the central subject of excitement among his followers. Yet if a date must be set when the dream was translated into program, it was probably at an all-afternoon-and-evening meeting at the old Duluth Hotel in Duluth, where Humphrey, having arrived for the ceremonies of opening the St. Lawrence Seaway on July 11th, 1959, assembled his innermost political leaders in his bedroom suite. Muriel, his wife, joined him there, for the decision would be a family decision, and there came also Governor Orville Freeman of Minnesota, Senator Eugene McCarthy, Congressmen John Blatnik and Joseph Karth, Minnesota party leaders Gerald W. Heaney and Ray Hemenway. Humphrey's personal aide, Herb Waters, was also present. Waters was a Californian—the others were all Minnesotans, a fact to be noted. Most of the campaigns for the Presidency, particularly those of 1960, have been launched from a single-state base, where a virile state organization with an acknowledged leader finds itself with the surplus vitality to descend upon the national scene and raid it for the grand prize. So, historically, developed the Ohio crowd of Warren Harding, the Albany crowd of Franklin D. Roosevelt, the Missouri crowd of Harry Truman. Leaders need "in-groups," and they draw them from their own kind. So, in 1960, was the Kennedy campaign to be an affair of Massachusetts boys, the Symington campaign one of Missouri men, the Johnson campaign one of Texans, and the Nixon campaign—despite the full eight years he had spent at the national center—one whose in-group was overwhelmingly Southern Californian.

Essentially, of this group that gathered for the all-afternoon-and-evening conference at the Duluth Hotel, it is best to remain fixed on Governor Orville L. Freeman and on Hubert Humphrey himself, for in their intertwined careers and visions they summed up the power of the Minnesota Democracy.

The events of the campaign year were to separate, then estrange Humphrey and Freeman, as it was to separate many old friends; but at that moment the two men were together, as they had been all their mature lives. They had met first in St. Paul when Humphrey was an instructor in government and Freeman one of his cherished pupils, a hungry depression lad working his way through college. "On Saturday nights," Freeman once recalled publicly, "I used to go to Hubert's house for dinner, and Muriel would cook us waffles, and it was the only hot meal I used to have all week."

Poor boys both, they had an almost romantic faith in The People; this faith had flared in the depression; with this faith alone they had acquired power. The essence of their faith was that government belonged to the people, that it must act for them, all the way, to the extreme limit and beyond the orthodoxies of liberalism. When Humphrey became Mayor of Minneapolis in 1945 at the age of thirty-four, Orville Freeman, then twenty-seven, became his secretary. Together they cleaned up the city, reorganized its police, cleaned the communists out of its unions. When Humphrey moved up to the Senate in 1948 (the first Democratic Senator elected in Minnesota history), behind him on the escalator was a file of young men he had trained, ready to take over the entire state. When Freeman became Governor in 1954, and Eugene McCarthy United States Senator in 1958, they had not only given their state one of the finest, most responsive, most practical yet visionary governments the nation knows, but had also made their Minnesota Democratic Party a model of clean and practical politics that was stimulating citizen groups all across the North Central belt of the United States. Led by intellectuals, untainted by scandal, solidly backed by the money and troops of the great labor unions, loved by the farmers of Minnesota, their state party seemed to them to possess a formula for unbroken victory. Colder men noted that this party seemed held together more by spirit and emotion than by hard organized machinery, that it rested on volunteer enthusiasm for an individual and beloved leader, plus the support of other organized groups the party could not control. Could this type of party be effective in other states?

The afternoon conference in Duluth, as later remembered by a participant, divided on just this question—whether the Minnesota model of politics could be generalized across the country. It was Freeman, a stocky former Marine officer, earnest, slightly brittle, who, reportedly, insisted they must now "fish or cut bait." A Presidential committee had to be formed immediately, insisted Freeman, for money had to be raised, and, since Humphrey could expect few big contributors, tiny donations would have to be raised in vast numbers. Freeman was supported strongly by Jerry Heaney, Democratic National Committeeman from Minnesota, as he was by almost all the other young men in the room, whom Humphrey had raised and who lived and governed Minnesota in his faith.

Three, however, were cautious: they were Humphrey, Eugene McCarthy and Congressman John Blatnik. Humphrey had been Senator in Washington for eleven years, McCarthy a Congressman there for eleven years, Blatnik for thirteen. This trio, which had observed national politics from the national capital, saw national politics quite differently from the politics of Minnesota or the Northwest. The pattern of politics that worked in Minnesota might not, they knew, necessarily work across the country. These three understood the mechanisms of national communications, the alliances of the political oligarchies and the cynicism of the great labor unions when they play politics on the national scale.

"I felt as competent as any man to be President with the exception of Stevenson," said Humphrey later, "but even then I was being compared to Kennedy constantly, and his publicity was incredible it was so good. It was in the right places, in the family magazines, in the good journals, in the quality spots. And I knew how I looked. I was always being talked of as being pro-labor, argumentative, testy, competitive, a far-out liberal. The only organization I had was in Minnesota, I had no money, no big press on my side, no public relations. My Minnesota crowd doesn't know how to use public relations. We had a certain pattern that worked in Minnesota, but they didn't know how the national press works. In Orville Freeman we had one of the best governors in the entire union—but nobody knew about him.

"There was only one chance in ten of making the nomination. Still, there *was* that chance. And besides, even if I didn't make it, I'd be able to do two things: first, condition the entire political climate of the campaign and then, second, *we* would write the platform, and whoever was the nominee, *he* would have to accept it. We'd make so much commotion that whoever got the nomination, our ideas would be accepted. And that was a way of evening the score with the Dixiecrats. I'd been looking for it from the day when Harry Byrd and his fellows first jumped me when I came to the Senate. That was the only reason that I could agree to it—the things I'd been saying to small groups were going to be said to a big audience. At no time did I think I would make it. I wanted it. But I could see what lay ahead."

When the evening ended and the group divided, there were obviously two interpretations of what had happened— the Minnesota people, safe in the bastion of their state, believed that the campaign had been decisively launched, that they were moving to the Presidency, and scouts were off and at work organizing committees, feeling for money, rounding up support in neighboring farm states. But in Humphrey's recollection, he had only agreed to *explore* the Presidency. It was they who had decided to set up their Humphrey for President committee. But he, publicly, was still uncommitted and could withdraw if he saw no way to move from the Minnesota base.

It was another friend of Hubert Humphrey who proceeded now to put the motor in the Humphrey campaign—James Rowe of Washington, D.C. One must stop and generalize about men like Rowe, for Washington holds perhaps fifty or a hundred such men, lawyers all, successful all, who in their dark-paneled law chambers nurse an amateur's love for politics and dabble in it whenever their practice permits. Where, in the regions, cities and states of the country, provincial lawyers love to counsel local politicians, promote names for the local judiciary, arrange the candidacies of lesser men, in Washington lawyers dabble in national politics, in appointments to places of high political destiny. Their influence, collectively, can never be ignored, because, collectively, they possess a larger fund of wisdom, experience, contacts, memories, running back over thirty years of national politics, than most candidates on the national scene can ever hope to accumulate on their own. Each of them, of course, is an individual and distinctive, Rowe more individual than most. Once one of Franklin D. Roosevelt's glowing, earnest young lawyers, Rowe had served the great chief as an anonymous aide in the White House, later had become a successful Capital lawyer himself, now affected a hard-bitten, cynical attitude toward the more practical aspects of American politics; yet, like so many graying New Dealers, he cherished the memory and emotions of the liberalism of the thirties. In Humphrey's camp of far-out liberals, Rowe was always seen as the conservative; among conservatives, Rowe is himself considered a far-out liberal.

It was Rowe who, in June, even before the Duluth meeting, had pointed out to Humphrey the only course his campaign could take. "In politics," says Rowe, "your strategy is never based on choice—it is forced on you."

In the case of Humphrey, Rowe pointed out, the dominant fact was that outside Minnesota he was unknown, and if recognized outside his state, recognized in sharp, negative terms as a wild and evangelical radical. To mobilize nationally the recognition and resources of warm emotion that he had mobilized locally in Minnesota over the years and then, with this recognition, to compel the acquiescence at Convention of the Democratic minorities and power brokers, Humphrey had, above all, to become known.

To become known, to be identifiable to voters in terms of their own gut reactions, is perhaps the most expensive and necessary condition of American Presidential politics. People cannot vote for a candidate unless they recognize him; this problem of political marketing dwarfs any comparable problem of mercantile marketing. Yet the purchase of recognition, or the staging of those performances that excite publicity, are rich men's games. Where renown cannot be purchased, it can be won only by the high patronage of a favoring national press (usually reserved for Republicans) or else by the high patronage of a Washington administration that exhibits a man before the nation as a Cabinet-rank Secretary or diplomatic dignitary. The administration that controls the White House can arbitrarily elevate any individual to attention on the national stage, as Roosevelt did for Truman, Harriman and half a dozen others or as Eisenhower did for Nixon.

But if a regional political leader cannot win national recognition in these simple and superior ways, then he must do it by showing muscle at the polls, where the voters can make him news—as did Estes Kefauver in 1952 and 1956. This is the route of the primary elections—the hard way. But for Humphrey, Jim Rowe insisted, there was no other way. What recognition he would win, he would have to win by stumping the primary states, by challenging John F. Kennedy, or any other, to public contest at the polls.

It was obvious, further, that there was not enough money to contest a truly broad spectrum of the primaries, à la Kefauver. In 1952 Kefauver had swept the Democratic primaries simply because he was uncontested. In 1956, making a second run over the same route in contest with Adlai Stevenson, Kefauver had collapsed first in Florida, then dramatically in California, when he ran out of money and vitality. This time it was certain that Humphrey would be fought every inch of the way by John F. Kennedy of Boston, a man at least equal to Stevenson in combat effectiveness, and lavishly financed.

Therefore, went the Rowe-Humphrey theory of planning, the primary clashes must be chosen carefully. Humphrey could not hope to win enough delegates in primaries to dominate the Convention and moreover, he could not foresee the funds to put on a major showing in more than one of them. The primary contests had to be chosen, thus, so that he would come into the Convention with a minimum of 150 to 200 votes, and the right kind of votes besides. He needed this minimum figure, first, to establish a bargaining position in Los Angeles; he needed it, next, to win the attention and support of the earnest citizen groups who play so large a role in Democratic politics; he needed it, above all, to buy the attention of the big-city political bosses of the East, the men who control the most disciplined platoons of merchandisable votes at Democratic conventions. It is difficult to buy the attention of the big-city bosses of the East with money (they can milk their cities of all the money they need for their own purposes); it is difficult, also, to buy them with patronage (federal patronage is largely a matter of honor in big cities—glamorous but not substantial; the patronage that counts in big cities are magistracies, judgeships, clerkships, licensing commissioners). Big-city bosses can usually be swayed only be a national candidate's demonstration of surplus disposable power at the polls, by a political glamour demonstrated as so appealing that voters will indiscriminately in November fatten the local ticket at the base and strengthen the machine's local candidates where it counts, at home.

If the primaries were rightly chosen and won, then Humphrey would have his minimum bargaining base of 150 or 200 Convention votes—he could then expect the support of the citizen groups and the old Stevensonian zealots; he would have shown his muscle to the big-city bosses of the Northeast; and then, with these two groups behind him, he would be able to overpower the Southern oligarchs in convention assembled.

But which primaries? If Humphrey chose only the easy ones, where his natural appeal was overpowering, victories in these would do little to release him from the narrow niche of extreme liberalism in which he was politically framed. Thus the District of Columbia primary could be easily won—but it would impress no one, because the District of Columbia vote is so largely Negro, and the Negroes were already emotionally committed in advance to Humphrey, the far-out liberal. The South Dakota primary could also be won easily—but it, too, would impress no one, for it was a neighboring state, in which farm issues were most important, and so considered agrarian territory that belonged to Humphrey in advance anyway. Wisconsin was good, though; a state of mixed loyalties, of diverse ethnic origins, both industrial and agricultural, highly Catholic (31 per cent)—and close enough to Minnesota to be sensitive to the over-the-border and week-end proselytizing of Humphrey's Minnesota staff. In theory, because Wisconsin was so close, a campaign there could be fought at minimum cost. West Virginia was also good—a state of vast unemployment, an attractive battleground, and far enough from home so that regional victory there would make Humphrey's appeal seem nationwide. Then there was Oregon, on the Pacific Coast, a wide-open, free-for-all primary, but one in which the state Democratic Party seemed to be reviving on the same citizen base that sustained Humphrey in Minnesota and the new Democrats in the upper Midwest.

This would make five primaries plus the Convention—which brought the Humphrey men to a consideration of money. There was never, from beginning to end, enough money in Humphrey's campaign chest to see him all the way through to the end of the primary parade, and always, from December on, as much of his energy and that of his aides was spent in raising money as was spent in active politicking.

Fundamentally, though, for all the talk of expenses, money and sources, the Humphrey campaign depended not on money, but on the ideas and the emotions that Humphrey could arouse, on his ability to communicate his crusader's enthusiasm to the people of the nation directly. If Humphrey's reading of the American mood were correct, if his romantic emotions were in harmony with those of the voters, if his techniques of cross-alliances of labor unions–intellectuals–farmers (so effective in Minnesota) could be generalized across the land—then he would win. And Wisconsin, so similar to Minnesota, was the place to begin. All resources, thus, had to be spent first in Wisconsin to get the word across. If Humphrey won on Wisconsin, that victory would generate the funds needed to carry West Virginia; if he won in West Virginia, then he could raise more money for the next round . . . and if . . . and if . . . and so to the Convention.

So Humphrey, as the fall of 1959 entered winter—a man

seeing a long-risk campaign based on however great or small his appeal to Americans might be in strange primaries in strange states where his fervor was untested. So into the fateful new year as on December 30, 1959, he called the ritual Washington press conference to make the ritual announcement of his formal candidacy; and Humphrey was first man off and running in the campaign of 1960.

"I never really said what I was running for," Humphrey remarked to a friend late in the summer of 1960 when, his Presidential hopes having been blasted, he was fighting desperately to be re-elected Senator back in Minnesota. "You notice," he went on, with a poor man's disarming smile at his own guile, "all those buttons and posters I printed? They said 'Humphrey in Sixty.' But they didn't say what for."

If the Humphrey campaign illustrated one Democratic approach to the Presidency, the campaign of Stuart Symington, simultaneous in conception, illustrated another.

The Humphrey campaign had set out to demonstrate power at the roots, with the voters; then, if successful, to deal with the power brokers of South and East who controlled delegates.

But the Symington campaign was aimed first and directly at the power brokers themselves.

No more than in the case of Hubert Humphrey can one be precise about the moment when the Presidency first glimmered in Stuart Symington's imagination. One can only mark when the thought was first uttered aloud, to whom, and what provoked the confidence.

In November, 1958, a season of spectacular Democratic triumphs and Republican defeats, the citizens of Missouri had re-elected Stuart Symington to the Senate by the shattering margin of 780,056 (66.4 per cent) to 393,847 (33.6 per cent). In American politics, any election that the voters settle by 55 per cent or better is a landslide; this was greater than a landslide. Exhausted from campaigning, Symington and his handsome wife, Evie, flew almost immediately to Puerto Rico, to recuperate there in the sun by the sea, as guests of Puerto Rico's governor, Luis Muñoz-Marín. While Symington rested, his mind projected the possible meaning of his recent triumph against the background of national voting. And so he sat down and wrote, in one of his rare longhand letters, to a fellow Missourian, Clark Clifford of Washington, that as soon as he returned to the capital they must have a very serious talk about the general situation.

Clark Clifford, too, is a Washington lawyer of the elite. He

is a man whose silken smoothness and handsome good looks
are almost cloying to an Easterner of the big cities, until one
observes that the smoothness stems from genuine good manners that accompany an impressively analytical mind. Clifford
(a protégé of Harry Truman's at the White House, where he
served as speech writer and general counsel while learning
politics from the Old Master as only the Old Master could
teach them) had been one of Symington's closest friends for
years; had urged him out into his first seemingly hopeless
Senatorial campaign in Missouri in 1952; had guided him
constantly in Washington in the years before and since.

The first meeting of the Symington campaign was, then, a
gathering of only two men, early in January, 1959, three or
four days after Symington's return from Puerto Rico; it took
place at the 150-year-old white farm house of Clark Clifford
on Rockville Pike, just beyond Bethesda, Maryland. The
ladies, Mrs. Clifford and Mrs. Symington, dined with the men
and, as soon as dishes were cleared, let the men depart to
Clifford's upstairs den, where they talked alone until 1:30 in
the morning.

There was no moment, as Clifford remembers it, when
Symington dramatically strode across the room, thrust out
his hand and said, "Clark, I'm going in." It was rather a long,
sober discussion in which Symington frankly stated that he
now was, indeed, seriously thinking about the Presidency,
that he knew Clifford had been thinking along similar lines for
him, that he wanted the honest net summary of Clifford's
thinking. The evening was exploratory, noteworthy only in
that it was the first time that Symington had ever permitted
himself to say openly to anyone else that he would attempt
the contest.

Months of conversation were to follow between that initial
meeting and the early fall of 1959, before, at a Sunday morning meeting on September 6th, again at Clark Clifford's home,
there came the final survey and decision to run. Between these
two meetings, contacts had been made across the country,
explorations pursued and the home base, Missouri, mobilized.
Now there were eight men. In addition to Clifford and Symington, there was the full Missouri team—James Meredith,
the late Richard R. Nacy, Denton Smith, Wilbur Daniels,
Stanley Fike (the Senator's personal aide), and Charles
Brown, Congressman from the Seventh Missouri Congressional District, later to be the field manager of the political
operation. From this gathering, there were missing only Governor James T. Blair of Missouri (like Governor Freeman of
Minnesota, Blair was to make the entire Missouri state ma-

chinery available for the national operation) and the greatest Missourian of all, ex-President Harry Truman.

The discussion that took place revolved around resources, rivalries and decisions.

The chief resource, all felt, was the candidate himself. He came, geographically, from the right part of the country for a Democrat—an industrialized border state. He had the handsome, silver-haired appearance of a President. His record of experience had been one of success in private business, success in the executive branch of the government, success in the Senate. His voting record was solidly liberal. And his ability, in the opinion of the men gathered, was unmatched by any rival.

His problem was similar to Humphrey's—that outside Missouri he was basically unknown, while to those who did recognize his name he was known as a single-issue man, a specialist who knew defense and nothing else, and who in that field was tagged "The Big Bomber Boy." Further, Symington's personal political contacts across the country, essential in the weaving of a national campaign, were limited. Finally, his press contacts were weak or worse, the Washington press viewing him generally as a monomaniac on the subject of defense and a lightweight in all else.

Even then the gathering could peg the other possible Democratic candidates and the conjunction of competition they might meet: there was Humphrey—but they felt certain Humphrey would never be accepted by the Southern oligarchy. Lyndon Johnson, they felt equally certain, would never pass muster with the powerful labor leaders of the Northeast. Pat Brown, Governor of California, they dismissed because if there was to be a Catholic contender, there was room for only one, and that clearly was Kennedy. Meyner of New Jersey, then regarded as a dark horse, they dismissed because they felt his youthful departure from Catholicism would lose him votes and delegates from both watersheds of bigotry, Catholic and Protestant. John F. Kennedy, they knew, was the chief competition. But he was young, he was a Catholic, he looked like a boy and had no record of executive experience. Stevenson's action could not be calculated at the moment.

The configuration of the Convention that emerged from their deliberations read simply: deadlock. One quarter of the Convention of Democrats would, as always, be held by Southern leadership. The rest of the Convention would probably split into all the component minorities that make up the majority party of the nation—a big-city, heavily Catholic bloc; a rural, farm-dominated Midwestern bloc; an egghead-citizen–group bloc. Besides that, there would be the heavy, splintering pressure of the crescent Negro lobby and the over-powering labor lobby. Plus any number of favorite sons. The Convention would almost certainly follow a Humphrey-Kennedy primary clash in the spring. And if, as seemed possible, the primaries would be inconclusive ("A good clean fight from which no survivors emerged," was the way some hopeful Washington wits phrased it), then the Convention of Demo-crats would divide into its component fractions, and it would be up to the power brokers who captained these groups to choose a compromise candidate.

Any way one looked at it, the Democratic Convention of 1960, seen from the fall of 1959, spelled deadlock. And if there was to be a deadlock, no more perfect candidate could be found than Stuart Symington.

There was, indeed, some discussion of whether Symington should enter the primaries. But, first of all, primaries required a huge sum of money—at least $200,000 was the estimate for a single major effort. Next, the national press image of Sy-mington as a lightweight had to be rectified before he could be presented in primary states where he was a stranger. Fur-ther, the august prestige of Harry Truman was cast against any participation in primaries. The Sage of Independence, Missouri, had now become the patron and biggest political asset of Stuart Symington. But Truman, like most men who have graduated in politics from big-city machines, sees open primaries as akin to sin, as civil war that periodically threatens to tear party organization apart, a quadrennial jousting in which victory guarantees nothing (*vide* Estes Kefauver), but in which defeat kills (*vide* Harold Stassen and Wendell Willkie). Besides—where? which primary? In Wisconsin, where Hum-phrey would take the farm vote and Kennedy the Catholic vote, Symington would certainly run a poor third. In West Virginia, could a man of Symington's patrician manners and executive temper compete with rough-and-ready brawlers like Humphrey and Kennedy? Further—a primary would open bitterness between Symington and all his rivals. For a man whose chief chance of selection lay in compromise, why arouse bitterness?

The decision on the primaries was left open as the 1959 fall meeting broke up. But, in essence and by default, a de-cision had been taken. Symington and his lieutenants would deal with the net of power brokers, the nerve system of politics that Harry Truman had so artfully mastered in his years in office and now hoped to transfer to his new choice,

Symington. Hopefully, it was felt that the king makers, real or imagined, in the big cities and states would see Symington as their only safe choice for the Presidency. Carmine de Sapio and Michael Prendergast, whose power then seemed enormous in New York, were friendly; Jake Arvey's dwindling but still potent influence in Chicago might be brought along; David Lawrence of Pennsylvania might be won; the remnants of the McKinney organization in Indiana would almost certainly follow McKinney, who followed wherever Harry Truman pointed. Southerners, if they could not have Johnson, expressed preference for Symington, and House Speaker Sam Rayburn was particularly warm. Beyond that lay the knowledge that Symington's record held potential appeal to Negro voters for an advanced civil rights position, to labor for advanced labor positions, to businessmen who could measure his achievements in private industry. Other candidates might be first choice in each of these areas—but none was every man's second choice.

Deep, deep, in the approach of Symington's managers was a conviction—almost naive for such seasoned politicians—that ability alone could sell a man for the Presidency. The kind of ability Symington possesses is caviar to the general; his is a personality that either in Germany or in Britain guarantees a brilliant parliamentary career but that in the brawl of American politics usually fails. The root of the matter is that Symington's effectiveness shows best in inverse proportion to the size of the group in which he gathers. In a public gathering Symington is flat and colorless; in a group of ten he is moderately persuasive; in groups of four, three and two he can be brilliantly dominant. An executive to the core, a man fascinated by the direction and proper organization of other men, he is a man excited by responsibility, one who likes to make things work. This is a person who appeals best to men who, like himself, deal in terms of organization and power.

These were the men at whom the Symington candidacy was pointed—the established leadership of the Democratic organization. For when one talks to political bosses, one is impressed over and over again by how seriously they, who are such narrow men, consider the Presidency. A favorite word of some politicians when talking about a Presidential candidate is "heft." ("Is he heavy enough?" they ask, or they say, "He's too light for the job.") Another word sometimes used is "sizable." ("Is he sizable enough for the job?" or, "He's got the size of a governor, he ain't got the size of a President.") And again measuring capacity, they ask, "Can he go all the way?"

Given their choice, small politicians prefer as President a man who will bring votes to fatten their base, one whose radiant name guarantees them victory in their local contests. This preference for a strong leader of the ticket is sometimes referred to as the Shorenstein rule, for Hymie Shorenstein was the man who best expressed it over a generation ago. Hymie Shorenstein was the large, rotund leader of the Brownsville district of Brooklyn, New York, many years ago, when that community was still solidly Jewish. A big man in his own territory, Hymie normally delivered majorities of fourteen or fifteen to one; and when Hymie grew passionate he could do better—in one Rooseveltian election he delivered 60,000 to 3,000 for the great FDR. Such a man was no negligible force in the larger Brooklyn machine of Boss McCooey, whom he served as satrap. Hymie believed in a strong leader of the ticket; it helped him all the way. One year—so the well-worn story goes—as the politicians divided up the local nominations, it was given to Shorenstein to choose a Democratic candidate for judge as his share of the patronage. The candidate so named thereupon contributed heavily to Shorenstein for campaign expenditures and watched the campaign's progress well into October—but could see no posters blazoning his name on walls, no organization working, no parades or demonstrations. Worried about his chances, the candidate marched into the anteroom of Boss McCooey one afternoon to complain about Shorenstein's sloth. There he met Shorenstein himself, also waiting to see McCooey; and when Shorenstein asked why his candidate was there, the candidate unburdened himself of his fears. "Ah," replied Shorenstein, "you're worried? Listen. Did you ever go down to the wharf to see the Staten Island Ferry come in? You ever watch it, and look down in the water at all those chewing-gum wrappers, and the banana peels and the garbage? When the ferryboat comes into the wharf, automatically it pulls all the garbage in too. The name of your ferryboat is Franklin D. Roosevelt—stop worrying!"

The Shorenstein rule no longer has quite the strength it had a generation ago, for Americans, with increasing education and sophistication, split their tickets; more and more they are reluctant to follow the leader. Politicians, of course, still look for a strong leader of the ticket; yet when they cannot find such a man, when it is they who must carry the President in an election rather than vice versa, they want someone who will be a good effective President, a strong executive, one who will keep the country running smoothly and prosperously while they milk it from underneath. In talking to some of the hard-rock, old-style politicians in New York about war and peace, I have found them intensely interested in war and peace for two reasons. The first is that the draft is a bother to them in their districts ("Always making trouble with mothers and families"); and the second is that it has sunk in on them that if an H-bomb lands on New York City (which they know to be Target A), it will be bad for business, bad for politics, bad for the machine. The machine cannot operate in atomic rubble. In the most primitive way they do not want H-bombs to fall on New York City—it would wipe out their crowd along with all the rest. They want a strong President, who will keep a strong government, a strong defense, and deal with them as barons in their own baronies. They believe in letting the President handle war and peace, inflation and deflation, France, China, India and foreign affairs (but not Israel, Ireland, Italy or, nowadays, Africa), so long as the President lets them handle their own wards and the local patronage.

Old-style big-city bosses are the most provincial of all political leaders, far more provincial than the stout little Radical-Socialist or M.R.P. politicians of Bas-Rhin or Marseille or any French provincial town who have opinions on everything. American big-city bosses would divide the world with Caesar, leaving to Caesar all the world without let or hindrance, so long as Caesar left them in control of their streets, parks, licenses and local appointments. Truman, one of our greatest Presidents on the grand scale of world history, was also a great President in their terms. In Symington, several of the big-city politicians were inclined to believe they would have a "safe" President. He looked the part, which was important to them. He knew all about such things as missiles, the Pentagon, foreign affairs, farm subsidies, inflation and deflation, and could govern the country safely. He was also safe as a boss: as a political executive, he gave the impression of a man who would recognize their domain and responsibility as they would recognize his.

Symington is, to be sure, a far more "sizable" man than this distorted picture reflects. He is a virtuoso of modern executive administration, whether in government or in business, a man who loves and understands administrative simplicities and complexities as few other Democrats do. He is a man who has made his fortune and, like so many such men, now offers his life for service.

Unfortunately a Presidential candidate must generate an extra-reasonable emotion; he must generate it across the press, across television and across radio, and through all the strange media of this enormous country, until it stirs the spirits of the men and women who vote. Symington had been able to generate a genuine magic in his home state of Missouri. But his managers saw no way of demonstrating a nationwide magic until, after the Convention, the power brokers once having chosen him, he could reach the people as Democratic candidate, heir to all the emotions and traditions of the Party.

Thus, Symington's strategy, like Humphrey's strategy, was inescapable.

Since Humphrey could expect no generosity nor any mercy from the power brokers until he showed muscle at the polls in the primaries, Humphrey was forced to choose the primary route. Humphrey would never be anyone's compromise choice.

Since Symington could hope for friendly audience from the power brokers and friendly appreciation of his abilities through the intercession of Harry Truman; and since, further, his hope lay in a deadlocked Convention; and since, even further, at the Convention he must emerge as the compromise candidate with the acquiescence of his rivals, the bitter fratricidal war of the primaries was a condition he must avoid.

Thus Symington and Clifford in the summer of 1959. They were not to announce the candidacy until March 24, 1960—too late.

The campaign of Lyndon B. Johnson, then Majority Leader of Senate and now Vice-President of the United States, illustrated yet another field of force in American political power.

Superficially Lyndon B. Johnson's campaign was the old Southern campaign. There has always been a Southern candidate at Democratic Conventions, from the days of Joseph T. Robinson and John Nance Garner down through Richard Russell and Lyndon B. Johnson. The South sends approximately one quarter of the delegates to the Democratic National Convention, and it expects to be listened to—or at least to return home having fought the good, if hopeless fight. Lyndon B. Johnson had been the traditional hopeless Southern candidate in 1956.

In 1960 he sought to be something more.

The Johnson candidacy was earlier in moving publicly off the scratch line than either the Humphrey or Symington candidacies, and when it did, it moved with apparent carefree gaiety from its home base in Texas. There, on October 17th, 1959, at a press conference in Dallas, Speaker of the House Sam Rayburn announced the formation of an "unofficial" Johnson for President committee, of which he and Texas Governor Price Daniel were co-chairmen. Shortly thereafter, a Johnson headquarters was established in the Littlefield Building in Austin, the state capital, and from this headquarters, all through the fall and winter of 1959 and 1960, proceeded the "noisemakers" of the Johnson campaign —local Texas politicians seeking to test their skills on a national level, supported by fuglemen of the Texas little-rich who provided bodies and manpower in kind if not in cash. Together they chanted "All The Way With LBJ" across the South and Far West. Instantly identifiable by their Texan garb, their yellow rose insignia, their ten-gallon hats (and, said their enemies, by the cowflap on their boots), they came and went in waves of frolic and fun, making tumult at every Democratic gathering between the Missouri and the Pacific. They kept Lyndon B. Johnson's name in audience, offered liquid hospitality, lobbied in Texas courthouse style for country delegates, and made much noise—but little else. Their activities absorbed the bursting energies of the Texas base; but whether they did more harm than good is still a matter of dispute.

What serious Johnson strategy there was lay in the conception of more impressive men. At this level of high calculation, only five men counted: two principals—Lyndon B. Johnson himself, and Sam Rayburn, sachem of the American Congress; and three others—John Connally,[1] the Majority Leader's most important political lieutenant for many years in his home state; burly George Reedy, the candidate's personal adviser and assistant in Washington; and Irvin Hoff, a field scout lent to Johnson for political reconnaissance in the West by Senator Warren G. Magnuson of Washington State.

The analysis these men made of the upcoming Convention of 1960 was not too different in departure from that of the Symington chieftains: the future read deadlock. But from there on, the Johnson approach to solution of the Convention deadlock was entirely different from that of the Symington captains. The power system on which the Johnson thinkers relied to master the Convention came from their command of the American Congressional system of politics. These men knew that the Johnson candidacy could not be muscled

---

[1] Now Secretary of the Navy.

by seeking individual Convention delegates. They knew, further, that whatever public image the nation might have of Johnson as the Convention floundered in anticipated confusion could come only from Johnson's record as the guileful, unflustered Mr. Fix-It of the Democratic Senate Majority. If the Convention deadlocked, if the Johnson image of a shrewd master of men were preserved across the 1960 session of Congress, then their plans could begin to work.

Their plans rested squarely on their control of Congress, on the enormous accumulation of political debts and uncashed obligations that, between them, Johnson and Rayburn had earned over years of the legislative trade. Scarcely a state in the union which did not domicile one political leader who, publicly or privately, freshly or for many decades, did not owe Rayburn or Johnson a repayment of favor for a bill passed, favorable legislation brought to the floor, some regional boon for state, city or district. Far-off Connecticut, the uncontested property of Governor Abraham Ribicoff and Boss John Bailey, was as solid for John Kennedy as was Massachusetts. But even in solid Connecticut, Junior Senator Thomas J. Dodd, trapped and bound over to Kennedy hand and foot by Connecticut's unit rule, belonged in heart to Rayburn and Johnson; if Connecticut broke after a deadlock, Dodd would lead for Johnson there. Across the country, the names of other beneficiaries were numberless. Even in Negro Harlem in New York, where greatest resistance to a Southern candidate might be anticipated by amateurs, Congressman Adam Clayton Powell could be counted on to support Johnson in return for validation of his claim on the committee chairmanship for which he yearned . . . and for other favors. All across the country the political season of 1960 would bring to the polls a fresh crop of Congressional and Senatorial aspirants, all of whom knew that their committee assignments in Congress and their first requests would be strained through machinery controlled by Johnson and Rayburn; where past gratitude could not be relied on, the Congressional system of politics could inspire enough fear or hope in such men to mollify or neutralize their hostility at the Convention. The system of American Congressional politics is a magnificent legislative process, perhaps the most effecfive in any Western democracy. But the congressional system of politics is as different from the systems of city-hall, state-house and Presidential politics as one system of specialized machine tools is different from another. It was Johnson's opinion that the machinery of Congressional politics could be applied to Presidential politics.

One other operational element in the Johnson front should
be noted, not for its effectiveness, but for the soft glow of
nostalgia it throws over American political history. This was
the New Dealers. If any candidate in the 1960 sweepstakes
was the candidate of the old New Deal, it was Lyndon B.
Johnson. A loose and highly ineffective coalition of aging
New Dealers operated as the Northern (Washington-New
York) wing of the Johnson campaign as awkwardly as did
the Austin regulars. These New Dealers included no less
eminent advisers than Dean Acheson, Oscar Chapman and
Tommy "The Cork" Corcoran (Johnson's back-room Washington lawyer—every Democratic candidate needs Washington lawyers). To these New Deal names should be added
that of Supreme Court Justice William O. Douglas, who
gave his blessing, and that of one-time New-Deal hortatorian,
now turned businessman, Eliot Janeway. Among them, and
chiefly in New York, they managed to raise no less than
$135,000 for the Johnson campaign; yet they were no more
effective than the Texas wing of the Johnson campaign, whom
the New Yorkers affected to despise as "Texas Rangers"
and whom they saw as wearing cowboy boots, reeking of
the stable.

These New Dealers are interesting chiefly as men clutching at the past. They were all of a generation that had found
new perspectives and great horizons when they were young
in the political architecture of Franklin D. Roosevelt, as had
Lyndon B. Johnson himself. Technically, their loyalties lay
with what the French would call "the class of 1948." For in
1948, with Truman's victory, the Democratic Party had bade
farewell to the world of Franklin D. Roosevelt—yet honored
him, in state after state, by thrusting to nationwide attention
a group of men, all of them his political children, who were
to dominate the party for the next decade. Nineteen-forty-
eight was the year when Illinois first chose Adlai Stevenson
and Paul Douglas, when Connecticut chose Chester Bowles,
when Minnesota first chose Hubert Humphrey, when Tennessee elevated Estes Kefauver to the Senate—and when
Texas lifted Lyndon B. Johnson from the obscurity of the
House of Representatives and named him Senator by a
margin of eighty-seven votes. All of these names were those
of men whose thinking had been shaped by the New Deal.
Now, as election year approached, seeking a standard bearer
for the New Deal in the sixties, most of the old back-room
New Deal operators fastened on the name of Lyndon B.
Johnson to back against the field. Instinctively they sensed
that they must close ranks against John F. Kennedy, a man

of the younger war generation. This decade of the sixties they had seen as their own. In their cluster about Lyndon B. Johnson, one could first notice that separation of generations which in both parties in 1960 was to range young against old; and if one were wise enough, one could note that not only did vitality and vision favor the young, but also the actuarial tables.

Yet as 1959 ended and 1960 began, neither the aging New Dealers nor the glandular Texans of Lyndon B. Johnson's native ranges had a sounder strategy than that of their shrewd principal—which continued to be to do as good a job as possible leading a Senate bursting with ambitions and to hope for a Convention deadlock, which the Congressional power system might master.

All these campaigns—those of Humphrey, of Symington, of Johnson—were thus, by the end of 1959, organizations in being, shapeless perhaps, yet captained by men who meant to be President of the United States and staffed by in-groups of three, five or ten men, whose lives and ambitions were now devoted to no other purpose.

At the end of 1959 there remained another man, uncertain, willing yet unwilling to be President, who was seven months later to be John F. Kennedy's chief rival for the Democratic nomination. He was Adlai E. Stevenson, whose motives and intentions no man could read—probably, at that point, not even himself.

To the outer eye, and even to his family and intimates, Adlai Stevenson was by 1959 a happy man. He had returned to Libertyville, Illinois, and his old farmhouse after the 1952 campaign, a lonely and melancholy man—defeated in election, his marriage broken, his children away at school, his home strange to him after being rented out for many years. The years between 1952 and 1956 he had spent with more than half a hankering for the Democratic nomination of 1956 and a deep sense of obligation to the party that had gone so deeply in debt on his behalf. With his defeat in 1956, however, a more philosophical turn seems to have come over him. Now his son Adlai Jr. lived just down the road from him; and young Adlai and his sweet wife, Nancy, would visit with the children on week ends. Home life was mending. Stevenson loved Libertyville and the quiet sound of the trees rustling when in summer, in blue sneakers and blue shorts, he would sun himself on the lawn. He slept in his own bed at his own choice; dignitaries and scholars from all the world made pilgrimage to his home; he could dash off to New York to taste the metropolitan excitement of the big city when and as he chose; and his trips around the world as a journalist kept him acquainted with great affairs of state at the level he preferred.

If this happy and placid man gave political calculators an impression of total schizophrenia, the reason was a simple one—Adlai Stevenson was and, I believe, remains torn in attitude to the two great systems of power that mesh in the unity of the American Presidency. Stevenson's attitude to public affairs approaches a nobility rarely encountered in the political system of any country; but his attitude to politics —the grubby, rooty politics of noise and deals and cruelties and chicaneries—is one of contempt. Yet public affairs and politics are linked as are love and sex. Stevenson's attitude to politics has always seemed that of a man who believes love is the most ennobling of human emotion while the mechanics of sex are dirty and squalid.

This seemed to be the quality of his reflections. "Deep down," said his closest friend during the winter months of 1959–60, "he wants it. But he wants the Convention to come to him, he doesn't want to go to the Convention."

With half his mind Stevenson shrank from memory of the sordid brutality of pre-Convention politics; nothing had so exhausted his vitality or good spirits as the murderous continental string of primaries he had fought to defeat Estes Kefauver in 1956—from New Hampshire through Minnesota through Florida through California. Indeed it is not too much to say that Stevenson's vitality has never recovered from the savagery of the 1956 primary campaign, followed so relentlessly and swiftly by the exertion of the 1956 electoral campaign. Stevenson knew and hated the intraparty warfare of domestic politics that, in the American system, creates and commands internal power.

On the other hand, there was the other aspect of the Presidency, the outer disposition of American power: that which lies at the disposal of a President once he arrives at the White House, the immense and majestic forces and influence that belong to any President. These fascinated Stevenson. His chief concern lay with America's position and role in the changing outer world; his journeys abroad for eight full years had made him intimately aware of the pressures in the world about us, of its dangers and promises. This concern, expressed in eloquent speeches, private conversations, many articles, had communicated itself across the country with sharper impact than that of any other private citizen of the

nation. To dispose of the power of America in the outer
world was a task that Stevenson, as a good citizen, could
not shrink from if called on; but he would not act, or deal,
or connive, or strike a blow to seize the Presidential nomination if his party did not offer it to him. Nor could any man
shake him from this simple stand until the last twenty-four
hours before the nominations at Los Angeles.

Yet many tried. There is an axiom in politics that a candidacy for any office is not simply the expression of individual
ambition—any great candidacy is the gathering place of
many men's ambitions. In Stevenson's case, this axiom was
raised to its highest degree. Stevenson would not act of himself. Yet he was, in political terms, a major property—he
could not be left neglected. His appeal was nationwide; in
Pennsylvania Governor David Lawrence, boss of that state,
still gave him an almost youthful adoration; in California
his zealots were the only genuine enthusiasts for anyone in
that state; in New York, in Illinois, in Wisconsin, in Oregon,
were other devoted forces. All across the country youngsters
he had summoned to politics with high morality in 1952 had
now matured and were unwilling in their maturity to forsake
him. If Stevenson would not act, others would act for him.

Organized Stevenson activity began as early as December
of 1959—and in all the months that followed, one must distinguish between volunteer fanatics who panted for the
leader of 1952 and 1956 at all costs, no matter what the
means; and the serious planners who slowly and silently
linked their efforts across the country to keep the nomination
open until they could persuade their principal to reach for it.

Four focal points marked the serious effort. One was in
Madison, Wisconsin, where James Doyle, former Wisconsin
Democratic State Chairman, was financed by Stevenson
friends from Chicago to keep a watchful eye on the wild
Stevenson amateur groups forming across the country, the
hope being that he might keep the responsible volunteers
responsible. Another was established in New York, where a
New York reform group won the financial help of Mrs. Ag-
nes Meyer of Washington to retain the full-time services of
author William Attwood[2] to prepare research and speech
material for Stevenson against the spring season of political
activity. A third group, largely devoted to fund raising for
the big push, operated out of Los Angeles, under the guidance
of moviemaker Dore Schary. Coordinating these three groups
was the fourth: a Washington center of four men, George

[2] Now United States Ambassador to Guinea.

Ball,[3] a Washington lawyer, and his youthful partner John Sharon, who worked in close partnership with Senator Mike Monroney and his able executive aide, Tom Finney. It was the Ball-Sharon-Monroney-Finney group that acted as strategy center.

These men could move no faster than their candidate—but against the day when he *would* move, or against the day when the primaries would split the Party open, or against the day when the nation would demand Stevenson, they meant to make plans. When opportunity came, they must be ready.

As December wore round the corner of winter into January and the candidacies of Humphrey and Kennedy were announced, the pressures on Stevenson grew. Still he remained firm; he would not seek the nomination. In the years since 1956 he had won in the crisp, hard-eyed world of professional lawyers an increasing respect as a cool, exact, skillful and effective attorney. Now as a member of the Board of Directors of the *Encyclopædia Britannica* he had some intricate legal work to do in South America in preparation for the Spanish edition of that massive work; as a lawyer, he was of counsel to Reynolds Metals, and they, too, required some work done in South America. At the end of January, still silent and perplexed, he set out on a two-months tour of business and sight-seeing in South America, leaving his candidacy without a candidate as the primaries approached.

Of all the groups that were then meeting in this germinal season of politics none, however, was more important than the group that met at Hyannisport, Massachusetts, on Wednesday morning, October 28th, 1959.

None weighed more heavily on the thinking of all the others than this one; and no other was to move on into American history.

They met in the living room of the home of Robert Kennedy, the same living room that one year and eleven days later was to be their command post on election night. It was, as the participants remember, a frosty New England day, quite clear; a child's football, half inflated, lay on the lawn outside; through the windows of the sunporch they could see the ocean; and through the windows beyond the fireplace they could see the turning fall color of the New England

---

[3] Now Undersecretary of State for Economic Affairs.

leaves, flaunting their red and gold against the dead winter green of the scrub pines of the Cape. Hyannisport sits on the underarm of Cape Cod; the magnificent sand beaches of the Atlantic that run from Florida through New Jersey through Fire Island to end in Massachusetts are at their most beautiful here in the simple, unimproved dunes of the Cape. The room in which the men met was a simple one too—furnished in yellow and green lounge chairs, several worn easy chairs and a hassock or two; open to the sun, dominated by a big fireplace, it was a comfortably large room for either party or conclave.

Sixteen people attended this conclave, and it is well to pause and study them, for their craftsmanship and vitality were in the next year to create a President—and with greater precision, against greater odds, across more contrary traditions, than had been shown by any group of amateur President makers since Abraham Lincoln's backers, a century before, had changed the structure of nineteenth-century politics. They were to act in a country at peace, moderately prosperous yet uneasily uncertain of its future, and totally unaware of what these men were planning for it.

Of these sixteen, nine at least should be starred for the record, for it was these nine who together created and directed the machinery that was to give them, a year later, in this room, their victory. Only two of these nine—the candidate and his brother—had ever participated in Presidential politics before; but each of the nine was in his way to prove indispensable. And though the campaign had been underway for a long time, this was the first time they had all gathered in the same room.

There were, to begin with, the candidate himself, John Fitzgerald Kennedy, and his brother Robert, host of the gathering; forty-two and thirty-three years old, respectively.

There were, next, two young men from Massachusetts. Kenneth O'Donnell,[4] thirty-five, a former Harvard football captain, team mate of Robert Kennedy at college, is a dark, lean, slight-figured man, taciturn, whose expression throughout the following year was to alternate publicly only between a quiet curiosity, expressed by raised dark eyebrows, and quiet amusement, expressed by the faintest turning of his mouth in a smile. O'Donnell's partner was Lawrence F. O'Brien[5] of Springfield, Massachusetts, forty-two, a placid, stocky man with a round benign face, an endless capacity

[4] Now Special Assistant to the President of the United States.
[5] Now Special Assistant to the President of the United States.

for work, never ruffled, almost unfailingly gentle. O'Donnell and O'Brien were a team, like quarterback and blocking center—O'Donnell the tactician, O'Brien the organizer. They thought in almost identical terms, and when they expressed an idea it was impossible to say whether it had come first from one or the other. They had been working in harness now for Kennedy for eight years; together they had overturned Massachusetts politics, victoriously battled the mucker element there in the name of their chief, and directed the 1958 Senatorial campaign of Kennedy that only a year before had swept Massachusetts by the incredible margin of 1,362,926 (73.6 per cent) to 488,318 (26.4 per cent) for Kennedy's nameless opponent. As a team, O'Donnell generally handled the candidate's person and reflections, transmitting the directives to O'Brien, who commanded the base of organization. Beyond these, but not at Hyannisport that morning, was a phalanx of other young men, *their* people, whom they had brought up in Massachusetts politics, who would staff and operate the campaign for the next year. These men were Kennedy's operating political arm.

There was, next, sitting beside the candidate, Theodore C. Sorensen,[6] then thirty-one. If O'Donnell and O'Brien were stewards of Kennedy's political personality, then Sorensen was steward of the candidate's intellectual personality. "My intellectual blood bank," Kennedy styled him late in the campaign. Tall, handsome, even more youthful in appearance than his age, quiet-spoken, shy, Sorensen, perhaps as much as any man, had helped educate the candidate to his present views. A gut-liberal (his father, in Nebraska, had been George Norris' campaign manager), Sorensen had now been with Kennedy for seven years; his introspection, his reading, his elegant writing, had stimulated many of Kennedy's finest thoughts and expressions. Hired originally as little more than an intellectual valet by the young Senator from Massachusetts in January, 1953, just after Kennedy had been elected to the seat, Sorensen had, by his learning, his dedication, his total devotion to his chief, become almost a lobe of Kennedy's mind. Through Sorensen were to filter, in the coming year, all major policy decisions on matters of national or international importance.

Sitting quietly, unobserved as usual, was Stephen Smith, thirty-one, a brother-in-law of the candidate, husband of his sister Jean. In January of 1959, ten months before, Steve Smith had come to Washington to open, unannounced, the

---

[6] Now Special Counsel to the President of the United States.

first Presidential headquarters of the Kennedy campaign. Slim, soft-spoken, absolutely discreet, business-trained (his family was one of the foremost of New York waterfront families), Smith was to be first office manager, then logistics manager, then unflustered administrative chief of all the impossibly complicated financial and personnel details of a campaign that eventually was to mobilize scores of thousands of volunteers and employees.

Present also was Louis Harris, a public-opinion analyst, thirty-eight, young, shrewd, vibrant, a man who found subtleties in statistics, a student of depth tides in American thinking. Proprietor of his own highly successful market-research firm, Harris had first been employed by the Kennedys as a public-opinion analyst prior to the Kennedy Senatorial race in Massachusetts in 1958. Accepting that job as little more than a routine professional contract, Harris had by now become so entranced by the Kennedy personality that his enthusiasm and excitement at practicing his craft at the summit of American politics made him a Kennedy zealot and a member of the inner circle. He was to poll in the following year more people across the country than had ever been done by any other political analyst in American history; upon his reports, upon his description of the profile of the country's thinking and prejudices as he found them, were to turn many of John F. Kennedy's major decisions.

Also there, for the first time admitted to the in-group, was Pierre Salinger,[7] then thirty-four. Salinger, an American of French descent, a man of dark, round face and broad cheeks, might, with ten or fifteen more years of age, be mayor of any Burgundian village—large in manner, full of gusto, a wine drinker and brandy bibber; his mind, in the French manner, is at once hugely jovial and quick, shrewd, practical. In the year to come, as his cigars grew bigger and his duties more responsible, Salinger was to harden from a boy to a man. Wartime skipper of a mine sweeper in the Pacific at the age of nineteen, then a newspaperman in California, then a Congressional investigator, he had twin loves—the craft of the press in general and the folklore of politics. It was, and is, a marvelous combination for press secretary, and no one who followed the Kennedy campaign through 1960 remembers Salinger with anything but respect and affection.

There was, lastly of the in-group, John Bailey, Democratic

---

[7] Now Press Secretary of the President of the United States.

State Chairman of Connecticut.[8] Bailey, a tall, cigar-smoking, baldheaded man, is one who affects an exterior hardness of manner, talks in a high, rusty, confidential tone of voice, and effectively conceals the fact that he is a Harvard Law School graduate. Bailey had in his fourteen years in office in Connecticut built the tightest New England political machine, which he operated with merciless efficiency. As a Catholic, he bears on his soul all the traditional wounds of the Protestant-Catholic clash in New England politics. But Bailey is in effect a transition political type. Able to talk politics in the toughest parochial terms with his fellow bosses across the Northeast, he is nonetheless able to go beyond that to an understanding of modern government too. Under his leadership Connecticut has had a succession of Democratic Governors among the ablest in the union. His role was to be that of shepherd of the Northeastern bosses in the Kennedy pre-Convention planning. None of the young men in the room, so youthful and so fresh, could win the confidence of the aging back-room power brokers who wield such influence in the Democratic Party; Bailey, then a ripe fifty-four years old but still youthful, was the man for such a job.

John F. Kennedy in his fourteen years in politics has had many servants, many aides, many helpers. As he has outgrown each level of operation, he has gently stripped off his earlier helpers and retained only those who could go on with him effectively to the next level. These men here assembled were those who had survived a decade of Kennedy selection. All of them were, in their own fields, quality men. In the personal Kennedy lexicon, no phrase is more damning than "He's a very common man" or "That's a very ordinary type." Kennedy, elegant in dress, in phrase, in manner, has always required quality work; these men by his standards were extraordinary; they were his choices.

The others in the room on the Wednesday morning were, all of them, in one degree or another, helpers and useful: his younger brother, Edward Kennedy; Hyman Raskin, a handsome, silver-haired Chicago lawyer; Mrs. Marjorie Lawson, an attractive Negro attorney from the District of Columbia; John Salter, a Washingtonian aide to Senator Henry F. Jackson; former Governor Dennis Roberts of Rhode Island; Robert Wallace, an administrative aide to the Senator; David Hackett, an old friend of Robert Kennedy. But these others were parts of the machinery, not leaders.

[8] Now Chairman of the Democratic National Committee.

Lastly, present on the roster, was Joseph P. Kennedy, one-time Ambassador to the Court of St. James, father of the candidate—a force unto himself.

The roots of this meeting lay deep. For three years now, ever since the defeat of Adlai E. Stevenson in 1956, the Kennedy strike for the Presidency had been underway. In the beginning, there had been but two men involved—Kennedy himself, and Ted Sorensen, his alter ego, Sorensen doubling as thinker, writer, contact man, field agent, political fingerman. After the Massachusetts Senatorial victory in 1958, more elaborate machinery had been required and staff began to grow. First Smith had opened Washington base offices. Then O'Brien had transferred to Washington from Massachusetts; then Harris had been launched and Salinger retained; local committees were quietly established everywhere that a possible regional Kennedy base might be of value.

A first survey meeting had taken place long since, in Palm Beach, Florida, on April 1st of 1959. Headquarters space and clerical help had been set up in ten rooms at the Esso Building in Washington in the spring, a quarter of a mile from the Senator's legislative chambers. By fall, Robert Kennedy, having resigned as counsel to the Senate Committee on Legislative Oversight and having also finished his own best-selling book, *The Enemy Within*, was ready to come aboard full time as campaign manager.

This was the meeting that was to see the final assault plans laid; it was to be a meeting for precise definition of functions. At its close, Sorensen, the effective campaign manager up to then, was to become national policy chief, and Bobby Kennedy, operational and practical campaign manager. All these men had been meeting week after week, traveling and reporting to the voluminous files and index system of headquarters for months now. But this was the first time all had gathered at one time away from Washington or New York or Boston or Hartford, away from telephone calls, away from press attention, to consider for a full day not the Yes or No of the Presidential strike, but the HOW: which levers, in what manner, must be pressed in the American structure of influence and control to bring about the occupation of the White House.

Each of those present remembers one fragment of the meeting, and no one can recall it all. Perhaps Sorensen's memory, for he has an historic memory, is best.

"Meetings are good for information," said Sorensen several months later, "for exchanging information, for clearing the air. Meetings are rarely the source of major decision. The fundamental note that morning, as of earlier meetings down in Palm Beach and in Washington, was the note of confidence. We were confident we knew how it would turn out, that we could meet them and lick them.

"There are no hard-and-fast, dramatic, black-and-white decisions that come out of a meeting like that. What comes out is a firming up of missions, after you decide from the top down what the problems are.

"Now the basic difficulties always boiled down to the facts that the country had never elected a Catholic, that the country had never elected a forty-three-year-old, that the country had only selected one Senator to be President in this century.

"This being true, you had to examine the nominating process, which is not a free open popular vote, but a process which is dominated and influenced by all the groups in the Democratic coalition—the farmers, labor, the South, the big-city people, etcetera. These groups are more influential in a convention than they are in the country as a whole. Therefore he had to prove to them that he could win. And to prove that to them, he'd have to fight hard to make them give it to him, he couldn't negotiate it. If the Convention ever went into the back rooms, he'd never emerge from those back rooms. So it evolved from the top down that you had to go into the primaries."

"From the top down" meant from the lips of the candidate to the attention and obedience of his staff, there assembled.

John F. Kennedy opened the meeting from where he stood, his back to the fireplace, facing the others as they sat, dressed in a sports jacket (which he later doffed), slacks and loafers, looking thoroughly boyish. (His hair was then still cut in the youthful brush cut with which the public was then familiar, later replaced by the more mature side cut of the present President.) He then proceeded to amaze them all by a performance that remains in the memory of all those who listened. Kennedy, who speaks from the platform in a high, resonant, almost melancholy tone of voice, is, in private, one of the more gifted conversationalists of politics, second only to Hubert Humphrey in the ease, simplicity and color with which he talks. On this morning he was at his best.

Now for three hours, broken only occasionally by a bit of information he might request of the staff, he proceeded, occasionally sitting, sometimes standing, to survey the entire country without map or notes. It was a tour of America region by region, state by state, starting with New England, moving through the Atlantic states and the Midwest, through the farm states and the mountain states, down the Pacific Coast, through the Southwest and then the South. "What I remember," says O'Brien, director of organization and keeper of the political ledgers, "was his remarkable knowledge of every state, not just the Party leaders, not just the Senators in Washington, but he knew all the factions and the key people in all the factions."

"We had," says Sorensen, "not only the best candidate there, but the best campaign manager, too. He knows the facts, who likes him and who doesn't, he knows where he should go and where he shouldn't, he has this incredible memory of places, names, dates, who should be written to and who shouldn't."

"He can still drive down an avenue in Boston," adds another, "and remember which stores put up his campaign posters ten years ago."

Now and then Kennedy would pause, ask for comment on a local political situation where one or the other of his staff men had particular knowledge, invite corrections, then go on. By the time he had finished and the group broke for lunch, the strategy had been clarified from the top down, as he saw it and meant to take it.

The nomination had to be won by the primary route. Not until he showed primitive strength with the voters in strange states could he turn and deal with the bosses and the brokers of the Northeast who regarded him fondly as a fellow Catholic but, as a Catholic, hopelessly doomed to defeat. And all the while the primary campaigns were being mounted, attention must be paid to the other states—contacts with the bosses in machine states, citizen committees in states where citizens were effective; and all of this with a projection beyond the Convention, with the organization so tooled that on the day after the Convention it could be converted into election machinery.

There were in all sixteen states of the union that were to hold primaries in 1960 for the choosing of delegates to the national Convention. Some should not be entered for fear of offending favorite sons; some should not be entered because they were unimportant. But of the sixteen, a broad enough number had to be chosen to give a national cast to the campaign, and those chosen had to be of value for their impact on neighboring states and on the big bosses who would be watching. And every primary had to be won —there could be no stumbling. "It has to come up seven every time," said Kennedy later, on the evening of the first contested primary in Wisconsin.

No hard-and-fast decisions on primaries were made at the morning meeting—except for New Hampshire. That had to be entered as the nation's first and as a matter of course. Ten of the other states were put on a list for consideration as opportunity and politics developed during the next few months.

Wisconsin was uppermost in the minds of all at the moment—a big victory there would destroy Hubert Humphrey for good; but Wisconsin was dangerous. Disagreement about Wisconsin was to divide the Kennedy staff for the next two months, until Kennedy, supported only by his father and Lou Harris, overrode his brother and all the others and entered there. There was Maryland, a strong possibility (later accepted); Indiana—interesting (if Stuart Symington could be lured to challenge in the Indiana primary and be wiped out there, it would be worth the effort; Symington, realizing the trap, briefly considered Indiana in the spring and then dodged it); Oregon was unavoidable, for the Oregon laws forced all candidates, willy-nilly, onto the primary ballot; West Virginia was vaguely discussed—no one at the moment could foresee the impact West Virginia would later have; Ohio and California were both special situations—they would depend on Kennedy's own relations with their favorite-son governors, Mike DiSalle and Pat Brown. Kennedy reviewed each of the sixteen primary states; explained the differing primary laws of each state; discarded the hopeless states or states where victory would not be worth the effort; and the morning meeting broke up.

The gathering now trooped across the lawn to the home of old Joseph Kennedy, where the usual hearty Kennedy board offered lunch—roast turkey and several sorts of pie, baked two thicknesses high by the Kennedy cook.

When the meeting reassembled in the afternoon, it reassembled under the chairmanship of brother Bobby. This, too, is a characteristic of Kennedy campaigning. The candidate is not only a flag bearer and leader, he is also a person and a resource. His energy is not to be over-used, as one does not drain a battery more than is necessary. ("We used the candidate perfectly in '58," said one of Kennedy's lieutenants, commenting on the technique of that campaign. "Some days we'd run him through fifteen towns and fifteen speeches and still have him in bed by eleven in the evening. It was perfect use of a candidate—we never wore him out.")

The morning's meeting had been analytical and strategic. Now, under Bobby's chairmanship, it was operational, for assignments were to be distributed and the nation quartered up by the Kennedy staff as if a political general staff were giving each of its combat commanders a specific front of operations:

§ New England and upstate New York went to John Bailey. New England's 114 Convention votes had to be absolutely solid for the home candidate, and there were slight ripples of disturbance in both Maine (Symington strength) and New Hampshire (Stevenson strength). In addition to New England, Bailey was assigned upstate New York—this was to be a covert over-the-border raid on delegates north of the Bronx county line, to round up all that was loose in the Empire State before the flabby downstate Tammany leadership realized what was happening.

§ New York City and northern New Jersey were not so much assigned as left, by silent understanding, to be worked out by the personal contacts of the candidate, the operations of John Bailey and the private resources of Joseph Kennedy.

§ Raskin was to be responsible for the Western states and his native Iowa. Raskin had first come to national prominence in the two Stevenson campaigns. His citizen and organizational contacts in the West were extensive and particularly valuable in the mountain states, Oregon, and California.

§ Young brother Ted Kennedy was to join Raskin in scouting the Rocky Mountain states.

§ Wallace was to survey and sound out West Virginia, preparing the ground if it were necessary to enter, later, the West Virginia primary.

§ Brother Bobby Kennedy, in addition to his general duties, undertook to establish contact with Southern leaders and seek out what friendship he could there as soon as possible.

§ O'Brien was to be responsible for drawing up a general master plan of organization and procedure for all states, to insure a standard operational procedure everywhere. In addition, he was to watch Maryland, Indiana and Wisconsin.

This left out such crucial states as Ohio, Pennsylvania, Michigan, California—but these were all states where negotiations had to proceed on a summit basis, between the candidate himself and their "favorite sons." Salinger's work, O'Donnell's work, Harris' work, was general across-the-board staff work. All had taken notes at the long session— detailed notes on their specific assignments, general jottings on the over-all shape of the campaign. Harris, leaving that week end for a vacation in the Virgin Islands, mentioned his trip casually—he was immediately given two contact men to look up there; after all, the Virgin Islanders had four votes at the Convention. Sorensen, now relieved of the detailed bookkeeping of political contacts and opportunities he had handled for three years, was to mobilize the thinking, the ideas, the speeches and issues of the campaign.

When at 4:30 in the afternoon the meeting finally ended, all were tired. They went out on the lawn and breathed the cold fresh air gratefully, watching the breeze blow the bay into whitecaps. They chatted in groups of twos and threes about their assignments and about the minutiae of politics until the cars came to pick them up and bring them to the Kennedy plane that would drop them off in New York and Washington ready for their new work. It had been a bread-and-butter day, a day of discussion of the nitty, gritty stuff and substance, names and places from which politics in America move; no one remembers any talk of greatness, or any drama, or of any of the perils of the outer world and America. That had happened long since or would come later and was locked in the mind of the candidate.

So, in the darkening afternoon, they were carried away, men with precise, deputized marching orders. Two months and six days later, on January 2, 1960, to the surprise of no one, John F. Kennedy announced to the press that he, too, was a candidate for President of the United States.

Chapter 3

THE REPUBLICANS:
FIRST STIRRINGS

ON THE Republican slope of the great political divide that separates America into two parties matters were wholly different.

Though Republican politicians use the same public phrases and private techniques as their Democratic rivals, the two great parties operate in different worlds of reality. Seizure of power on the Republican side is so different from seizure of power on the Democratic side that it sometimes seems that the fauna who contend in these separate jungles come of different orders of political zoology. For despite the cynic's dictum that the national parties offer Americans only the choice between Tweedledum and Tweedledee, the Republican Party is completely different from the Democratic Party. What these differences are we shall explore later. But one cannot begin to describe Republican reality, as the Party leadership approached 1960, without exploring that spectacular Republican schizophrenia which for a century has baffled all observers.

The Republican Party, to be exact, is twins and has been twins from the moment of its birth—but the twins who inhabit its name and shelter are Jacob and Esau: fratricidal, not fraternal, twins. Within the Republican Party are combined a stream of the loftiest American idealism and a stream of the coarsest American greed. These two political streams have mixed their waters from the days of the Party's birth, when the unbearably pure New England abolitionists let their conscience be joined with the skills of some of the most practical veterans of the old Whigs to form a party that would end slavery. Between them, the Adamses of New England and the Thurlow ("Let's not be too damn virtuous") Weeds of New York assembled Pennsylvania Camerons, Missouri Blairs, Illinois McCormicks, with a basic following of solid Northern, Protestant farming stock, and chose Abraham Lincoln to guide their party through an inevitable and noble war. Out of this war some Republicans harvested honor, while others harvested great fortune. For the next forty years,

74

as America swelled with industry and new immigrants from
Europe, these twins of the Republican Party, the good and
the greedy, fought each other for control of the Party and
the nation's power.

Now that the Democrats have captured the liberal imagination of the nation, it is forgotten how much of the architecture of America's liberal society was drafted by the Republicans. Today they are regarded as the party of the right.
Yet this is the party that abolished slavery, wrote the first
laws of civil service, passed the first antitrust, railway control, consumer-protective and conservation legislation, and
then led America, with enormous diplomatic skill, out into
that posture of global leadership and responsibility we now
so desperately try to maintain.

The fact that all this has been almost forgotten by the
current stylists of our culture is in itself significant. For until
this century and down through its first decade the natural
home party of the American intellectual, writer, savant and
artist was the Republican Party. Its men of state and diplomacy were, as often as not, thinkers and scholars; and it is
doubtful whether any President, even Wilson or the second
Roosevelt, made the White House so familiar a mansion to
writers and artists as did Theodore Roosevelt (who, indeed,
was also one of the founders of the Authors' League of
America).

The alienation of the Republican Party of today from the
intellectual mainstream of the nation stems, actually, from
the days of Theodore Roosevelt. For when in 1912 the twins
of the Republican Party broke wide apart in the Roosevelt-
Taft civil war, the "regulars" of the Taft wing remained in
control of the party machinery, and the citizen wing of progressive and intellectual Republicans was driven into homeless exile.

From 1912 down almost to date, then, the machinery of
the Republican Party has remained in the hands of the regulars, the descendants of Thurlow Weed and Mark Hanna.
These are men who, with unflagging loyalty and granite
resolution against the future, hold the Party together, do its
grubby daily duties, raise its funds, maintain its discipline
and, through the long lean season of politics, perform its
essential tasks. They are, by and large, whenever in convention assembled, very dreary men, difficult to speak to, suspicious of the press and book learning, convinced that the
world betrays them. But their climactic quadrennial exasperation is, nonetheless, completely human when, every four
years as they gather at their great national Convention, they

find themselves overwhelmed by an inrush from the old citizen-progressive wing, which insists on claiming its share of the ancient Republican patrimony, babbling in phrases that to the regulars are almost indistinguishable from those of liberal Democrats.

Now and then, over the course of the past half-century, there have, to be sure, been major uprisings of the liberal-progressive wing of the Party—but, except in New York State, those electoral triumphs the liberal wing has won have been fleeting and regional, leaving behind such names in history as Norris in Nebraska, Borah in Idaho, Johnson in California, Stassen in Minnesota, and a party whose machinery still belongs to the Old Guard. Only at the quadrennial national conventions does the liberal wing of the Party show its real muscle; and this usually happens only after the liberals have, by a sort of palace coup, succeeded in winning over the men who fund and finance the regular party machinery, the executive class of the nation's great corporations. Now, although this alliance between the liberals and the executive direction of the nation's economy had dominated the Republican Conventions of 1940, 1944 and 1948, it was not until 1952 that the liberals and the executive class could produce a candidate who would also sweep the national electorate and win the Presidency.

The campaign of 1952 must be seen as a political classic in the primary, convention, and electoral rounds of the contest—a classic equal to the Rooseveltian campaign of 1932 or the Kennedy campaign of 1960. But the victory of 1952, which gave the nation a man of fundamental decency as President, gave the Republican Party a leader whose life had been spent apart from politics and to whom the sordid, subterranean mechanics of partisan politics were distasteful. That same lack of compelling initiative that was soon to show in his direction of the executive arm of American national government showed almost immediately in the political direction of his own party. A man accustomed by military training to deal with and command specialists, Dwight D. Eisenhower left the direction of his party machinery in the hands of specialists, men drawn almost entirely from the old regular wing of the Party. That infusion of strength, that revitalization of party philosophy, direction and personnel that liberal Republicans had so hoped for, anticipating in Eisenhower a Republican Franklin D. Roosevelt, never came to pass. Instead, election by election, while Dwight D. Eisenhower as President swept the nation, the Republican Party lost ground.

Divorced from the personal carrying power of his great name, in each measurable off-year Congressional election under his administration the Republican Party lost ground. It carried 49 per cent of the electorate in 1950. In the off-year election of 1954, its total polling strength had sunk to 43 per cent. In only one of the four Congresses he was supposed to guide did Eisenhower have a Congress of his own political persuasion. And with the Democratic triumphs in the elections of 1958, the fortunes of the Republican Party, as a party, had sunk to their lowest ebb since the zenith of the New Deal in 1936. On the morrow of the 1958 election, Republicans woke to find that they controlled only fourteen of the forty-eight state legislatures chosen in the previous day's elections.

It was this gloomy scene that Richard M. Nixon and his friends surveyed from the soft and balmy warmth of Key Biscayne, Florida, where they gathered in December, 1958, a few weeks after the Congressional election, at the home of a local Florida realtor, C. B. ("Beebee") Rebozo, to survey the wreckage of the Party—and to face up nonetheless to the strategy of making Richard M. Nixon, Vice-President, full President of the United States two years hence.

Of all the in-groups involved in the seven major campaigns of 1960, this certainly was the most curious. The setting, first, was alien to any of the sources of these men's power; their host was an undistinguished though wealthy Florida businessman, whose hospitality had been lavishly extended to Richard M. Nixon since his first prominence as a young Congressman in the late 1940s. Most of the men had brought their wives, and except for two individuals—Len Hall and Bob Finch—they were persons bound by old intimacies and personal friendship rather than by common achievement, political know-how or power control.

Jack Drown and his wife, Zelda, were there because they were the oldest friends of the Nixon couple from Southern California. Drown, a bluff, cheerful, entirely pleasant executive, directs one of the best regional magazine distribution companies in Southern California, but his knowledge of high politics is restricted. Ray Arbuthnot and his wife were likewise early Southern Californian friends, bound by old intimacy. Arbuthnot is a California-style farmer, shrewd, efficient, but similarly unskilled in national politics.

The two operative men were first quality, however, and together they, with Nixon, were for the next fifteen months to form the entire high command of the Nixon campaign. One was a Californian, the second a New Yorker, and as the Nixon staff—always small—later grew, it was to consist exclusively of Southern Californians and New Yorkers. The more conspicuous of the two was Leonard W. Hall, former Chairman of the Republican National Committee, former Congressman, now at loose and brooding over the humiliation Nelson A. Rockefeller had recently inflicted on him in the summer struggle for the Republican nomination for New York's governorship. Hall was a long-standing friend of Nixon's, a political operative with experience almost but not quite comparable to John Bailey's on the Democratic side; substantially motivated by friendship, Hall was motivated even more, one may assume, by a desire at this point to even the score with Nelson Rockefeller, who had snatched party control from him in New York. The second, and lesser known, was a young thirty-five-year-old California lawyer named Robert H. Finch—a neophyte in national politics, but about to develop into the ablest man Nixon was to recruit for his labors. Tall, handsome, pleasant of manner, incisive of mind, graceful of phrase and expression, he was "classy enough" (someone said) "to make the first team on the Kennedy side of the fence if he had wanted."

As they surveyed the scene and the perspectives in a long three-day conference, there developed, in the memory of those who participated, several postulates:

§ First, that no campaign perspectives could be shaped until Nelson A. Rockefeller's position was defined. For Rockefeller, within two weeks of his victory, was already beginning to obsess the imagination of citizen Republicans. His victory in New York (by 573,034 votes) was not only stunning in itself but doubly impressive in this season of Republican disaster. Only Barry Goldwater in Arizona had scored a comparable personal success on the Republican side in 1958, and Goldwater was an odd one, out there on the extreme, no menace to anyone for the 1960 season. What would Rockefeller do? Did he want the Presidency? Would he contest the nomination?

The answer to these questions was, obviously, yes.

There followed the next postulate:

§ Second, the Vice-President had an enormous equity with the regulars of the Party machinery. For seven years, dry season and full season, the Vice-President had crisscrossed the country, delivering himself to regular Party organizations, helping them at their dinners, their banquets, in their campaigns. He had done their chores and their work for six years in an administration whose President was—as they put the phrase delicately but negatively—"not politically conditioned."

§ Thus, in the long civil war between regulars and liberals in the Republican Party, the regular base was safe for Nixon. Thus, further, the Vice-President did not need to tool up a large professional organization, as Robert A. Taft had done in 1948 and 1952. Therefore it was unnecessary, and probably unwise, to be caught in the public stance of the Party's partisan candidate, the choice of the regulars. The Vice-President, all felt, should be presented in areas where his exposure was chiefly nonpolitical and statesmanlike.

§ Third, there remained the long-range problem of the primaries. If Rockefeller ran, he would have to run via the primary route. But primaries are always a terrifying and demeaning brawl; the Democratic Party would certainly explode in a nationwide donnybrook in the spring of 1960; it was probably unwise for the Vice-President immediately to present himself in the same cadre and frame. The image of statesmanship was his vital asset; it must be preserved. But no decision was made on primaries—it was too early.

All this was of the soundest planning. Finch resigned from his law practice in Los Angeles and moved immediately to Washington in January, 1959; a public-relations officer, Herbert Klein, also of Southern California, was recruited and moved to Washington in June, 1959; Len Hall prepared to liquidate his affairs in New York and come to join them. And all through 1959, the Nixon operation proceeded smoothly, quietly, watchfully—waiting on Nelson Rockefeller.

The structure of this planning was, in its way, a classic reflection of the principle of Legitimacy in American Presidential politics. The Presidency hovers over the popular American imagination almost as a sacerdotal office, a priestly role for which normal political standards are invalid. The President—any President—is part of history, something that Americans, however mute they may remain, take very seriously. They choose their Presidents from men who seem to them familiar on the scene of history—great chieftains of war and diplomacy, men who have previously sat in the Cabinets in Washington, men who have already inherited the White House as Vice-Presidents. This succession of Legitimacy has been broken only three times in our century —once by accident, when in 1912 the Republican Party broke in two and the Democrats installed Woodrow Wilson; next in 1920 when, revolting against the war, the people cast out Wilson and installed Warren G. Harding; lastly in 1932 when, in the cataclysm of the depression, the people had to seek out new and untried leadership. From 1932 down to 1960, "Legitimacy" prevailed in an unbroken succession. After Roosevelt came Harry S. Truman, Vice-President and a Roosevelt appointee; and after Truman came Dwight D. Eisenhower, a war hero, also an early Roosevelt choice to act in history.

Richard M. Nixon now, at the end of 1958, in choosing to adopt the nonpolitical posture of statesman was acting with the most astute appreciation of the value of Legitimacy. His political phrasing of this principle in his campaign chant—Experience—was to prove, throughout the 1960 campaign, his soundest appeal. Though the spectacular Rockefeller victory in New York could arouse and alert Republicans across the country to new leadership, such emotions come and go easily. Private polls financed by the Vice-President's friends showed him, early in the spring of 1959, behind Rockefeller in Republican appreciation—at one point (according to a Nixon poll) Rockefeller led Nixon among Republicans by a margin of 40 to 38 per cent, with the balance undecided. In the summer of 1959, however, the weight of "statesmanship" began to make itself felt. The Nixon trip to Russia that summer gave his popularity, as measured by the pollsters, an enormous surge; and his role in the steel settlement (another statesmanly privilege of the Vice-Presidency) produced a further surge—but by then, the first act of the Rockefeller campaign had risen like a rocket, claimed its headlines and burst. For Nelson Rockefeller and his lieutenants had much to learn about American politics in 1950.

There is no artful way of describing the difference between Richard M. Nixon and Nelson A. Rockefeller, for they are almost stock characters in the panel of American types.

Poor from boyhood, able, intense, dark and watchful as he surveys the world about him, Richard M. Nixon has brought from his impoverished middle-class youth many strange qualities—the thrust of enormous internal drives, an overwhelming desire to be liked and, where he is rebuffed, a bitter, impulsive reflex of lashbacks. Having made it on his own, he has had to learn to court people whom he has necessarily disliked. He has had to realize how vulnerable a naked man, without money or family prestige, can be in a hostile world that over and over again savages him for no reason he can define. He has thus come to regard the world about him with a wary, forbidding suspicion. A brooding, moody man, given to long stretches of introspection, he trusts only himself and his wife—and after that his confidence, in any situation, is yielded only to the smallest possible number of people. No other man, for example, in such a situation of American politics as that in which Nixon found himself during the Chicago Convention in 1960 would have concluded a secret compact with Rockefeller in New York and left his closest personal aides totally and mercilessly uninformed of the transaction. No other candidate of the big seven operated in 1960 with fewer personnel or kept more of the critical decisions in his own hands. Richard M. Nixon is a man of major talent—but a man of solitary, uncertain impulse.

There is something perhaps especially Californian about this strange Nixon uncertainty—and the manner in which the apparently firm and resolute man suddenly changes course and takes new directions. It is as if the changing unsettled society of Southern California in which he grew up had imparted to him some of its own essential uncertainty. His was an almost Horatio Alger boyhood, first on the citrus farm that his parents (transplanted Midwesterners) operated until he was nine, then in the peaceful Quaker town of Whittier, California. He plodded the sidewalks selling newspaper subscriptions, was janitor of the town swimming pool, cranked homemade ice cream for parties, played piano at church, starred on the high-school debating team. Yet even as he grew, peaceful Whittier, surrounded by its orange groves, was being engulfed in the suburbs of Los Angeles as the California southland doubled its population with wanderers and homeseekers from all over America, then doubled again. And it is in this culture of Southern California, where the synthetic and the genuine, the exquisitely beautiful and the grotesquely ugly, mingle without distinction that Nixon grew to manhood searching for identity.

Not even political success of the highest order seemed to give him what he wanted. An able and effective conservative young Congressman and Senator, he was chosen to run with Dwight D. Eisenhower in 1952 on the Republican national ticket because, as one of his Californian sponsors who was present at the conclave that chose him said, "We took Dick Nixon not because he was right wing or left wing—but because we were tired and he came from California." His near-repudiation by Eisenhower during the 1952 campaign embittered him deeply, and all through the four years of the first Eisenhower term a distance of personality separated them. It was as if Eisenhower, who sets great store by men's achievement in war, in finance, in industry, could not recognize the purely political achievement and talent in Nixon. One of Nixon's friends still remembers a telling scene at the beginning of the 1956 campaign. In early fall of that year, the Republican National Committee had decided to launch the national campaign against the Stevenson-Kefauver ticket from Eisenhower's Gettysburg farm. Republican dignitaries large and small had journeyed from Washington to the Gettysburg farm, where TV and press waited for the ceremonies that would begin their effort. When the ceremony was over, President Eisenhower jovially beckoned to two of his cronies and invited them into the farmhouse with him. Nixon, standing beside his friend on the lawn, watched the little group enter the farmhouse, then turned to his friend and remarked bitterly, as the friend remembers, "Do you know, he's never asked me into that house yet." There was always this sensitivity in Nixon, this seeking of a fixed point and a fixed position of his own in American politics and leadership. And as 1960 approached, this desire to establish his own independence, his own place in the sum of things, was apparently among the strongest of his motivations.

The personality and background of Nelson A. Rockefeller, his chief rival in the Republican Party, is entirely different. It is one of total security, total confidence, total cheeriness. Born into what is America's closest counterpart to a royal family, raised within the walls of the greatest private fortune known to man, Rockefeller has escaped the weight of wealth that makes all but one of his four brothers and one sister such shy, withdrawn and reticent people; instead, the assurance of wealth has made him radiant. Rockefeller is, in image and in actual person, one of the sunniest, most expansive and outgoing personalities of American politics. Life has treated him well ("I've never found it a handicap to be a Rockefeller," he once said) and his constant smile is genuine, his great bear hug an authentic expression of delight in meeting people. His pleasure in the rituals and costuming of American politics—Indian war bonnets and Texan boots, blintzes-eating and pizza-picking—is unfeigned.

Underneath this countenance of a grown-up Boy Scout there exists, however, a hard, shrewd, vigorously responsible man. If one presses too hard through the surface joviality, one encounters a frosty and unyielding stubbornness. Living in a family where affairs of state and the condition of the Republican Party have been dinner-table conversation for several generations, he has come to have a citizen's concern with the course of American destiny more closely akin to the dedication of Adlai Stevenson than to that of anyone else on the Republican side. Having served in Washington under Roosevelt, under Truman and under Dwight D. Eisenhower, he had finally, early in 1956, quit the Eisenhower administration in total frustration and returned to New York to enter politics.

Rockefeller's entry into electoral politics and its motivation should be underlined. Fundamentally it was his opinion that the Eisenhower administration, which he had served, was drifting from crisis to crisis, was preparing its plans and managing matters of state on a month-to-month, year-to-year basis, while America's position in the changing world required planning that reached from today over five years, over ten years, into the farthest foreseeable future. This conviction was buttressed by his education over the years in Washington and his final realization that federal appointive office, of which he had held many, brings no political strength; only the people, voting at the polls, give a man true power in American government.

Neither of these observations was secret to the Republican high command of New York State, and for a brief while early in 1958 the Republican leadership of New York had tried to shunt him off into the fall Senatorial race. But the Rockefeller family had so lavishly financed the Republicans of New York over the years that Nelson Rockefeller could not regard their decision as binding on him, as it might be for a lesser man. It was the first time Republican leadership was to meet his stubbornness; Nelson Rockefeller flatly refused the Senate candidacy. In the Senate he would be trapped—he would be a talker, a follower, coerced into supporting Eisenhower policies. He wanted to be Governor of New York, an executive post to be won from the people directly; he meant to have it. His summer pre-Convention campaign in 1958 across New York, and his later electoral campaign that fall were his first ventures into the field of electoral combat; they were superbly managed, superbly conducted and thunderingly successful.

Now from 1956 on the thought of becoming President of the United States had never been entirely alien to Nelson A. Rockefeller. When, however, he became Governor of New York in November of 1958, another of the classic pressures of American politics began to work on him. This is the law that every Governor of New York suffers, and must suffer, from the disease of *Presidentitis,* a condition of instantaneous inflammation of ambition. In the twenty-one national elections between the Civil War and 1948, no less than thirteen times did one or the other (and sometimes both) major party choose as its Presidential candidate a Governor or former Governor of New York. The Empire State is so various in complexion, so rich in manpower, resources and votes, so dominant in the web of communications that shape America's mind, that a Governor of that state is considered Presidential timber from the moment the votes are counted that give him victory. Public and press attention begin to focus on his next step forward even before he assumes office —and, in the case of Nelson A. Rockefeller, from the pre-dawn hours of Wednesday, November 5th, 1958, while the votes for Governor were still being counted. "I am really not interested," said Nelson Rockefeller of the Presidency to the first questioner of the press that night in flush of victory. But the next afternoon at a skeptical press conference he said he was, indeed, aware of the wide speculation that he might seek the Republican Presidential nomination in 1960. Yet he considered it "unwise to cross bridges ahead of time." For that reason, he continued, he could not promise categorically to spend four winters in Albany, the state capital, although he had "every intention" of "doing the job."

Yet the pressure was inescapable. He was Governor of New York. His concern with the affairs of the nation—and particularly national defense and foreign policy—was public knowledge. He was vulnerable to attack as moving too fast and too soon. But he was fifty-one years old, and in 1960 he would be fifty-two; if he did not move in 1960, and if the succeeding Republican President held a normal two terms, he would be sixty in 1968, too old. In Presidential politics, one must move at the proper season of life; one hopes that the tide is right at that season. If the proper season of life comes too soon or too late in the tides of history, one remains a might-have-been—a Daniel Webster, a Henry Clay, a Henry Stimson, a Robert Taft, a Samuel Rayburn, an Estes Kefauver. Besides, above all—and Nelson Rockefeller made no bones of the fact—he disliked Richard M. Nixon and considered him incapable of the role of President.

Rockefeller, unlike Nixon, is a man who believes in survey, consultation, conference, planning and staff work. The apparently casual and easy-going Governor of New York has a passion for organization; although not the most meticulous administrator, he is an incorrigible initiator—and as he initiates, he organizes. By June of 1959, six months after assuming office in Albany, the first antennae of the Rockefeller

Presidential campaign had been raised to monitor the political wave bands of the Republican Party. By fall, active exploration had begun and the elaborate Manhattan offices of the Governor of New York hummed with purpose that reached far beyond the horizons of the Empire State.

By mid-December, when the private staff of the Rockefeller family had been combined with the political resources of the New York Governor, the Rockefeller Presidential exploration was a thing of political wonder, large enough to make even the Kennedy operation seem like a Montana roadshow. Two large buildings on New York's West Fifty-fifth Street (Numbers 20 and 22), which the Governor had bought years before to shelter his philanthropic activities, now housed his official gubernatorial staff and served as command headquarters for the national attempt. Restored and renovated, the two old brownstones glistened, their interiors broken by glass partitions hung with modern paintings, furnished with modern furniture resting on gray wall-to-wall carpeting. A darkroom, a press room, several conference rooms, a mimeograph room, a room wired for television, all made it a far more efficient headquarters than Republican National Headquarters itself on I Street in Washington.

A political division directed crosscountry reconnaissance of leadership in various state Republican parties; a speechwriting division researched and prepared great statements on national and world affairs; an "image" division of top-drawer Madison Avenue talent pondered the problems of personal public relations; a logistics division scheduled and arranged the Governor's trips almost as carefully as the advance men of a fully staffed Presidential campaign; routine press relations were shunted to the Governor's Press Secretary in Albany; and a citizens' division linked itself with this headquarters, corresponding with local grass-roots Citizens for Rockefeller Clubs that seemed ready to sprout fully armed, like dragon seed, all across the country. In addition, a campaign biography was being written, as well as a history of Mr. Rockefeller's long career in public services and philanthropy.

Normally a staff so huge and elaborate develops its own instinct for self-preservation and swamps its principal with such information, advice and confusion that it can never be liquidated except by outside force.

In this case, Nelson Rockefeller, an experienced staffmaster, knew exactly what he was doing, what his staff was to do, and what was to be the object of his first exercise. It was to explore a candidacy, not launch a candidacy. If the exploration showed hope, the candidacy would be launched later.

Some seventy people of the official gubernatorial staff or Rockefeller acquaintance were involved in the exploration, most of them adding this new excitement to other full-time official or private jobs that absorbed their chief energies. Yet the in-group of the Rockefeller exploration was as small as any of the other campaigns. These men, to be specific, were the political leaders of the New York Republican Party (George L. Hinman, L. Judson Morhouse, Lyle W. Hornbeck), and the quality leaders of the Rockefeller empire's personal staff—the late Frank Jameson, a genius at public relations, whose death is mourned by all who ever met him; Richardson Dilworth, chief investment counselor of the Rockefellers, one of the most civilized and responsible younger personalities in American industry; John Lockwood, the family's reticent chief legal counsel; and the candidate's abnormally shy yet abnormally dynamic younger brother, David Rockefeller.

To these must be added at this point the name of Emmet J. Hughes, a man not only fascinating in himself but fascinating as a symbol of the homeless American political intellectual. Emmet Hughes, then not quite forty years old, had been summa cum laude at Princeton; had served with distinction in Spain during the war; had then become one of the luminaries of the distinguished corps of Time Inc. correspondents overseas after the war; and had, finally, joined the inner Eisenhower group in the campaign of 1952 for his first taste of American national politics. In both style and rhetoric he was one of the few men in either the early Eisenhower regime or the recent Time Inc. development who fully warranted the adjective "brilliant." Yet, in the Rockefeller entourage, as much as in the Eisenhower entourage, Hughes was an anomaly—basically a Democrat by family background and by early orientation, he had come to prominence first as Eisenhower's sharpest thinker and had now developed into the chief ideologue and strategist of the Rockefeller campaign, the 1960 expression of the permanent citizen insurrection within the Republican Party. In himself Hughes was symbolic of that intellectual traffic that no longer respects any party lines in American politics, whose leverage is that of the impact of ideas on individual personalities. Rockefeller had first met Hughes in Washington when both were growing restless in the service of Eisenhower; had come to regard Hughes as an ally there, and invited his help and rhetorical services when finally, in 1958, he was elected Governor of New York. Now as Rockefeller, the organizer, organized his tactical exploration of Republican politics across the country, Hughes must be seen, disdainful of detail and tactic, interested far more in ideas than in partisan Republican purposes, as the man closest to the Governor in ideology and in defining the strategy of the Rockefeller hopes.

Three great considerations shaped the Rockefeller exploration in the fall of 1959.

The first, simple as it may seem, was to test the strength of ordinary citizen concern for the welfare of the United States, a motivation akin to that which fueled the Adlai Stevenson candidacy on the other side. Here the explorers reflected the intense propelling drive of their principal. In his heart, in his soul, in his innermost private conversations, Nelson A. Rockefeller believed that the United States was entering a period of terror and torment in a world that might destroy it. His family had helped make this country; he felt responsible for it; he must do something about it; and, as he phrased it once to an intimate, "I hate the thought of Dick Nixon being President of the United States." Rockefeller was almost equally concerned about domestic affairs—about the problems of racial integration across the country, about American medicine, about American education, about juvenile delinquency. In all these areas he believed that the nation could not afford to rest planless and programless—it must prepare now.

This kind of concern was strength—but the appeal of this strength was to the liberal-progressive wing of the Republican Party, the citizen wing, the wing that lies dormant three and a half years out of four and then, in the fourth year, erupts to choose a Willkie or an Eisenhower. Nixon certainly possessed the regular wing of the Party—but how much of the citizen wing had Nixon neutralized, too, in his years as Eisenhower's public protégé? This, first, had to be explored.

The second consideration was to take a practical measure of the mechanics and acquisition of delegates. You could not approach the Convention unless you sampled the posture and attitudes of the regulars who controlled party organization, and thus delegates, in state after state. To do this, a political intelligence operation was carefully set up from the Fifty-fifth Street headquarters, the country being quartered in four. Northeast political intelligence was to be gathered by Roswell P. Perkins, a thirty-year-old Wall Street lawyer. The South was to be investigated by R. Birdell Bixby, a law parner of former Governor Thomas E. Dewey. George

Hinman, an upstate New York lawyer and one of the most elevated men to make politics his concern in New York, was responsible for the West. Lyle W. Hornbeck, secretary of the New York Republican State Committee, was responsible for the hostile Midwest.

Thus the New York men looked out over the country, as the Minnesota men of Hubert Humphrey and the Missourians of Stuart Symington and the Bay Staters of John F. Kennedy looked out on the other side. But they were seeking, and sought, no delegate commitments, they were offering, and could offer, no deals. What they wanted to know, precisely, was just how complete and firm was Mr. Nixon's grip on the men who managed the herd of delegates who would come to the Republican National Convention, and whether their attitudes to Rockefeller were of warmth, indifference or outright enmity.

The third area of exploration was, perhaps, the most interesting—and certainly the most instructive to the Rockefellers.

This was the financial exploration.

The Rockefeller family has been in national politics long enough (since long before McKinley) to know how Republican politics are managed. The family recognizes the twins within the Republican Party and, for the last twenty years, has thrown its weight with the citizen wing. Yet the gross fact is that the regular wing of the Republican Party depends for support on the executive class of the great corporations as intimately as does the liberal wing of the Democrats on support from labor-union leadership. As a matter of fact, the men who raise the money for the Republican Party control it, generally, to a far greater degree than the men who raise the money for the Democratic Party. In almost every state with a major Republican Party, except New York, if one knows the name of its Finance Chairman, one knows where the roots of power twine. And even in upstate New York it is wise to know where Bausch & Lomb stand in Rochester, where Gould Pump stands, where the Corning Glass Works stand. This is no more cynical a requirement than to know, on the Democratic side, where Walter Reuther stands in Michigan or David Dubinsky in New York—except that control on the Republican side is rarely as recognized or as open as on the Democratic side. In Washington State, it is always sound to start Republican politics with the Weyerhaeuser family, in Idaho with Idaho Power Co., in Ohio with George Humphrey, in Illinois (now that Colonel Robert McCormick is dead) with Edward Ryerson. These corporate executives are not generally backward forces; by and large, they are far more enlightened than the regulars they finance to control the Party machinery; on many occasions in recent Republican history they have broken the back of the regulars and forced the regulars to support the liberal citizen wing.

Now it was always obvious to the Rockefeller forces that a Presidential campaign, expensive as it might be, could be financed, technically, out of their own stupendous private fortune. But it was equally obvious that even if they were successful, a nomination purchased only by fortune would be politically worthless; and obvious, further, to the in-group that the morality and conscience of Nelson Rockefeller would not stand for it; and, lastly, that if the great "club" of American executive business leadership chose to finance Richard M. Nixon in opposition, not even money could buy the regulars over.

Exploration of the various branches of the "Business Club" was therefore in order to find out whether the "Business Club" found the national crisis of a high enough order to join the Rockefellers and compel their local regulars to help.

This exploration was left in the hands of two men: David Rockefeller, the candidate's brother, and Richardson Dilworth, his chief investment counsel. (Dilworth is a namesake and first cousin to the Democratic Mayor of Philadelphia.)

What happened next was shock.

The Rockefellers had always assumed that they were the first family of American business. The Rockefellers had been, for decades, the largest influence in the financing of the Republican Party. Now they discovered that not even they were large enough or powerful enough to *control* American business.

They met courtesy wherever they went. Mr. Ryerson, who raises the funds for the Illinois Republican Party, held a dinner at the Chicago Club for Nelson Rockefeller. So did the men of the Johnathan Club in Los Angeles, of the Pacific Union Club in San Francisco. Rockefeller emissaries were received courteously everywhere they went: by the Ohio crowd (George Humphrey of National Steel Corp. and Mark Hanna & Company, Charles White of Republic Steel Corp., Ralph Lazarus of Federated Department Stores, the Cleveland Trust Company), by the Michigan crowd (Walker L. Cisler of Detroit Edison, Joseph M. Dodge of the Detroit Bank and Trust Company), and in Wisconsin. No one likes to offend a Rockefeller.

Yet the doors were barred.

Few of these business leaders are individually of the Mark Hanna philosophy, either socially or in the conduct of their businesses; but collectively their philosophy is essentially negative, for, quite naturally, they must seek a veto power to check the excess of government as it intrudes on the working of the economy. Nor do they have a high respect for politicians, even of Republican stripe. ("Let's face it," said one of the Ohio proprietors of the Republican Party, speaking of a moderately important Ohio Republican leader whom he supports, "in politics, you have to put up with second-rate people, they're the only choice you have to deal with.") These men are, furthermore, as industrial managers, endowed with an overdeveloped organizational sense: one works in the ranks of a large industry; one slowly rises to the top of the organization, and the organization owes the hard worker a prior loyalty over a sudden interloper. This loyalty they owed Nixon, not Rockefeller, the political newcomer. (Interestingly enough, Henry Ford, a maverick in his own business leadership, turned out to be among the few mavericks among Republican big-business men—he thought, as early as 1959, that Richard Nixon would lose and that the party ought to try Rockefeller.)

In the words of one of the Rockefeller in-group: "The doors were locked, barred and closed. I'd always read these things that the Democrats say about us and thought they were naive. But here was the club, not only against Nelson because he was a liberal, but also committed to Nixon. Richard Nixon is a shrewd man; he spotted where control of the nomination lay seven years before. When he was traveling, he wasn't just making friends with State Chairmen and the regulars; he was dining with the big interests at the same time. It was perfectly clear that Nelson would get no support financially except from the family purse. These people liked Ike. But they liked Nixon even more. Here was a boy who would continue the Eisenhower policies, who was not only very able but also amenable. They thought Nelson was too god-damned independent; he was too brilliant and unpredictable; Nelson's money hurt him because he didn't need them—he was too independent."

In the papers and in the headlines, the Rockefeller "campaign" lasted a total of eight weeks, from early October to early December. His speeches (except for his poor Alfred E. Smith Dinner speech, a ritual in American politics) were excellent—he discussed our foreign policy, our farm policy, our need of economic growth, always with good sense and fine tailored eloquence. He made two serious scouting trips, the first in November, the second in December. On his first trip he reconnoitered the West Coast—to be shabbily mistreated by Nixon zealots in Southern California, and handsomely received in the state of Washington. On the second trip he toured the Midwest and South—Missouri, Indiana, Minnesota, Wisconsin, Oklahoma, Texas and Florida. In some of these states he did well, in others (such as Wisconsin) he was chilled. The people—students, housewives, men and women of the citizen wing—turned out to see, listen and be charmed. The regulars, who controlled the delegate machinery, ignored him. He became an honorary Pawnee Indian (complete with feathered headdress) in Oklahoma, and an honorary Texan (complete with ten-gallon hat and cowboy boots) in Dallas. But the bony skeleton of the Party, the hard-core descendants of Thurlow Weed, Hanna and Taft, would have none of him.

The problem of the nomination hinged on the primaries; and the problem of the primaries focused on the first primary in New Hampshire, to be held on March 8th, with filing required by January 28th. The Rockefeller trips and the Rockefeller speeches had created a drumbeat of headlines and a cascade of letters from citizens.

But Len Hall, now installed at the Sheraton-Park Hotel in Washington for Nixon, operating against his old fraternal enemy of New York, was triggering counterheadlines. If Rockefeller warmed Republicans in Washington State, Hall could spring a statement from the Republican leaders of New Jersey that they were adamant for Nixon. Using his long-distance phone as his instrument, Hall was tireless in defense. Let Rockefeller discover a pocket of strength in Indiana, where Senator Homer Capehart declared his friendship; Len Hall would spring the announcement of Governor Wesley Powell (Republican) of New Hampshire that he was going to lead Nixon's campaign in the New Hampshire Republican primary. And the New Hampshire primary was the most important.

By mid-December the Rockefeller clan was ready for its final reading. Report from the four quarters of political intelligence on the "regulars": zero. Nixon had the regulars sewed up.

Report from Rockefeller's personal trips about the country: zero. Support and cheers from the people, pockets of strength in Indiana, in Washington, in Minnesota, but the delegate brokers there and everywhere else, totally opposed.

Report from the financial exploration: zero. Business was against Nelson A. Rockefeller, it wanted Nixon.

Beyond this were personal factors. Rockefeller had tasted the campaign trail—and was tired of it. Overscheduled, over-speechified, exhausted, he knew now that a political war fought by primary contests could be fought only by a man who had no other duties or responsibilities to claim his energy. Yet he was Governor of New York, and desirous of being a good governor. His second session with the New York State Assembly was approaching and he could not master that, make a good program and also find the energy necessary to fight the New Hampshire primary—or those that might follow.

On Thursday morning, December 24th, four men—Emmet Hughes, George Hinman, John Lockwood and Frank Jameson—gathered with Nelson A. Rockefeller in the Governor's private office in Fifty-fifth Street. The Governor had just returned from his last Midwestern swing, but even while he had been on the road they had been drafting, at his suggestion, a statement of his withdrawal from the race.

It was clear to all these principals that Nelson Rockefeller's road to the Republican nomination of 1960 was, for the moment, effectively blocked. Not only could they not challenge Nixon within the Party, but to hail him to primary war would confuse and obscure the Rockefeller position itself. Rockefeller would have to fight within the primaries against a Nixon who would champion Eisenhower positions; he would thus either have to fuzz his disagreements with the Eisenhower position or else hopelessly summon Republican voters in their own primaries to repudiate the most popular Republican President of modern times. Withdrawal from the primary race and direct contest would free the New York Governor to speak out as he wished on national issues; withdrawal at the moment would let him adopt the Churchillian posture of the leader who raises alarm. What he might achieve in this role would be far more significant than a string of tight and possibly losing primary races.

The advisers had briefly considered a "good-sport" statement of withdrawal endorsing Richard M. Nixon. This suggestion was now abandoned. Another suggestion was made that morning that the statement include the bitter phrase "the men who control the convention and the financial powers behind them . . ." But Emmet Hughes edited that phrase out and his editing stood. The final statement read:

". . . I believe . . . that the great majority of those who will control the Republican convention stand opposed to any contest for the nomination. . . . Therefore any quest on my part for the nomination would entail a massive struggle in primary elections throughout the nation demanding so greatly of my time and energy that it would make impossible the fulfillment of my obligations as Governor of New York. . . . My conclusion, therefore, is that I am not, and shall not be, a candidate for the nomination for the Presidency. This decision is definite and final."

The decision was, however, not definite and final. The statement of withdrawal had been issued on a Friday afternoon in Albany. The Governor himself was, about that time, boarding a week-end train at Pennsylvania Station in New York to visit his wife's family in Philadelphia for the Christmas holidays. He chatted casually with a friendly newspaperman about the wide range of world affairs with which he had had to familiarize himself in recent months; how you could never be sure what kind of question was coming next, of what the motives of the questioner were. He talked of the challenge and techniques of being a public figure—he said it meant liking people and being relaxed. But he said, almost wistfully, that it had all been "great fun."

In New York, the exploratory operation was put on ice. The campaign biography was canceled; some of the speech writers released; the advance men sent back to their law offices. But those who lived in the inner Rockefeller circle knew that the emotional drive, the intense concerns that had stimulated this exploration were only momentarily banked.

"He said to me," related one of them, " 'The more I campaign, the more I put Nixon on the front pages and the better I make the Party look in general. Besides, the more I take this line, the more I drive the Party to the right.' " Then, reflecting, the friend continued, "Anyway, he has at least as good a chance of getting the nomination this way as any other way. The other way he couldn't have won except by driving a personal assault on Eisenhower."

For the moment, in Christmas week of 1959, as John F. Kennedy and Hubert Humphrey prepared their formal announcements of candidacy, Nelson Rockefeller had withdrawn —and rested, waiting on events in the outer world to propel his next moves.

There are those who insist that Nixon had, through his intelligence agents and friends, heard of the Rockefeller decision to withdraw several days earlier. Yet there are hard contrary reports that the first newspaperman bearing the news of Rockefeller's withdrawal to the Vice-President's office at the Capitol in the afternoon entirely surprised and instantly dismayed the group of friends he discovered with the Vice-President. "We've just been kicked in the groin," is the way one member of the Vice-President's personal staff reacted to the first report in the newsman's presence.

Whether or not they had known a few hours or days in advance, the Vice-President's staff had good reason to be dismayed at the news. For in the year since the first meeting at Key Biscayne, they had finally hatched the decision to contest with Nelson Rockefeller any primary he might enter. The Nixon thinkers had written a drama for the election year, on the Republican side, in which Nixon would be the active campaigner through the primaries and Nelson Rockefeller his sparring partner, cast for defeat. They had begun to look forward to the primaries as an action that would enliven the spring, race the Party's blood, take newspaper space and television time from the Democrats—and, above all, tune up the personnel and human machinery they would need in the fall election for President.

All this was now denied them. They could play statesman for several more months, watching the progress of John F. Kennedy on the other side of the political divide—yet always with one eye on Nelson A. Rockefeller, wondering what his concerns might persuade him to do.

Chapter 4

THE ART OF THE PRIMARY: WISCONSIN AND WEST VIRGINIA

A PRIMARY fight, at any level, is America's most original contribution to the art of democracy—and, at any level, it is that form of the art most profanely reviled and intensely hated by every professional who practices politics as a trade.

In theory a primary fight removes the nomination of candidates from the hands of cynical party leadership and puts it directly in the hands of the people who make the party. When, indeed, theory matches fact (for, in some states, primaries are absurdly meaningless), primary contests result in disastrous and unforgettable explosions. A genuine primary is a fight within the family of the party—and, like any family fight, is apt to be more bitter and leave more enduring wounds than battle with the November enemy. In primaries, ambitions spurt from nowhere; unknown men carve their mark; old men are sent relentlessly to their political graves; bosses and leaders may be humiliated or unseated. At ward, county or state level, all primaries are fought with spurious family folksiness—and sharp knives.

Bosses and established leaders hate primaries for good reason; they are always, in any form, an appeal from the leaders' wishes to the people directly. Primaries suck up and waste large sums of money from contributors who might better be tapped for the November finals; the charges and countercharges of primary civil war provide the enemy party with ammunition it can later use with blast effect against whichever primary contender emerges victorious; primary campaigns exhaust the candidate, use up his speech material, drain his vital energy, leave him limp before he clashes with the major enemy.

And whatever ill can be said of local primaries can be multiplied tenfold for the Presidential primaries. For the amount of money used in a series of Presidential primaries across the breadth of this land is prodigious; the stakes of the Presidency are so high and dramatic that a horde of self-winding citizens and amateurs suddenly insists on participation; and the wreckage that a primary usually leaves of a well-organized local machine is as nothing compared to the wreckage that two political giants from alien states can make of an instate organization, whose private ambitions they abuse and whose delicate local balances and compromises they completely ignore as they strive for power to command the whole country.

Yet, when all is said, there remains this gross fact: were there no Presidential primaries, the delegates sent to the National Conventions would be chosen by local party bosses, and the decision of the Convention, made blind by inability to measure candidates' voting strength, would rest in the back room, with the bosses. When, for a period of thirty-five years, from 1865 to 1900, the choice of Presidential candidates was left to the bosses in convention assembled, their selections resulted in such mediocre leadership of this country that it could be truly written that "No period so thoroughly ordinary had been known in American politics since Christopher Columbus first disturbed the balance of American society." It was only with the turn of the twentieth century that the Presidential primary was introduced, soon to spread over the union. Many states in the next half-century experimented with the Presidential primary—some making it a permanent feature of their politics, some finally abolishing it, most of them altering its rules from decade to decade. By 1960, only sixteen states still retained a legal, open primary, in which all seekers for the Presidency of the United States, of either party, might offer themselves to the people directly. These sixteen states were as diverse in their politics and sociologies as the diversity of American civilization itself; they had been chosen by no superior reason or plan. Altogether to the foreign eye they must have seemed the most preposterous field of battle on which men who aspire to the leadership of American freedom and control of its powers should choose to joust. Yet these states were, and remain, vital to the play of American Presidential politics.

For John F. Kennedy and Hubert Humphrey there was no other than the primary way to the Convention. If they could not at the primaries prove their strength in the hearts of Americans, the Party bosses would cut their hearts out in the back rooms of Los Angeles. Thus, as they approached their combat, they had a sense of multiple audience—first, the folksy audience of the primary state to be won directly, along with the local delegates that could be harvested in the primary victory (this, of course, was the least of their considerations); next, the national audience, as the nation first paid its attention to the combat and assessed the men; and, last, there were the bosses of the big Eastern states and the smaller organized states who would coldly watch the race to observe the performance of political horseflesh.

Of the sixteen primary states, Hubert Humphrey had by late winter chosen five as his field of battle; of the same sixteen, John F. Kennedy had similarly chosen seven. And they were first to clash head on in Wisconsin on April 15th.[1]

Of all fifty states of the union, Wisconsin is probably that state in which professional politicians most hate to tempt a primary. It was Wisconsin, as a matter of fact, that in 1903 first invented the Presidential primary, which so many other states have since copied. And the political philosophy that inspired that revolutionary invention has made and left Wisconsin in political terms an unorganized state, a totally unpredictable state, a state whose primaries have over many quadrennials proved the graveyard of great men's Presidential ambitions.

It is worth examining the roots of Wisconsin's political philosophy and its kinship with that of a sister state, California. It would have been difficult at the end of the nineteenth century to pick two states more thoroughly Republican or more thoroughly corrupt than Wisconsin and California. The ownership and management of the political machinery of these states by their railways, their bankers and their industries had become so knavish that from within the Republican Parties they owned, there burst forth twin revolutions, with twin leaders who were to blow fresh air through the entire American political system. If today, half a century later, the maverick politics of Wisconsin and California remain alike, as do their magnificently decent and efficient systems of state government, it is a tribute to the ability, in our political system, of individual men to change the life of their communities. Decades after their death, both Wisconsin and California are better states to live in because fifty years ago

[1] The actual technical opening of the 1960 campaign was, to be sure, the New Hampshire primary of March 8th. In previous years—as in the Eisenhower-Taft clash of 1952, or the Kefauver-Stevenson clash of 1956—the technical opening of the season in New Hampshire had been its true political opening, for the New Hampshire primaries in those years were battles. But in 1960 Kennedy's over-the-border strength from Massachusetts made any challenge to him in his New England backyard political folly. Kennedy won, contested only by a ball-point pen manufacturer, by a margin of 9 to 1 in what was, politically, a trumpet flourish for national publicity but of no real meaning.

Hiram Johnson of California and Robert LaFollette of Wisconsin decided to make them better.

The philosophy of Robert LaFollette saw the state of Wisconsin as servant of the people and the open choice of state government as the citizens' prime right and responsibility. The source of all evil, by his philosophy, lay in political bosses, the pressure groups that controlled the bosses and the system of patronage and machine-made convention candidates who did their will. Over thirty years of furious political activity, Robert LaFollette succeeded in changing the politics and constitution of his state so thoroughly that professional politicians still shudder at his memory.

Candidates in Wisconsin are today still chosen not by conventions but by wild open primaries. Organized, incorporated, legal party machinery is forbidden (as in California), and the formal receptacles of party responsibility are denied official recognition. Patronage in Wisconsin (as in California) is almost negligible—the Governor of Wisconsin has only eight major patronage jobs at his disposal. Paid political advertising is forbidden in newspapers and magazines, over radio and TV, for twenty-four hours before election day. No political candidate can hire cars to haul voters to the polls, or pay poll workers. And, above all, when it comes to the sacred office of the Presidency and the Presidential primary, the maximum is achieved in frustrating political discipline and party control: in a Presidential primary voters may vote, without regard to their registration, either in the primary of their own party or of the opposition party, so that crossover Republicans may frustrate Democratic aspirants they hate, or crossover Democrats may frustrate Republicans they hate. This system so nearly approaches anarchy that there is much talk among the best of men in Wisconsin of abolishing the crossover privilege (as, indeed, California did six years ago when it abolished cross-filing in primaries, a Hiram Johnson legacy similar to the LaFollette legacy).

Having thoroughly disorganized formal party politics in Wisconsin, the LaFollette family went on, in 1934, officially to divorce their Progressive wing from the Republican Party, and establish a Wisconsin Progressive Party that was to dominate the state's politics for the next twelve years. In Wisconsin, Progressives were the first party, Republicans the second and the Democrats a poor third. The Republican Party rested heavily on old colonial American stock, the suburban middle class, big industry and farmers of German origin, and chose through the open primaries, now horrible leaders like Joseph McCarthy, and now fundamentally decent men like Alexander Wiley. The Democratic Party became a fossilized, parochial group in the industrial cities along Lake Michigan, a receptacle for crumbs of Washington patronage, regarded in the words of one of its leaders as "little more than a Polish-Irish marching society." As late as 1938, Democrats could claim only 8 per cent of the general vote. The dominant party, the Progressives, combined many elements: intellectuals of the campus and the middle class, proud of LaFollette's innovations and achievements; working-class voters in the largely Germanic big cities, tinged heavily with Teutonic beer-hall socialism (Milwaukee for decades elected a Socialist Mayor); and in the countryside the predominantly Scandinavian farming vote, oriented toward a more puritan Danish-American socialism.

It was the collapse of the Progressives immediately after World War II that upset this pattern of Wisconsin politics— that plus the rise of Joe McCarthy. Though at war's end the son of the great LaFollette rejoined the Republican Party, which his father had dominated a generation before, not even his LaFollette name could lead the basically decent voting elements of the Progressives back to the party whose standard bearer was now McCarthy. The homeless drift of these scores of thousands of Progressives coincided, moreover, with the citizen revival in the Democratic Party. The nationwide surge of citizen participation in politics, which in the past decade has become one of the Democratic Party's greatest promises and problems, had begun early in the upper Midwest. Hubert Humphrey and his citizen groups had triumphed in 1948, to take over the Minnesota Democratic Party; in the same year G. Mennen Williams, Neil Staebler and Walter Reuther had taken over the Michigan party. In 1952 Adlai Stevenson's campaign beckoned thousands of high-minded amateurs to new enthusiasm for politics and new participation; and though Stevenson's influence in reshaping the structure of American democracy was nationwide, nowhere was it more permanently effective in changing the nature of a state party than in Wisconsin. (Madison, Wisconsin, is not only the state capital, it is the capital of Stevensonian strength across the country.) The new young men of the Wisconsin Democracy, largely amateurs in 1952, and the old homeless Progressives, thus began to pour in on the fossilized sectarian Democrats of the lake shore to obliterate older Democratic leadership. By the mid-fifties they had taken over the Democratic Party. In 1957, for the second time in the century, one of them—William Proxmire —became a United States Senator; in 1958, again for the

second time in the century, one of them—Gaylord Nelson
—became Governor. Democrats were fashionable, full of
vigor, victorious.

In March, as the primary approached, Wisconsin still lay
beneath its snow. The snow stretched in a crystal carpet all
across the hills as the plane flew west from New York, a
white blanket across the slopes of the Appalachians, em-
broidered by the black of leafless trees; the snow covered the
gray ice of the frozen lakes, just beginning to show the
seams and cracks of coming thaw; the snow covered Wisconsin.

Under the snow it is impossible to tell poor farm from rich
farm, for snow forces farmers to shelter their automobiles and
equipment indoors; the snow gives a white uniformity to
the landscape, to dairy farm and corn farm, to German-Amer-
ican and Polish-American homestead, to Anglo stock and
Scandinavian stock, to Catholic and Protestant.

The campaign was about to begin.

A very forlorn and lonesome young man and a long preposterous day remain as this writer's first outdoor memory
of the Kennedy campaign of 1960. In retrospect I can still
see a bareheaded, coatless man, lithe as an athlete, his face
still unlined, his eyes unpuffed with fatigue, wandering solitary
as a stick through the empty streets of the villages of Wisconsin's far-northern Tenth Congressional District, which juts
out into the Great Lakes.

The Tenth Congressional is cold and desolate country. Once
heavily forested and a major mining center for lake iron, it
passed its peak at the turn of the century. The great fir forests
have all been cut now and the log jam of 1886 (the greatest
log jam in the world: 700,000,000 board feet of timber) is
only a memory; scrub oak and jack pine have replaced the
primeval fir forests, and black bear and deer are returning.
The iron ore has been depleted by years of mining, and the
locally notorious mining camps no longer know revelry. ("The
four hottest places on earth on Saturday night," the local
saying used to run, "are Cumberland, Hurley, Hayward and
Hell.") The glacial soil here in northern Wisconsin is too
thin for rich farming, and the farmers scratch for a living.
Predominantly Scandinavian and Lutheran on the farm, the
Tenth is notorious in civilized south Wisconsin for its other
pockets of oddballs—colonies of Finnish Trotskyites and
Latin miners, plus transplanted Kentucky mountaineers, who
came decades ago to cut timber, then became bootleggers

when the timber ran out and now live by game poaching and smuggling from Canada. Steadily losing population, the Tenth Congressional will probably be wiped out in the current Congressional reapportionment and become a memory.

For Kennedy this was hostile territory (a Lou Harris sampling had told him the Tenth Congressional was 60 to 40 against him) and day it showed its hostile face to him. He had risen at 6:30 in the morning, and his motorcade had sped from Eau Claire (in the Ninth Congressional District) over the black-top roads through the villages of the Tenth. He had first poked his head into the N-Joy Café at Cornell in the morning, hoping to find a rally waiting—and had found eight people sitting before a cake with green icing, waiting to listen to him. He had stopped at Ladysmith, Ingram, Prentice and Phillips, finding few people in the streets and cold indifference in the stares of those who observed him. Occasionally his advance men had persuaded a high school to let him talk to its civics class, and he would speak to the children, giving them little lessons in Presidential politics and anecdotes of history,[2] urging them to study hard, for their brains were the true "gold reserve of the nation."

At noon he stood at the head of the street in the one-street village of Phillips and looked down its length and saw no one; he entered its hardboard factory and spoke to the workers on the line, who grunted and let him pass; he visited the local newspaper, which was totally indifferent to the fact that a Presidential candidate was pausing with them; he circulated the cafés on Phillips' main street, courteously interrupting the men and women slurping coffee and eating sandwiches,

---

[2] His two favorite anecdotes for the high-school classes were one of General Winfield Scott and another of Madison and Jefferson.

General Scott, the candidate would relate, was the first Presidential candidate ever to barnstorm the country looking for votes. But General Scott used the pretext, as he traveled, that he was exploring the country looking for sites for veterans hospitals. "I'm not here looking for sites for hospitals," Kennedy would say, "I'm here running for the Presidency and I'm here because this is a key primary in a key state and your votes count." Then laughter.

The Madison-Jefferson anecdote, when told to children, was much the same. In the 1790s Madison and Jefferson had come north from Virginia on what was theoretically a naturalist expedition in which they claimed, they were looking for butterflies along the Hudson. While in New York, however, they had made the first alliance of Virginians with the Knights of St. Tammany, out of which the present-day Democratic Party was to grow into an alliance of Southern and big-city blocs. "But I'm not here looking for butterflies," Kennedy would say, "I'm looking for votes. Because this is a key primary in a key state for the key office of the Presidency. The Presidency is important, etc. . . ."

saying, "My name is John Kennedy, I'm running for President in the primary"; and they went right on eating. He left the town shortly after noon and the town was as careless of his presence as of a cold wind passing through.

All afternoon he drove the roads of the Tenth Congressional —larger than his native state of Massachusetts, with a population that could be squeezed into five wards of Boston—and spoke only to schoolchildren or walked the streets alone, reaching for hands. Not until late afternoon did the insolent silence pucker in friendship. At the crossroads called Mellen five people were waiting for him—and one was jovial with drink. The drinker insisted that since it happened to be St. Patrick's day, the candidate must, absolutely must, have a drink to the patron saint right there at the crossroads bar. With difficulty the candidate unglued the drunk and went on his way, still alone.

He had, by nightfall, traveled some 185 miles through the Tenth Congressional, and all that day had seen no more than 1,600 people, of whom probably 1,200 were children too young to vote. He had not even once lost his dignity, his calm, his cool and total composure. Yet to the observer this exercise here on campaign terrain seemed even more preposterous a stab at the Presidency of the United States than it had seemed from the distant political heights of New York and Washington.

Except that it did not seem preposterous to Kennedy himself. As he drove on the last lap of the day, at nightfall, from Hurley toward the even more desolate town of Ashland, he explained it, and it was quite clear to him: the day was a fragment in a master plan that reached all the way to the Convention and beyond. The Tenth, overwhelmingly Protestant, socially patterned to fit most neatly into Humphrey's farm appeal, was, he thought, the toughest of the ten Wisconsin districts to carry. If he could carry the Tenth, he might carry all Wisconsin's districts, farm and city, Protestant and Catholic alike. It was important to campaign where it was tough. It was important to talk to schoolchildren because schoolchildren talked to their parents when they went home.

Here he paused, for the car had come round a bend, and over the snow one could see for the first time that day the flat gray ice-bound expanse of Lake Superior, and the driver was talking. The driver, a local boy, pointed out that the ice was gray and rotten; in a few weeks it would break; then would come the smelts, the Lake Superior smelts that came in vast shimmering schools to make black patches over the water. People from all over Wisconsin and Michigan, said the driver, would be coming here in a few weeks with nets and baskets to haul in the smelts. Only, you couldn't eat more than a meal or two of them—they were so rich they made you sick.

Kennedy, interested as always in techniques, listened attentively to the driver, asked a question or two about the smelts, absorbed the information carefully as one more bit of local lore that a President might some day have to know, and resumed, almost without a break, his projection from this miserable day in the Tenth Congressional to the Convention. If he could carry the Tenth, he would carry all of Wisconsin. If he swept the entire Wisconsin delegation, he couldn't see how "they" (the big Eastern bosses) could deny him the nomination at the Los Angeles Convention. From there his mind made a transit to the big bosses who would control the Convention—he mused on the effect a victory here would have on the thinking of Governor Lawrence, boss of vital Pennsylvania; from that he made the transit to the similarity of Lawrence's problems in Pennsylvania to the problems of Governor Rosellini in the state of Washington. And then the car was approaching Ashland, a mournful little city on the shores of Lake Superior—site of the first home of a white man built in Wisconsin (1661)—once a busy iron port, its lakefront piers now rotting since the ore trade has petered out, too many houses closed, a grim and ugly portrait of a depressed area. And then the candidate began to talk about the problems of depressed areas and what the government ought to do. Nothing seemed preposterous to him about the entire day, neither the children nor the drunk nor the lonesomeness, nor the need and possibility that he do something about Ashland.

The comparison memory is of an evening with Hubert Humphrey, the romantic—for, with a romantic's clarity of mind, Humphrey could see how wildly preposterous was this primary route to the Presidency. Humphrey could see himself, with utter frankness, as he must look to the outer world on such exercises as these. My notes, of that evening, jotted down fragmentarily in the cold, are scarcely an accurate reproduction now. But his tone and attitude remain forever firm in my memory.

A number of newspapermen had waited at Humphrey's hotel, the Kaiser-Knickerbocker in Milwaukee, until late in the evening to learn whether he was or was not actually planning to campaign the next day in south Wisconsin. Humphrey was waiting for a telephone call from Washington to find out whether his vote was needed on some particularly crucial bill in the Senate. (Such matters as his own vote in the Senate bothered Humphrey far more than Kennedy who, single-mindedly, felt that running for the Presidency was his most important full-time business and Senate attendance took second place.) At 10:30 that night Humphrey had decided he could safely remain to campaign the next day in Wisconsin and so, with the three remaining newspapermen, two aides, his seventeen-year-old son and his prospective son-in-law, he loaded himself into his cold campaign bus for the long icy journey to Madison two hours away.

It was cold outside, the snow packed to cake; the drifts blew powder snow over the windshield; and it was colder inside the bus than outside. Humphrey was tired—he had been busy for a full legislative week in the Senate in Washington, had then flown to New York to plead for more money with his New York backers, had then flown on to Wisconsin, had then campaigned over the week end, and he now knew he would arrive in Madison at about one in the morning and that he must rise at 5:30 to shake hands in the dark dawn at the gates of the Oscar Mayer meat-packing plant before hitting the road for more campaigning. A cot had been placed in the bus for his cat napping, but it was too cold to nap and Humphrey was nervous. So he sat there on the edge of the cot as the bus jounced over the ice, the ruts and the snow; and all the while two pencil-thin shafts of reading light came down from the baggage ledge of the bus to carve his normally sharp features into something paler and sharper than normal.

One of the newspapermen, feeling the chill too, pulled out of his briefcase a bottle of fine expense-account whiskey and some paper cups, then poured a round for everybody against the bitter cold and offered a cup to Humphrey. We hunched forward about him, for he is a very lovable figure, and someone asked him why he too wasn't filing in the Indiana primary against Kennedy—for Kennedy had just filed for the Indiana primary.

Humphrey twirled the cup in his fingers and, as I remember his fine voice above the hum of the bus, began to talk in a monologue that lasted for fully an hour.

"Now, you ask me that? And why didn't I file in Florida too? Well, I'll tell you—any man who goes into a primary isn't *fit* to be President. You have to be crazy to go into a primary. A primary, now, is worse than the torture of the rack. It's all right to enter a primary by accident, or because you don't know any better, but by forethought . . ." He shook his head and some thought or some question carried him off to the farm problem.

"These people aren't leaving the farms, they're being driven off the farms, it's worse than in the thirties; these boys on the farm are taking a thirty-per-cent cut in their living; these auctions are going up every day; the rate of auctions is as high as it ever was in the thirties, they're driving farmers off the farms, the farmers aren't leaving. Oh, I know all the economics of it, I know all the economics of agricultural production, but I just say it's *good* for this country to have family farmers, I just *feel* that way. Socially, there *have* to be family farmers making a living on the farms in this country. Now that Benson, he's an idiot, he has brains one degree less than a moron, and this country is going to have some bills to pay for him some day . . . if I just had the power to investigate. . . . I was mayor once, in Minneapolis, we had a fine young crowd of men. A mayor is a fine job, it's the best job there is between being a governor and being a President, and I could investigate . . ."

He looked at us sharply as if we were asking him questions.

"You say, *why* does Humphrey want to be President? Why does any fellow want to do this, and especially me, the odds aren't good for me— But sometimes I wake up in the middle of the night and I say to myself, My God, what if I *should* be President, what if it should happen to me . . . and the country going into this difficult time."

Almost all I know of Humphrey's philosophy comes of that long night—that romantic, almost quaint faith in ordinary people. We passed a shopping center; and he hated it, and the facts tumbled out—only the big firms, the Sears, Roebucks and the Montgomery Wards and the Piggly-Wigglys could lease space in these big new shopping centers; the little merchant was being squeezed out, as his father had been squeezed out. The government ought to take care of the little merchant by a federal guarantee of small commercial leases. He talked of the farmers, and how the young ones were leaving the farm to go into the big cities to work on wages—and it was as if he coddled and cosseted every dark farmstead he passed that night. To Humphrey, it was a nation of little people, of individual individuals, and he their only tribune.

What is amazing about Humphrey is the wealth, the diversity, the detail of his knowledge, which runs from internal labor-union politics to the price of milk to the support price on peanuts to the tonnage on the St. Lawrence Seaway to his favorite Food for Peace plan to nuclear disarmament. Name a subject and somewhere, from his reading, Humphrey has picked up an expertise that he has digested and can now deliver, fused with intensity and passion within the frame of his own philosophy: that this is a nation of individuals, of yeoman and country merchants, and government's job is to keep the big man from crushing the little man. "The purpose of politics," he said talking to a group of farmers in mid-Wisconsin, "is only to give people a sense of direction."

With this brilliance goes also a strange detachment by which he can see himself apart. When he talks of politics he says "I think" or "I want" or "I did." When he speaks of issues it becomes, "Humphrey advocated" or "Humphrey first suggested" or "It was Humphrey who pointed out that . . ." as if he were a third person. In him a sharp knack of politics ("You wonder why I visited that Veterans Hospital on Sunday—maybe *they* can't vote, but on Sunday, they've all got visitors") mixes with a sweet love of the helpless. Visiting a school for deaf mutes in mid-Wisconsin, he would stop to make a full-dress speech to the children (translated by finger language), then leave with tears in his eyes because they were so sad. All through the primaries this strange detachment hobbled him. He found it difficult to hate deeply. He would dictate to a crowd of newspapermen a stinging statement against Kennedy—then, off the record, hang his head like a boy and take the edge off by saying, "I'll have a lot more to say later, and it'll all be petty and cheap, too."

What spoiled the Humphrey campaign—apart from the underlying fact that this country, Democrats and Republicans alike, was unwilling to be evangelized in 1960—was the very simplicity, the clarity, the homely sparkle he could bring to any issue. He could talk on almost any subject under the sun —to farmers, to workers, to university intellectuals. And when he finished there were no mysteries left; nor was he a mystery either. He was someone just like the listeners. There was no distance about him, no separation of intrigue, none of the majesty that must surround a king. Humphrey in a druggist's jacket explaining the problems of druggists in small towns and their inventories (which he could, spectacularly), or Humphrey, joining a picket line to sing "Solidarity Forever," was just like everyone else; and a President, unfortunately for Humphrey, must be different from everyone else. Humphrey yearned for the attention of the national press; yet the national press, which bore him so deep an affection, considered him almost too easy a friend. Humphrey was always good for a fine, sparkling quote or a quick disquisition in almost any realm of national policy. But the quick disquisition and his opinions, by being so easily available, were devalued. There was missing a restraint, and always present a friendliness too easily given.

When restraint was artificially imposed, Humphrey could sound very close to greatness. On the last week end of the Wisconsin campaign his fine, high, metallic voice cracked and suddenly disappeared entirely. All Sunday morning doctors worked on his throat; his voice was his chief combat weapon, and it had to be in shape for three critical TV appearances that afternoon. Yet he had promised a Jewish group that he would speak to them that morning, and so he arrived, direct from doctors' ministrations and an hour and a half late, at the Jewish Community Center of Milwaukee, under sternest orders not to raise his voice above conversational level. Under such restraint, and since he could not entertain with typical ringing Humphrey oratory, he gathered the audience to him in a soft tone and spoke first of his career in Minnesota and of the young men who, with him, had remade the Democratic Party in that neighboring state. Then, extemporizing, he continued somewhat like this:

"We believe liberalism is more than intellectual capacity—intellectual liberalism must be buttressed with an understanding of people and a love of them that goes far beyond texts or documents. For if you can't cry a little bit in politics, the only other thing you'll have is hate.

"The real contest in this world is not a military one; our real competition with the Soviet Union is not an economic one. Our struggle with totalitarianism and communism goes far beyond economics, science, education. It's a conflict over a system of values. . . . It may be necessary for a moment of history to let other systems have their claim on areas—but it's another thing to accept it. We have to live with it—not accept it. This is a struggle between good and evil, between tolerance and intolerance, over the very nature of man; and we come from a civilization that believes as an article of faith that man is created in the image of his maker, of a spiritual heritage in which human dignity can never be debased or abused by sheer power. No man has the right to govern another without his consent, and unless people understand this real moral value they can be duped. All of history is a constant struggle for emancipation from fears, from tyranny, from ignorance. And we are the emancipators, that's what this is all about, even if we don't recognize it. What we're trying to do is to get people to think about their own role in government, their own role in history.

"To select a President it's more important that he be good of heart, good of spirit, than that he be slick, or clever, or statesmanlike-looking. To be a leader means a willingness to risk—and a willingness to love. Has the leader given you something directly from his heart?—or has it all been planned in advance, all been scheduled? Is it efficient? If you want efficiency in politics, you can go to the communists or totalitarians.[3] I believe politics is simply to deal with people and to be human. Every now and then I read in the paper how disorderly Hubert Humphrey's campaign is and I say, THANK GOD."

With the "Thank God," Humphrey's voice suddenly found itself again; the doctors' work on his throat had taken effect; and the solemn, thoughtful man disappeared with a boom, as, whango, the current of sound was turned on in his voice box.

"Thank God," Humphrey bellowed, as if thanking God both that his campaign was disorderly and that his voice had come back in time for his TV appearance.

"Thank God," he said again, happy, "we *are* people, *just* people. Maybe we aren't efficient. But you can read the Declaration of Independence and the Constitution and the Gettysburg Address, and you won't find even once in them the word 'efficiency.' And you can read all of Marx, all of Engels, all of Stalin, all of Lenin and you won't find even once in them the word 'love.'"

Triumphantly Humphrey concluded, and it had been a fine speech, and had he made more like it, under similar restraint, he might have won.

Yet there were very few speeches like that, for a primary does not lend itself to that kind of oratory. A Presidential primary, the first direct appeal to the people in the shaping of their destiny, is always fought low, low down. And the art of the primary, for the candidate, is to appear as intimate and close as the local Congressman yet maintain a separation of dignity that makes him seem like a President also. It is an extremely difficult art, usually performed in short snatches of stump talking of five or ten minutes each, of talk at union halls, at tea parties, at wienie roasts, at student groups, at minority halls. One set speech, one handful of phrases, must cover all occasions. In a primary a candidate must not waste the great utterances of state that should be used later in the grander electoral campaign if he is successful; he cannot really cut the heart out of his rival, for he may have to sup-

[3] Many months later I learned that reports of this speech carried back to Kennedy held that Humphrey had compared him and his organization to "Nazi" efficiency. This envenomed and embittered Kennedy more than anything else that Humphrey was reported to have said. Since I was there and know this report to be untrue, I am pleased to set the record straight.

port his rival if he is defeated—or seek his support if he wins.

Humphrey solved his problem partly by a too-folksy folksiness, partly by a series of talks on substance, detail and issue, a series that proved that he knew more about Negro problems in Negro wards, dairy problems in dairy country, union problems in union country, than did even the local Congressman. He stuck to issues, always a mistake in a primary campaign. And it was as a man running for Congress, not for the Presidency, that he was accepted.

Kennedy solved his problem on two levels. The first was his own personal appearance, his incessant storm-driven campaigning, in which, over and over again, he presented himself as young Lochinvar running against the big bosses (which was true), as a man summoning all of his listeners to consider the nature of the Presidency: that the Presidency is the key office in American life, that the President alone can shape, create, revive and protect the nation, and that therefore they, who in Wisconsin were privileged enough to have first voice in this selection, should take it as seriously as did he.

The second level was organization. For the Kennedy organization, on its first run outside of New England, was having its trial breaking-in period.

Technically the two candidates for the Presidency were challenging each other for the allegiance and possession of Wisconsin's thirty-one delegates to the Democratic National Convention. Ten would be chosen on a statewide, winner-take-all popular-vote basis. Twenty others would be chosen, two each, from the ten Congressional Districts of the state. The National Committeeman and Committeewoman would split the remaining vote. The three Congressional Districts of the western tier of Wisconsin—the Third, Ninth and Tenth—were farm and dairy country, close to Minnesota and Humphrey's home base, vulnerable to his farm appeal. The two southern districts—the Second and First—were rich dairy and farm country with some admixture of industry. Milwaukee held two more districts—the Fourth and Fifth—and these were industrial districts, where Kennedy's Eastern appeal might be greatest. The Seventh Congressional, smack in the middle of Wisconsin, was unpredictable. The Sixth and Eight Congressional Districts along Lake Michigan were old Joe McCarthy territory, part industrial, part lumbering, part farming.

Each of these districts was soon to be seen in a different light. The University of Wisconsin, a magnificent institution, had some years before, in its Department of Rural Sociology, prepared a map that attempted to show the incredible mingling of ethnic stocks that make Wisconsin's share of America's political harmony. It had found no fewer than twenty-three parent stocks[4] as being dominant in one or another of the seventy-one counties of Wisconsin. Americans of Germanic origin predominate in Wisconsin, followed by those of Scandinavian origin (chiefly Norwegian), followed by British stock, followed by all the others.

But Wisconsin was soon to be seen as more than just an American state of different stocks. Each stock was soon to be split by analysis and by publicity, then by pressure groups, into its Protestant-Catholic cleavage. And whether or not originally this was the way the Democratic voters split by inclination (for in Wisconsin the "balanced ticket" of the big Eastern states had been unknown), soon, by amplification and dispute over their religious loyalties in the press and on TV, they were to do so in fact.

As we shall see later in this book, no one can state with accuracy the Protestant-Catholic percentages of any American community. All figures are guesses. But in Wisconsin the best guess is that 31 per cent of the population is of Catholic faith. In the East, generally most Catholics still vote Democratic; but in Wisconsin, more than in most states, there has been a heavy break-away during recent years of Catholics to the Republican Party. Given the open crossover privileges of the Wisconsin primary, Republican Catholics and Republican Protestants could both, if they chose, vote in the Democratic primary rather than in their own. Would Republican Protestants and Republican Catholics take advantage of this privilege to invade the Democratic Party and vote for their kinsman-in-faith? And if so, who would benefit most by such religious crossovers? Neither of the two candidates, men whom I have known to be beyond any stain of prejudice, wanted such crossovers or sought them. But the lens of national reporting was soon to focus attention on this religious imponderable as the central political question of the campaign. The hate merchants and the prejudiced of both faiths were to flourish in this reporting. Both candidates were to denounce the prejudice; but neither could erase the intrusion of religious feeling.

Religion and ethnics have always been important in Amer-

[4] The dominant ethnic stocks, listed in no apparent order, were in 1940: Latvian, Italian, Icelander, Croatian-Slovene, old-stock American, Norwegian, Indian, Swedish, Danish, Polish, Finnish, Bohemian, mixture [?], Russian, Irish, Scotch, English, Swiss, German, Belgian, Hollander, Welsh, Lithuanian, French.

ican politics[5]; they can be overcome, as every candidate knows, only by the sharpest differentiation of his program, policy and personality from his rival's. But when, as in the Wisconsin primary, the advanced liberal programs of Humphrey and Kennedy matched so closely, such differentiation of political purpose was impossible, and "kinship politics" were loosed to play their dominant role.

Both candidates threw all their energy into Wisconsin; each spent roughly the same sum—approximately $150,000. But money could not measure their efforts. As Humphrey phrased it, he was like a "corner grocer running against a chain store." Humphrey had billboards, advertisements, a bus, radio and TV time, literature—all the technical needs of a campaigner. But his Minnesota team were men engaged in their daily jobs across the border; they could give him only week-end help and little else; and his national headquarters, the seat of organization, consisted of six men in four rooms in a Washington hotel.

Kennedy had been preparing for this first campaign for months. Kennedy fidgeted in no airports waiting for a plane —his own plane flew him about the country and in and out of Wisconsin at his convenience. (It was cheaper, Kennedy pointed out characteristically—and he was right—to have one's own plane, for mileage cost of a campaign actually cost less this way than by commercial plane.) Kennedy had Louis Harris on his staff—and Harris' polling of 23,000 Wisconsin voters was not only the largest ever done in a single state but invaluable in informing his candidate of moods. Above all, Kennedy had organization and the beginning of his national press cult.

Where Humphrey could staff but two offices in Wisconsin with first-caliber personnel—one in Madison (the Second District) and one in Milwaukee—Kennedy could staff eight of the ten Congressional Districts of the state with superior personnel. Nor was the Kennedy staffing done by money. It was the long-established connection of Kennedy's friendships and social background that provided him with the talent. His sisters and brothers—in themselves a small troop of unpaid political talent—operated all across the state. Four of the ten districts were staffed by Ivy League college classmates, able to devote full time to the organization of Kennedy volunteers. In the industrial First District, he could invite a talent as large as Artist Walton to create his volunteer organization.

[5] See Chapter Eight for a fuller treatment of religion and ethnics in politics.

From Gloucester, Massachusetts, a former mayor, Ben Smith,[6] arrived to take over organization in the Tenth District; and the Kennedy Senatorial staff—all but Sorensen—moved out to Wisconsin en masse. Humphrey had relied on his credit over the years with the Wisconsin State Democratic Organization, the help he had given them in organization, the voice he had been for them in Congress; Humphrey relied too on his good name with the great unions to provide manpower, funds and help. The Kennedys relied chiefly on themselves. They expected the elected Democratic state officials (Governor, United States Senator, Congressmen) to stay neutral lest they be torn apart in this contest of out-of-state candidates. But they won to their counsel Patrick J. Lucey, Wisconsin State Democratic Chairman, and chose the attractive young Democratic Mayor of Madison, Ivan Nestingen[7] to head their statewide Citizens Committee. Beyond that, the Kennedys entered with their own organization, their own techniques, their own staff to call their own meetings, to hold their own receptions, to set their own targets.

It is activity that creates news, and activity in Wisconsin lay chiefly with Kennedy—in the flight of his personal plane, the Mother Ship; with the candidate's glamorous family; with his revolving circus of Ivy League performers and organizers. The press, charmed by Kennedy, entranced by the purr of his political machinery, slowly fastened on the candidate from Massachusetts as the winner. Gradually, as primary day approached, the estimates rose—Kennedy would take six of the ten; Kennedy would take eight of the ten; Kennedy would take nine of the ten. The political wise men of the Wisconsin Governor's office in Madison were of the opinion that Kennedy might even take all ten of the ten districts and wrap up the nomination right there.

By Tuesday, April 5th, as Wisconsin prepared to vote, it was (or so the prognosticators felt) a walkaway.

The fact that it was not a walkaway, as shown by the actual result of the voting, was to shape all the rest of Kennedy's strike for the Presidency, from then until November.

He received the returns in privacy with several members of his family, in the third-floor corner suite of the Pfister Hotel in Milwaukee, in the pattern that was later to become familiar—Brother Bobby and Analyst Lou Harris receiving the direct results in a separate communications center, linked

[6] Whom President Kennedy has now caused to be appointed United States Senator from Massachusetts.

[7] Now Undersecretary of Health, Education and Welfare.

to him by direct line. Within two hours after the polls had closed the profile of voting had become apparent. He was to lose the Western tier conclusively—the Third, Ninth, Tenth—whether because they were farm districts or Protestant districts he could not judge. He was to lose the Second equally heavily—whether because it was Protestant or loved Humphrey or was Stevensonian again he could not judge. He was to carry the Seventh narrowly; the Sixth and Eighth (heavily Catholic, old Joe McCarthy country) substantially; the First District and Milwaukee's Fourth and Fifth (again heavily Catholic) decisively. No one could tell whether Humphrey's districts had voted against Kennedy because they were Protestant or because they were farmland closest to Minnesota; nor whether Kennedy had won his own six districts because they were heavily Catholic or because they were heavily industrial. The returns had shown their character by eight o'clock; by ten, the entire message was clear to him.

He had been reading the newspapers, slowly sipping a bowl of chicken-noodle soup, now and again watching the television set or accepting a call from his brother Bobby at the communications center. In that attitude of intellectual alertness that he was to maintain constantly through the full year, in narrow victory or sweep alike, he showed his emotion only once.

"What does it mean?" asked one of his sisters.

"It means," he said quietly yet bitterly, "that we have to do it all over again. We have to go through every one and win every one of them—West Virginia and Maryland and Indiana and Oregon, all the way to the Convention."

He had read the meaning of the results instantly and clearly. His margin of 56 per cent of the popular vote was not decisive. The break of the popular vote would convince none of the bosses who controlled the delegates of the East that he was a winner. He had lost all four predominantly Protestant districts and had carried the unclassified one (the Seventh) only by a hair. His popular margin had come entirely from four heavily Catholic areas—the Sixth, Eighth, Fourth and Fifth. All that he had said, the entire imagery of the Presidency as the key office, the deciding force in war and peace, would be obscured by these totals. They would be read, he knew, wherever men read politics as a Catholic-Protestant split. He had tried to dodge this issue as skillfully as he knew; so had Humphrey; but now he would have to face it head on—and in West Virginia, where Protestants measured out at 95 per cent and Catholics at 5 per cent. Taut of face, unsmiling, sensing himself wounded, he prepared to leave for the TV studios to thank the people of Wisconsin for the victory he knew was not a victory.

If Kennedy received his six-district-to-four margin as a setback, Humphrey received the short end of 4 to 6 almost as a victory.

Humphrey had expected defeat, had accepted the prognosis of the experts as certain tidings of devastation. Yet here he now was, having run a tight race, finding in the figures hope, cheer and comfort. Nixon on that day had run a poor third in the Republican primary—the total Democratic vote being more than 2 to 1 greater than the Republican. To Humphrey it seemed that Kennedy had won only because of Republican Catholic crossovers. Obviously, it seemed, the Republican Catholics of the Fox River valley, of Green Bay, of Sheboygan, of Manitowoc, and of other centers of the Sixth and Eighth had crossed from the Republican side to vote for one of their own on the Democratic side. Exultantly Humphrey sat in his hotel room at the Kaiser-Knickerbocker with wife and friends. As if presiding over a celebration, he scooped up onion dip on his potato chips and waved guests to his victory board.

He emerged from this inner scene of homespun gaiety to greet the TV cameras and the press briefly. Exuberant, he told them, "You can quote me as being encouraged and exhilarated and sorry it's all over." He quipped for a few minutes, then said he was going directly back to Washington the next day and on to West Virginia.

"I was going to try and get a ride with Jack on his plane," he laughed, "but he thought I ought to catch the next bus. Why don't you fellows come along? We're selling popcorn concessions down there."

Then, just before darting back to his wife and his celebration, he turned and smiled at the newsmen whose predictions he had upset. "I always told you fellows politics could be fun, didn't I?" he said.

It is quite clear now, in retrospect, that John F. Kennedy owes his nomination as much to Hubert Humphrey's decision that night in Milwaukee as to any other man's decision except his own.

For that night, on the field of battle, having carried, despite all prediction, four out of ten districts against the "chain store" Kennedys, it seemed to Humphrey that he had won a moral victory.

But the reading of politics by hard men across the nation could only be otherwise. If Humphrey could not carry Wisconsin, a neighbor state so similar in culture and sociology to his own, then he could carry nothing in the Midwest. Thus, in hard politics, he could not deliver his base; therefore, he had been eliminated.

If, realizing this, Humphrey had withdrawn at that moment, Kennedy would have faced zero opposition in the West Virginia primary; thus, any Kennedy victory there would have proved nothing and been meaningless in terms of bargaining power vis-à-vis the big Eastern bosses.

Realistically, again, Humphrey could get nothing for himself out of a West Virginia victory; Wisconsin had eliminated him as an active contender for the nomination. If he won in West Virginia, he could at most only create that Convention deadlock for which the Johnson, the Symington, the Stevenson forces so yearned.

It was Humphrey's decision alone—and it was made impulsively, instinctively, in the flush of primary night at the Kaiser-Knickerbocker Hotel in Milwaukee, before morning and a few days' reflection could give him another perspective. Had Humphrey really wanted to hurt John F. Kennedy, withdrawal from West Virginia that night would have done it.

Many people in the next few days tried to shake Hubert Humphrey's decision. Pressure came from the East, from Alex Rose who speaks for the labor leaders of New York and the Liberal Party of that city. Pressure came from Walter Reuther, who saw the two liberal candidates for the nomination about to tear each other apart in West Virginia, thus deadlocking the Convention and probably throwing it to Lyndon Johnson. Pressure came from as far off as California, where Pat Brown, the Governor, decided to telephone Orville Freeman and ask him to persuade Hubert Humphrey to withdraw. Even within Hubert Humphrey's own camp, the astute Jim Rowe read the portents and urged that Humphrey bargain with the actual winner in Wisconsin now, while his strength was at its peak.

But the combat wrath had been aroused in Humphrey. The odd cleavage of the Wisconsin voting had convinced him that Republican Catholic crossovers into the Democratic primary had been chiefly responsible for his apparent defeat. He wanted to run in a primary limited to Democrats. He had accepted and raised large sums of money from friends across the country, and he owed them a real fight for their money. He recognized that many of these friends were Stevenson people, using him only as a tool to deadlock the Convention against Kennedy, so that Stevenson might sweep it later—yet the commitment to fight seemed binding on Humphrey. Furthermore, some forms of pressure by men unauthorized to speak for Kennedy yet assuming to speak in his name were so vile as to amount to little short of blackmail. Humphrey reacts to pressure like a man of courage, and to this kind of pressure Humphrey offered fight.

So he would enter; he refused to withdraw.

The Kennedy leadership, observing Humphrey, also misread the instant situation. In retrospect, they would come to recognize that Humphrey's battle in West Virginia, a solidly Protestant state, would certify their victory as an authentic expression of national appeal. But at the moment they were furious. They had fought a clean and elevated campaign in Wisconsin. Now Humphrey refused to accept the decision. He was preparing to frustrate them in West Virginia—not, it seemed to them, out of any hope in his own eventual triumph at the Convention, but only to deny it vengefully to John F. Kennedy in the name of shadowy third persons who disdained the ardor of field combat in the primaries.

Whatever Humphrey's personal reading of his chances in West Virginia, the Kennedy reading was that Humphrey faced them chiefly as a spoiler. In the Kennedys too the combat venom rose. They had played by Wisconsin rules in Wisconsin; they would play by West Virginia rules in West Virginia. And they meant to win.

In American life political patterns are rarely determined by geography, and the states of the union group themselves in distinct political families more by past history than by simple neighborliness.

Only 640 miles separate Madison, the capital of Wisconsin, from Charleston, the capital of West Virginia. Yet centuries of time and tradition, immeasurable gulfs of culture, separate these two states. If one were to choose as a proud grouping those American states whose politics are probably the most decent and worthy of respect, one would group Wisconsin, certainly, with Minnesota, California and Connecticut. And if one were to choose those states whose politics (excluding the baroque courthouse states of the South) are the most squalid, corrupt and despicable, then one would add West Virginia to that Jukes family of American politics that includes Indiana, Massachusetts and Texas.

The platform on which West Virginia politics are shaped is a bulge on the inner slope of the Appalachians, 24,282 square miles in extent (forty-first state in the union in size), on which dwell 1,850,000 people (West Virginia was one of only three states in the union to lose population in the last decade). Centuries ago the sturdy Welsh-Scots-English pioneers of the frontier, moving from tideland over the crest of the Appalachians, entered this hill country and settled on its slopes like men making homes in an amphitheater that faces out west over the Ohio River and the vast rolling plains of the midcountry. Finding it a lovely state, with scarcely a patch of flatland as big as a baseball field, they hunted the hills and farmed the hollows, then broke from the slave-holding aristocracy of Virginia to form their own Free State in the Civil War ("Montani Semper Liberi" reads their state motto); thereafter they watched the westering tides of post-Civil War migration, with all its varied ethnic stocks from Europe, sweep around their hills to the rich and fertile plains states beyond.

Almost unchanged in speech or colonial courtliness of manner, they learned that they sat on what are quite probably the greatest coal beds the world knows. As America's industry grew in the last century, and as coal fueled it, West Virginia became *stupor mundi* in the coal-bearing provinces of the world. (So involuted and multiple are the coal beds beneath her hills that the standard geological estimate is that the underground expanse of West Virginia's coal seams is one and a half times the entire surface expanse of the state.) Producing between 100,000,000 and 173,000,000 tons of coal a year, in some years the state mined more coal than did all of Germany. But coal made only a few men rich; and although coal was West Virginia's basic industry (employing 116,000 people, or one fifth of all nonfarm employment in the state until ten years ago), it was an industry of low wages, of bitterness, of violence and union combat.

Over the past thirty years coal has molded West Virginia politics. Starting with the era of Franklin D. Roosevelt (who let John L. Lewis organize the miners against an industrial savagery unique in American industry), West Virginia became a Democratic state; the Mine Workers Union became a force in politics equal to the United Automobile Workers in Michigan or the clothing workers in New York.

When coal began to die some fifteen years ago, West Virginia began to die with it. Technology helped kill coal; as gas and fuel oil became the predominant source of American energy, coal's portion of America's energy supply dropped from 51 per cent (in 1945) to 23 per cent (in 1960). American industry and railways no longer need coal for energy—

gas, hydroelectric power, fuel oils are more efficient energy sources. Only steel, requiring soft coal for coking, and the electric-generating industry still sustain the stricken industry.

High union wages also helped kill coal employment—as the union shoved wages up and up, it became not only cheaper but also imperative for the operators to automate mines with the superb new machines of the postwar era. Gradually, as these pressures made themselves felt, the miners were dismissed, then they hungered. In 1960 West Virginia still produced 119,433,000 tons of coal—but the miners, who had numbered 116,421 thirteen years before (when they dug 173,000,000 tons of coal), had fallen to a miserable 42,900. New chemical industries have grown up in the West Virginia valleys of the Kanawha and Ohio Rivers— using West Virginia's gas, coal and clean waters. But these new automated giants reflect the mysteries and triumphs of industries that produce by skill and engineering—they need few men. In 1960, of West Virginia's fifty-five counties, no less than twenty counted 15 per cent of their people as recipients of federal government relief. In some counties like Mingo (41 per cent) or McDowell (26 per cent) a quarter or more of the population required and received miserable federal food packages.

West Virginia's politics rise from this hunger, and they are sordid politics. When men are unemployed, any job looks good, and government in many West Virginia counties is the chief source of jobs. Until 1947 county sheriff's offices, by antique tradition, operated on the fee system, and the jobs of several county sheriffs were estimated to be worth about $30,000 a year in "take"; some county assessor offices are worth more—up to $70,000 a year in take. Posts on local school boards are bitterly contested, from one end of the state to the other. "Hell," one local politician answered me, "curriculum? They don't give a damn about curriculum, half of them don't know what the word 'curriculum' means. School board means jobs—it means teachers' jobs, janitors' jobs, bus-driver jobs. They'll pass the curriculum in five minutes and spend two hours arguing about who's gonna be bus driver on Peapot Route Number One. Bus driver means a hundred and sixty dollars a month for a part-time job."

Politics in West Virginia is not only part-time jobs but full-time gossip, and it gets more intense as one descends the levels from statehouse to county courthouse, where the local bosses are established, barons of little realms, forming and breaking their alliances. Politics in West Virginia involves money—hot money, under-the-table money, open money. Politics in West Virginia can be violent (the Hatfields conducted their feud with the McCoys of Kentucky out of West Virginia's Logan County). And politics in West Virginia is complicated. On election day the West Virginia voter is presented with probably the most cumbersome ballot in America; crowded with individual names, it seems that everyone, his cousin and his uncle are running for public office. In 1960, the Charleston *Gazette,* printing sample ballots on Monday, May 9th, for the next day's primary, used *three* full-size standard newspaper pages to reproduce the ballots offered in the subdivisions of Kanawha County. On one huge ballot the Charlestonian was offered *fifty-three* individual choices of candidates if he wished to ponder his selections. Such a mystifying ballot requires simplification for the voter; and simplification is supplied by "slating." The local bosses, the union chiefs, the statewide candidates, the education-board candidates, even the veterans organizations, all make cross-alliances to settle on, then print, a "slate" of approved candidates among the multitude of names. Their followers and faithful are supposed to carry this printed slate to the polls, then use it as guidance. It is quite obvious that no one without an avocation for politics and at least five full minutes in the booth can use a West Virginia ballot without a "slate." The West Virginia ballot, with its multitude of choices, strains reasonable choice to the point of unreason. A printed "slate" is essential; and money is spent lavishly—and legally—in providing such "slates."

To this bleak picture of hunger and politics one should add, in all justice, a condition that most of us who reported West Virginia in the spring found little time to note: that these are handsome people and, beyond doubt, the best-mannered and most courteous in the nation. These are people who teach their children to say "Sir" and "Thank you" to their elders; they speak in soft and gentle tones; their relations with their Negroes are the best of any state with any significant Negro population, north or south. The Negroes, being treated with respect and good manners, reciprocate with a bearing of good manners and respect. Whether on a West Virginia bus or in a crowded West Virginia store, men and women are well-behaved and friendly. Moreover, these are brave people—no state of the union contributed more heavily to the armed forces of the United States in proportion to population than did this state of mountain men; nor did any state suffer more casualties in proportion to its population. That they should live as they do is a scar and shame on American life, an indictment of the national political system as well as of their own.

Of these good people, two last dominant facts remain to be noted: that they are white, and they are Protestant. Negroes in West Virginia come to about 4 per cent of the population; Catholics in West Virginia come to 5 per cent of the population; almost all the rest are seed of the frontiersmen, of the men who bore their Bibles with their rifles across the mountains; and who still take their religion, like their bootleg liquor, strong and neat. As the two candidates prepared to campaign in West Virginia, the discovery of West Virginians' poverty would attract only secondary national attention. It was to be West Virginians' religion that engaged the chief attention of American politics.

West Virginia had long attracted the interest of John F. Kennedy—perhaps longer than any of the other states in the union outside his own. Two years before, while running for re-election as Senator from Massachusetts, he had retained Louis Harris to make the very first probe of public opinion outside his home state—in West Virginia, in June of 1958. (The result of the poll then was 52 for Kennedy, 38 for Nixon, balance undecided.)

A shadow organization had been set up early in 1959 in West Virginia, its local chief being Robert McDonough, a printing-plant proprietor of Wood County, a lean, taciturn but imaginative student of his home state's bizarre politics. The original Washington strategist and director had been Ted Sorensen. Slowly, through 1959, from county to county, from center to center, the Kennedy people had woven an organization called West Virginians for Kennedy—not so much to act as to be ready to act if necessary. In December of 1959, Lou Harris had reported out of West Virginia again— this time with a 70-to-30 break for Kennedy over Humphrey. Still there was no Kennedy decision to act in West Virginia. A small state, its primary verdict not binding on the delegates actually elected, it seemed only conditionally worth a campaign effort in a spring of frantic exertion. The condition on which it would be worth the effort was simple: that "the trap could be baited for Humphrey to enter," as one of the Kennedy early planning papers said. When in February of 1960 Humphrey did indeed "enter the trap" by filing his primary papers in Charleston, the Kennedys jubilantly followed suit and closed the trap about him.

By April of 1960, however, after the Wisconsin primary, it was uncertain whether it was Humphrey who was caught in the trap or Kennedy himself. For between February and April the political atmosphere of the country had begun to heat. The Wisconsin primary had attracted the attention of the national press and the national television networks; and the nation had become aware that a religious issue was beginning to develop in its national politics for the first time since 1928; men and women from West Virginia to Alaska were slowly learning the identity and religion of the major candidates; and the tide in West Virginia had turned against the Boston candidate. Sampling in Charleston now, three weeks before the primary voting day of May 10th, Harris discovered that the citizens of Kanawha county—which includes Charleston, the capital—had shifted vehemently in sentiment. They were now, he reported, 60 for Humphrey, 40 for Kennedy. When Kennedy headquarters inquired of their West Virginia advisers what had happened between his 70-to-30 margin of December and the short end of the present 40-to-60 split, they were told, curtly, "But no one in West Virginia knew you were a Catholic in December. Now they know."

Only two moments of discouragement seemed seriously to shake Kennedy confidence in victory in the long year of 1960. The greater was the late-August abysm, following the Convention, when the candidate was trapped in Congress' special session. But the first was the period after Wisconsin, as the Kennedy men approached West Virginia. They had been overconfident in Wisconsin; they had been misled by the press; the vote had broken on strictly religious lines. Now they faced trial in West Virginia with every survey showing against them, fighting a man who could not win at the Convention but who, if he won here, would throw the nominating decision into the back room.

As usual with the Kennedy operation, solutions proceeded at two levels—one strategic and one organizational. Both are worth examination, for both were in their way classics of American politics.

The organizational solution was, of course, O'Brien's. After ten years in the service of John F. Kennedy, Lawrence F. O'Brien is certainly one of the master political operators of the new school.

What distinguishes the new school from the old school is the political approach of exclusion versus inclusion. In a tight old-fashioned machine, the root idea is to operate with as few people as possible, keeping decision and action in the hands of as few inside men as possible. In the new style, practiced by citizens' groups and new machines (Republican and Democratic alike) the central idea is to give as many people as possible a sense of participation: participation galvanizes emotions, gives the participant a live stake in the victory of the leader.

It is always easy for a glamorous candidate to arouse the bowels of people who hear him. What is much more difficult is to give these people, once aroused, the sense that they are usefully participant. In 1958, for example, John F. Kennedy in his Massachusetts Senatorial campaign had circulated nominating petitions signed by 256,000 citizens of the Bay State—some fervid, some perfunctory. At the same time the Kennedy headquarters in Boston were overwhelmed with the offer of service from some 1,800 volunteers for whom no easily useful function could be found. The O'Brien solution: to put the volunteers to work sending out letters of thanks to each of the 256,000 signers of the nomination petitions. This is what politicians consider a nearly perfect solution; it made happy the receivers of the letters of thanks and, more importantly, gave to each volunteer the illusion of service. There are still men at the bars of South Boston who boast of the letter that Jack Kennedy sent them for signing his nominating petition in 1958. All this, of course, is codified in the O'Brien Manual—a sixty-four-page black-bound book that gives the diagram of organization for every Kennedy campaign from beginning to end. It would be superfluous to summarize this book. Its burden is that every vote counts; that every citizen likes to feel he is somehow wired into the structure of power; that making a man or woman seem useful and important to himself (or herself) in the power system of American life takes advantage of one of the simplest and noblest urges of politics in the most effective way.

Heavy with gloom, O'Brien arrived in West Virginia, sleepless from Wisconsin, on the Wednesday following the Wisconsin primary. There were at that moment four weeks to go before the voting of May 10th; and the organization then available had been prepared not for an emergency but for easy victory. Bob McDonough, as Executive Chairman, had, in the weeks preceding, added only one paid full-time worker, the hulking Matt Reese, to his staff; together Reese and McDonough had found chairmen for Kennedy volunteer organizations in thirty-nine of West Virginia's fifty-five counties. These county chairmen had been informed of what was required by O'Brien two weeks earlier: subordinate district chairmen; telephone chairmen for the women's workers; primary day chairmen for rounding up cars to haul voters to the polls; two stand-by deputy chairmen available day or night for literature distribution, whether at church socials or factory gates, by dawn or by dusk. Only twenty-five of the thirty-nine county organizations had, in whole or in part, fulfilled these assigned tasks. Now, on the day after the Wisconsin primary, with the middle-European accents of Wisconsin still ringing in their ears, O'Brien and Bobby Kennedy, with no rest or vacation, arrived in West Virginia to pull the organization together for emergency action. This was crash work; neither needed to tell the other that defeat in West Virginia would all but end John F. Kennedy's chance of nomination.

A first meeting in the morning for the northern chairmen took place at the Stonewall Jackson Hotel in Clarksburg. A second meeting for the southern chairmen took place that afternoon at the Kanawha Hotel, 100 miles away, in Charleston.

Jobs to be done:

§ Organization of volunteers for door-to-door distribution of the Kennedy literature.

§ Rural mailings.

§ Telephone campaign. (The West Virginians explained the problem of telephoning in a state where the party line still reigns, but O'Brien insisted nonetheless.)

§ Receptions to be organized. (And since tea and coffee receptions were too effete for West Virginia, it was all right to call receptions an "ox roast" in the northern part of the state, a "weenie roast" in the southern part.)

§ Finally, all county chairmen were told which members of the Kennedy family (plus Franklin D. Roosevelt, Jr.) would be available to tour in what areas on which day.

§ Above all: work.

Five days later, on the Monday following the Wisconsin primary, area commanders had arrived. Kennedy area commanders are in themselves also worth study, for so much has been written and will be written on the use of Kennedy money to buy elections. The controversy over Kennedy money revolves largely about the money paid out in actual campaign (legitimate and aboveboard) and the money value of the services the Kennedys commanded without payment (staggeringly large). There were to be eight main headquarters of the Kennedy campaign in the emergency program for West Virginia, and to these were later added eight more subheadquarters. These, however, were to be staffed by volunteers of such talent (and of such independent means) that the money value of their talents defies definition. Even at this late date no complete listing is available of the Kennedy volunteers who invaded West Virginia for the primary; but even a partial listing of their names would bring the total to fifty people (as against Humphrey's talent total of less than ten). There were Lem Billings, a roommate of the candidate at Choate School, an advertising man; Bill Battle, a Navy comrade of the candidate, son of a former governor of Virginia; Artist Bill Walton (assigned to the bleak deprivation of McDowell County). Other volunteers included: Benjamin Smith (Harvard), former mayor of Gloucester, Massachusetts, independently wealthy; Claude Hooton, Harvard classmate; Chuck Spalding, Harvard classmate, independently wealthy; R. Sargent Shriver[8] (Yale), brother-in-law, independently wealthy; Richard K. Donahue,[9] Vice-chairman of the Massachusetts Democratic Committee, a corruscatingly brilliant young lawyer from Lowell, Massachusetts; Paul B. ("Red") Fay,[10] a comrade of his PT boat days. And besides these, the total staff of Kennedy's Senatorial office (except for the strategic-intellectual arm of Sorensen-Goodwin-Feldman), plus girls, drivers, typists, press men, chauffeurs, TV men. When Kennedy is denounced for his expenditures in West Virginia, this staff is commonly cited as an illustration of extravagance; but the key men of this staff were volunteers; they could not be recruited by money and were, indeed, worth more than money.[11] An FBI investigation later authorized by Richard M. Nixon's friend, Attorney-General William P. Rogers, could after exhaustive study turn up no evidence of wrongdoing.

Each of the eight area commanders, plus their deputies, were in West Virginia six days after the Wisconsin primary. They met on Monday evening in the Kanawha Hotel, preparatory to being dispatched to the hills.

First instruction: to inspect all the machinery outlined by the O'Brien Manual, see whether it was functioning under the

[8] Now Director of the Peace Corps.
[9] Now a White House assistant.
[10] Now Undersecretary of the Navy.
[11] As a matter of political technique, it should be noted that while this full Kennedy first team was employed in West Virginia, a complete second team was simultaneously being deployed in Maryland, whose primary was to follow West Virginia's in a week; a third team was being simultaneously fielded in Oregon, whose primary was to follow three days after that; and a primitive fourth team was being simultaneously fielded in Indiana.

local chairmen already designated, then telephone back in three days with a full report on their area.

A week after the telephone report they were to submit a written report on their area, describing its problems, potentials and needs in exact detail. One other instruction: since all of them were alien, out-of-state and Eastern men, suspect by the mountaineers, they were enjoined to pay their first call in each district upon the local county courthouse political leader—whether friendly or hostile. Whatever they were about to do, they were instructed, they should report frankly to the local political leader before doing it. This was to be no secret Papist conspiracy. The candidate—now vacationing in Montego Bay in Jamaica—could give West Virginia no more than ten days of his time (he had Nebraska, Maryland and Oregon primaries to fight simultaneously); but when he came he would rouse the people. Their job was to harness the manpower that the candidate's leadership would trumpet up.

So spoke O'Brien—tired, benign, still unruffled.

If organization could do it, he would do it. This was his trade, and in West Virginia he was performing what will remain a masterpiece in the art of the primaries. But beyond organization was the raw stuff of American politics: those things blurted out by simple people that show their emotion, their misgiving, their trust.

And there could be no doubt about the issue that bothered these people, at least no doubt from the memories of this correspondent:

§ Woman on a lawn at West Hamlin, West Virginia, as the school band plays and the incomparable tulips wave in the breeze: "I'm not prejudiced. A man's religion shouldn't have anything to do with it. But a man ought to be a good Catholic if he's going to be one. And they believe in church-and-state and I don't."

§ Little old lady, under a dripping umbrella in the rain at Sutton, West Virginia ("Home of the Golden Delicious Apple" says the sign): "We've never had a Catholic President and I hope we never do. Our people built this country. If they had wanted a Catholic to be President, they would have said so in the Constitution."

§ Big burly man, heavy jowls, good face, limping (the limp from World War I, in which he had been hit): "I'm a Lutheran—and you know how we feel. I haven't been in New York since we came off the boat in 1919, I hear it's changed."

§ A man in front of the courthouse in Putnam County,

West Virginia; the man is angry because somebody on the
outskirts of the crowd is making a noise: "What's that goof-
ball blowing off for? I'm a Baptist, but I got nothing against
no man's religion."

The issue, it was clear, over and beyond anything O'Brien's
organizational genius could do, was religion: the differing
ways men worshiped Christ in this enclave of Western civilization.

All other issues were secondary. The Kennedy tacticians
had already refined several minor lines of attack on Humphrey. They had begun and continued to stress the war
record of John F. Kennedy, for in West Virginia, a state of
heroes and volunteers, the stark courage of the Boston candidate in the Straits of the Solomons in the Fall of 1942
found a martial echo in every hill. ("To listen to their
stuff," said an irate Humphrey man, "you'd think Jack won
the war all by himself.") The Kennedy men continued to
hammer at Humphrey as being "front man" for a gang-up
crowd of Stevenson-Symington-Johnson supporters who refused to come into the open. They stressed their candidate's
sympathy and concern for the hungry and unemployed.
Humphrey, who had known hunger in boyhood, was the
natural workingman's candidate—but Kennedy's shock at the
suffering he saw in West Virginia was so fresh that it communicated itself with the emotion of original discovery.
Kennedy, from boyhood to manhood, had never known
hunger. Now, arriving in West Virginia from a brief rest in
the sun in the luxury of Montego Bay, he could scarcely
bring himself to believe that human beings were forced to
eat and live on these cans of dry relief rations, which he
fingered like artifacts of another civilization. "Imagine," he
said to one of his assistants one night, "just imagine kids who
never drink milk." Of all the emotional experiences of his
pre-Convention campaign, Kennedy's exposure to the misery
of the mining fields probably changed him most as a man;
and as he gave tongue to his indignation, one could sense
him winning friends.

Yet the religious issue remained, and as the days grew
closer to the voting the Kennedy staff divided on how it must
be handled. His native West Virginian advisers said that West
Virginia was afraid of Catholics; the fear must be erased, the
matter must be tackled frontally. Lou Harris, with his poll
reports in hand, concurred. But most of the Kennedy Washington staff disagreed—raise no religious issue in public, they
said, religion is too explosive.

It was up to the candidate alone to decide. And, starting on

April 25th, his decision became clear. He would attack—he would meet the religious issue head on.

Whether out of conviction or out of tactics, no sounder Kennedy decision could have been made. Two Democratic candidates were appealing to the commonalty of the Democratic Party; once the issue could be made one of tolerance or intolerance, Hubert Humphrey was hung. No one could prove to his own conscience that by voting for Humphrey he was displaying tolerance. Yet any man, indecisive in mind on the Presidency, could prove that he was at least tolerant by voting for Jack Kennedy.

The shape of the problem made it impossible for Humphrey, himself the most tolerant of men, to run in favor of tolerance. Only Kennedy could campaign on this point and still win in good taste and without unfairness. If his religion was what they held against him, Kennedy would discuss it. And by exquisite use of TV, he did indeed discuss it.

There remains with me now a recollection of what I think is the finest TV broadcast I have ever heard any political candidate make. It is also one of the few slip-ups I know in the efficient Kennedy organization, for no transcript, no tape recording, no TV tape is known to anybody who heard Kennedy address the people of West Virginia on Sunday evening, May 8th. What I write is from memory and scattered notes.

Over that week end before the West Virginia voting, Kennedy had paid a flying visit to Nebraska, where he was required to face a primary on the same day as the West Virginia primary. He had already been hammering night and day, for ten days, the issue of religion ("I refuse to believe that I was denied the right to be President on the day I was baptized"). In Nebraska, home state of Ted Sorensen, he had asked this closest of his aides to write down the four or five questions that bothered Protestants most when they worried about Catholics. Sorensen stayed up all night pondering the problem and came up with the questions. In West Virginia the next night, Sunday, Franklin D. Roosevelt, Jr., was summoned as the interlocutor, and on the paid telecast Roosevelt now questioned the candidate on his religion.

The religious question was planted by Roosevelt, Jr., about three or four minutes after the broadcast began, and Kennedy, as I remember it, used almost ten or twelve minutes of the half-hour show to answer. Later the same phrases were to grow sterile, but at this moment Kennedy spoke from the gut. He reviewed the long war of church on state and state on church and that greatest of all constitutional decisions: to separate church from state. Then, peering into the camera and talking directly to the people of West Virginia, he proceeded, as I remember, thus:

> . . . so when any man stands on the steps of the Capitol and takes the oath of office of President, he is swearing to support the separation of church and state; he puts one hand on the Bible and raises the other hand to God as he takes the oath. And if he breaks his oath, he is not only committing a crime against the Constitution, for which the Congress can impeach him—and should impeach him—but he is committing a sin against God.

Here Kennedy raised his hand from an imaginary Bible, as if lifting it to God, and, repeating softly, said, "A sin against God, for he has sworn on the Bible."

Against this issue of the campaign Humphrey was powerless. Savagely the Kennedy team increased the pressure.

In every hollow, hill and city the Kennedy operational team cultivated the courthouse bosses; they had played by the rules in Wisconsin and won squarely; they would play by the rules in West Virginia and win here, too. Under O'Brien's lash, the volunteers multiplied and then multiplied again, until by primary day O'Brien could estimate that he had 9,000 volunteer primary day workers engaged in some task or other.

In the newspapers Kennedy advertisements drummed away at the record of their war hero, or flayed Humphrey as the puppet of faceless men afraid to show their courage in a West Virginia primary.

Up and down the roads roved Kennedy names, brothers and sisters all available for speeches and appearances; to the family names was added the lustrous name of Franklin D. Roosevelt, Jr. Above all, over and over again there was the handsome, open-faced candidate on the TV screen, showing himself, proving that a Catholic wears no horns. The documentary film on TV opened with a cut of a PT boat spraying a white wake through the black night, and Kennedy was a war hero; the film next showed the quiet young man holding a book in his hand in his own library receiving the Pulitzer Prize, and he was a scholar; then the young man held his golden-curled daughter of two, reading to her as she sat on his lap, and he was the young father; and always, gravely, open-eyed, with a sincerity that could not be feigned, he would explain his own devotion to the freedom of America's faiths and the separation of church and state.

With a rush, one could feel sentiment change. Harris'

pollsters, now operating across the state on a day-by-day basis, would check and recheck certain streets in specific towns at weekly intervals. "You could see them switch," says Harris. "You would meet a Madame LaFarge type all dressèd in black, and she would say, 'I don't care about Humphrey, but I just don't want a Catholic.' When you had one like that, you had a germ cell infecting everyone in the street. I remember going back to one particular one the Monday before the election, after the TV speech on religion, and she took me in, pulled down the blinds and said she was going to vote for Kennedy now. 'We have enough trouble in West Virginia, let alone to be called bigots, too.' "

Kanawha County, the most populous county of West Virginia, seat of Charleston, the capital, had checked out in the first poll after Wisconsin as being 64 for Humphrey, 36 for Kennedy. Two weeks before the election, the Humphrey margin had dropped to 55 to 45; the day after the Humphrey-Kennedy TV debate it had fallen to 52 to 48; on Saturday before election, the Harris sampling showed 45 to 42 for Humphrey, the rest undecided; and after the final TV week end on religion, it had switched to a narrow Kennedy lead. (On primary day itself, Kanawha County was to go 52 to 48 *for* Kennedy.)

The orchestration of this campaign infuriated Humphrey. Once the issue had been pitched as tolerance versus intolerance, there was only one way for a West Virginian to demonstrate tolerance—and that was by voting for Kennedy. Backed against the wall by the development of an issue for which there was no conceivable response either in his heart or practical politics, Humphrey fell back on the issue of money. ("There are three kinds of politics," he would say. "The politics of big business, the politics of the big bosses, and the politics of big money, and I'm against all of them. I stand for politics of the people.")

Here, indeed, one could mourn for Humphrey. Tired from his exertions in Wisconsin, tired from his efforts in the meaningless District of Columbia primary, tired from his travels (flying by commercial airliners and carrying his own bags through the air-gates), half of Humphrey's time was spent in raising money to continue, the other half barnstorming in his lonesome bus (OVER THE HUMP WITH HUMPHREY read the bus's sign). Humphrey was being clubbed into defeat in a gladiatorial contest far from home, without funds, in a contest where victory could bring him little, and defeat would erase any influence he might have in the campaign of 1960.

Already heavily in debt for his Wisconsin campaign

($17,000 of unpaid debts hung over his head as he entered West Virginia), Humphrey had exhausted every resource and friendship he knew to raise money for this new campaign. He had been deserted now by all the old labor leaders for whom he had battled so heartfully for so many years in Washington; they wanted him out after the Wisconsin primary; they would give him no help here. And where desertion was not voluntary, the ever-efficient Kennedy organization, knowing its own fate to hang in the balance, moved to chop off the flow of support. In New York, from which so much Stevenson money had originally come to Humphrey's coffers, Governor Abraham Ribicoff,[12] acting on Kennedy's instructions, warned all Stevensonians that if they continued to finance the hopeless campaign of Hubert Humphrey, Adlai Stevenson would not even be *considered* for Secretary of State. Where necessary, Kennedy lieutenants were even rougher; in Connecticut, Boss John Bailey informed former Connecticut Senator Willian Benton, publisher of the *Encyclopædia Britannica,* that if he continued to finance Humphrey (Benton had already given Humphrey $5,000 earlier in the spring), he would never hold another elective or appointive job in Connecticut as long as he, Bailey, had any say in Connecticut politics—which is a statement equivalent to permanent political exile in the Nutmeg State.

Strangled for lack of money (Humphrey's expenditures in West Virginia were to total only $25,000—nothing, in the scale of American politics), knowing himself in debt, aware of the nature, depth and resources of this final Kennedy drive, as the final week end approached Humphrey became a figure of pathos. He needed advertising, he needed workers, above all he needed TV to show himself across the state.

I remember the final Saturday morning, shortly after it was revealed that Kennedy's TV expenditures alone across the state had mounted to $34,000. Humphrey had had but four hours' sleep that morning and was up at seven, prepared to barnstorm north from Charleston in his bus on a rainy morning; at that point one of his assistants informed him that the TV stations that had booked him for a Sunday night half hour were threatening to cancel unless they were paid that day, cash in advance, for the time.

It was one of the few times I have seen the temper of that genial man snap.

"Pay it!" snarled Humphrey. "Pay it! I don't care how,

[12] Now Secretary of Health, Education and Welfare.

don't come to me with that kind of story!" Then, realizing that his crestfallen aide was like himself, destitute, Hubert pulled out his checkbook at the breakfast table and said, "All right, I'll pay for it myself," and scribbed a personal check of his own.

Mrs. Humphrey watched him do so, with dark, sad eyes, and one had the feeling that the check was money from the family grocery fund—or the money earmarked to pay for the wedding of their daughter who was to be married the week following the primary.

My memory tells me that the sum of that check was $750—not a particularly large sum for a statewide hookup of half an hour. But such a grocery-money check buys time only—it does not buy the production, the preparation, the care a major television manipulation of the public requires.

What happens when a man goes on cold on TV in politics with such a grocery-money investment was grotesquely shown by Humphrey's final appeal to the voters of West Virginia on that day before the election. From somewhere he had raised another $750 for another half hour of TV time, and now (like Richard Nixon much later in the year) he was prepared to save all with a telethon. A telethon is a political gimmick in which a candidate, theoretically but not actually, throws himself open to any and all questions from any voter who cares to call the broadcasting station. A good telethon requires good staff in order to screen questions and artfully sequence them so they give the illusion of spontaneity yet feed the candidate those pretexts on which he can masterfully develop his themes. It is commonly one of the most spurious and obnoxious devices of modern political gimmicry.

What happens when such a telethon is authentic—not spurious—Humphrey demonstrated with his modest $750 investment on that Monday. For when authentic, unscreened questions are fed to the candidate the effect is comic. Except that, watching Hubert Humphrey fight his last national battle with family grocery money, the effect was more sad than comic.

The telethon opened with Humphrey sitting alone at a desk; before him was a manual telephone with switch buttons for two lines, which he was supposed to punch alternately as questioners telephoned in. The viewing audience was to hear both unscreened question and answer over the TV set.

The first question was a normal mechanical question: "What makes you think you're qualified to be President, Senator Humphrey?" So was the second question: "Can you be nominated, Mr. Humphrey?"

Then came a rasping voice over the telephone, the whining scratch of an elderly lady somewhere high in the hills, and one could see Humphrey flinch (as the viewers flinched); and the rasp said, "You git out! You git out of West Virginia, Mr. Humphrey!" Humphrey attempted to fluster a reply and the voice overrode him, "You git out, you hear! You can't stand the Republicans gitting ahead of you! Why don't you git out?"

Humphrey had barely recovered from the blast before the next call came: what would he do about small-arms licensing for people who like to hunt? Then, what would he do about social security? None of the questions were hitting anywhere near the target area of Humphrey's campaign program, and then a sweet womanly voice began to drawl on the open switch, "How about those poor little neglected children, Mr. Humphrey, I mean how can we lower taxes like you say and take care of all those little children who need more schools and more hospitals, and more everything . . ." On and on she went, sweetly, as Humphrey (his precious, costly minutes oozing by) attempted to break in and say that he, too, was for the poor little neglected children.

By now the telethon was becoming quite a family affair, and the next voice was a fine mountain voice, easy, slow, gentle with West Virginia courtesy, and it said, "Senator Humphrey, I just want you to know that I want to apologize for that lady who told you to git out. We don't feel like that down here in West Virginia, Senator Humphrey, and I'm very sorry that she said that. . . ." He would have rambled on and on, but Humphrey, desperate, expressed quick thanks and pressed the other button.

He had barely begun to answer the question when a clipped voice interrupted on the party line of the caller, "Clear the wires, please, clear the wires, this is an emergency!" Humphrey attempted to explain that they were on the air, they were answering questions to a TV audience. "Clear the wires, clear the wire at once, this is an emergency," repeated the operator on the party line that straggled down some unknown West Virginia hill on which, perhaps, someone was trying to summon a doctor; and Humphrey, his face blank and bedazzled, hung up, shaken, to press the button for another call (a gruff voice, with a thick accent, asking what he and Kennedy were going to do for the coal operators, they'd only been talking about the miners up to now, not the operators). From that point on the telethon lost all cohesion

—proving nothing except that TV is no medium for a poor man.

West Virginia voted on May 10th, a wet, drizzly day. By eight o'clock the polls were closed. With 100 names on some of the local ballots, all of them more important as jobs to West Virginians than the Presidency, the count was very slow. Shortly before nine o'clock, however, came the first flash: Old Field Precinct, Hardy County, Eastern Panhandle, a precinct acknowledging only twenty-five Catholic registered voters, had counted: For Kennedy, 96; for Humphrey, 36.

The count dragged on. By 9:20, with ten precincts out of 2,750 in the state having reported, the first trend became visible: Kennedy, 638; Humphrey, 473—a 60-to-40 break. Yet these were from northern West Virginia, the sensitized civilized north. How would the candidate do in the fundamentalist, coal-mining south? By 9:40 the count read Kennedy, 1,566 and Humphrey, 834; and someone in the Humphrey headquarters muttered, "We're dead."

By ten o'clock the sweep was no longer spotty but statewide. Down in Logan County, Kennedy was outrunning the local boss; in McDowell County he was doing better than 60 to 40. Hill pocket, hill slope, industrial town, Charleston, Parkersburg, Wheeling, suburb, white, Negro—the Kennedy tide was moving, powerfully, irresistibly, all across the Protestant state, writing its message for every politician in the nation to see.

There remained then only the ceremonies of burial for the Humphrey candidacy and of triumph for Kennedy.

It is no easy thing to dismantle a Presidential candidacy, and though Hubert Humphrey had decided to yield by ten in the evening, two and a half long hours went by as, from his room in the Ruffner Hotel, he telephoned his supporters and contributors all across the land (in Minnesota, in Washington, in New York) that the end had come. At one A.M. the Western Union messenger arrived at the Kennedy headquarters with Humphrey's telegram of concession; at 1:15 Bobby Kennedy, representing his brother, who was sheltering in Washington that evening, walked through the rainy streets of Charleston to pay a graceful thank-you call on Humphrey at his hotel. Equally gracious, Humphrey announced that he would be coming to the Kennedy headquarters to greet Kennedy on his night flight in to Charleston to claim victory. Together the two walked out into the rain and turned the corner down Capitol Street toward Kennedy headquarters at the Kanawha Hotel.

On Capitol Street, Humphrey paused a moment to enter his main (and practically only) headquarters in West Virginia. A few bitter-enders remained among the litter of wadded paper coffee cups and cigarette stubs, staring blankly at the desolate posting boards where the totals had been listed. All through the hills and hollows of West Virginia, Humphrey had been accompanied by a folk singer, singing the old depression songs, fervid with the old faith of yesterday's New Deal.[13] Now the folk singer, Jimmy Wofford, stepped out to twang his guitar for the last time. "Vote for Hubert Humphrey," he sang. "He's your man and mine."

The Senator's eyes gleamed with tears in the bright lights that television had installed to catch the surrender. It took him a moment to get his voice under control.

"I have a brief statement to make," he said. He read the words, "I am no longer a candidate for the Democratic Presidential nomination."

Jimmy Wofford tried one last serenade. "Vote for Hubert Humphrey, he's your man and mine——"

But he could not go on. He put his head down on his guitar and cried.

Senator Humphrey went over and patted him on the shoulder. "Aw, Jimmy," he said.

Bobby Kennedy, no dryer-eyed than anyone else, walked over and put his arm around the Senator. Then they all went out into the rain again and marched in a body to the Kanawha Hotel, where Kennedy would soon be arriving. It was the end of a campaign, the end of a long year of planning and hope. The first of the seven had been scratched from the list of candidates for the Presidency of the United States by the people of the hills. In the morning, when Hubert Humphrey woke, the Presidential image had evaporated. Outside the Ruffner Hotel his parked bus had overnight been given a ticket for illegal parking.

Kennedy, depressed and gloomy on primary day, feeling that here in West Virginia, despite his last-minute surge, he could not hope to win, had chosen that night to hide from the public, the press, and the West Virginians who were vot-

[13] I take the following incident from the superb report of Mary McGrory of the Washington *Star*, who was there at the moment to observe, as I was not.

ing. If he were to be beaten, he would receive the defeat in private, not under the scrutiny of the world. He had flown to Washington on the morning of primary day, addressed a woman's group at lunch, retreated to his Georgetown home and invited two friends for dinner with himself and his wife. The two friends brought with them a bottle of champagne, and the candidate had said, "Well, one way or another we'll crack it open this evening."

Perfectly self-possessed while every political mechanic, operator, and prognosticator worried about his reaction and his whereabouts, Kennedy calmly invited his two friends to sneak out with him to see a movie—the returns would be late in coming in, and they might as well relax. They did not return from the movie until 11:30—to find a message on the banister from their maid to please call Charleston, West Virginia, at once. A grin split Kennedy's face as he talked to his brother Bobby at the Kanawha Hotel, and then, as he put the telephone down, he burst out with a very un-Senatorial war whoop. The champagne cork popped, the guests drank; the Senator sipped, then put his glass down and prepared to leave for West Virginia. He called to assemble his plane crew; went upstairs to dress; called his father in Massachusetts; telephoned Charleston again to make sure that no reverse trend had set in, and then drove to the airport; boarding the plane, he called for a favorite drink—a bowl of hot tomato soup—and began to enjoy the evening.

By three in the morning he had been into Charleston, thanked West Virginians over TV, met Hubert Humphrey and shaken hands ("It was very nice of you to come over, Hubert"), held a press conference ("I think," he said, "we have now buried the religious issue once and for all") and was leaving again. In the lobby of the Kanawha Hotel the throng glued itself about him, and with difficulty he pushed his way to the door into the rain.

"What are you going to do now, Jack?" asked a newpaperman of the candidate.

"I have to study up on the problems of Maryland tonight," said Kennedy. "I'm campaigning there tomorrow—Friday is primary day there."

Chapter 5

PRE-CONVENTION: DEMOCRATS

WHEN morning rises over the Appalachian hills of West Virginia, afternoon is already slanting over the farmlands about Sverdlovsk, Russia.

A seemingly galactic space separates the politics of Sverdlovsk from those of West Virginia. Yet on the morning of May 1st, 1960, while Hubert Humphrey and John F. Kennedy were rising to bounce once more over the roads of the Appalachians, a mountain boy raised in these same hills was already parachuting through the air to fall in the flat farmlands near Sverdlovsk. His mishap was to link the two systems of politics in a manner that warped both world events and the American electoral exercise for the rest of the year.

Late the night before, by West Virginia time, when dawn was already clearing the High Pamirs, Francis Gary Powers, born in the hills of Kentucky, raised in the hills of Virginia, had taken off from Peshawar, Pakistan, in a high-altitude plane called the U-2, a marvel of American aeronautical engineering. Flying over the Russian border and directly across the heart of the Soviet Union on a flight planned to end in Norway, he was exposed as prey to Soviet fighter craft and was to become, when shot down that afternoon, the first acknowledged American spy ever seized by the Soviet Union. And while the politics of Washington waited on tidings from West Virginia, it may be assumed that the politics of the Kremlin quivered instantaneously in response to the tidings from Sverdlovsk.

In a few days, however, with the announcement of Francis G. Powers' plight and later confession, the politics of Washington and of America were to become more concerned with the U-2 disaster and its implications than with the events of West Virginia. For the shooting down of the U-2 and its consequences were to tear apart the illusory world in which millions of Americans lived; and their alarm for the peace and safety of their country was, over the next two months, to shake all the involved domestic calculations of the Presidential candidates who strove to lead them.

Many diverse and profound matters of history were engaged by the fate of the lone aircraft shot down that day over mid-Russia.

§ The U-2 incident preceded only by days the opening of a summit conference of the great chiefs of state, headed by President Eisenhower and Premier Khrushchev, who were to discuss the problem of Berlin. The U-2 incident was to provide the Russians with a pretext for rupture of the conference; thus a decade of idiot's dialogue in Soviet-American diplomacy was to be ended.

Eleven years before, at the first such conference in Paris, in May of 1949, when Americans and Russians first met to discuss the Berlin blockade, their three-point agenda had read: (1) the problems of Berlin; (2) the problems of East-West relationships; (3) the problems of disarmament and peace. Now, eleven years later, in May of 1960, their agenda read: (1) the problems of Berlin; (2) the problems of East-West relationship; (3) the problems of disarmament. The word "peace" had been left out of the new agenda, but after eleven years the rest of it stood unchanged. In May, 1949, however, as NATO was being tooled up, Americans had negotiated at the first crest of the Marshall Plan, at a moment when the great initiatives of the Truman administration were about to bring their predictable pressure on the Soviet system —and the American negotiators at the Pink Palace on Avenue Foch had fairly earned their triumph: the peaceful lifting of the Berlin blockade. Now, in May, 1960, they were about to negotiate at the ebb tide of these earlier initiatives, under the insistent eighteen-month pressure of Mr. Khrushchev, at a conference in which, it was apparent, they could gain nothing. Only the clumsiness and extravagance of Mr. Khrushchev's use of the U-2 incident, with its consequent rallying of Allied support, was to prevent this dismal new summit conference from being an utter catastrophe.

§ The U-2 incident raised the problem of Presidential command. Who had ordered the flight of the U-2 over the Soviet Union so shortly before such delicate negotiations? If Eisenhower had not—as apparently he had not—then where in the chain of American military and intelligence bureaucracy did such orders issue? How far had the chain of command decision degenerated in the American system when orders of such delicacy and peril could be issued without senior political control? Both Russia and America now possessed hydrogen bombs. Both Russian and American systems of radar surveillance and air defense were approaching a degree of such instantaneous response and complexity that atomic war could be triggered by errant mechanisms almost of themselves. Who exercised American authority in such critical matters as the penetration of Soviet air space?

§ The U-2 incident raised the matter of America's honor and prestige. There was no question that America, as much as the Soviet Union, requires constant and careful espionage to protect its security in an uneasy world. Concerned men could sincerely debate whether the U-2, with its teasing of Soviet trigger mechanisms of retaliation, was or was not a technically sound method of espionage. But there could be no dispute over the fact that American spokesmen had, after the event, lied to the world and to their own people, and then compounded the lies with contradiction, uncertainty and confusion.

All these were deep problems of statecraft, too detailed, too complex, too sophisticated for the American public at large to grasp. But the events that were immediately to demonstrate these problems were clear and brutal in impact on the Americans' image of themselves and their leadership, and thus on the Presidential campaign of 1960.

From May 5th, when Mr. Khrushchev gloatingly told his Soviet Congress of the shooting down of the U-2, until July 11th, when the Democratic Convention opened in Los Angeles, American statecraft reeled through a period of chaos and humiliation unknown since the elegant diplomacy of the great John Hay had given America its posture as one of the senior powers of earth.

From May through June all the following events occurred.

§ The U-2 was shot down and our spokesmen were exposed as false.

§ President Eisenhower flew to Paris for a summit conference that immediately collapsed; following the collapse, he was denounced by Mr. Khrushchev as a "hypocrite" and a "liar."

§ Rioting in Turkey shook and nearly wiped out a friendly government.

§ Student riots in Korea reached a violence so great as to overthrow the government of Syngman Rhee.

§ Our slowly deteriorating relations with Fidel Castro of Cuba arrived at a permanent and total hostility as the bearded maniac expropriated American interests in Cuba and welcomed the rocket-rattling support of Mr. Khrushchev from the Kremlin.

§ In the Far East, the last good-will mission of our peaceloving President (who had flown 60,000 miles around the world in the previous eighteen months, seeking peace) ended in humiliation as he was excluded from Japan.

§ The current disarmament negotiations between Russia and the United States, after earlier hope, conclusively broke down and were ended.

§ And finally, American statesmanship, which had hitherto given only the most perfunctory attention to the surging discontent of Africa, became aware, as the Congo was freed, of a development of anarchy and savagery that might tear the entire United Nations apart.

All these events beat like a fusillade on the minds of thinking Americans. None of these individual events could approach in global importance or future portent their own choice of the next President, who would dispose American power in management of such affairs. Yet these thunderous outer events, when fed into the stream of internal American politics, into the plans, calculations, aspirations and emotions of the men who were seeking the Presidency, were to produce explosive changes in the politics of the pre-Convention months.

Both parties were to suffer this same internal explosion of concern; in each an almost dormant candidacy was instantly to be revived by the outer events.

In its solution and mastering of such explosions, each party was to shape its stand and posture for the later electoral campaign addressed to the nation.

First, then, the Democrats.

And at the period into which we now enter, as world events beat like a distant drum, the primaries are over,[1] the cards are all publicly dealt, and political attention focuses on the magic figure of 761—the number of votes required to make a majority of the delegates preparing to meet at Los Angeles to choose a Democratic candidate.

The first candidacy to feel the impact of these foreign events was that of Adlai E. Stevenson.

[1] From West Virginia on, the primaries were all downhill for John F. Kennedy. He had taken New Hampshire overwhelmingly March 8th; taken Wisconsin as we have seen; won Indiana unopposed; swept West Virginia on May 10th. The same day that West Virginia fell to him, the Democratic voters of Nebraska also gave him that state. Maryland gave him its mandate on Tuesday, May 17th; and Oregon, the last of the contested primaries, gave him a 60 to 40 margin over its native son, Wayne Morse, on May 20th. Political students will note, for whatever significance the fact may bear, that of the seven states in which John F. Kennedy campaigned so brilliantly to earn the Democratic nomination, Richard Nixon was to claim no less than five for his own in the later November election.

Over the previous eight years, Adlai Stevenson had become the most clear and eloquent voice on foreign policy in the Democratic Party. By his travels, by his writings, by his speeches, by the simple seepage of his ideas, he had, in good season and bad, outlined a picture of the world and the direction of American movement that, though frequently abused on first enunciation, had become so accepted as to have become a cliché of everyone's thinking by the spring of 1960. The strengthening of the UN, the cessation of bomb testing, the reorganization of the Atlantic Alliance, the search for a modus vivendi with the Soviet Union in Europe—all these positions, first pioneered by Stevenson, were now the common utterance of all Democratic speakers.

Thus, when in May of 1960 American policy in the outer world crumbled and a new architecture seemed necessary, Democrats high and low, who had been neutral and indifferent before, suddenly took note of Stevenson again. His unauthorized headquarters in Washington now rang busily with telephone messages from governors and senators, from volunteers and contributors. Across the country, the leaderless troops of his 1952 and 1956 campaign began to stir. If he would lead, they would march. But would he lead?

Early in June, 1960, I visited Governor Stevenson at his home in Libertyville, Illinois, outside Chicago. I had last visited him at his home in the summer of 1955—an earlier time of decision. In that summer he had been resolute and firm. He then felt certain that any Democrat to run against Eisenhower in 1956 would be defeated. He had been approached by many friends, including eminent and powerful Republicans, urging him not to run in 1956, when he must face certain defeat; Republicans and Democrats alike, these friends had offered him the promise of full, material support against Nixon if Nixon chose to run in 1960. Yet Stevenson had spurned them. A party, he had said in 1955, was not something you used or did not use when the time was ripe for you. A party stood for something; it was a force and an education of the people; you served it in time of need as its leader, speaking its principles, whether it was convenient for you or not. So he would run in 1956.

Now, in 1960, he was not so much irresolute as unwilling to consider politics any longer. There were greater matters on his mind.

He sat on the lawn of his farmhouse, a white country home edged with black window trim. From the lawn, his eighty acres stretched away in the green summer beauty of the American midlands, broken only by an adjacent tennis court and the picket fence that penned his black-faced Suffolk sheep. We sat close to a flower bed of peonies and iris under a maple tree and the sun beat down, even in early morning, with the heavy June heat of the plains. A flight of enormous tangerine-colored butterflies swept back and forth across the lawn; the maples rustled softly; just above the threshold of sound the occasional drone of a distant high-flying plane hummed now and then in the distance; Stevenson sprawled in a beach chair in faded khaki shorts and an orange sports shirt, shod with torn blue sneakers, and, his eyes closed against the sun, he talked of his concerns.

There were so many areas of his concern—there were the manifold domestic problems of the nation. "This contrast of public squalor and private opulence, this failure of emphasis in our economy, this preoccupation with private consumption against public consumption," he said. "How do you make people see these things? The other side is so easy to take— employment for most people, ever-rising living standards while the long-term problems of our water system, of our school system, of urban transportation, can't be made visible to people, and these problems never come back in time to plague the people responsible for them. . . ."

But these were not his chief concerns. His chief concerns were in foreign policy, and with that sturdy, lucid thinking he reserves for high affairs, Stevenson let his thoughts ramble about the world.

"We're a self-indulgent consumption society," he said, "and our standards have been so terribly tarnished around the world. What we have to preserve is not only our strength but our moral leadership, and we've made such errors—that whole panorama of stupidity starting with the 'unleashing' of Chiang K'ai-shek to the collapse of the summit. I think I've talked with more heads of state than any other American, and when you hear them talk of American foreign policy, it's a thing of wonder and mirth to them.

"Look at Europe and the trouble there—we can't let Europe subdivide into the Six and the Seven, we can't let the old nineteenth-century equalization of trade operate again. There has to be an Atlantic conference, and for six years there's been no evidence of our moving in that direction, though, I must say, I think Dillon[2] has been moving correctly recently. We have *got* to reorganize Europe's resources for

---

[2] C. Douglas Dillon, at that time Undersecretary of State in Eisenhower's cabinet; now Secretary of the Treasury in Kennedy's cabinet.

the major cold war conflict or it can be extremely disadvantageous for us.

"When I went to Washington after the sputnik crisis, I wrote reams of copy for Eisenhower and Dulles to use at the NATO meeting, and none of it was ever used. I felt that we had to call on all the NATO nations to put their top priority not on launching pads and missiles but on the concert of our resources to help the emerging nations, so that we could offer them the maximum efficiency with the maximum celerity. This is a job that will take all we have from all of us. It means not just us, but includes the capital exporting skills and technical skills of countries like Austria and Sweden and Switzerland. We need a new agency, bigger than NATO, for this job. This should have, at least, the urgency of national defense—but they couldn't envision it, didn't want it."

We were talking, on that day, several weeks before the Congo dissolved into jungle barbarism, and Stevenson, as if prescient, went on, saying, "I class this urgency very high. Once they achieve their independence, these emerging nations deteriorate so rapidly that it takes all our skill and the greatest sense of urgency to meet their needs. It takes all the resources of the civilized world, the Japanese and the Italians, too, to handle the emergency—and we shouldn't do it on a bilateral basis, it has to be done by pooling.

"So there's the problem of creating a genuine Atlantic community. We have a perpetual commitment to Europe. But we can't do it all, we can't afford to. We ought to allocate our resources, we have to backstop them with our navy and nuclear forces; but they must pay for their own defense."

He discussed Europe at length, reaching always as he spoke for directions in policy; he contrasted the "linear thinking" of American defense policy in Europe with the strategic necessity of inducing Russian troop withdrawal from central Europe. He defined the complications such a new seeking of policy might meet with on the part of our more rigid European allies, particularly the Germans. It was necessary, he insisted, that we start thinking in new strategic terms, now.

"We have to get Russian troops out of central Europe. Mutual withdrawal is conceivable, when the time comes we have to be ready for it, we must be exploring it. I know that none of these steps is easy, nor is any early attainable. But there must be a sense of direction in what we're doing."

We were talking now in terms of direction of policy, of shaping strategies, and his mind switched to Asia. "We live in Asia with this mythology of Chiang K'ai-shek's return to China, and so we keep Quemoy and Matsu as landing stages back to the mainland. The opportunity we missed in 1955 is one of the greatest political crimes of our times, for in 1955 we had a chance to talk to them, to begin to resolve some of the problems there. It's not impossible that we could relinquish those islands in return for their relinquishing the use of force in the Orient and agreeing to a plebiscite in Formosa.

"We lost that opportunity and fortified the islands; and we did it again in 1957—how do you make Americans see these problems?"

At this point our conversation was abruptly broken off by the summoning of a telephone in his house. Up to that point it had been a coldly lucid, roving analysis of great affairs. It was the Adlai Stevenson and the clear voice for which Americans in search of leadership were aching. But when he came back from the house to the lawn a full forty-five minutes later, it was another Adlai Stevenson, the baffling, stubborn, reluctant leader. He bustled out to the lawn with a yellow pad in his hand, annoyed, angered.

He had just received a telephone call from New York, he said. He had been told that Eleanor Roosevelt, either in her column or in an open letter, was about to insist that he declare publicly whether he sought the Democratic nomination or not. But he felt his position was clear. He had stated it over and over again. He felt the Party *must* beat Nixon, the country would be unsafe in Nixon's hands. Thus, if the Party called on him to serve, he would serve as citizen or as leader or as nominee. But the Party had given him the chance twice. He would not demand it again, nor would he reach for it. Nor would he declare himself out of the race. He was not trying to stop anyone, or help anyone—why was not all this clear?

For an hour there in the sun he tried to resolve these turbulent thoughts into some clear answer that Eleanor Roosevelt could make public; and the telephone rang from Washington and again from New York, and one had the sense of a distant clamor calling for executive leadership. Yet he would not act. He would wait.

The clamor on the telephone was real. All through the Democratic Party Stevenson's motives, Stevenson's inaction, Stevenson's words were being weighed, analyzed, pulled apart. And most of all by his own people.

Few men in public life have ever suffered from Adlai Stevenson's good fortune. The inner nature of the man needs privacy and solitude for reflection; yet his personality and eloquence are such that he automatically invites the public attention that other politicians hopelessly crave; and this attention frequently suffocates him. Like other men in American history denied the supreme prize—like Norris, like La-Follette, like Taft—the devotion he arouses in the hearts of his loyalists can be erased neither by time nor defeat. Now, and until the closing of the nomination at Los Angeles on July 13th, he was to be tormented by friend and foe alike, all clamoring that he declare his stand publicly.

A Stevenson campaign had been under way without Stevenson since early in the year (see Chapter Two). Quietly, through the spring months, it had waited on the results of the West Virginia primary, when, the Stevenson leaders felt, after Kennedy and Humphrey had killed each other off, the Democratic Party must turn to its most eminent national leader. All through this period the sober and responsible control elements of the Stevenson campaign had tried to sit on the bursting spontaneous enthusiasm of Stevenson amateurs across the country. At one point, when the California volunteers telephoned to New York (to George Backer, one of the finest minds in American politics and, at this point, a Stevensonian), Backer had insisted that they must not use the money they had collected in the West Virginia campaign to block Kennedy's chances, or they would be tagged as anti-Catholics. "But what can we do, George?" said the caller from California. "We have a hundred thousand dollars, and they keep shoving more money at us."

Early in April the four centers of the Stevenson campaign (see Chapter Two) had combined to set up headquarters in the Letter-Carriers' Building at 100 Indiana Avenue in Washington, where general intelligence from across the country was to be collected. As delegates were chosen, names and addresses were filed, then cross-indexed for pressure that could be brought to bear as the Convention approached. Kennedy's West Virginia victory was a body blow to these leaders; but the summit collapse a few days later made the need of Stevenson as candidate and President seem all the more urgent. In New York the anti-Tammany reform clubs, grouped under the Roosevelt-Finletter-Lehman leadership, were in daily telephonic communication. In early June James Doyle, who had shepherded and restrained the volunteers from his Madison, Wisconsin, office, was brought to Washington, where he officially announced the launching of a Draft Stevenson movement. By late June Draft Stevenson clubs operated in forty-two states of the union; metropolitan newspapers in New York were carrying full-page Stevenson advertisements appealing for funds (the first of these drew $40,000 in contributions, larger than any response to any single advertisement in 1952 or 1956).

From Indiana Avenue, broadside after broadside of mail (polls, analyses, pleas) now went out to every delegate and politician who would attend the Convention, proving that Stevenson could indeed save the country from Nixon and Khrushchev. In Los Angeles the Stevenson chieftains leased the empty Paramount Building across Pershing Square from the Biltmore Hotel (which was to be official Convention headquarters), and a banner a hundred feet long by nine feet high went up, demanding of arriving delegates: DRAFT STEVENSON. Across the continent volunteers hired planes to tow sky banners over the beaches of Coney Island, the Rock-aways and Fire Island as New Yorkers sunned themselves on the July 4th week end; the banners in the sky demanded: DRAFT STEVENSON. Over the country, to all the clubs, went the word to start moving on Los Angeles, as if to storm a fortress. And giving up their vacations, riding coaches, driving jalopies, the volunteers set out, marching as to Armageddon, to battle with John F. Kennedy.

This was the carnival coating of the movement, the neces-sary noise to pressure the politicians, the delegates, the press. More quietly, however, Stevenson leadership worked with a more precise plan, a more realistic appreciation of the structure of the Democratic Convention. The frenzy of the volunteers would be necessary to stampede the Convention; but before any stampede could begin, the Convention had to be structured to break under the pressure.

Leadership for the Stevensonians, at this point, devolved on as odd a pair of American political operators as the year 1960 was to see. The senior operator was Senator Mike Monroney of Oklahoma, fifty-eight, a man risking his entire career with no real hope of reward or any hope of mercy from the high political forces he now challenged; and thirty-three-year-old John Sharon, junior partner in the Washington law firm of Cleary, Gottlieb, Steen and Ball, a young man first blooded in politics four years earlier, when he had pro-posed the "open-convention" approach to the Vice-Presidency of 1956.

The strategy of these two men required a Convention dead-lock, and all deadlock revolved around the magic figure of 761—the Convention majority. Of the necessary 761, Ken-nedy—so estimated the Stevenson managers—already had 604. Johnson, they estimated, had between 450 and 500.

Symington they estimated at perhaps 100 or 150. Further, they knew they had in their own "noncampaign" accumulated a "beachhead" Stevenson vote of between 45 and 50 votes—easily expandable, they calculated, to 75 or 80 on the first ballot.

Then there were the unknowns: the favorite-son states of Minnesota, New Jersey, Kansas, Iowa, California, along with the uncommitted states of Illinois and Pennsylvania. If the favorite sons could all be held firm through the first ballot without going over to Kennedy; if the vote of the Illinois, Pennsylvania and California delegations could be split or frozen for the first ballot—then Kennedy could be stopped at his estimated first ballot figure, 150-odd votes short of nomination. And if he were held there for one, two or three ballots, then the Convention must break away from him, seeking another leader. Johnson, they figured, would be the next leader—but Johnson, they felt, could never convince the Northern states (sensitized by labor-union and Negro pressure), to give him the necessary majority. Symington might move into the lead later. But by that time the break-aways from Kennedy and Johnson would be coming to Stevenson. Their man, Stevenson, twice the nominee, was the only truly national figure in the Convention. Ultimately, as the deadlock moved from Kennedy to Johnson and perhaps to Symington, weariness and frustration would overtake the delegates, and the stampede to Stevenson would be on.

Thus the Stevenson thinkers on strategy.

To prepare the strategy, to firm up the wavering favorite sons and the undecided bosses, Monroney and Sharon now, in late May and all through June, took to the road, to mark up in four weeks some 30,000 miles of travel and missionary work around the country. In California they dined with Governor Brown at his Sacramento mansion; they shook him as they described the glowering clouds of war and disaster in the outside world. Yes, Brown admitted, Stevenson was far and away the best-qualified man to be President. On into the night the conversation went, Brown wavering in indecision. As they left, the perplexed and troubled Governor of California pleaded with them to remember what he owed Jack Kennedy—if Kennedy had come into the California primary, he would have clobbered the California governor.

Illinois, Sharon and Monroney sensed, was for Kennedy because the hard, cold Mayor of Chicago, Dick Daley, controlled three quarters of its sixty-nine Convention votes. But they tried nonetheless. To Daley the Stevensonians sent Carl Sandburg, Poet Laureate of Chicago, to plead the case of fellow Illinoisian Stevenson. Daley made no commitment; yet the Stevenson people now hoped that if Kennedy faltered on the first or second ballot, Daley would be with them—certainly on the third or fourth.

Governor David Lawrence of Pennsylvania, master of that state, was reached. Lawrence, an old Stevenson loyalist, knew himself to be under intense pressure from his own big-city delegates for Kennedy; he gave the Stevenson people friendship and hearing—no commitment. He had only recently returned from a European voyage and now sought to sample the political winds of home before making up his mind. Through Lawrence, however, connection was made with Governor Robert Meyner of New Jersey, and the word came back: Meyner would hold his New Jersey delegation, despite all internal Kennedy pressure, firm against the Massachusetts Senator throughout the first ballot. Meyner was solid.

Back and forth, Monroney (tall, gaunt, handsome, well-mannered) and Sharon (young, glowing, enthusiastic) spread the message: hold the line—the dream ticket is coming up, Stevenson and Kennedy. And, although they could not measure their work in votes, they could sense movement. David Lawrence, disturbed by conflicting loyalties, journeyed to Illinois to talk to Daley, to Jake Arvey, to Stevenson himself. That was the rub: Stevenson himself. Pat Brown, unsettled by his evening with Monroney and Sharon, his contrary spring promise to Kennedy weighing on his conscience, telephoned East to speak to Stevenson personally. He located Stevenson in his New York offices, and over the long-distance telephone Stevenson gave Brown a brilliant and eloquent lecture on the meaning of the summit collapse, the portent of trouble for the free world, the significance of all this to the Party in November—but as for himself, Stevenson told Brown, he was not a candidate, he was not going to endorse anybody, make a deal with anybody, stop anybody, or say anything privately or publicly to deny anyone else a fair, clean shot at the nomination he had twice won.

Working thus without command leadership, denied the base of a home-state delegation from Illinois to place the name of their candidate in nomination, the Stevenson chieftains strove to keep their leaderless confederacy marching in the direction that strategy demanded: deadlock.

An hour or two in the law offices of John Sharon in Washington at the end of June was an hour or two of constant flutter and telephoning. One could listen to Sharon's end of the conversation as the phone incessantly interrupted his conversation. "Yes, Senator. . . . Yes, Senator. . . . No, we have that under control. . . . Yes, Senator, I'll pass the word to him." Or: "Yes, Governor . . . yes, Governor. . . . Contact Senator So-and-So . . . he's handling that. Yes, Governor . . ." and then "Yes, Senator" or more practically "All right, if you people [this was a Symington call] can add an extra vote in the Arizona delegation, we think we can deliver you a vote and a half . . . yes. . . . If we all pull together, I think we can tie the Arizona delegation up and take it away from him."

The Monroney-Sharon leadership strove desperately to keep their growing corps of supporters clean; but if there was a stop-Kennedy movement rolling, it rolled wherever Sharon and Monroney moved. Aloof and seemingly undisturbed, Adlai Stevenson and his two permanent aides, William McCormick Blair[3] and Newton Minow,[4] prepared during the week of July 4th to fly to Los Angeles, to dwell in two rooms at the Park-Wiltshire Hotel. On July 4th, however, Monroney and Sharon had preceded them, and behind Monroney and Sharon volunteers were coming by train, bus, plane and jalopy, literally in thousands.

It was not so much the summit that destroyed the Symington candidacy, as the West Virginia primary.

The entire Symington strategy (see Chapter Two) had been built on a simple prognosis and recipe as follows: Stuart Symington was the candidate most readily acceptable to *all* the various minority groups of the Democratic Party—labor, Negro, South, big-city bosses, border states; the necessity of such a compromise candidate would ultimately become apparent to the leaders of the Democratic Party after the West Virginia primary—for the West Virginia primary would result in such religious bitterness that neither Kennedy nor Humphrey would emerge with a clear mandate; after West Virginia, the Symington net could begin to deal with the power brokers.

Now this strategy had evaporated. Kennedy had won a stunning victory in West Virginia. If there was to be a deadlock, it would depend on other forces than those Symington could muster—it would depend on Stevenson or Johnson. Symington was out of it as an active force. He could only travel prodigiously—displaying himself to Party conventions over the nation as a man to be considered as a possible safe

[3] Now Ambassador to Denmark.
[4] Now Chairman of the FCC.

port in a storm if the Convention were to break up completely. But his heart was not in it.

Perhaps the best description of the outer Symington of this period is that of Robert D. Novak of the *Wall Street Journal*, who in June reported:

> Amid the turbulence of this election year there exists one island of tranquility: Senator Stuart Symington's campaign for the Democratic Presidential nomination. Indeed there's nothing quite like it on the political scene. . . .
>
> . . . the Symington campaign has a somnambulistic air, a feeling that the Senator and his aides are going through the motions of the social convention that requires every candidate to campaign.
>
> Consider his recent California stumping. Although most would-be Presidents are up at the crack of dawn, Mr. Symington did not leave Santa Monica airport in California oilman Ed Pauley's Lockheed Lodestar until the unbelievably civilized hour of 11 A.M. As it was, he was 30 minutes early in arriving at Ontario—and calmly waited in the plane until his official greeters arrived.
>
> Later in the day, Mr. Symington took in his stride the experience of riding through the streets of Pomona in an open convertible at the head of a carefully planned caravan —and gazing at almost deserted sidewalks. A few days later, he arrived in San Francisco and promptly canceled a press conference in order to get some rest—a not uncommon occurrence in the Symington campaign but something most politicians would do no more lightly than a British subject would cancel an audience with the Queen. . . .
>
> This irrelevance of Mr. Symington's travels contributes to the curiously bland quality of his campaign. But its nonchalance derives not only from its apparent purposelessness but also from the personality of the candidate.

· · · · ·

> One factor more than any other sets off the Symington campaign from those of his rivals: The lack of a demon within the urbane Missourian driving him irresistibly toward the White House. The collapse of their Presidential ambitions could leave Mr. Kennedy or Mr. Johnson embittered men. But Mr. Symington gives the impression that life would go on for him much as it has before even if he never becomes President of the United States. . . .

How much at variance this outer Symington was with the inner Symington only his intimates knew, for the events of the outer world and the lengthening series of American humiliations abroad stirred him deeply. I met Stuart Symington for the first and only time during the campaign at a luncheon, on the day following my visit to Stevenson at Libertyville. It was a day on which Symington had been sorely tried. He had just come from a hearing of the Senate Armed Forces Committee, and as he strode down the corridor he was talking, in obvious exasperation, to two of his aides about the hearings just concluded. ". . . do you realize that some of our troops in Berlin are still armed with World War I rifles, not even World War II rifles? . . . Do you know something else . . . guess how much of our total budget for new arms they were going to spend for ground force equipment, the stuff we need in limited war? . . . Go on, guess . . . not even one tenth of one per cent of the entire budget for new equipment for the ground forces. Not even that, only thirty-seven million dollars. . . . I told them I wouldn't go along with it. . . . I won't. . . . Do you know that half the Soviet divisions have been completely equipped with modern weapons, new since World War II? . . ."

He sat down at the lunch table; ordered a hamburger; wondered whether there'd be any government at all left to defend ten years from now, the way we were being pushed back all around the world; commented on the Russian growth rate as contrasted with the American growth rate; and then calmed down to talk about what he saw as the job of the Presidency.

"What I want to do is to pull back into the operation this one fundamental concept of government being a partner of business, a partner of labor—and we have to work it out for the farmers too. This Republican talk of pulling the federal government out of business is not only stupid . . . it's dangerous. Look, you get up in a plane, you want to make sure it lands safely—we can't give up the FAA. You buy stock in a mine, you want to be sure that the mine is really there—we can't give up the SEC. You buy a bottle of medicine in the store, you want to be sure that what the label says is really in that bottle—we can't give up the Food and Drug Administration. You tune in your radio, you don't want to find five stations on the same channel—we can't give up the FCC. . . . This silly Republican prattle of pulling government out of business! This country's become strong because government *is* a partner of everybody, and we have to recognize that kind of strength is our only hope. . . . a new road is strength, a new bridge is strength, a good school is strength, above all, a good teacher is strength, she's playing with the greatest national resource we have.

"This business talk—the greatest danger there is in government is when people don't know what they're doing. When Charlie Wilson came into the Pentagon he put the General Motors system in there. Now, I know General Motors, they were my second-biggest customer when I was in business, they're a great crowd, with a one-for-all, all-for-one spirit. They all have options and profit sharing, they all share in the profits. But in the Pentagon this system worked in reverse. In business there's the profit motive, the less people you have the better, if there's an extra body in the operation, you cut it off. But in government, there's no profit motive—the sole desire is power, and the more people you have under you the better, the more power. When I worked in the Pentagon there were eight Secretaries, and that was two too many. Now there are thirty-six! For years I've said we could save billions by reorganizing the Pentagon."

Someone at the table made a partisan remark to the effect that the pieces of government seemed to be lying about Washington that day like a child's watch taken apart. Symington was now in full flow of eloquence and he took this as a cue.

"If you want to put it together again, you have to get the plumbers out and the watchmakers in. You have to set up a government to handle changes. You've got to set up a chart and an organization so that everyone knows what they're doing. Take space—the whole space thing is as fouled up as the All-American Chinese puzzle. We've split up space the way Solomon split the baby. We have a space agency, NASA, reporting directly to the President—and its Executive Secretary hasn't even been appointed. And the Defense Department has a space agency, the ARDA. And then there has to be a coordinating body between NASA and ARDA. And the Navy is in space, and the Army is in space, and the Air Force is in space. And if the Navy wants something for its program from the Army, the Army says to the Navy: Go kiss my foot. Then the Air Force says to the Army when *it* wants something: Go kiss my foot. And then all three of them turn on ARDA together and they yell: Go kiss my foot! And then people talk of making a special Secretary for Peace—we need a Secretary for Peace the way we need a Secretary for Love! You have to organize these things in functions so people know what they're doing, where the final decision is. The basic theory of government has to be a pyramid, where decisions reach the top in an orderly way—not a rake where everything reaches the top."

Here he was growing angry, and his knuckles grew white as he clenched his fists, his handsome mobile face furious at such offenses to his executive spirit.

"This government," he said. "You've got to grab it! You run the government, or they run you, and there's no middle ground. I'll tell you a story. When I was made Assistant Secretary of War for Air, I called in an industrial engineer named C. D. Cline and I said, 'Cline, the relationship between the War Department, Patterson's office and Air Force procurement is absurd. Every contract over a hundred thousand dollars has to be negotiated out in Wright Field and then renegotiated and reduplicated back here in Washington, and it's taking weeks of red tape to clear anything. I want you to go out to Wright Field, talk to them and look into it all.'

"Well, forty-eight hours later he came back to my desk and told me about this project director out there. Cline said, 'I talked to him for five minutes and he said, "I've only three things to say to you: one, I don't believe in industrial engineers; second, if I did, I wouldn't hire you; third, I don't want to talk to you at all."'

"It was about nine o'clock in the morning then and I walked into 'Toohey' Spaatz' office, he was Chief of Staff of the Air Force then, and I said, 'I want you to fire that man by ten o'clock in the morning.'

"Twenty minutes later Spaatz comes back and tells me that it couldn't be done, this man at Wright Field had Civil Service status, you couldn't fire him.

"Well, I went back to my office and telephoned the head of the Civil Service Commission. I made an appointment for three o'clock that afternoon. I walked right into his office, explained it, asked if I could fire that man, and said, 'Before you answer that question, I want to say one thing—if you tell me I can't fire him, I'm going directly from this office to the White House to resign.' So it turned out at the Civil Service, after they heard me, that I could fire him: for simple insubordination.

"I remember leaving that office with one of my Air Force generals and giving him my car to drive directly to the air field to get a plane to Wright Field and fire that man that afternoon and bring him back to me. When he came into my office the next day, that fellow was a very different man—he cried. He told me what it would do to his career and his family, and his retirement was coming up, that stuff. So I told him it was production I wanted, not punishment—could he give me his word he'd go back there and do a job. He said he could. The fact is—he did.

"But you have to run it—you have to run this government, or it runs you!"

We talked of many things in the long lunch: of housing; of urban decay and renewal; of the farm problem; of Castro; of the shrinkage of American strength around the world; of American and Russian science. Over each subject the same executive mind cut with the same bold stroke of action. Yet all the while we talked, all four of us knew that the Symington campaign had come to a dead stall—for American Presidential politics are not determined by executive action and ability; they are a world of their own, and in that strange world of politics Symington's only hope lay in quiet waiting, in the fortuitous accident of compromise, in behaving with dignity and observing without bitterness a mobile situation where leadership decisions were being made by other men with stronger troops, more positive controls—and a better grasp of the mysteries of American politics.

So, as Congress moved to suspend its sitting for the Convention interlude, Stuart Symington and his Missouri men planned their journey to Los Angeles.

From his offices of Majority Leader of the United States Senate Lyndon B. Johnson watched the unfolding events of May and June like a man trapped. He, like Stevenson, enjoyed an instant appreciation in political weight as the world's events, beginning with the collapse of the summit, made the youthful Kennedy seem ever more like a boy. But the unqualified Kennedy victory in West Virginia, proving the Massachusetts Senator could win in Protestant country, more than balanced what advantage international affairs gave Johnson. Kennedy, with his ever-clear perception of immediate reality, was heard to remark to a friend at the time that the kind of help Lyndon needed he wouldn't get from Paris or Moscow—he needed it from the Northern big cities and from the West.

Thus Johnson was cast back on his original concept of strategy, and the strategy hobbled him. If he was to win, so went that strategy (see Chapter Two), he must prove himself master of an unruly Senate, the senior legislator of the nation, a man mature, liberal and managerial. And now as the Senate, with its attention diverted by foreign affairs and stewing domestic politics, crawled through the hot spring months toward the Convention, that program of "responsible moderation" that Johnson, as chief Democratic legislative architect, had hoped to erect was still unfinished. The bills for increase in minimum wages, for medical aid to the aged, for school-construction subsidies, for increased public housing, for repeal of the Communist disclaimer oath, for new farm legislation—all these were inching through the complicated legislative machinery of Congress. Johnson's presence was required to nurse them one by one through the hidden ambuscades and open hostility of the Washington jungle. Kennedy, away and on the road, could cultivate delegates and leaders at will, returning to Washington only for vital roll calls. But the leadership of legislation that was to establish Johnson as liberal, sound, wise, masterful—that required Johnson's constant presence in the capitol.

There were other Johnson handicaps: chiefly his outer bearing and his experience.

In many ways the Lyndon B. Johnson of 1960 resembled the Alfred E. Smith of 1928. Alfred E. Smith was the first man of his Catholic minority to be considered seriously for the Presidency of the United States. In 1960 Lyndon B. Johnson also represented a minority, perhaps the most embittered in the nation—the Southern whites; and he was the first representative of them to be considered seriously for the Presidency in over a century. Between 1928's Irish-Catholic Smith of the lower East Side of New York, with his cigar, his derby, his grotesque accent, and 1960's Irish-Catholic John F. Kennedy, Harvard-trained, immaculately tailored, superbly eloquent, there had intervened a generation of American experience. Between the Lyndon Johnson of 1960 and some future Southerner who will have entered the mainstream of American life a generation hence there must come a similar experience.

For the Lyndon B. Johnson of 1960, however astute and familiar with the affairs of Washington, presented himself nationally as something essentially provincial. To watch Lyndon B. Johnson perform oratory on his native heath is to see something like an act out of a show-boat production. He normally begins in a grave, serious tone, strictly out of Washington. Then, as his fists clench, flail and thrash the air, his voice changes. It roars like a bull's; it drops to a confidential whisper as he tells grassy jokes; it achieves a high-pitched Southern resonance; all texts are discarded, and the flavor of the slow drawl, the snapped phrases, the smirked confidences are never recaptured in the printed text. His face, which is, with the exception of Eisenhower's, the most mobile and expressive in national politics, seems a wad of India rubber—his mouth draws tight in anger, opens wide in a bellow of indignation, sucks in about the corners as he ruminates aloud, turns up in a great smile after the joke, turns down in sorrow as he wails of the nation's problems. When Lyndon B. Johnson is in good form and seen in the proper setting—say, at a small-town Masonic temple at a dinner for small-town Southern Democrats where the hot food is being served by the good Ladies of the Eastern Star— one can observe a master performance of native American political art. Yet when the same performance is transferred to a dinner of Brooklyn Democrats, say, in New York, or is delivered on television, it has no smack of Presidential quality about it. It is, sadly, what is called in the cynical North and the citizen West "cornball"—and as remote from the dignity of the Presidency as was Alfred Smith's bad grammar, Eastside enunciation and New York provincialism.

A third and even graver burden lay on Lyndon B. Johnson. This was the quality of his experience and the difficulty of demonstrating this quality in Presidential politics. If Symington's mind is as fine an executive instrument as Washington possesses, Johnson's is as fine a legislative mind—and as difficult to make known to the commonalty. For Johnson, the United States Senate is more than the Senate: it is faith, calling, club, habit, relaxation, devotion, hobby and love. For him the Senate, with its hallowed traditions, is the most glorious instrument of government known to man, and each facet of its life—its majestic decisions, its sordid little deals, its prickly personalities, its open clashes and back-room intrigue—fascinates him. Over twelve years the Senate has become almost a monomania with him, his private domain, and he confuses the United States Senate with life itself. By the time that the politics of 1960 were coming to a crisis, Lyndon B. Johnson all but believed that the *Senate* was America, and that *he* was the Senate. It was a confusion that many in Washington shared with him, for it is a condition and a disease in Washington that men in that capital confuse delegated power with real power. Both in the Washington administrative bureaucracies and in the Congress, the men who pass on billions of foreign aid, on appropriations for missiles, on great public works (as well as the lesser men who court these decision makers) believe that the enormous power in their hands is substantive. Long service in Washington at the court of power decisions causes men to forget that power rises ultimately from beyond the Potomac.

For Johnson, this was particularly unfortunate. His art of legislation over twelve years of Senate service and eight years of Senate leadership was one that could be summarized only for political scientists. Translated in the clipped shorthand of public images North and West of the Potomac, Johnson appeared more often than not as a "cute operator," a man who knew all the tricks of the Senate. Nor was it possible to explain briefly his creative efforts, which found so little reflection in the arid tomes of law and enactment that were their fruit. To take one expression of his art, however, of particular relevance in 1960, it is simply necessary to examine his achievements in the field of American race relations. Ever since the first slaves were landed in Virginia in 1619, the problem of race has been the most difficult of resolution in American politics. It embrangled the original Constitution makers for months; it split the politics of our first seventy years; it caused the Civil War; it remains today, now that its violent frontier has moved North, the most explosive problem of our society. The Civil War in 1861 proved that the problems of Negro and white Americans could not then be discussed or solved legislatively, and so the country went to war. For almost a century after that, by tacit consent and use of the filibuster, this, the most difficult of all American problems, was never *reasonably* discussed in the halls of Congress. Lyndon B. Johnson's achievement over the past eight years has been to make the matter of race relations again a subject for discussion and legislation in Washington. By his secret and sinuous arts—of cajolery, of threat, of promise, of bluff—he has succeeded in making it possible for Southern and Northern Congressmen *actually* to discuss, *actually* to seek, *actually* to strive to find a meeting ground across the gulf. The minimal civil rights legislation of the past eight years reflects as yet no real solution. That lies beyond the halls of Congress, in society. But the fact that the subject of race relations is open to reasonable discussion and minimally open to legislative management, however cautious, is Johnson's achievement. Yet this is an achievement as difficult to make clear to voters as Symington's executive talent; and throughout the campaign Johnson was distrusted in the North as a race-prejudiced Southerner and in the South as a traitor to White Supremacy.

These were the burdens under which Johnson labored; he was aware of some and blithely ignorant of others. And his strategy through May and June reflected all of them.

Since the target enemy in the immediate pre-Convention period was John F. Kennedy, the Johnson campaign focused

on Kennedy and, focusing on Kennedy, foreshadowed in curious fashion the later campaign of Nixon. Kennedy, Johnson
repeated over and over again, was too young, too inexperienced
—the country needed a man "with a touch of gray in his hair."
Kennedy, Johnson repeated again and again, had been wrong
on the U-2—this country must face the Russians without
giving an inch. To "apologize" for the U-2, as Kennedy suggested, was appeasement. Beyond that, and certainly without
Johnson's authority (as later, similarly, without Nixon's authority), his lieutenants pumped the divisions of religion,
insisting that a Catholic could not win, stimulating the deep
springs of bigotry that were later to poison the general election campaign.

Belatedly now the real Johnson campaign began. Jim
Rowe, master tactician of the Humphrey campaign, switched
his talents to Johnson, and a touch of practicality became
apparent. The Majority Leader's week-end absences from his
legislative burdens in Washington grew longer. His private
plane carried him to North Dakota, South Dakota, Washington, Nevada, California, Iowa, New York, New Jersey,
Pennsylvania. His Washington headquarters began to announce names of prominent supporters: Senators Mansfield,
Bible, Anderson, Oren Long, Magnuson. But the Washington
press cynically noted that these were all Senate names, men
dependent on Johnson's Senatorial favor and long captive
to his cause. On the road, at all the conventions of the
mountain states, his agents multiplied and redoubled their
efforts; the old freewheeling Texas amateurs were now replaced by shrewder, tougher men. And on July 5th, only
five days before the Convention was to open, almost as a
perfunctory afterthought, Lyndon B. Johnson called a press
conference to tell the world that yes, he was really a candidate
for the Democratic nomination for President of the United
States.

Long before then, however, the nature of his chances had
been clearly silhouetted against the configuration of the Convention. He could not win as the Southern candidate. He must
win by being the candidate of the West. If he could add to
his base strength in the South another 150 delegates from the
West and a score of other votes from the Midwest he could
stand as the candidate of the wide-open spaces, the candidate
of the William Jennings Bryan crescent, against the preponder-
ant Northeastern bloc. Let Kennedy be stopped—by the
combination of Stevenson, Johnson, Symington and favorite
sons—on the first ballot or two, and this crescent would close
on the Northern delegates and roll east to victory. The last

pre-Convention Johnson estimate of Johnson strength—two weeks before the nomination—came to 502½ votes (the Johnson estimate of the Kennedy total: 602½ votes) of the 761 needed for nomination. Of these 502½ Johnson votes, 385 came from the Old South and the border states, another 80 from the West and the mountain states, the balance from scattered friends in the industrial Northeast.

If this arithmetic were correct, and other candidates and favorite sons held firm, then Kennedy could be stopped. But if it were not correct, then Kennedy was within a fingertip of the nomination. The doubtful figures in this arithmetic lay mostly in the 80-odd votes that Johnson claimed in the mountain states. Were these Johnson figures valid or imaginary? Were the men whom these figures represented firm or waverers, friendly or committed, cautious or indifferent? And the Kennedy clan was already at work on the men behind these figures.

Several strands of identifiable philosophy run back to the very beginning of John F. Kennedy's political career, and of these perhaps the most significant is his Carlylean approach to society.

In any conversation with the candidate, on almost any level, on any phase of American domestic politics, it was immediately apparent that he saw American politics differently from other men. Politics, in his conversation, were groups of men led by other men. To know who the leaders were and understand them was to know and understand how the group worked. This sense of the value of leadership, of personality, of quality in other men, is personal to him and independent of any valuation set by press or public opinion. It results in a meticulously cordial but utterly cold indifference to men the rest of the world sees as great but whom he, personally, regards as hollow; and at the same time an intense concern and flattering cultivation of men unknown to the world at large whom he regards as individuals with qualities of mind, speech, brain, eloquence or influence that may be useful to him. There are hazards in this kind of thinking, but there is also a gripping realism in the approach; and to watch this thinking govern and deploy the vast Kennedy forces in May and June of 1960 was to see American politics afresh.

There are fifty states in this union, each of them endowed with a separate sovereignty by the Constitution. These sovereignties are genuine; they create in each state two major parties; and within each party from two to four separate political groups contend for capture, first of the state party's leadership, then of the state's sovereignty. Where true power lies in these hundreds of revolving, dissolving, nascent and fading political groups is known only by local folklore, below the threshold of public report. Such information is the trade gossip of politicians, the treasures of wisdom that political reporters exchange among one another from state to state, a baffling perplexity for academic political scientists who seek permanent truths, the aspect of mystery that the average voter confronts as he seeks to understand who controls his government.

The laws of libel, the decencies of political reportage, the conventions of friendship and custom, the obstacles of distance and parochialism, all effectively conceal the ever-changing topography of American politics. It is impossible to report publicly which world-famous governor of what state was commonly called "The Boob" by his political boss; which apparently sinister boss is only a paper tiger in the hands of other men; which labor leader can really deliver votes and money and which cannot; which great industrialist is a political eunuch while his neighbor is master of the state; which nationally eminent Negro is considered an "Uncle Tom" by his people, while some unknown kinsman really controls the wards; which aging leadership no longer controls its county leaders and which does. The root question of American politics is always: Who's the Man to See? To understand American politics is, simply, to know people, to know the relative weight of names—who are heroes, who are straw men, who controls, who does not. But to operate in American politics one must go a step further—one must build a bridge to such names, establish a warmth, a personal connection. The country is so vast, and its political worlds so many, that these local leaders, groping as they leave their home base, crave contact with one another and are grateful to any man who can give them the sense of strength in multiplication.

All this the Kennedys had learned in their upbringing; all this they had always coupled with their cold indifference to famous names and their search for unknown leadership of quality and talent. From their earliest days in the barbarian wars of Massachusetts politics they had sought out and created their own local leadership, seeking talent within or without the political rosters of that state's mad politics, finding bright young men to do their bidding from Springfield to Lowell, creating out of such bright young men an entirely personal organization, which cuffed aside and momentarily dispersed the rotten party organization that had gutted the state for years.[5]

In 1956 the Kennedys were to observe that the same pattern worked on a nationwide scale. In one wild night, at the Democratic National Convention of 1956, as John F. Kennedy and Estes Kefauver contended for the delegates' mandate for the Vice-Presidency, the Kennedys learned that national politics also depended, simply, on knowing people. "I remember a wonderful Maryland delegate and his wife," recalls Bobby Kennedy. "They were entirely friendly. They liked us. But Kefauver had *visited* them in their home. He had sent them Christmas cards. We couldn't shake them. Believe me, we've sent out lots of Christmas cards since."

Since national politics was only people, the Kennedys set out from 1956 on to learn who the people were—the right people. Between 1956 and 1960 no Democrat, not even Adlai Stevenson, spoke in more states, addressed more Jefferson-Jackson Day dinners, participated in more local and mayoralty campaigns of deserving Democrats, than did John F. Kennedy. By the spring of 1960 Kennedy had not only visited every state of the union, but his intelligence files bulged with what was possibly the most complete index ever made of the power structure of any national party. And where he had passed, his organization was seeded; under Sorensen first, then O'Donnell, then O'Brien, then under Bobby Kennedy himself, organization cultivated what the master had planted, until all across the union outside the solid South, Kennedy organizations existed—frequently better informed and occasionally better organized than those of the men who fancied themselves masters of their state. The epitaph of the Johnson campaign was written, for this reporter, by a Kennedy organizer who said with a flat simplicity, "Why, do you know, Lyndon actually thought that Carmine De Sapio and Tammany controlled New York!"

Now, in May and June of 1960, the harvest of this knowledge was about to begin. Since the previous fall and the Hyannisport meeting (see Chapter Two), Kennedy command had divided the country into regional areas of his lieutenants' authority. All through the spring months the first team, the election machinery, had been concentrated on the primary wars, seeking votes from the people, proving to all observers

[5] The relapse of the Massachusetts State Democratic Party between 1958 and 1960 to its normal disorderly and vulgar pattern can be ascribed almost completely to the stripping of the state of its best young men to man and operate the Kennedy Presidential operation across the country.

everywhere what the appeal, what the magic, of a Kennedy campaign could be like, exploding (so it seemed) the myths of prejudice, demonstrating how nationwide was the Senator's appeal. The primaries were now over, and the primaries had netted some 134 delegate votes. Now the rest of the harvest proceeded, state by state, across the nation, fitting itself to the manners and morals of each state's politics like an exercise in the diversity of American life.

The political harvest in Michigan was conducted with Spanish punctilio, the honors of grandees being paid to its leadership. Leadership in Michigan in 1960 lay in the hands of three men, C. Neil Staebler, Walter Reuther, Governor G. Mennen Williams.[6] High-minded yet hard-knuckled, each of these three had been measured and analyzed. In the course of twelve years Neil Staebler, State Chairman and one of the most moral men in American politics, had built one of the most efficient citizen-politics organizations in the upper Midwest; he would brook no outside intrigue disrupting his smooth state organization; though a one-time Stevensonian, Staebler now most wanted a winner in 1960, a winner of liberal cast. Kennedy had proved himself a winner in the primaries, a winner on liberal terms, and he had scrupulously kept Kennedy organizers out of Michigan itself. Kennedy had won Staebler's respect, possibly his affection. Walter Reuther, whose United Automobile Workers are to Michigan Democrats what the Chase Manhattan Bank is to New York Republicans, had originally been neutral in choice between Hubert Humphrey, Adlai Stevenson and John F. Kennedy. As the last apostle of the creative trade unionism of the thirties, Reuther wanted first to be sure that labor would have a place at the White House table; he wanted next to be sure that the Democratic nominee would pass his personal tests of purity on civil rights and union rights; he wanted last, but above all, to have a Democratic winner. By mid-May, even before the Oregon primary had closed, Kennedy had passed all Reuther's tests.

As for Williams, it is only necessary to quote one of the earliest (January, 1960) analyses of the Kennedy lieutenants on this strange personality: "Everyone seems agreed that Williams is a man of strong convictions," read the report to Kennedy's headquarters. "He takes himself very seriously and believes that he is an instrument of God's will in furthering liberal, humanitarian causes. He is a devout Episcopalian and will show moving pictures of his trip to the Holy Land

[6] Now Assistant Secretary of State for African Affairs.

at the drop of a hat. Williams apparently sees himself as having been tapped to put the Sermon on the Mount into governmental practice. This is not a pose but reflects a sincere, if unusual, conviction. I go into this in some detail because I think that any approach to him which overlooks this strong religious drive—which is completely intermeshed with his personal ambition—will miss the mark."

With Kennedy's smashing victories in West Virginia and Oregon, the Michigan triumvirate was now convinced that Kennedy was their man. The Massachusetts Senator had proved himself a clean, hard, organizational fighter in Staebler's terms; had given his commitments and friendship to labor clearly enough to satisfy Reuther; and had passed all of Williams' tests of liberalism and humanitarianism. Michigan was ready to join the bandwagon. With ceremonial dignity all arrangements were now made for the Michigan endorsement.

Kennedy had spent the evening of June 1st in San Francisco. He had stopped in Chicago on the morning of June 2nd to accept the endorsement of the Textile Workers of America. Now, to lend dignity to ceremonial, his plane was loaded with reporters and flown to northern Michigan to be met by Governor Williams and his handsome wife. For no apparent reason, reporters and dignitaries were then driven forty-five miles to the Mackinac Bridge, then ferried to historic Mackinac Island, where the Governor maintained his summer home. A private conversation of an hour and a half proceeded in the Governor's cottage while reporters shivered in the chill outside and sipped warm coffee served by Mrs. Williams. Then, on the ferry back from the island, Governor Williams announced to the assembled press that he had had many matters to discuss with Jack Kennedy about the future and that he had finally decided to endorse the Massachusetts Senator personally; no, he said, the candidate had had no "knowledge" of what was going to happen at the meeting until he arrived. (On the plane up to Michigan, the candidate had told the reporters it was a safe guess he was going to receive an endorsement.) The Governor expressed his belief that he was speaking for a "majority" of Michigan's fifty-one Convention votes, a statement equivalent to Mr. Khrushchev's belief that he speaks for a majority of the Supreme Soviet. Gravely, in Williams' presence, Mr. Kennedy underlined the "importance" of this endorsement and declared it to be "extremely important in the fight for nomination and election." He then motored to his airplane and took off for Colorado to harvest more votes.

The harvest in New York came next. But this was a leadership operation on an entirely different level. Michigan had been won by the loftiest and most punctilious methods, with no offense given to its high-minded leaders. New York was won, with equal art but by other political methods.

The Democratic Party of New York State, once the greatest in the union, its fatherhead and fountain of creative thinking, has fallen on evil days. Split at least five ways by the classic ethnic clashes of the Northeast (Irish, Italian, Jewish, Negro, white Protestant), the leadership of the New York Democrats has long ceased trying to bind these groups together into any coherent community pattern; it divides rather than unifies the tribal groups of the Empire State. No great ideas, no great visions, have been offered either the state or the city by the leadership of the Democratic Party since the days of Franklin D. Roosevelt. In no other state of the union, outside the South and Massachusetts, does so vast a gulf separate the thinking intellectuals, the responsible executive class, the fertile minds of the universities, from the political leadership of the Democratic Party. Divorced thus from the perspectives and realities of popular concern, the machinery of party leadership has fallen into the hands of coarse men, who have concentrated control more and more into their own narrow groups, separating themselves more and more from the people, their needs and aspirations. The Democratic leaders of New York—still the largest state of the union, voting 114 votes at the Democratic Convention, or one seventh the total needed to nominate—still believed well into the spring of 1960 that they would cast these votes themselves.

That it was not to be was the result of the quiet, unnoticed and brilliantly effective work of five men: John Bailey of Connecticut, Congressman Charles A. Buckley of the Bronx, Congressman Eugene Keogh of Brooklyn, Erie County Chairman Peter Crotty—and Joseph P. Kennedy, the candidate's father, himself.

These men saw New York with absolute reality, not as political mythology has it, but as decay has enfeebled it. The outsider who comes to New York comes first to Manhattan, bearing in his mind the legendary power of Tammany and recognizing National Committeeman Carmine DeSapio as boss of Tammany. Yet Boss DeSapio controls only one county (Manhattan) of New York State; and within this county he is under intense enemy pressure from citizen reformers. Four other counties make up the rest of New York City, and fifty-seven more comprise the state.

The Kennedy plan was to work from upstate down. Starting in the fall of 1959, John Bailey, National Committeeman from Connecticut, had been allotted upstate New York as his area of reconnaissance, and he proceeded, thereupon, to move through the flabby Empire State Democracy in an over-the-border political raid unmatched in domestic politics since Huey Long raided Arkansas from Louisiana. Quietly winning to Kennedy purposes Buffalo County leader Peter Crotty and New York Democratic State Secretary Ben Wetzler, Bailey proceeded carefully, without arousing the slumbering Manhattan leadership, county by county, to sound out, with the help of Crotty and Wetzler, the loyalties of the upstate counties. By spring Bailey could report some forty-odd upstate New York delegate votes as safe for Kennedy.

Westchester, the Bronx, Queens County and Albany were left to father Joseph Kennedy's jurisdiction; and there he was working his old friendships and compelling persuasions. Two Congressmen—Buckley of the Bronx and Keogh of Brooklyn —joined him as allies. By May within New York City the Kennedy-Buckley-Keogh forces could safely count forty more votes—for a total of eighty out of 114.

Alerted to what was going on too late in the spring to countermove, Boss DeSapio and his docile partner, Michael Prendergast, were now left hoping (as were so many others) that in West Virginia the Kennedy campaign would explode in religious warfare; that the Convention would then dead-lock; that they could then persuade the pro-Kennedy upstate county chairmen to hold neutral; and might then still be able to swing New York's massive 114 votes for maximum effect in the deadlock. But with the Kennedy victories in West Virginia, in Maryland, in Nebraska and in Oregon, the Kennedy bandwagon had begun to roll. The upstate county chairmen and the Bronx, Queens and most of the Brooklyn politicians had secured themselves spring seats early. There was now nothing to do for the DeSapio-Prendergast leadership but to scramble aboard the rolling bandwagon with what little grace and dignity they could muster.

The candidate arrived in New York on June 16th for a reception tendered him by the mayor of New York, Robert Wagner, on the green and beautiful lawn of old Gracie Mansion. June 16th had been a day of long knives and dirty politics in New York; the DeSapio-Prendergast machine, venting its spite on the reformers, since they could not vent it on Kennedy, had that morning excluded former Governor Lehman, one of New York's most revered Democrats, from the Convention delegation. The candidate sat there on the lawn, handsome and tired, with just a fleck of gray now in his glossy brown hair, relaxed, soft-voiced—yet distant and frosty. He had been angered by the machine's affront to Lehman, whose support he felt essential to carrying New York later. He had the Tammany delegates now in the squeeze of his hand. And so he let the Tammany chieftains approach him, as a Roman proconsul of Augustus' time might receive barbarian chieftains on the marches of Empire. The reformers stood on one side of the lawn (in New York, it is the reformers who can raise the big money to fund a war chest) the old-timers on the other. Several Negro politicians stalked between groups, one of them arguing with a reform politician about whether or not the Negroes should back the reformers. ("We won't be a tail to your kite, you should have called us in before.")

The old-line politicians of Tammany blinked at the scene in the sun, their cigars put away, their predatory faces baffled yet not hostile. This handsome young man was seed of their seed, stock of their stock, both his grandfathers had been ward-heeling politicians, just as they were. Yet he had gone to Harvard and was tailored in England and was somehow different from them—as they hoped their sons would be different. All three groups stared at the young man, for somehow he had captured New York, and none of them could say precisely how. They stood in line to shake his hand and he treated them with correct yet distant courtesy; occasionally, with barely suppressed boredom, he would look up from conversation and beckon another to come over; it was not quite a surrender ceremony; but the warmth in his inflection and manner was little greater than when he had prowled the main street of Phillips, Wisconsin. "How are you," he said as they filed by. "How are you, pleased to meet you, good of you to come, how are you." The next week, the New York State delegation to the Democratic Convention met in Albany, polled its membership and discovered that it was 87 of 114 for Kennedy; but Kennedy did not bother to appear.

For Kennedy, May and June were weeks of supreme exertion as, without pause or rest, he flew about the country harvesting the previous four years' exploration of leadership. It is almost impossible now to re-create the schedule of travel that shuttled him across the country in the five weeks between the May 20th Oregon primary and the June 27th Montana State Convention, last of the delegate-picking conventions. A partial schedule, starting in Oregon, goes something like this: Chicago (for a visit to Adlai Stevenson to plead for his support, which was refused); to Hyannisport;

to Washington, D.C.; to New Jersey; to New York; to Washington, D.C.; then on to Washington State; to San Francisco; to Chicago; to Michigan; to Colorado; to Minnesota; to New Mexico; to Colorado; back to New Jersey; to Harvard; to New York; to Massachusetts; again to Colorado; to South Dakota; to North Dakota; once more to New York; and again to New Jersey; to Pennsylvania; to Washington, D.C.; to Massachusetts; to Iowa; to Montana; and finally home to Massachusetts and rest. Nor does the mileage, the physical exertion or the delivery of person reflect in any measured sense the number of votes he sought to harvest in any area. For Kennedy, the value of the votes to be gathered lay not in their simple arithmetical total so much as in their contribution, as multiples, to his over-all strategy.

In all the Rocky Mountain states, for example, there were fewer votes to be won than in either New York or Pennsylvania. Yet the Rocky Mountain states were, in May and June, entering their weeks of state conventioneering and delegate selection; and strategy required, no matter what the exertion, that he give the mountain states his attention.

This strategy had come clear at the end of May when his May 21st visit to Stevenson convinced him that Stevenson would not withdraw. The major opposition at the Convention, therefore, would come from Stevenson loyalists if not from Stevenson himself. Yet it was obvious, too, that the Stevenson thrust could not be mounted until after the Convention had deadlocked for the first and second ballots. If there was to be a deadlock on the first and second ballots, the major actor in the opening deadlock would be Lyndon B. Johnson. If Lyndon B. Johnson did have eighty or ninety votes from the Rocky Mountain states, then Johnson could, indeed, present himself to the nation not as the Southern candidate but as the Western candidate. To whittle down the Johnson total in the mountain states, to isolate and portray Johnson as the Southern candidate, was essential to Kennedy; and if personal exertion was required, then strategically it was worth it.

The Mountain states had been, since the Hyannisport meeting, the supervisory domain of Brother Teddy Kennedy, and Teddy had worked early and late recruiting young leadership for his brother. Now, as the Western state conventions met in late spring, the candidate added his personal pressure to that of his deputies. In almost all of these states, Johnson's Senatorial allies or Stevensonian zealots held apparent control. But under each set of controls, the Kennedy organization had built new strength. In New Mexico, Senators Dennis Chavez and Clinton P. Anderson were both with

Johnson, and Johnson expected all seventeen of New Mexico's delegates. But Kennedy's young men had worked hard, and as the New Mexico Democrats met in their State Convention to pick delegates, the Massachusetts candidate blitzed them with a personal visit, to come away with four of Johnson's expected seventeen votes. In Arizona, former Governor Ernest W. McFarland was expected to hold that state in line, by its unit rule, with all seventeen Arizona votes for Johnson—but young Congressman Stewart L. Udall[7] had been organizing the state for Kennedy and delivered—all seventeen votes for Kennedy. In Colorado, Senator John A. Carroll was a Stevenson man, while Governor Stephen L. R. McNichols and ex-Senator Edwin C. Johnson leaned to Johnson; but young Byron (Whizzer) White[8] and Teddy Kennedy had been organizing Colorado from county level up and could claim ten of Colorado's twenty-one convention votes by late June (at the first ballot in Los Angeles, later, they lifted this to thirteen and a half). Exhausted, one day in June Kennedy slumped in a green leather couch in the waiting room of the Durango airport in Colorado, waiting for his Convair to taxi up, and said to Whizzer White and Brother Teddy, "Now let's be honest—just how many delegates did I get for this two-thousand-mile flight—a half of one?" "But you cheered us all up," said White. And he had.

As June closed, as Kennedy addressed his last state convention (in Montana, June 27th), the configuration of the Convention had begun to be clear. Kennedy could count as solid 114 votes from his native New England; he could count another 265 from the Northeast (Michigan, New York, Delaware, Indiana, Maryland, Ohio); he could count only 36 for sure in the farm states; he could count only 31 in all the South; he had netted 61 in the mountain states; he had 28 on the Pacific Coast; he had another dozen scattered votes in the territories; all in all, he had some 550 publicly certified votes.

Beyond these were the unknowns. There were three native-son states that were delicate to tamper with: Iowa (26), Kansas (21), Minnesota (31). And then there were a big four, the great question-mark states that would determine whether or not he would fail: Illinois (69), Pennsylvania (81), California (81) and New Jersey (41). In this packet were 350 more votes—more than enough to nominate. In each of them the candidate had assurances, promises, hopes, friends;

---

[7] Now Secretary of the Interior.
[8] Now Deputy Attorney-General.

he had worked them early and worked them late; with an even break in these states, he would win. But he could not be sure, and no one could be sure until the Convention met and, by its own chemistry, decided on a Democratic nominee for President.

Except for one major speech on foreign affairs on the floor of the Senate in early June, the events of the outer world might, to the reader of newsprint, have seemed as remote from John F. Kennedy's reflections as events on the far rim of the moon. He had been invited to visit England and make several speeches there in May; he had briefly considered the invitation as an opportunity to give his candidacy the luster of prestige abroad. Then he had rejected it. The primary target was the Convention, the primary need was delegates. Let others adopt whatever line they wished; he knew his trade. He, Kennedy, meant to have delegates. First things first.

Whoever runs for the Presidency of the United States can, however, never shape his own problems. America and America's problems at home and in the world shape it for him; and always, whether traveling or at rest, there was another Kennedy concealed from the public eye under the delegate seeker.

I flew with the candidate on the last of his trips to the West—a day-and-night-and-day-and-night-again flight out to Iowa and Montana, then back to Massachusetts. He was tired then, at the sick edge of exhaustion from six months of campaigning; and the Convention yet to come, and after that the campaign against the Republicans. Sitting in the back of the empty plane with a few friends he trusted, he let his mind travel an ungoverned span of thoughts, which came and went as his mind flicked across the country. It was the range, the extent, the depth and detail, of information and observation that dazzled, then overwhelmed, the listener.

He had taken off on a clear, hot, sunny morning from the Hyannisport airport, having hugged his wife, cuddled his daughter, raced up the stairs and buckled himself into his seat—en route to Iowa and a meeting with the Iowa Convention delegates. His mind was on Iowa as he left, and he studied the latest polling report on Iowa by Louis Harris. Someone asked about Loveless, the Governor of Iowa, as a possible Vice-Presidential candidate. He responded and then began to play on the personalities of the Democratic Party, all the potential Vice-Presidents, as if their names were musical chords—Orville and Hubert and Herschel and Gaylord and Henry and Claire and Symington and Albert, and on and on, as if he were casting roles in a play, a two-sentence personality sketch attached to each and then on to the next, drawing a laugh or a chuckle with each description. From the possible Democratic Vice-Presidents he moved on to the nature of the Vice-Presidency, and thus to the personality of Mr. Nixon; and from that to Mr. Rockefeller. (Mr. Rockefeller, he felt then, would be a far tougher candidate to beat.)

He was in his candid mood at that moment, the words sharp, his personality portraits merciless; and having entertained us, he turned to his newspapers and read them, gulping columns at a time. A Drew Pearson column caught his eye and aroused him again to a disquisition about Lyndon B. Johnson; once, he averred, he had thought Lyndon B. Johnson the best-qualified man to be President of the United States; but now, as the combat venom welled up in the candidate, he spoke briefly, pungently, bitterly about the gang-up, the Stop Kennedy coalition of Stevenson and Johnson and Symington and Humphrey. He touched now in his survey of America on New York politics, border state politics, mountain state politics, farm politics. He spoke of campaigning and how, no matter where you were, you could always tell a farmer as you clasped hands and shook with him in a line of many people. He liked the feel of a farmer's hard hand. And thus on to the Iowa farm problem; and then he fingered and was diverted by a scholarly survey on farm surpluses that he was studying.

He touched down twice in Iowa, in afternoon and evening, at Cedar Rapids and Des Moines, speaking to delegates in both places: to a farm picnic outside Cedar Rapids, to a TV audience and a press conference in Des Moines.

Then the plane was aloft again, and he was somber in the dark as it moved through the air toward the mountains and Montana. The stewardess brought him a steaming bowl of hot tomato soup; with complete relish he stirred in a thick gob of sour cream and supped. At almost any moment of afternoon and evening on the road, soup is the favorite Kennedy dish—almost any kind of soup: chicken soup, tomato soup, bean soup and (if anybody at Hyannisport has thought to prepare it for the journey) his favorite New England clam chowder. Having finished his soup, he moodily stared out of the black windows; a lightning storm was flashing across the distant sky, and as the lightning burst, the great ranges of the Rockies were clear beneath while the plane bobbed back and forth in the air. He hunched a knee up under his chin and swung his chair back away from the window to his friends.

Somewhere outside in the stormy night, as the plane tossed and he took his soup, he had left Iowa and the farm problem behind and his mind was not yet on Montana. It was in another range.

It was on Khrushchev. After Nixon, it would be Khrushchev. And there was Berlin to think about. He talked about Berlin now, very slowly, as if picking his own way through his thoughts, and then went on to China. Now he was questioning about China, and his questions came sharp, fast, as the interlocutor responded. Could China have been saved in 1945 and 1946? he asked. What had happened? The interlocutor tried to recall a sequence of decisions far away in Chungking in the fall of 1945, and the candidate cut in: Who made that decision? When? Who had command decision? Why was command decision not exercised? What was Chou En-lai like? Mao Tse-tung?

One of the group had been in France shortly after the war and brought up the problems of American intervention in other countries and the intervention against the Communists there in 1947, under the Ramadier cabinet. Kennedy wanted to know how the decision had been taken. How had it worked? His mind jumped to the State Department, its personnel; he mentioned names; he was familiar, obviously, with all its workings—he was somewhere between Iowa and Montana in the night en route to the Democratic nomination, yet he was playing President. He was inquiring, demanding opinion, in question after question: Should Presidents go to summit conferences? Was personal diplomacy an effective technique for American presidents? How much of the reservoir of good will had Eisenhower used up in these recent trips round the world? Had the President of the United States been seen too often and too familiarly abroad? He brooded about the matter aloud, then, as the plane pitched and tossed and sheet lightning lit the hills, he buckled on his belt and turned back to the dark windows, watching silently for the next burst of illumination to light up the far and beautiful country. When he came out of his reverie, the plane was coming down to Helena airport, it was one o'clock at night and he was in Montana, in mind and in body: Who was the advance man here in Helena? Who was handling arrangements?

He was up at 6:30 the next morning, answering telephone calls, hearing reports. He breakfasted in his hotel room, received Montana politicians, politicked, lunched, encouraged his Montana men as the Montana Convention met. Montana had only seventeen votes, but they were important. Established in the Placer Hotel, on Last Chance Gulch, as Montana's delegates met across the street in the Marlowe Theater, he had left China, Berlin and France far behind—he was a tactical general commanding a raid far in Lyndon Johnson's rear.

Outside, the mountains of Montana were fragrant with early summer; pine and fir glistened as they reached to the sky on a June day of absolute purity; the dandelions had passed to seed, but the mountain slopes twinkled with daisies, with primroses, with bluebells, with black-eyed susans, with purple lupine. But Kennedy had indoor work to do: he told his public stories again for the benefit of the good, sober Democrats of the mountain capital, earnestly deciding on the best President of the United States (Stuart Symington was also there that day, and so was Jim Rowe, field-general for the Johnson forces). He told them of the California delegate who could not make up his mind which was the best candidate ("All I can say," the California delegate had remarked, "is that even though I can't make up my mind, when I do, I'll be mighty bitter about it"). He told them of the Massachusetts delegation to the 1924 Democratic Convention, which had watched the Convention creep upward toward its 104th ballot while its money ran out; the Massachusetts chairman had then assembled his delegates and said, "Gentlemen, we are faced with a choice—either we have to move to a more modest hotel or to a more liberal candidate."

In the evening he dined with the delegates and spoke briefly, pleadingly, eloquently to them of the importance of the Presidency, and of the importance of the West in this choice, the importance of the West in general ("Eastward I go only by force," he said, quoting another son of Massachusetts, Thoreau. "Westward I go free." He continued, "This is why I have come to Montana"). And when he had finished it was nine in the evening and he was through with the long, long planning of the steps to the Convention, because now all the delegates had been chosen and he was to board the plane to go to Massachusetts and rest for ten days before the Convention began.

He boarded the plane as the summer sun fell beneath the hills at the airport. In the dry mountain air, the purple and gray tones of the Rockies that cupped the airport were very crisp and very near, almost close enough to touch, and above them lay the gold-and-lavender, pink-and-red bars of the sunset. He was tired now, his eyes deep and heavy, his movements still graceful but slow. The few tired men in his plane sat apart from him, giving him privacy, and he sipped another bowl of hot soup, sat up refreshed, then looked around as if inviting conversation.

The conversation began in a burst of anger. A story had appeared in a New York newspaper that evening that an Eastern Governor had claimed that Kennedy had offered him a cabinet post in return for his Convention support.[9] His anger was cold, furious. When Kennedy is angry, he is at his most precise, almost schoolmasterish. It is a federal offense, he said, to offer any man a federal job in return for a favor. This was an accusation of federal offense. It was not so. It did not happen that way. It never happened that way. That was not the way politics worked. The matter was discussed, and then someone offered the observation that that day, in Helena, its best bookstore (Miss Susan Eaker's bookstore, an excellent one) had sold out completely of copies of his *Profiles in Courage*. The information pleased him, and he began to talk about books. Now he was off in the literary range of his experience, and it obviously pleased him to talk of it; and so to history writing and American history. Someone brought up Simon Cameron of Pennsylvania, quoting Lincoln on Cameron, and Kennedy corrected the quotation and went on to other passages of history. How much, for example, he had enjoyed Churchill's history of Marlborough. Kennedy quoted with amusement Churchill's ironic passage on his illustrious ancestor: "In his youth he prized money more than passion, in his age money more than fame." He inquired whether any of us had read a magnificent piece of historical reporting he himself had just read—Theodore Roosevelt's report on the funeral of Edward VII. He ran through the historians of America's past, the known and the obscure, and wondered whether modern historians were really better because they knew more or just seemed so because they saw the stage of American history lighted as we saw it.

From Marlborough and the writing of history to the personality of Adlai E. Stevenson and the quality of the American intellectuals. Then to a long, tender and perceptive disquisition on the Irish and the Jews in American life. From that to the American Negroes and what their problems were— and their search for leadership. Did so-and-so really control in Harlem? Was so-and-so really a reader of history, as reported, or was it just a story? Then to the Chinese again. Then to his own role in the great debates on China in 1946

---

[9] No cabinet post was later offered this Governor.

and 1948—and an apology to those present for having, in his ignorance, publicly slurred at that time and thus injured a man whom now he knew to be innocent.

All the while the plane had been flying back eastward through the night, and the hours had been stretching on to midnight and beyond. He had called for another bowl of soup while his two exhausted aides slept, completely worn out, in the back of the plane and his two conversational companions bent close to him. Now and then he would turn off the light above his head as he spoke. Then, when one or another of the conversationalists would respond, he would flick on the light nervously so as to observe his expression. The time came when he must sleep, and unwound now from the tension of the day, he made his way to the twin bunks in the rear compartment of the plane where he slept in flight and closed the door.

At dawn the plane was descending over Cape Cod, and it was both hot and cool, as it can be only on the Cape in June. The salt air of the Atlantic in the June morning slapped at us who remembered Montana and the mountain air only the night before. The candidate came off the plane by himself, walked across the field to the car waiting for him, and motored to his home alone.

The next time I was to see him, ten days later, was at the International Airport at Los Angeles, just before the Convention opened. Three thousand people were there, banners waving, bands playing, girls screaming. As he descended from the plane in Los Angeles that later day, the crowd burst and overwhelmed him. I remember the Los Angeles police, among the most efficient, if the most cruel, in the nation, being swamped by the crowd, and in the crowd a large man in a brown suit hammered his way through to the candidate. The large man in the brown suit seized John F. Kennedy by the lapels, and for a moment I thought it an odd greeting before I realized that the man was probably a maniac. The Los Angeles police realized it a moment before I did, for by the time I was aware this was danger, they had knifed into the crowd and, brutally, they were chopping the man's frantic arms from the candidate's person. He was, from that moment, never to be solitary in public again nor private in person— he was the stuff of a President and, as such, more than himself, and a man to be guarded and shielded.

Yet that was ten days later, and in those ten days much was to happen.

Chapter 6

RENDEZVOUS AT LOS ANGELES:
THE DEMOCRATIC CONVENTION

EVERY convention is a universe in itself, with its own strange centers of gravity, its own fresh heroes and fools, its own new resolution of pressures and forces, its own irrecapturable mood of stage and place.

Los Angeles was the stage of the Democratic Convention of 1960, and as the delegates began to gather in the first week of July, Los Angeles gave of its best. Smogless and milk-blue, the skies stretched on day after day, as gentle and pure as they must have been a generation ago, before industry and the automobile fouled the air of the city with their wastes.

Normally a national convention gathers in a huddle of close-clustered downtown hotels at the center of some clotted city, so that simple nearness throws delegates together at café, bar, sidewalk, lobby. Then in the daily bustle and jostle they rub on one another and rub and rub and whisper and gossip and mill and churn, until summer heat, strained emotion and growing tension bring them to a common boil out of which decision erupts. But Los Angeles is huge, and the delegates were scattered all across the great city, tucked away in hotels over a belt of thirty-five miles of palm-starred boulevards. Dispersed thus and scattered across Los Angeles' vast spaces, unwilling to trust their own driving skillls to the freeways' lunatic traffic, most of them unwilling to spend the five of ten dollars for a taxi ride from one center of their sprawling dispersion to another, the Democratic delegates of 1960 were atomized. (From Pennsylvania delegation headquarters in Pasadena, for example, to New York delegation headquarters in midtown Los Angeles was a fifteen-dollar taxi ride; which discouraged casual visiting between these two traditionally friendly delegations.) They caucused, therefore, by state, in the hotels allotted to their states, and when not caucusing, they lounged, lured by the perfect weather, by the hotel swimming pools under the palms, or took their wives and children to Disneyland (Disneyland outdrew all the night clubs of Los Angeles combined during the Convention fortnight), or enjoyed the hospitality of the Hollywood studios, which ran special buses from the Ambassador Hotel for delegates wishing to make the tour of movieland.

Diffuse as the Convention was, it nevertheless had, as it must, a nerve center: the Biltmore Hotel, an enormous, tawny, old-fashioned hostelry, which stands eleven stories high, dominating the green rectangle of Pershing Square, where the tired old men, the loafers, the time wasters and the free-speech enthusiasts make their permanent open-air headquarters in Los Angeles. Here at the Biltmore were not only the headquarters of the Democratic National Committee, the headquarters of the great TV networks, the headquarters of all the major candidates (Kennedy, Johnson, Stevenson, Symington, Meyner) but also the press bowl and the rooms of hundreds of correspondents, officials and hangers-on. It was the Biltmore that made the news.

Here, slowly, in the first week of July, as the first of the 4,509 delegates and alternates and 4,750 news representatives, as well as uncounted hundreds of party officials and untold thousands of candidates' workers, began to arrive, the Convention began to simmer.[1] Through the Biltmore lobby paraded two rival Puerto Rican delegations, with their steel drums and guitars, making music and dancing in Latin costume. Here floated the pretty girls, almost indistinguishable from one another in their official red-white-and-blue striped dresses and skimmer hats, soliciting delegates, giggling, jiggling, pinning badges on any one who lingered at their headquarters for a moment; offering taffy for Lyndon Johnson (who had flown in half a ton of taffy from Austin, Texas); offering Pepsi-Cola for Stuart Symington; offering orange juice for George Smathers; offering coffee, moving pictures, buns at John F. Kennedy's headquarters. Here were distributed the leaflets of Brigadier-General James A. Holdridge, U.S. Army Ret., Vegetarian Party candidate for President, proclaiming the 1960 elections a violation of the Constitution and hence, NULL AND VOID. Outside in the evening, hymn-singing Angelenos paraded with sandwich boards, their message (in red, homely lettering on white background) proclaiming: PRAY MUCH, CHRISTIANS. WE WANT A GOD-FEARING MAN, NOT A MAN RULED FROM ROME OR FROM MOSCOW.

All this the TV camera caught and showed the nation. TV displays events, action, motion, arrival, departure; it cannot show thought, silence, mood or decision. And so the TV

---

[1] The Los Angeles Convention Bureau estimated that the Convention brought, in all, 45,000 visitors to the city.

camera caught the carnival outer husk of the Convention in
all its pageantry and motion: the girls in their summer dresses,
the bands and the music, the suicide-seeker trying to jump
from the hotel roof, the lounges of each major candidate,
where were entertained the still-undecided delegates arriving
from uncertain states. And the TV camera, like a magnet, began to draw people from all Southern California into the
Biltmore—the curious who wanted their faces on camera just
for a moment; hucksters seeking to display their little signs
for an instant of promotion before the national eye; politicians
from the dispersed hotels, seeking sixty seconds of national
attention; children and mothers and con men and civic students, all thronging and crowding one upon another. (Burly
Mother leading Timid Boy plows through the packed Stevenson headquarters as newsmen clamor at his public-relations
officer for news; she buttonholes the overwhelmed press officer, points to her boy and says: "You see, he's editor of his
high-school newspaper, he's got to have an interview with
Stevenson, you hear? He's just got to have it, I know Mr.
Stevenson will do it.")

And the special pleaders: the good-citizens group demanding that this Convention save the dunes of Lake Michigan;
the efficiency expert presenting his plan for revitalizing the
Civil Service (automatically, by law, fire the ten per cent least
efficient in every government department at the end of every
year); the Negro leader insisting that this Convention go on
record as demanding a Negro in the Cabinet; and on and on.
As the Fourth of July week end closed and the planes began
to unload their passengers in thousands, delegates would un-
pack, telephone their leader, then, wandering and uncertain
in the strange city, they would drift to the Biltmore. There
delegates and sight-seers crowded together until the lobbies
seemed about to burst; policemen guarded the press bowl
from invasion; above the bowl the crowds thickened and
thickened until they no longer moved but oozed, inch by
inch, in a slow whirlpool with the consistency of lava, reaching final and complete unmanageability at the passageway
where the doors of the eight-elevator bank opened to take
people upstairs to the headquarters of the candidates, where,
perhaps, some of their questions might be answered.

For the delegates were perplexed. If there was any mood
at all to the Convention, it was perplexity. All of them
strangers, all of them having, by political war or long service
in their home states, earned the right to come to Los Angeles
to choose a President, the delegates took themselves seriously.
It was a more sober Convention than any other I can re-

member attending. Moreover, it was a concerned Convention. All across Los Angeles, from Pasadena on the east to Beverly Hills on the west, the great bookstores reported a run on books: sell-outs on Kennedy's *Strategy of Peace*, sell-outs on Stevenson's *Putting First Things First*, sell-outs on Kennedy's *Profiles in Courage*. (In Hollywood, The Pickwick Bookshop reported they had sold out of Blanshard's *American Freedom and Catholic Power* too.)

The matters that concerned the delegates were many and diverse. But one could take their very presence in Los Angeles as symbolic. Almost all of those who had come from the East Coast had flown here on the new swept-wing jets, which now spanned the continent in five hours. Four years before, had they flown to Los Angeles, they would have come by the now obsolete propeller-pulled airplane, and it would have taken them from nine to eleven hours. The continent had been cut in half. So much had America shrunk since 1956—so much had the world shrunk about America. So much had space itself shrunk, as man-made satellites now orbited the distant moon. It was as if the delegates sensed, if they did not know, that now halfway around the world missiles with hydrogen heads coded for Los Angeles, as well as Chicago and Washington and New York, were already in place.

Nor would anyone let them forget that the world was closing in on their country: this shrinkage of the world, this changing world, this world of challenge and chaos and Communism, was the central theme of all oratory; and the speakers—in caucus, on TV, in convention later—seized on the theme, repeated it, hammered it, flattened it, until the entire Convention seemed a continuous drone of great worries, fogged in overlapping redundancies. Whenever one tuned the inner ear to attention to strain phrases out of the drone, the same words came shimmering through the blur: "This world, half free and half slave" . . . "the ramparts of freedom we guard" . . . "leadership" . . . "uncommitted nations" . . . "the revolution of technology" . . . "this, the most powerful nation on earth reduced to" . . . "people who look to us for leadership" . . . "revolution of rising expectations" . . . . . . "twenty-five minutes away from the push button on Khrushchev's desk . . ." and on and on. By the time, on Monday evening, the keynote speaker, Senator Frank Church of Idaho, rose to set the note, all he had to say had already been reduced to cliché.

That it had become cliché was simple of explanation. The newspaper headlines that the delegates were reading in

Los Angeles as they sought rumor and gossip and reflection of their own doings drummed at them with the sounds of a universe far larger and more ominous than the universe of the Convention. CUBA SUGAR OFF read the morning headlines Thursday before the Convention, and the afternoon headline: KHRUSHCHEV THREATENS AUSTRIA. On Friday it became obvious that Africa was in chaos: THOUSANDS OF WHITES FLEE CONGO IN PANIC said the local headline. RUSSIA SHOOTS DOWN AMERICAN PLANE said the papers reporting the fate of the RB-47 on Monday as the Convention opened; and Tuesday afternoon, as delegates weighed the votes they were about to cast, came a streamer headline in the Los Angeles *Mirror-News:* ANY MORE U.S. SPY FLIGHTS MEANS WAR, NIKITA WARNS.

The Democrats were not divided on these issues of the future, of war and peace, as a fortnight later the Republicans were to be. By unspoken consensus, they were united on foreign policy and defense. What divided them were matters of the past, the emotions that reached into the origins of America rather than into the whither of America. They were divided on the relations of white and black, and divided on the attitude of Protestant and Catholic. And they were divided, above all, on the matter of leadership—who could be trusted? What manner of man should be selected to lead the country? What kind of personality might best straddle the past and turn to face the future? In this intermingling of past and future, the nature of the election was for the first time foreshadowed.

In a matter of days another dominant note was struck by the mysterious process of common press observation. From the sounds and sights, from the hundreds of lost and milling faces in the Biltmore, the press distilled a swift truth that was a remarkably accurate historic assessment: that this was the convention where the young faced the old, this was the convention where one generation gave way to another, this was —in James Reston's felicitous phrase—the assembly that witnessed the Changing of the Guard.

A convention is usually made up of older, if not wiser, men than the common voters who send them there. In most states delegates are chosen by party leadership to honor long-time trusted servants of the party; or from men of eminence in culture, diplomacy or the professions, who can give the luster of their achievement and their names to the delegation; or, particularly in the organization-controlled states, very heavily from those who contribute the big money to campaign chests and now crave the honorable symbol of a national delegate badge and the sense of high participation. Most of those who come to a convention have thus earned, over many years of achievement or contribution at some level, the right to be considered important. Delegates from the primary states are usually younger and more vigorous than the delegates picked by the big machine states, but they are in a minority; one way or another, a convention is an assembly of older men, averaging in age over fifty, some of whom boast of unbroken attendance at conventions that reach back to the time of the nomination of Woodrow Wilson. Almost as much as the national Congress, the delegates (at both conventions) preserve the continuity of American politics.

It was these older men who first reflected what was happening; it was visible in the various shades of melancholy on their countenances. One could see drifting through the lobbies of the Biltmore such former powers as James Farley, Tommy Corcoran, Scott Lucas, Claude Pepper—but they were powerless now, ghosts at a banquet over which they had once presided. Even such currently active politicians as Carmine DeSapio and Mike Prendergast, leaders of New York's huge but impotent delegation, seemed of an ineffectual age, dazed and somewhat bemused. They strolled through the lobby of the Biltmore on their first day almost hand in hand, as if afraid to be alone in this sunny city and alien mingling of strangers, then retired to lounge by the swimming pool of the Ambassador Hotel. The authentic ringing applause for Mr. Sam Rayburn when the Convention opened, the warm emotional applause for Eleanor Roosevelt, the tumultuous applause for Adlai Stevenson when he first appeared at the Convention, came from the heart; yet such applause was for these people not only as individuals but as symbols of a familiar past, a safer, more glorious past. Even Averell Harriman, a man who earned enormous credit from this Republic before he wasted it in the tribal wars of New York politics, was received with unfeigned and genuine enthusiasm when he rose to second the nomination of John F. Kennedy. It was as if here in Los Angeles, at this time, only his triumphs in Moscow, Washington, London and Paris were remembered from the larger days of American triumphs. Of all the master figures of the past of the Democratic Party, only Harry Truman was absent. By instinct, knowing that time had passed him by, he would not expose himself to this tide of youth.

American politics has witnessed very few such sharp breaks in the flow of time. It was so when in the 1850s the generation of Clay-Calhoun-Webster passed from the scene and the younger men who were to make a Civil War seized command; it was so when the senior echelon of the Civil War finally, in the 1890s, broke in age, and national leadership passed from the command level of those who had directed that war to the level of men like McKinley, who had enlisted as a private in the 23rd Regiment, Ohio Volunteers. It was happening now in the Democratic Party (as, less conspicuously, it was to happen in the Republican Party, too, in 1960).

The vantage point from which best to view the change was the far corner of the 8300 Wing of the Biltmore Hotel. There, on the eighth floor, Room 8315 opened into a four-room suite that was the command post of the Kennedy operation. From Suite 8315 four entirely relaxed young men surveyed the throng and the chaos about them and, unflustered, operated across the body of American politics. It was their ages that fascinated one. In one of the rooms was Robert Kennedy, chief-of-staff, a common sailor in the war, now only thirty-four. In another was Kenneth P. O'Donnell, a bombardier-navigator in the war, now only thirty-six. In another was Pierre Salinger, a nineteen-year-old master of a mine sweeper during the war—now only thirty-five. And the oldest of the four was Lawrence F. O'Brien, a ripe and majestic forty-three. Downstairs on the ground floor of the Biltmore, in the herd where the thousands milled and the lost delegates wandered from headquarters to headquarters shopping among the candidates, questioning on issues, on pledges, on promises, were the older Kennedy men—John Bailey, fifty-five, and Hy Raskin, fifty-one. But upstairs and in command was a new generation. One of the young men said to me, "You know, old-timers are afraid of us. We have to have older men like Bailey and Raskin downstairs to deal with them, just to make them feel we're safe."

By good fortune I had been assigned during the Convention to a room in the 8300 Wing, adjacent to the Kennedy command post. One morning late in Convention week, after Kennedy had already been nominated, one of the weary young field men, coming to report to headquarters, wandered in and lay down to relax on my couch. As he lay there, he mused. "You know, I used to think during the war that people who stayed home in their jobs were getting ahead of us. There we were overseas, losing all those years. And there they were at home getting ahead. Now I feel sorry for the older men. I think we learned something during the war about how to do things; we learned how to work in a way the generals didn't understand. They'd tell us what to do, but then we had to go out and organize the thing—cut the red tape, get the stuff there on time, no matter how, throw away the rule book. We learned to work together without any fussing. The other day when they tried to change the rules here against us, nobody got frantic or excited. Larry just said to Kenny, 'I think we ought to get our fellows on the rules committee to work on it,' and Kenny said, 'I guess you're right. I'll round them up and give them the word.' And that was it. No conferences or planning. I think we learned to work that way during the war, and I feel sorry for the older fellows who never learned."

If there was control anywhere in the Convention, it came from Suite 8315.

And if there was any major testing of this control, it came from a second group of young men, the Stevenson leaders, who made their headquarters across the square from the Biltmore in the deserted Paramount Building but maintained a beachhead for the reception of delegates in an impossibly crowded and overflowing two-room suite on the mezzanine of the Biltmore.

All the other participants in the Convention—the Symington leadership in the 6300 Wing, the Johnson leadership in the 4300 Wing, the lesser favorite sons at the Biltmore and elsewhere—were actors in a drama shaped by these two superior external forces. And as the rumors multiplied and multiplied again in the course of any single day; as the delegates crawled from room to room at the Biltmore, and then back to their own hotels; as question, confusion, resentment, noise, tumult grew—only the Kennedy young men in 8315 and the pilgrim leadership of the Stevensonians knew what was happening as they dueled.

Control as exercised from 8315 was precise, taut, disciplined—yet as casual as that of a veteran combat army, blooded in battle, which has learned to know all its own component parts and recognizes the full reach of its skills and courage. The combat-proved Kennedy area commanders of the spring primary wars had all arrived in Los Angeles on the Saturday before Convention. To their forces had been added almost a score of young men from the Massachusetts delegation, hand-picked the previous spring by the Kennedy organization for style, poise, political savvy, and for the precise purpose of operating on the Convention floor, as now they were supposed to do. In all, some forty delegate-shepherds were assigned each to a particular state delegation that was theirs to cultivate; each was given packets of name cards listing the assigned state delegates by name, profession, hobby, children, wife, peculiarity, religion, and sent out to operate. They were instructed, as they found shifts in any delegation, to report such changes to a private tabulating headquarters in Room 3308 at the Biltmore; and there, every hour on the hour from Friday through balloting day, a new fresh total, accurate to the hour, was to be prepared. For five days, the shepherds were told, they were not to sleep, see their wives, relax, frolic or be out of touch with 8315. Each morning, for the five Convention days from Saturday to the Wednesday balloting, they were to gather in Room 8315 for a staff survey at nine A.M., then disperse to their tasks.

At the Chicago Convention in 1956, in the tumultuous balloting for the Vice-Presidency between Kefauver and Kennedy, communications had broken down between the Kennedy floor lieutenants and the Kennedy off-floor command. Having learned the overriding importance of instant convention communications, the Kennedys had now, in 1960, strung their own independent net of communications between all the parts of their field and headquarters command. A cottage beside the Los Angeles Sports Arena had been assigned by lot to Kennedy as his liaison post. This now became an early model of the communications control post later set up at Hyannisport. From the cottage out to the Convention and under its beaverboard floor ran a net of direct communication lines to special telephone posts fixed on the chairs of friendly delegations (Massachusetts, Illinois, Michigan, New York, Wyoming, Rhode Island). Eight of the forty state shepherds were to carry duo-com walkie-talkie sets as they roved the floor of the Convention to link them also, as they moved, to communications control at the cottage. Governor Ribicoff of Connecticut and Robert Kennedy were to be floor managers, disposing and directing the forty state shepherds as they roved the floor. From the cottage control board another labyrinth of lines ran to the special switchboard of 8315 control downtown, another line to the Senator's own private hideaway in Hollywood, another line to the Senator's public Presidential suite.[2]

By the week end before the Convention, the shape of the duel was clear, its elements agreed on both by the men who sought to make Stevenson President and the team that Jack Kennedy had built.

[2] Several Stevenson leaders assert that the Kennedy walkie-talkies were powerful and sensitive enough to monitor their own more primitive radio communications with the floor.

Without any debate at all, both sides would agree that John F. Kennedy now had 600 certain votes on the first ballot: from six New England states, 114; from six Northeastern industrial states, another 265; from four farm states, another 36; from four Southern states, another 31; from eight mountain states (as the result of his May and June drive), another minimum 61; from four Pacific states, another 40; and in addition to these solid clusters, another certain 50-odd scattered votes, to give him an unshakable 600.

There remained, then, the areas of possible increment where Kennedy must pick up another 160 votes: two farm states (Kansas and Iowa) with 52 votes still backing their favorite-son governors (George Docking and Herschel C. Loveless); plus the big five of unknowns: Pennsylvania, 81; California, 81; New Jersey, 41; Minnesota, 31; Illinois, 69— for a total of 303. It was for the loyalties of these five states or their leadership that the main Kennedy and Stevenson forces dueled, while their guerilla commandos contended in every other delegation for the ones, twos, threes of the waverers, of the sincerely perplexed citizen Democrats trying to make up their minds how to cast their votes for President of the United States.

It is impossible to report the total activity of a free convention. As each state gathers its delegates far from home to caucus, the internal politics of every state becomes tangled with the greater national issues, and with the ambitions and personal hopes of their leaders. In each, new wounds are cut, new enmities are seeded; and as the major Presidential candidates revolve from caucus to caucus, pleading and exhorting, urging and seeking, displaying themselves five or eight or ten times a day, tuning their antennae to the particular wave length and concern of each state's worries, whether it be wheat surplus, school desegregation, unemployment in steel mill or coal mine, no unifying theme or purpose is ever instantly apparent.[3] Since it is thus impossible

---

[3] A partial schedule, covering only the personal morning activities of John F. Kennedy, at the Convention and starting on Monday, July 11th reads like this: On Monday, between 8:30 A.M. and 1:30 P.M. he addressed the caucuses of Nevada, Pennsylvania, Michigan, North Carolina, Arkansas, New York, South Carolina, Florida, Alaska. The afternoon was equally crowded. On Tuesday, between 8:45 and 1:30 he made it to North Carolina, a collective New England breakfast, Wyoming, South Dakota, a nationalities group and California. On Wednesday morning, the day of the balloting, between 9 A.M. and 1:00 P.M. he made it to Indiana, a farm-state caucus, Virginia, Colorado, Hawaii. At this period, it should be added, the activities of the Stevenson and Johnson people were equally frantic.

to make reason out of all these simultaneous activities and caucuses, it is best to focus, as the contenders did, on the big five unknowns—each of them in their differences reflecting the entrancing diversity of the American political scene.

Both Kennedy and Stevenson strategies reflected the same analysis: that if Kennedy could be stopped long enough, his first-ballot strength might crumble. The very efficiency of the Kennedy organization frightened older men; the independence of the Kennedys from political commitments still annoyed several of the big-city bosses, who had hoped to have a President dependent on them; the ugly headline echo of world events disturbed the citizen delegates, who measured the youthful face and voice of John F. Kennedy against the dimensions of the problems the President must face. If Kennedy could command 700 or 750 votes by the time the first ballot opened, then there would be no contest; but if he were held substantially below 700 votes on the first ballot, then would come a real testing of his strength. How many of the politicians here (like the Indiana delegation), compelled to vote for Kennedy on the first ballot (by his primary victory in Indiana), would stay with him on the second? How many of the Rocky Mountain delegates, acquired in late spring, would shift away if a Stevenson surge seemed to be developing? Would Mike DiSalle of Ohio remain firm on the second ballot? Could the Stevenson and Tammany groups in New York combine to whittle down Kennedy's expected 100 of the 114 New York votes if a second, and then a third, ballot came?

To hold their first-ballot strength firm and then add to it from the big five was the scheme of the Kennedy strategists. To freeze the big five about their own favorite sons or urge them to anyone else against Kennedy became the plan of the Stevenson strategists.

New Jersey froze first. In this state an internal war meshed with the larger national picture. Pledged to its own Governor, Robert Meyner, with all forty-one votes on the first ballot, the New Jersey delegation was split internally and bitterly. Joseph P. Kennedy had, through the long spring of 1960, won the loyalties and votes of the north New Jersey political leaders for his son, the Massachusetts Senator. Yet the quiet operation that had won them had simultaneously embittered their Governor, who felt himself bypassed and his machinery of state politics threatened. If Meyner released New Jersey, some thirty New Jersey votes would go to Kennedy and the balance to Symington and Stevenson. Now, however, become adamant over the week end, Meyner refused to release.

Illinois broke first. Of Illinois' sixty-nine votes Mayor Richard Daley, boss of Cook County, controlled an estimated fifty-five. Once Daley had been a friend of Adlai Stevenson; in 1955 Stevenson had delivered his great local influence in the Chicago mayoralty primary to help make Daley Mayor. But all spring Daley had been under the persuasion of Joseph P. Kennedy, whose real-estate interests in Chicago had given him a master's knowledge of Cook County politics. Would past gratitude to Stevenson or present inclination to Kennedy prevail in Daley's mind? Or had he already made up his mind? Illinois caucused on Sunday afternoon in secret, and when the door opened Mayor Daley announced that Illinois would vote fifty-nine and a half for Kennedy, two for Adlai Stevenson, one uncommitted, the balance for Stuart Symington. First blood for Kennedy.

Monday was Pennsylvania's day. Here, too, the drama centered in a single man. Pennsylvania's eighty-one votes lay, theoretically, at the disposal of Governor David L. Lawrence, a grizzled veteran of American politics who has made honorable transition from political boss to responsible public leader. The respect and affection that David Lawrence had paid Adlai E. Stevenson over the previous eight years had come close to public adoration; this affection still remained and all who dealt in national politics recognized it. Scrupulously respecting Lawrence's political authority inside Pennsylvania, as they had respected Williams' in Michigan, the Kennedy strategists had built no organization of their own inside Pennsylvania against its Governor. Yet in eastern Pennsylvania, Philadelphia's able Congressman William Green, boss of that city, had in early spring begun to mobilize delegate sentiment for Kennedy, and Lawrence could ignore neither Green's pressure nor the astounding, spontaneous Kennedy write-in vote in the Pennsylvania spring primary. Would Lawrence release his delegates to vote their conscience, thus splitting Pennsylvania's eighty-one votes ineffectually between Kennedy and Stevenson? Or would he, as an astute political leader, throw the full weight of Pennsylvania for maximum effect one way or the other—and which way?

Lawrence, a man of great honor, is one of the most silent leaders in American politics. On his arrival at the Los Angeles airport Saturday evening, July 9th, Lawrence had been met by John Bailey, who, offering the Pennsylvania Governor his car, had driven him directly to the Biltmore, all the while earnestly pressing the Kennedy cause on him. Bailey pressed on the Governor the candidate's invitation to private conversation at eleven the next morning. Kennedy and Lawrence conferred alone at the Biltmore for half an hour. No announcement was made. Quietly, late that night, David Lawrence drove all the way to the Beverly Hills Hotel, eight miles away, to visit Adlai Stevenson, the man he so admired, for a two-hour conversation that went on long after midnight. Still no announcement. Lawrence's decision was not to become public until Monday. And on Monday at 11:30, as the Pennsylvania caucus broke up in Pasadena, Governor Lawrence announced: Pennsylvania would vote sixty-four for Kennedy, eight for Stevenson, the rest being scattered. Now without doubt the Kennedy total was over 700 and victory was close enough to taste.

There remained only two major unknowns, Minnesota and California.

Minnesota had only thirty-one votes—but Minnesota's influence in the Convention was nationwide. Still floating through Los Angeles, still drifting and questioning, were perhaps several hundred delegates and alternates, heavy of conscience and burdened with citizen responsibility. For such people as these, the Minnesota delegation, conscience-heavy itself, could set an example. Hubert Humphrey had freed his state's delegates of all personal loyalty to him and urged them to vote their conscience. But what did conscience dictate? Was it Stevenson, whose international experience seemed best to meet the challenge of the headlines? Or was it Kennedy, who had taken his cause directly to the people and won in seven primaries across the country? Who was the best man? Should they listen to G. Mennen Williams, pleading the cause of Kennedy? Or Eleanor Roosevelt and Herbert Lehman, so vividly and evocatively pleading the cause of Stevenson? The Minnesotans caucused on Sunday and on Monday (twice) and on Tuesday (twice), and still they could not make up their minds. Symbolically, the high command of their hitherto united party split—Governor Orville Freeman[4] would nominate Kennedy, Junior Senator Eugene McCarthy would nominate Stevenson; and their leader, Hubert Humphrey, would make no decision at all.

By now, Tuesday, all Stevenson hopes focused on California; and California was even more confusingly divided than Minnesota. Over the long week end preceding the Convention, the control of Governor Edmund G. (Pat) Brown over his delegation had collapsed. A clumsy sequence of political blunders had in the course of the previous eighteen months already undermined the authority with which his 1958 elec-

[4] Now Secretary of Agriculture.

tion (by a million votes) had endowed him. Now, in Los Angeles, indecisive, vacillating, unsure of himself, torn between a pledge to Kennedy and a fondness for Stevenson, aware of several simultaneous revolts among the citizen Democrats who had planned and staffed his earlier electoral victories, Brown presided over a series of increasingly unstable California caucuses, until finally, on Tuesday evening, July 12th, California split wide open: thirty and a half for Kennedy, thirty-one and a half for Adlai E. Stevenson, the rest scattered. Now for the first time (although too late), the Stevenson forces had a cluster for maneuver; their belated, leaderless, but spectacular last-minute exertions had begun to pay off.

To see what their exertions had provoked and what had influenced the Californians, one had to withdraw from the Biltmore, from the hotel caucus rooms, and drive to the Sports Arena, where, on Monday evening, the Convention began. There, at the entrance to the new arena, glistening with its glass panes and ceramic tile, on the first day of ceremonies, it seemed that all the political oddities of Southern California had assembled to greet the delegates.

VOTE FOR PROHIBITION said one parader's placard; and he was followed by a lady with a banner demanding FREEDOM NOW. WARNING read one huge sign and continued THE WRATH OF GOD IS UPON US AS INDIVIDUALS AND AS A NATION UNTIL WE TURN FROM OUR SINFUL WAYS AND TO JESUS CHRIST AND THE BIBLE.

RELIEF FOR THE ISLE OF MAN read another sign, and ABOLISH THE WALTERS-MC CARRAN ACT read another.

BACK JACK said another sign; and DESEGREGATE NOW; IT'S ONLY JESUS THAT WILL SAVE US; NO MORE EXECUTIONS; WALK FOR LIFE.

The delegates and visitors filed in to the Arena through this outdoor reception, sat down, began to listen to the opening tattoo of oratory; then about an hour after the Convention began, all of us became aware of a rumble outside.

A brief investigation outside showed a total change of scenery there. The Convention hall was now ringed by an endless chain of people, yelling and chanting. Young and old, boy and girl, husband and wife, some wheeling babies in carriages, some in overalls, others in the business suits in which they had just left their offices, others in the loud violet, orange and floral sports shirts that Californians enjoy —all of them together were marching, close-locked, chanting, "We want Stevenson!! We want Stevenson! We want Stevenson! WE WANT STEVENSON!"

They carried a forest of banners: ADLAI IS A MORAL MAN; ADLAI IS A LOUSY GOLFER; A THINKING MAN'S CHOICE—STEVENSON!; WIN WITH ADLAI!; STICK WITH STEVENSON; NOTHING LESS THAN THE BEST—STEVENSON!; FACE THE MORAL CHALLENGE—STEVENSON; WE WANT STEVENSON!

This was more than a demonstration, it was an explosion. All that first evening the endless chain paraded around the Sports Arena; on the second day it had seemingly doubled in numbers. Frenzied, angry, yelling, screaming, the marchers shouted in thousands: WE WANT STEVENSON! WE WANT STEVENSON! And catching contagion from one another, feeling strong in numbers, they made the throb of their voices heard clearly inside the Convention hall itself.

To politicians, all people are votes. Were these people solid voters or were they Southern California crackpots? One could not tell by looking at them. The baby carriages, the children toddling, the old folks marching, these, certainly were Southern Californians—yet not crackpots. And the others, in their thousands, where did they come from? From how far away? What did they represent?

Monday had been Kennedy's day; Tuesday was Stevenson's day. California's delegation, shaken by the impact of the demonstration, had cracked under the pressure on Tuesday afternoon. And as the demonstrations grew outside the Biltmore now, in Pershing Square, outside Stevenson's new suite at the Sheraton-West—other delegations began to wonder. Governors Docking and Loveless (of Kansas and Iowa)[5] had promised their support to Kennedy over the week end; now, infected by the excitement of the Stevenson demonstrations, the Kansas and Iowa delegations revolted against their leadership; they would vote for their Governors on the first ballot whether their Governors wanted them to or not; they would hold the ring open and see.

Ever since his arrival on Saturday afternoon, the clamor and excitement of the Convention had been working on Adlai Stevenson, always a cool, stubborn and precise man. He had been shaken first on the Sunday morning after his arrival, when Tom Finney, the extraordinarily able and articulate executive assistant of Senator Monroney, had briefed him on the full range of operations being conducted at Los Angeles in support of his candidacy. Successively and hour by hour other old friends whom he had first brought into politics but

[5] Governor Loveless is now a member of the Renegotiation Board. Governor Docking is now a member of the Board of the Export-Import Bank.

who now marshaled independent political power pressed him to act. Over and over again neutral delegates as well as his own faithful waited for word of leadership from him, wondering whether finally he would say, "Yes, we march."

On Tuesday morning the troubled Minnesota delegation implored him to come and speak to their caucus. To Minnesota he yielded; he came to a caucus room full of delegates parched for leadership, ready to ignite, ready to break for him, and he spoke; yet he refused to summon them to follow. On Tuesday afternoon he decided to visit the Convention floor and take his seat as an Illinois delegate; galleries and delegates alike erupted in affection, their applause overwhelming him, their enthusiasm crushing him until he could be extricated and brought safely to the platform. Now, at midnight on Tuesday, his lieutenants assembled 250 delegates and alternates in the LaFayette Room of the Sheraton-West Hotel and insisted that Stevenson come down from his suite upstairs to address them. The following day was balloting day. The Kennedy leaders were insisting that they could win without the California vote; but the Stevenson leaders knew that beyond the thirty-three publicly announced California votes for Stevenson they held commitments for twelve more California votes, which they could trigger at will as switches after the first ballot—and the reserve twelve votes were not so important for their number as for the trend they could set in motion. Iowa, North Dakota, Alaska, were all unit-rule states that Kennedy held by half-vote margins. Kansas, too, was a unit-rule state. A switch of one or two votes within any of these delegations could switch an entire state's vote. Kansas and Iowa were already in revolt against their state leadership. North Dakota's delegates were convening that night in open split. Mountain delegates were said to be breaking one by one. A rump faction in New York State's delegation was meeting that night at the Ambassador to reconsider Stevenson's chances. Would Stevenson come, would he lead?

For the first time now, at one o'clock in the morning, Stevenson came down from his private suite to greet his followers new and old and consider his candidacy publicly. For the first time the old warmth came back into his voice as the emotions of the yearners reached and stirred this man who, knowing politics so precisely, understood their emotions so completely, and stood before them transfixed between reality and dream. He spoke briefly and movingly, but cryptically. He ended by observing that a previous speaker that evening had urged him to fix his wagon to a star, and this reminded him of a poem by Robert Frost; and so, as if he had made up his mind, he concluded he could stay no longer with them, for "The woods are lovely, dark and deep,/ But I have promises to keep,/ And miles to go before I sleep,/ And miles to go before I sleep." [6]

On this line Stevenson left, returning to his suite to ponder what he must do; and the Stevensonians felt that now, at last, it was possible that they would be led.

In the incubation of a Convention, rumors have the force of fact. On Monday the delegates had accepted as fact the rumor that Stevenson himself was about to nominate John F. Kennedy. On Wednesday, as they woke, they accepted as fact that Stevenson was running and had decided to fight for it. By four o'clock on Wednesday afternoon, July 13th, the endless chain of demonstrators about the Sports Arena had swollen into ranks of six and eight abreast as they chanted WE WANT STEVENSON. An evening paper now proclaimed in its banner headline: KENNEDY BANDWAGON FALTERS; and another: KENNEDY TIDE EBBS.

In the Convention hall, the nominations began, one after the other. With endless mechanical tedium and artificial demonstrations they went on and on, stretching the tension of boredom that begets excitement. One could see the galleries filling with Stevenson placards and Stevenson banners. Outside, the Los Angeles police called for reinforcements as the marching thousands of Stevensonians threatened to storm the Convention. Minute by minute one could detect a seepage through the barred gates, rising to flood. Observers speculated on how the Stevensonians were slipping their demonstrators into the hall, where every seat was numbered and ticketed; some charged forgery of tickets; others described an elaborate plot of ticket smuggling in and out of the hall. ("If we had packed the galleries by a dirty trick like this," growled a Kennedy man, "they would have said—Kennedy machine").[7] But the galleries were now quivering with impatient Stevensonians waiting to demonstrate.

Certainly the high point of drama in the Los Angeles Convention was the placing in nomination of Adlai E. Stevenson by Senator Eugene McCarthy of Minnesota. In magnificent

[6] This Robert Frost quotation is also a favorite of John F. Kennedy's, much quoted by him during his own campaign.

[7] The packing of the galleries by the Stevensonians was the result of sharp, well-planned organization. They had been allotted, prior to the Convention, only thirty-five tickets for all their cohorts. They had proceeded thus: first they solicited all members of the 750 Club (a Democratic money-raising device which promised two tickets to each con-

voice, holding the crowd with the rhythm of his cry, toying with the crowd, letting it respond when he asked questions, McCarthy pleaded for Adlai Stevenson. "Do not reject this man," he pleaded. "Do not reject this man who has made us all proud to be Democrats. Do not leave this prophet without honor in his own party."

It was a superb speech, flawed only by the logic that held it together. For McCarthy pleaded that these delegates set themselves free of their instructions, that they pause and reconsider before going on to vote their pledges. Yet Kennedy held honest title to these instructions from common voters in New Hampshire and Wisconsin, in West Virginia and in Maryland, in Oregon and Indiana. He had piped up control of these instructed delegates by his own voice and own effort, in village squares and school gymnasiums from one end of the nation to another. It was only after he had won confidence from the voters that he had turned East again to the big cities and, with the mandate of the primaries, clubbed the big-city bosses into submission. Only then had they become his allies here on the Convention floor—and, like defeated chieftains, his most solid allies. As Caesar, after he had conquered Gaul, used the Gallic cavalrymen to mop up Pompey in the ensuing civil wars of Rome, so now was Kennedy using the big-city bosses to mop up Stevenson.

This the delegates knew; but not the galleries. And as Eugene McCarthy concluded, the floor erupted. In from all the gates poured the demonstrators, snake-dancing, chanting, wriggling, yelling. Gold balloons burst from the ceiling and drifted over the mob, and the mob yelled: WE WANT STEVENSON. From all the galleries, paper banners unfurled, saying WE WANT STEVENSON. Now the chant became a drumbeat and the hall echoed rhythmically: WE WANT STEVENSON, WE WANT STEVENSON! The Convention floor was now so congested with people that no more could crowd in, and demonstrators in the packed galleries began subdemonstrations of their own, marching around and around the gallery rims, the thud and

---

tributor of $1,000) for their unwanted tickets and thus collected 1,000 free tickets; next, they pressed their friends on the host committee of the California Democratic Party to turn over most of their 1,000 tickets to them; finally, learning that the Kennedy organizers expected to draw 2,500 tickets from the regular machinery of the Convention, they had lined their own people up at the special distribution lines for these tickets, pinned on them large KENNEDY buttons, and claimed from the earmarked Kennedy supply an estimated 1,500 tickets as their own. The Stevenson people thus, on the night of the Convention's nomination, were in possession of almost 4,000 tickets to pack the galleries; which they did with lusty delight.

tramp of their feet picking up the chant: WE WANT STEVEN-SON. A huge papier-maché ball bounced, to the same rhythm, up and down over the sea of demonstrators. As they passed the state delegations, the Stevenson demonstrators tore loose the state standards at each delegation enclave, and now the California, the Nevada, the Montana standards bobbed in the tide on the floor, waving to the cadence of WE WANT STEVENSON. The chairman pleaded for order; McCarthy pleaded for order; the Convention band attempted to blare above their shouting; the lights were turned out; and still the chant went on: WE WANT STEVENSON.

A convention in American politics is very frequently a place where the naked act of history and decision takes place in public. In 1860, 1912, 1940 and 1952, American conventions, both Republican and Democratic, had seen such acts take place. Here now was the greatest and most authentic demonstration of emotion since the galleries of Philadelphia had overwhelmed the Republican delegates of 1940 with their chant of WE WANT WILLKIE. Yet if demonstration and noise alone can sway a national decision at a nerve center of national politics, then American politics would be reduced to that naked violence that has so frequently and tragically swayed the history of France and of Germany. To be effective, such a demonstration as the Los Angeles Convention was now witnessing must cap, not begin, a campaign that has long since previously established other bases of power. Of all the Stevensonians, Adlai E. Stevenson alone that afternoon probably knew this. For, late and tragically for his chances, Stevenson had, that morning, finally responded to the clamor for his leadership and had failed; and although his faithful on the Convention floor were unaware of it, the Stevenson campaign had ended some three hours before.

If there had been a moment during the entire season of 1960 when Stevenson had sought the Presidency of the United States, it had happened that morning. Waking early on Wednesday, after the turbulent demonstrations and late-night meeting of Tuesday, Stevenson had decided that if, against his will, he was to be propelled into active contention for the nomination, it should be done realistically. Distasteful as Stevenson finds sordid politics, he understands their mechanics as well as any man in American public life. To be realistic about it meant that on the Convention floor there must be one home base of strength actively pushing his nomination, fanning out its delegates to seek others, as the

Massachusetts men were fanning out to seek more strength for Kennedy.

This meant, then, that Stevenson must have his home base with him—Illinois. Which logic, in turn, led to Mayor Daley, his one-time friend. At some time on that Wednesday morning Stevenson had first lifted the telephone to reach Daley. All that morning Daley, with an instinct for the request that was coming, had dodged him. At one in the afternoon, Stevenson located his old friend, Jake Arvey, boss emeritus of Chicago. Arvey in turn found Daley on the floor of the Convention at four o'clock, as the nominations were beginning, and he insisted that Daley return Stevenson's call, a courtesy due their former leader. From the Convention hall Daley returned the call. To Daley, Stevenson said that he had heard the results of the Illinois caucus (Kennedy, 59½; Stevenson, 2) and wanted to let Daley know the following: that it was true that he had not sought the nomination; but he hoped he was not being passed over by a formula of words; he hoped the Illinois delegates' vote did not reflect a feeling that he, Stevenson, would not campaign against Richard M. Nixon wholeheartedly, with all the fire and courage he possessed; he pointed out that he was the first Illinoisan to be considered for the Presidency since Abraham Lincoln— to have won only two votes from his home state was a melancholy measure of his career. Daley, in haste and on the floor, informed Stevenson he had no support. Stevenson asked whether he had no support, period, or whether he had no support because it was the delegates' impression he was not a candidate. Daley replied that Stevenson had no support, period. He might have left it there. But he felt called on to add that Stevenson had had no support in Illinois' 1956 delegation either—and that he, Daley, had personally held it together for his former Governor.

With that the hope of a real Stevenson candidacy had ended, and the demonstration in the Sports Arena four hours later was meaningless. Those Stevenson demonstrators who left Los Angeles a few days later, left, some in sorrow and some in bitterness. Yet neither sorrow nor bitterness was warranted. Stevenson himself, as a man, was later to be given a role[8] to play in that field of power that he preferred above all others; and Stevenson as an agent of American politics had left behind him such an infection as no other defeated aspirant for the Presidency ever left. He had left behind the virus of morality in the bloodstream of both

---

[8] Stevenson is now United States Ambassador to the United Nations.

parties; there was a permanent monument to him in the behavior and attitudes of the victorious candidate; and also of his antagonists, the Republicans.

John F. Kennedy had risen that Wednesday morning in his secret hideaway on North Rossmore Boulevard, only slightly perturbed. He was fully aware of what was happening, for the Kennedy intelligence was sleepless. There had been a revolt against him in the North Dakota delegation the previous night. But all through the night brother-in-law Sargent Shriver had worked on the wavering North Dakota delegate whose half-vote carried the necessary majority to invoke the unit rule, and North Dakota's eleven votes were safe again.

That morning Kennedy breakfasted at North Rossmore alone with an old friend (David Powers of Boston), eating the breakfast he ate every morning—two four-minute eggs, a rasher of broiled bacon, orange juice and milk.

In room 8315 Bobby Kennedy had assembled the team of state-shepherds for the last time, and they had taken their last exact count of each state's vote. The reading that morning was 739½. New Jersey was still to caucus, and that meant that the command post had still to operate on New Jersey. Let Bob Meyner have his forty-one votes on the first ballot, but thereafter, on the switches after the first ballot, New Jersey must be broken open and the thirty Kennedy delegates there permitted to add their votes for the majority.

Still running hard (for John F. Kennedy is a man who runs all the way), the candidate addressed six more caucuses that Wednesday morning before returning to his hideaway at 3:30 in the afternoon, half an hour before nominations were to begin. When he arrived, the news media and television had finally discovered where he had been sojourning in secrecy for the previous four days, and he was ringed about. Privacy was over now, but the candidate wanted to swim and relax. With Powers, he slipped down the back fire escape of the apartment and leapfrogged over the back fence to escape the newspapermen guarding his front door. He drove directly to the Beverly Hills villa that his father had rented from Marion Davies and spent the rest of the afternoon there at the swimming pool, dining on Irish stew with his father, his mother, Dave Powers and his cousin, Anne Gargan.

When he returned to his apartment, still unobserved, at eight o'clock, the nominations at the Convention had already begun, and he picked up a copy of the tabloid his headquarters published daily and on its sample balloting sheet began to

mark the vote he expected from each of the fifty states of the
union. He had no need to refer to notes; he had them all in
memory, down to half-votes. He checked now by his special
phone with his brother Bobby, and found that his own final
tally matched Bobby's to the half-vote. According to Dave
Powers, he sipped a Coca-Cola, waited, fidgeted at the TV
set and then, as the TV set began to call the roll for balloting,
Kennedy began to mark.

"Alabama?"

"Alabama casts twenty votes for Johnson; Kennedy, three
and a half; Stevenson, one half; Symington, three and a
half."

At Illinois the candidate was over the 100 mark. With
Iowa, over the 200 mark; with his native Massachusetts, over
the 300 mark; just short of 500 with New York; and over the
650 mark with Pennsylvania. In each case the morning tally
of Room 8315 had been within two, three or four votes of
actuality, and always conservative, as it was now developing.
All along the way, as the Rocky Mountain states gave their
vote, the Johnson tally was one vote, two votes, three votes,
short of Johnson calculations. Earlier in the morning Bobby
had instructed the floor managers and shepherds to be ready
at the call of the state of Washington on the roster; if at
Washington in the alphabetical list the tally had passed 700,
one could hope that with a little extra pressure 761 would be
made before the alphabet was concluded. At Washington,
the count read 710; West Virginia was sure now for 15 to
make it 725, and Wisconsin with 23 to make it 748.

The candidate leaned forward—Wyoming, on the next
call, could make it. On the floor Bobby and Teddy were
equally alert, and the TV camera showed Teddy Kennedy
deep among the Wyoming delegates, whom he had cultivated
since the previous fall.

"This could do it," said the candidate to Powers who was
alone in the room with him; and this did it.

"Wyoming," chanted Tracy S. McCraken, Wyoming's national committeeman "casts all fifteen votes for the next
President of the United States."

And so it did, to make a total of 763; and the rest was
anticlimax.[9]

As Wyoming voted, the hall heaved. Without waiting for
the final tally to give Kennedy his closing 806, those who
knew their politics darted from the Arena to seek the man who

[9] The final tally of the first ballot at the Democratic National Convention of 1960 was: Kennedy, 806; Johnson, 409; Symington, 86;
Stevenson, 79½; all others put together, 140½.

was now the Democratic candidate for President of the United States.

Across the concrete rim of the Arena, from which in the past twenty minutes the Stevenson chain had disappeared as if by a witch's malediction, was the cottage that held the Kennedy communications post, linking the floor operators to the candidate in his hideaway. If he had any plan to come here this evening, it would be known first at the command post.

One by one, they slipped in with the jugular instinct of men who know the beat and pulse of power. John Bailey, bald and happy, was the first to arrive. He alone of the big-city bosses of the Northeast had been a loyalist of John F. Kennedy's troops before conscription. There arrived next the Governor of Ohio, Mike DiSalle, the first reluctant chief conscripted by Kennedy early in the winter. There arrived next Dick Daley, Mayor of Chicago, boss of Illinois Democrats. Then came two Pennsylvanians, Governor David L. Lawrence of Pennsylvania and Congressman William Green of Philadelphia. One by one they arrived; the word had now spread through the Convention hall that Kennedy would stop here for a moment of private greeting with the leadership before going to the rostrum of the Convention itself. To this correspondent, who watched them from a corner of the cottage living room, it seemed as if political types were evenly divided either into long-and-thin or short-and-stocky men. Daley, DiSalle, Lawrence, McCloskey, Prendergast, Green were the short and stocky. Averell Harriman of New York, G. Mennen Williams of Michigan, John McCormack of Boston were the tall and thin. Ribicoff of Connecticut, slender of build, darkly handsome as ever, an original loyalist, was an indeterminate type. Yet, collectively, long or short, they represented the system of power that policed the industrial civilization of Northeast America; nor had I ever observed so many of them, all shuffling restlessly in the same room, so strong yet so ill at ease. It was not a back room as I had imagined it; no one smoked cigars; no one drank hard liquor, for the Kennedys frown on hard liquor; only Coca-Cola and beer were available. Restlessly, the bosses waited.

In the tiny patio of the model cottage, by the tiny model swimming pool, three of them convened aimlessly—Bailey of Connecticut, DiSalle of Ohio and another. And then one of them, I cannot remember which, said, "There he comes now."

A hush fell on the trio. Far off in the distance they could see a winking row of red lights, pricking a serpentine across a Los Angeles Boulevard. All of them recognized the blinking, winking, ominously tantalizing, flashing train of light; for they were bosses, mayors, governors, masters of police themselves. This they recognized: it was a police cavalcade, bearing the possible next President of the United States from his hideaway to this cottage.

Kennedy loped into the cottage with his light, dancing step, as young and lithe as springtime, and called a greeting to those who stood in his way. Then he seemed to slip from them as he descended the steps of the split-level cottage to a corner where his brother Bobby and brother-in-law Sargent Shriver were chatting, waiting for him. The others in the room surged forward on impulse to join him. Then they halted. A distance of perhaps thirty feet separated them from him, but it was impassable. They stood apart, these older men of long-established power, and watched him. He turned after a few minutes, saw them watching him, and whispered to his brother-in-law. Shriver now crossed the separating space to invite them over. First Averell Harriman; then Dick Daley; then Mike DiSalle; then, one by one, in an order determined by the candidate's own instinct and judgment, he let them all congratulate him. Yet no one could pass the little open distance between him and them uninvited, because there was this thin separation about him, and the knowledge they were there not as his patrons but as his clients. They could come by invitation only, for this might be a President of the United States.

After a few moments of conversation it was time to go to the Convention hall, which an hour and a half before had thudded and pounded to the screaming of people who loved Stevenson.

Outside the cottage the instantaneous throng had gathered, the mob that always coagulates about power. The mob was thick over the few hundred feet from the cottage to the Convention, and it was conceivably dangerous, as all mobs are. The men in the cottage knew such mobs. All of them—mayors, governors, bosses—clustered together and formed a flanking escort about the candidate, led by the white-helmeted police of Los Angeles, to protect the nominee as they brought him to the Convention. By now many more had arrived, but all sensed their duty: the short—DiSalle (Ohio), Wagner (New York), Green (Philadelphia), Daley (Chicago)—and the tall—Harriman (New York), Williams (Michigan), McCormack (Boston)—followed by all the rest, put their heads down and squared their shoulders to plunge through the crowd and protect him, bowing, as it were, to another man and another era. No one of them, perhaps, could remember back to six months or a year ago, to the day when they had had other candidates, other dreams. Kennedy was now their candidate, he had compelled their loyalty; as he had compelled the loyalty of this Convention, which had no other choice.

He spoke to the Convention and returned briefly to the gathering, then went home to his North Rossmore apartment. There was to be no celebration; he was too tired. He asked Dave Powers to cook something, and Powers fried him two eggs in butter, offered him toast and jelly, and served him two glasses of milk, and the nominee went to bed.

I came back much later to the Biltmore. There, in the bar, the Convention crowd was drinking; all the lieutenants of the lost causes were relaxing in deep, almost uncontrollable, relief—as if passion had been spent, and now that it was over, this moment of release was permanent.

Then, in the early hours of the morning, I went upstairs, in the now empty elevator, to the 8300 Wing where I slept. There was one other man in the elevator with me, and since we did not know each other and I was tired, I said nothing but wondered where he was going. He came out on the eighth floor as I did and strode briskly down the corridor as I did; and as I opened my door I watched him knock on the door of 8315 very briskly, as if he belonged, and was not afraid to wake anyone. A very sleepy and tired Bobby Kennedy opened the door, blinked, and let the guest in. It was James Roosevelt, son of Franklin D. Roosevelt, who had come to pass on whatever words were important at that moment between the family of one President and one generation, and the family of another. It seemed altogether appropriate. The door closed.

The true story of the choice of Lyndon B. Johnson for the Vice-Presidency of the United States must remain an exercise for tomorrow's historians, not for today's reporters. Time and years will eventually hammer the conflicting recollections of the participants into a commonly accepted truth, which will then become the final truth. For within days, indeed only hours, after the event, any one at the Biltmore Hotel in Los Angeles could have his choice of three or four certified versions of the transaction, all purporting to be the only truth, all interlocking, yet all conflicting.

Thursday, July 14th, the day after the nomination, was a day of weariness for the high command of the Democratic Party; and after principals, emissaries, intermediaries had climbed up and down the stairways of the Biltmore's top floors more times than they could remember, their recollections of their own roles blurred and faded in exhaustion and cross-purpose. What can be reconstructed now out of the contemporary recall of those present must be seen as a fog-shrouded range of facts in which occasionally one peak or another appears at a given hour of the day, but whose connection to the next peak of facts is obscured by the clouds in between. History is always best written generations after the event, when cloud, fact and memory have all fused into what can be accepted as truth, whether it be so or not.

When, at two o'clock in the morning of Thursday, after his nomination for the Presidency, John F. Kennedy returned to sleep at his North Rossmore apartment, he had left his lieutenants and back-room chieftains at the Arena cottage with the impression that the Vice-Presidency was a choice between only two men: Senator Henry M. Jackson of Washington and Senator Stuart Symington of Missouri. If the thought of Lyndon B. Johnson had crossed his mind before that moment or persisted in his mind that night, it was known to none of the big-city leaders. Many weeks earlier Kennedy had said, replying to a questioner, that if he could not be President himself he thought Lyndon B. Johnson better qualified for the Presidency than any other man he knew. But the poison of the spring contest for the nomination had so changed his mind later that his remarks about Johnson in the final pre-Convention weeks were of the same colorful bitterness as Johnson's remarks about him. And yet the underlying respect must have continued, for at the height of their clash in Los Angeles, on the Sunday before the Convention opened, Kennedy, seemingly idly, remarked to Washington publisher Philip Graham that if he thought Johnson would accept the Vice-Presidency he might offer it. Whether Kennedy expected the thought to be carried back to the Southerner is not known; but Graham, a man of great influence in Washington politics, is a trusted confidant of Johnson's, and by the next evening Johnson had been told of the feeler and, still in his prenomination anger, had answered with a single earthy expletive.

Yet in the small hours of Thursday morning after his nomination when Kennedy returned from the Convention to his North Rossmore apartment, he found that Johnson had sent the warmest and most cordial telegram of congratulations. It was cause for reflection. Until that moment Kennedy had accepted at face value Johnson's statement that he would never, never, *never* trade his Senatorial vote for the Vice-Presidential gavel. Was it possible that Johnson *was* now available for the second spot? And if so, was placing him there desirable? What Kennedy's reflections were that night he has not said—nor did he share them with his personal staff, all of whom supported other men for the Vice-Presidency. At eight the next morning, however, he telephoned the suite of Lyndon B. Johnson at the Biltmore, reached Johnson's wife, who waked her husband, and thereupon made an appointment to visit the Texas Senator in his suite.

By nine o'clock he had telephoned his brother Robert in Suite 8315 in the Biltmore, and a few minutes later, when press secretary Salinger and tactician Kenneth O'Donnell entered Bobby's room, they were immediately put to work on the simple arithmetic of electoral votes: add the votes of New England to the votes of the Solid South, and how many more would be needed to carry the election? I happened into Suite 8315 a few minutes thereafter, and the surprise of the occupants can be described as total.

The substance of the early-morning telephone call is a matter of conjecture, perhaps forgotten in the memories of the principals. Yet Johnson must have known what was coming. When I arrived in the Johnson suite at about 9:30, in the quiet that still prevailed before news of the Kennedy visit spread, I found a sleepy aide hurriedly dressing for the day's work. Of his own, the sleepy aide volunteered: Well, yes, he supposed Lyndon would take the Vice-Presidency if it came up—Lady Bird Johnson, the Texan's wife, felt that the Majority Leadership was too strenuous a job for a man who had had a heart attack; she felt the Vice-Presidency or the Presidency was a lot better. And besides, the Party needed Johnson on the ticket if they were going to carry anything in the South or Midwest.

The Majority Leader made a few telephone calls to close friends as he waited for Kennedy's arrival. One of them observed that his power would be far less as Vice-President than as Majority Leader; to which Johnson replied, "Power is where power goes." At any rate the Majority Leader was fully composed when the new leader of his party arrived at 10:15 to talk. Kennedy's recollection, a few weeks later, was that he had sounded out the Majority Leader as to his "availability" and that the Majority Leader allowed that he was available. The impression of the Kennedy staff on this day of action was that the subject of the Vice-Presidency came up almost casually in a general exchange of courtesies and political talk and that it was only during the course of the visit that Kennedy realized that the Majority Leader would enjoy a change in rank and status. "It was always anticipated," said one of the headquarters staff numbly at the end of Thursday's events when all was over, "that we'd offer Lyndon the nomination; what we never anticipated was that he'd accept."

Three floors of the Biltmore Hotel now witnessed a rump convention. One knot of the curious, of reporters, of television and radio men gathered in the 7300 Wing, outside Johnson's Suite 7334. Another group gathered in the 8300 Wing, about Suite 8315. And the third and largest mob gathered in the 9300 Wing, where in Suite 9333 John F. Kennedy now held personal court. By 10:45, when Kennedy had climbed back the two flights of stairs from the Johnson suite (having conferred briefly and alone with Sam Rayburn in the corridor on the way back), the day's pandemonium outside the Presidential suite had begun. In the narrow corridor outside 9333 were strung television cables, installations, power packs and cameras of the three major networks and several local stations; radio networks strung an independent vineyard of wires up and down the stairs; reporters pushed and pressed to get close to the Presidential door. Gradually, in the course of the day in the hot packed corridor, the press of human beings built up a sweat that hung like a meaty animal odor over the whole matter of choosing a Vice-President of the United States.

Now the leadership elements of the Democratic Party began to filter through the suite of the nominee in a parade that was to last the rest of the day, to assist him in making up their mind. First of the big-city leaders to arrive was David Lawrence of Pennsylvania. Following him came the New York crowd—Wagner, Harriman, DeSapio and Prendergast; then William Green of Philadelphia; then DiSalle of Ohio; then Bailey and Ribicoff of Connecticut; then all the others.

Most of these men—apparently led by the grave Lawrence, who swings the heaviest influence among them—thought that Johnson was a fine choice—fine for the country, even finer for the ticket.

But then followed the deputation of labor's leaders—Arthur Goldberg,[10] the most important labor lawyer in Washington, Alex Rose of the New York Liberal Party, Walter Reuther of the United Auto Workers. These men of labor violently

[10] Now Secretary of Labor.

and vehemently objected to Johnson; in their view the critical Negro vote of the North must not be alienated. The labor leaders agreed that it might be expedient, if Johnson seemed to want the Vice-Presidency, to make a *pro forma* offer of the post—but to word the offer so as to make its rejection almost certain. To this the nominee objected: if there was to be an offer of the Vice-Presidency, it must be a genuine offer, a real one, not a fake. Raising strenuous objections, the labor leaders withdrew to Walter Reuther's suite at the Hotel Statler-Hilton, and Kennedy said he would call them back by two o'clock. Meanwhile the two other minor candidates— Jackson and Symington—still waited for word of their fate; and leaders entering and emerging from the room baffled and confused all their questioners with their various interpretations of what was going on inside. Johnson was in; Johnson was out; Symington was in; Symington was out; Jackson had it; Jackson did not have it.

What was happening in the Presidential suite was that two of the three major elements of the Democratic Party—labor and big-city leaders—had come into direct collision.

The third major element of the Democratic Party—the Southern element—swirled about the Johnson headquarters in the 7300 Wing. Here, as the perplexed Majority Leader of the Senate listened to his Southern friends, he found counsel equally divided. Some insisted with absolute violence that for Johnson to run on such a ticket of civil rights and Catholicism would be treason to the Old South; others insisted just as vehemently that he must take it—the Southern branch of the Party could not be left without a voice in the executive arm of government. At one point, it is reported, Johnson put through a call to John Nance Garner, another Texan who had been chosen as running mate to another Harvard man almost thirty years before in just such circumstances. "I'll tell you, Lyndon," the Sage of Uvalde is reported to have remarked to his perplexed fellow Texan, "the Vice-Presidency isn't worth a pitcher of warm spit."

Early in the afternoon the scene in the Johnson suite had reached absolute confusion. Bobby Kennedy and Kenneth O'Donnell had descended from Suite 8315 to review matters with Speaker Rayburn, Johnson-adviser Jim Rowe, publisher Graham, and other members of the Johnson inner council and to describe to them the split between big-city and labor leaders upstairs—along with the danger that this split might lead to a violent floor fight over the Vice-Presidential nomination itself. While these men conferred in the Johnson suite, and the telephone rang and Graham, reaching Kennedy directly, urged that Kennedy now make the offer hard by a direct call from the nominee to the perplexed Majority Leader, every possible pro and con was thrashed out. And while they continued thrashing out whether or not it was wise to risk a floor fight, the nominee telephoned Johnson directly and Johnson, sitting on the bed in his inner bedroom, listened to a draft statement announcing his choice; he asked whether Kennedy *really* wanted him or not, and when the Presidential nominee informed him that he really did, Johnson agreed to accept, floor fight or not; then he emerged on the scene of conference in the other room with his decision made.

Upstairs, however, matters had to be tidied up. The big-city leaders considered again the report of Lyndon's willingness to fight and the threat of a split with labor. It is axiomatic in the Democratic Party that when any two of its three major components (the South, the big-city leaders, labor) choose to gang up on the third or any other of the fractional elements of the Party, the two-thirds decision prevails. It was obvious to the big-city men that the AFL-CIO leadership would not endorse Richard Nixon, the probable Republican nominee. Where could labor go if not to Kennedy and whatever running mate he chose? It was obvious, further, that an offended and sullen Lyndon Johnson, teamed with Sam Rayburn, could make of the forthcoming summer Congress session a trap in which Jack Kennedy could be destroyed.

And besides, the big-city men liked Johnson; they do not, as a group, like big labor leaders except for the money they provide in campaigns. One big-city leader offered the thought that labor always talked big—but when it came to delivery, labor never really could deliver votes at the polls. Furthermore, not all of labor's leaders were united. David MacDonald of the Steelworkers Union favored Johnson too.

Shortly after three it was decided in the Presidential suite, finally, that Lyndon B. Johnson was to be nominee for Vice-President. There remained then the amenities of informing all the other disappointed aspirants for the job. Kennedy now managed to clear his room. (At the same time the Police and Fire Departments of Los Angeles were clearing the repertorial herd and the television equipment from the stinking corridor outside the door; the security officers had finally decided that there was danger of both fire and floor collapse.)

The nominee dictated to one of his press secretaries, Charles Roche, the final draft of an announcement of Johnson's selection; as soon as it was typed he read it over the telephone to the Majority Leader; he passed it on for release as soon as it was approved; he announced a press conference for 4:30. And with that the politics of the Vice-Presidential nominating process had come to their end.

There remained now only the Friday ceremony of acceptance; and the balmy weather of Los Angeles held perfect as it had for the previous fortnight. John F. Kennedy sat on the platform, surrounded by mother and sisters, flanked by all the men he had defeated—Humphrey and Symington, Johnson and Stevenson. As the sun set he spoke, facing the west, to eighty thousand in the Los Angeles Coliseum. His face was tired and haggard from a year of strain and a week of sleeplessness, his voice was high and sad.

. . . I think the American people expect more from us than cries of indignation and attack. The times are too grave, the challenge too urgent, the stakes too high to permit the customary passions of political debate. We are not here to curse the darkness, but to light the candle that can guide us through that darkness to a safe and sane future. As Winston Churchill said on taking office some twenty years ago: if we open a quarrel between the present and the past, we shall be in danger of losing the future. . . . Today our concern must be with that future. For the world is changing. The old era is ending. The old ways will not do. . . .
. . . The problems are not all solved and the battles are not all won—and we stand today on the edge of a New Frontier—the frontier of the 1960's—a frontier of unknown opportunities and perils—a frontier of unfulfilled hopes and threats.
Woodrow Wilson's New Freedom promised our nation a new political and economic framework. Franklin Roosevelt's New Deal promised security and succor to those in need. But the New Frontier of which I speak is not a set of promises—it is a set of challenges. It sums up, not what I intend to offer the American people, but what I intend to ask of them. It appeals to their pride, not their pocketbook—it holds out the promise of more sacrifice instead of more security. . . .
Can a nation organized and governed such as ours endure? That is the real question. Have we the nerve and the will? Can we carry through in an age where we will witness not only new breakthroughs in weapons of destruction—but also

a race for mastery of the sky and the rain, the ocean and the tides, the far side of space and the inside of men's minds. . . .

It has been a long road . . . to this crowded convention city. Now begins another long journey, taking me into your cities and homes all over America. Give me your help,
　　[and the crowd cheered]
　　give me your hand,
　　—[and it cheered again,]
　　your voice and your vote.
　　[And it stood and cheered and cheered on]

Thirty-five million Americans watched on their television sets as John F. Kennedy accepted the call of his party in Los Angeles that Friday evening.

Two groups among them are worthy of note.

Across the continent, in Washington, D.C., Vice-President Richard M. Nixon had decided that the time had come for him to watch his rival in action on the television screen. He therefore invited two intimates of his campaign to his home to watch and measure the performance of the enemy. They sat rapt, then content, then pleased. The rapid delivery, the literary language, the obvious exhaustion of the Democratic candidate, the mechanical flaws inherent in an open-air telecast from a camera one hundred feet away in uncontrolled conditions, all combined to invite in them a sense of combative good feeling. The Vice-President offered the observation that he thought it a poor performance, way over people's heads, too fast. He could take this man on TV—so he felt. Already the Republican and Democratic parties had been exchanging an interfire of telegrams over a proposal for a series of national TV debates between the candidates. The Vice-President, according to those who discussed it with him, was now unworried by the tired image on the screen before him that night; he could not foresee what time, illness and strain would do to his own image on such a screen in the fall; he looked forward to the meeting.

The other noteworthy TV viewing group met in New York. All that week Joseph P. Kennedy had secluded himself in the villa of Marion Davies in Beverly Hills, screened from the public eye, as he had always sought to be during the long year. Yet Joseph P. Kennedy had labored hard in his privacy and through his purposeful channels: it was he who had master-minded the coup of delegates in New York City; he who had organized the north New Jersey delegates out from under Governor Robert Meyner, thereby engendering the continuing Kennedy-Meyner bitterness; he who had been most influential in bringing Dick Daley of Chicago into camp and thus also the votes of Illinois. Now with the first phase of the campaign over, the restless one-time Ambassador did not propose to stay in Los Angeles to witness his son's acceptance of nomination; he wanted no eye distracted from his son's moment of honor. Joseph P. Kennedy that Friday morning flew from Los Angeles to New York. Arriving in New York late in the evening, yet presumably not wanting to waste his time viewing the nomination on a TV screen in solitude, he telephoned the home of Henry R. Luce, publisher of *Time, Life* and *Fortune.* Henry Luce was dining alone with his son that evening and courteously invited the father of the Democratic nominee to join them and watch the telecast. There, in an atmosphere of warmth and good fellowship, in the company of the single most powerful influence on the minds and opinions of America, Joseph P. Kennedy watched his son accept his nomination and launch *his* contest for the American mind and American loyalties.

On Saturday morning, July 17th, the candidate held a press conference in Los Angeles and announced the nomination of his National Chairman, Senator Henry M. Jackson. He went swimming in the afternoon. The next morning, candidate, brothers, sisters, children, staff, newspapermen, all took off by chartered plane for a long-awaited Hyannisport vacation.

By Sunday the staff of the Biltmore Hotel had begun to dismantle the many headquarters strewn through its corridors and rooms. By Sunday evening the crowded, partitioned press bowl had again become a supper club. By Monday the last strands of TV cables, cord, and electronic ganglia had been removed. On Monday morning a crew of painters moved into Suite 8315. Furniture, carpets, telephones were all removed as the painters redecorated Suite 8315 to remove the smoke, grime and dirt it had acquired in its few short weeks of drama and purpose. By the next morning, completely repainted, decked out with new rugs and furniture, Suite 8315 was just another four-room suite in a hotel of hundreds of such rooms. The floral carpeting had been scrubbed and vacuum-cleaned all down the corridor; the 8300 Wing was whisperingly empty in midsummer Los Angeles. From Room 9333 all the way to the basement bowl, the hotel was hollow;

traveling salesmen and passing tourists rattled about in emptiness. There are no Smolny Institutes or Rue des Jacobins remembered in the political history of Americans—only hotel rooms.

Chapter 7

THE REPUBLICANS:
FROM THE SUMMIT
TO CHICAGO

THE MOST hopeful adage of political folklore is: "One man plus the truth makes a majority."

Never, however, has this adage been more strenuously tested by one man than by Nelson A. Rockefeller in the twelve weeks between the shooting down of America's U-2 and the choosing of Richard M. Nixon as Presidential nominee on July 27th at the Republican Convention.

For the impact of events abroad on the Democratic Party was as nothing compared to the explosion they provoked within the Republican Party—an explosion that rose from Nelson A. Rockefeller's sole conviction that disaster had now amplified his truths enough to shake a majority of his Party.

For Rockefeller, the winter and spring of 1960 had been months of hard work. Publicly he had thrust the Presidency from his ambitions. His new tax program in New York State, criticized by Democrats yet respected by all, was not only a monument of fiscal rectitude and responsibility but magnificently successful. Almost embarrassed by a new surplus, the state government could now finance a whole variety of programs, and with great zest Rockefeller proceeded to give New York an administration that, if not creative, was nevertheless the most spankingly efficient and warm-hearted since that of Herbert Lehman sixteen years before. If it was not creative (as it was not), it was because events in Washington and abroad continued to obsess Rockefeller's private imagination. All along, as we have seen, since his December withdrawal, he had planned to raise the alarm on America's drift in national defense and in foreign policy. But from January into May events imposed a gag on him—a summit conference of the American President and the Russian Premier was scheduled for mid-May, at which they would discuss world affairs, war and peace. It was impossible for Rockefeller to attack the administration of his Party at a moment when its President was approaching negotiations of such importance and delicacy. So, privately, he brooded with as much sullenness as his happy character can effect.

This sullenness disturbed Republican headquarters and Mr. Nixon. On May 1st Nixon leaked to the national press that Rockefeller was his personal choice for Vice-President in 1960. Rockefeller publicly spurned the offer. That same week the Republican National Committee offered Mr. Rockefeller his choice: he could be either chairman or keynoter of the National Convention. Mr. Rockefeller responded that he did not plan even to attend their Convention.

And then came the U-2, and thereafter the Summit and disaster. Mr. Rockefeller's mood began to change; he was free now to speak.

In mid-May a seemingly casual announcement was made by L. Judson Morhouse—Republican State Chairman of New York, one of Rockefeller's closest lieutenants—that the Governor of New York might conceivably be available for a Presidential draft. Events abroad moved faster, more ominously; Mr. Khrushchev rattled the headlines day after day; Mr. Castro in Cuba was entering a manic phase; Turkey, Korea, Japan, sputtered with street riots and violence.

From his offices on Fifty-fifth Street, Rockefeller declared that the United States and the Republican Party must openly and frankly debate all the events leading to and following from the collapse of the Summit. Two days later, in Albany, at a meeting of the State Republican Executive Committee, Governor Rockefeller acknowledged he was indeed open to draft to meet the national crisis; his lieutenants proceeded to freeze the New York State delegation to the Chicago Convention in an uncommitted posture; Rockefeller avowed he might now possibly attend the National Convention as his delegation's leader.

One must understand the attitude of the Rockefeller family toward public affairs to understand the nature of the drive that now began.

To a Rockefeller, all things are possible. This is a family that examines New York City, decides to clear a midtown slum and then erects the greatest executive building complex in the world; it examines a rotting tenement area and decides it must be abolished and begins there to realize such a dream as the Lincoln Center of the Performing Arts, designed to be the most fantastic monument of man's spirit since Athens; it decides that the congestion of Wall Street threatens to blight the world's financial center, clears five acres for greensward and building in a plaza larger than Piazza San Marco in Venice, and blows fresh air through the canyons of Manhattan. Whether in missiles, electronics, real estate, oil or Latin-American investments, when the Rockefellers decree, that which they decree comes to pass. This sense of public power, moreover, has always been accompanied by a strange, pietistic sense of responsibility. Universities, museums, foundations, all have flourished when the Rockefeller taste or conscience has been touched; let Americans witness modern art, decrees their taste—and the Museum of Modern Art comes into being; let American medical education be reorganized—and so it is; let malaria be abolished—and research scientists of the Rockefeller Foundation move to the assault. Let housing be built in Puerto Rico —let the Negroes of Alabama be educated—let this happen, let that happen, and where imagination sees opportunity the Rockefellers, if they agree, cause it to happen. Their attitude to America as a whole is not a patronizing one; rather, America is their patrimony. Their stupendous fortune—estimated now at between three and six billion dollars—is so vast that it is affected by every rustling and turning of America's mood and destiny. They are so big they cannot help being concerned by all America's problems. Whatever happens, it must touch on a Rockefeller interest, either financial or philanthropic, somewhere on the national scene.

Since 1880 the Rockefellers have, quietly and discreetly, been in everything—oil, steel, art, the market, science, missiles, the Congo, medicine, real estate, banking, education. Only two areas of American life were ruled out, by common family consent, from Rockefeller activity. The first was any investment or exertion in communications (that mesh of radio, TV, newspapers, magazines and publishing in which so many rich families love to dabble); the second was politics. Public service was always to be performed privately, out of the public eye; political activity was limited (since the early brutally corrupt practices of the original John D. Rockefeller, founder of Standard Oil) to the discreet financing of the Republican Party nationally and, in New York, locally.

Nelson Rockefeller ruptured this family tradition as early as 1940, when the war emergency encouraged him to accept Franklin D. Roosevelt's offer to be Coordinator for Inter-American Affairs. He later served as a special adviser on international affairs for Harry Truman. He had further served the Republican administration of Dwight D. Eisenhower, until he became frustrated and disenchanted. He then entered the electoral lists as a contending politician and won the Governorship of New York. But he still retained, even in politics, the family tradition of piety, enlivened by the family sense that all things are possible. In all his private conversations there was an attitude to government occasionally so naive as to touch on the absurd—yet now he was Governor of New York, most populous state in the Union.

I had had occasion to enjoy several rambling talks with Rockefeller in his gubernatorial campaign of 1958. I must paraphrase from memory his remarks then, but there ran through them all one theme: here was this country, in this world, both of them growing increasingly complicated—science coming along, administration becoming more complex, technologies changing our way of life and our security. Could democracy in its old-fashioned way master all these things? Would our political system work in the face of these challenges? This "wonderful system of ours" (his phrase), could it rise to the challenge?

One can only assume that now, at the end of May, 1960, as the international problems of America grew more complex, these personal attitudes had become more intense. Nelson Rockefeller had brooded for several years over the whole range of American problems, establishing as a philanthropist, all manner of study groups to report on American problems, none spectacularly brilliant or creative, but all of them well-informed and studious. Of all the nation's problems, however, one had become an obsession with him: the interlocked perils of defense and foreign policy. He had come to believe so violently that America lived in imminent danger of destruction, that the security of America was being clipped to America's purse rather than the purse being stretched to provide security, that his position had become one of the far extreme. He was obsessed with the thought that the years 1961 through 1964, the years of the impending missile gap, were years of instant national emergency. And now, in May of 1960, the disarmament conferences with Russia were breaking down in Geneva; and from Africa through Asia, from Paris to Peking, America's position was crumbling.

All these matters, presumably, as well as the qualities of Richard M. Nixon, were discussed at his long conference with his chief thinker, Emmet Hughes, on Memorial Day, May 30th, 1960, at the imperial Rockefeller estate in Tarrytown, New York. And from this conference emerged the Rockefeller decision to assault—an assault on American complacency. If Messrs. Eisenhower and Nixon were hurt in the process, so be it. From this decision, eight days later, came his famous pronunciamento of June 8th.

Few American campaign documents in a Presidential election have ever been more sincere, more straightforward—or more apparently naive. It was pointed out to him by George Hinman that the statement would make his nomination impossible. "That's irrelevant," replied Rockefeller and went on to release it to the press.

> I am deeply convinced [said the Rockefeller statement] and deeply concerned that those now assuming control of the Republican Party have failed to make clear where this party is heading and where it proposes to lead the nation. Now is the time to face and weigh these facts. . . . A new period now begins, it summons new men. New problems demand new ideas, new actions. . . .
> I cannot pretend to believe that the Republican Party has fully met this duty. I know it is unconventional—on the political scene—to mention lack or lapses in one's own party. But the times we live in are not conventional. And the scene we must view is not simply one of partisan politics, but the politics—perhaps the destiny—of all the world. This is not extreme, it is merely realistic.
> In this spirit, I am compelled to say two things bluntly. One: I find it unreasonable—in these times—that the leading Republican candidate for the Presidential nomination has firmly insisted upon making known his program and his policies, not before, but only after nomination by his party. Two: I find it reasonable—and urgently necessary—that the new spokesmen of the Republican Party declare now, and not at some later date, precisely what they believe and what they propose, to meet the great matters before the nation . . .
> I can no longer be silent on the fact. We cannot, as a nation or as a party, proceed—nor should anyone presume to ask us to proceed—to march to meet the future with a banner aloft whose only emblem is a question mark . . .

There followed a nine-point program, hard and specific, calling for actions of foreign, military and domestic nature repudiating the entire policy of the Eisenhower administration, and the statement closed:

> The people, I am convinced, are ready. The question remains: Is the party ready? The path of great leadership does not lie along the top of a fence. It climbs heights. It speaks truths. The people want one thing above all others— leadership of clear purpose, candidly proclaimed.

With this, the old civil war between citizens and regulars in the Republican Party was opened anew, and for the next five weeks the Republican Party resounded to the crash of Rockefeller artillery as, from every encampment, from New

York (upstate and downstate), from Washington, from Chicago, from North Dakota, from Montana, wherever he happened to be, Nelson Rockefeller loosed his salvos. The collection of nine major documents[1] that he delivered in addition to his many radio, TV and ordinary appearances between June 1st, 1960 and July 19th is one of the most remarkable collections of political documents in American campaign history. What the documents all added up to, however, was open warfare with the leadership of his own Party and implicit denunciation of its conduct of national affairs over the past eight years. Rockefeller regarded Democratic leadership with equal contempt and bitterness and so stated explicitly; but the Republican Party was his battleground, and there he fought.

Whether or not Nelson A. Rockefeller really believed at this time that he might win, thus belatedly, a Presidential nomination, as had Wendell Willkie in 1940 and Adlai Stevenson in 1952, is still a matter of debate among his closest advisers. Most insist that he realized (or they realized) from the very beginning that Nixon's grip on the nominating process was unbreakable; most insist, further, that the Rockefeller purpose from the very beginning was only to arouse concern and serious consideration for platform and program. One of them said to me at this time: "It's impossible. Everyone knows it's impossible. Maybe only Nelson, when he's alone by himself in his shower in the morning, lets himself dream that he can be President this year; but, anyway, if he has got a chance to be President, he isn't hurting it any by attacking on the platform first."

What went on in Rockefeller's own mind must remain forever a matter of speculation. In early July, in his fantastically busy activities of assault, I managed to pause with him for a few brief minutes and ask him then how he, with such a program, could manage to govern across the grain of his Party. He responded crisply: "I have to get my hands on the decision-making apparatus," and went on to describe in detail what he had, in the previous eighteen months as Governor, actually managed to achieve across the grain of the Party in the New York Legislature, dominated by upstate Republicans of the old regular wing. Yet he would not say

---

[1] The documents, all of them study papers hard in proposal, specific in fact, covered: American economic growth, civil rights, foreign affairs, national defense, government reorganization, health care for the aged, disarmament and arms control, education, Latin-American unity and a general summation prepared for the Republican Party Platform.

whether he was, formally, running for the Presidency or not.

Whatever it was he meant to do—to become President, or mobilize the Republican Party for international emergency—it was clear, however, that his only leverage in either case lay in ideas. With these he must win or lose, and in playing out his course over the July weeks, stretching the strength of his ideas to the peril point, he was illustrating another grand theme of American politics. European social scientists, familiar with the European political parties, frozen in their intellectual dogmas, like to see American political parties as entirely pragmatic and barren of ideas. It is true that almost any British, French, German or Italian politician can ideologize in his party's tradition in the flossiest intellectual terms; but these ideologies have long since become sterile and only a substitute for live thought. In American politics, a good set of fresh ideas can sweep through the nation like a gale, shaking people and party alike until the once fresh ideas, too, become dogma and die.

Now in June and July the ideas of Rockefeller began to beget in the Republican Party a ferment similar to that which the Stevenson ideas, amplified by the same international crisis, were achieving on the Democratic side; and that yearning of citizens to participate in politics that comes to crest every four years began to work on the Republican side.

To see what happened in the reverberation of the Rockefeller uprising, it is perhaps wisest to shift across the continent to the office of a young lawyer, named William M. Brinton, in San Francisco on a hill overlooking the Golden Gate, the great Bay and the rocky island of Alcatraz. Brinton was one of those young men (again of the war veteran generation) who, like John Sharon on the Stevenson side, believed that citizens can be organized to be heard. He had in the summer of 1959 organized the first Citizens for Rockefeller organizations in California, set up the first radio programs supporting Rockefeller (paid for out of listeners' contributions) and was approaching a smooth-working national net of Citizens for Rockefeller when, in December of 1959, Rockefeller's withdrawal from the race had pulled the rug out from under him. Now, however, in the spring of 1960, as the sounds of storm and strife resounded from the East, he reacted like a Lexington minuteman to the bell and call of Paul Revere. (To arms, to arms, the British are coming.)

The Rockefeller blast of June 8th was released on Wednesday, the day after the California primary. Brinton and his friends had test-flown Rockefeller, without his consent, in the primary, and in four metropolitan areas (San Diego,

Los Angeles, San Francisco and Sacramento) they had urged all those who preferred Rockefeller to cut Nixon on the primary ballot. Analyzing the vote, the Brinton headquarters concluded that no less than 18 per cent of the hard-core Republicans who had voted in the primary had heeded their instructions and cut Nixon for Rockefeller. Now, with the June 8th blast and the fusillade of following statements, Rockefeller was in the open as a moving force.

On June 27th, Brinton flew from San Francisco to New York to plead with the Rockefeller staff that he be allowed to set up a national Draft Rockefeller movement. On June 28th, the Rockefeller high command said he might go ahead—but with no formal authority from them. On June 29th, before flying home, Brinton telephoned his friends in San Francisco to establish National Draft Rockefeller headquarters in his offices. By July 8th, a newspaper advertisement seeking support had appeared in twenty-nine newspapers in twenty-one states where Citizens for Rockefeller headquarters had been reactivated. A paid public-relations analysis had told Brinton to expect some 16,000 responses. Before the Democratic Convention opened on July 11th, he had received some 40,000 replies. Now he was financed with contributions and was in business.

It was too late, however, to organize the personal pilgrimages and pressures that the Stevenson volunteers had arranged for their man in Los Angeles. On July 18th Brinton transferred his operation from San Francisco to the Conrad Hilton Hotel in Chicago to invoke another type of pressure. Now, with yet another round of national newspaper advertisements, with yet another volley of national TV spot appeals, Brinton demanded that Republicans everywhere write, wire, telephone their delegations in Chicago to press for a Rockefeller nomination.

And press they did. Although the physical Rockefeller demonstrations in Chicago were thin and unimpressive by the standards set by the Stevensonians in Los Angeles, what the Citizens for Rockefeller did achieve in the last week end before the convention was, in its own terms, a spectacular demonstration of what the citizen spirit can evoke. Within twenty-four hours of the week-end TV appeal, 260,000 pieces of mail had arrived at the Chicago Convention, accompanied by an outpouring of telephone calls and telegrams of unprecedented volume. Within fifty-six hours after the appearance of the advertisements, more than a million pieces of mail and telegrams poured into the hotels, special post offices and Convention facilities, to swamp mail delivery, so that by Wednesday of the Convention some hotels were still sorting mail forty-eight hours late.

To Brinton and his earnest volunteers, now headquartered in the Conrad Hilton Hotel, with a base camp across the street in the Blackstone Theater, with five independent national Rockefeller for President organizations finally coordinated in one effort, it seemed momentarily possible to shake the Convention. Said one of the midwestern Rockefeller leaders, a patent developer and sober businessman: "When the Taft people came here in 1952, they marched their 532 delegates to the Convention on opening day singing 'Onward Christian Soldiers'—we've got to do the same thing."

But volunteers and citizens' groups are the guerilla forces of American national politics, a maquis that becomes effective only when a regular army already in being has engaged the enemy while the guerilla volunteers rip at his rear and roots. And already by the time the flood of mail and pressure was reaching its peak, the regular army that the Rockefeller volunteers hoped to support had fought its climactic engagement with the enemy and made its armistice in a silent clash by night. Outside in the streets, in the hotels, at the Convention hall, in the stockyards, the Rockefeller volunteers sang, pinned buttons on passersby, yelled and cheered, and it seemed they were participating in a Convention. But the real Convention, the deciding Convention, had already met and all but concluded its work before the gavel pounded and called the public Convention to order.

If conventions epitomize the mythology and legendry of American national politics, then Chicago epitomizes the convention city. For one hundred years, ever since the nomination of Abraham Lincoln at the Wigwam, it has been the favorite city of political convention-goers. Counting notches for fourteen Republican and nine Democratic national conventions in the last twenty-five quadrennials, Chicago can boast that here were first named all the following Presidents of the United States: Lincoln, Grant, Garfield, Cleveland, Harrison, Theodore Roosevelt, Harding, Coolidge, Franklin D. Roosevelt, Truman and Eisenhower.

Knowledgeable and experienced in handling hordes of visitors, Chicago loves conventions. When conventions assemble, the police hack bureau orders all taxi drives to don clean white shirts. The sanitation department strings the core of the convention area with gaily colored special litter baskets. The motorcycle police are mobilized and Lake Shore

Drive swept of traffic whenever any candidate wants his parade. The night clubs are ready and their prices rise, as from simple beanery to the awful splendor of the Pump Room the bonifaces prepare to feed the visitors. Most of all, there are hotels—hundreds and hundreds of them for every purse and taste, squeezed and crowded one next to the other between the Loop and the lake front, prepared to handle any conceivable problem of housing and accommodation. And as the delegates (2,600-odd delegates and alternates with 1,331 votes attended the Republican Convention of 1960) gather in these hotels, they squeeze together, meet each other, interlock and interweave, all in this tiny area by the lakeside, until they boil up at the center point, the junction of Michigan Avenue and Balbo, where all traffic stops between the Blackstone Hotel on the north and the Conrad Hilton on the south.

Every convention in American political history, since the first invention of the device by the Anti-Mason Party in 1832, has been not just one convention but a constellation of little conventions. The unifying embrace of the Convention hall, the balloting process, the summary of the proceedings in later historical records all combine to hide this multiplicity of lesser conventions within the greater convention, but it is of the essence. America is so huge that, to function politically and effectively, leadership groups of strange states simply must learn to recognize each other. Thus, as a convention jells, a score of smaller conventions go on within its larger framework. Individual state delegates caucus first, by state, and here, in strange cities far from home, the delegates of individual states come to know each other best because they share an adventure. Farm states caucus individually, then together; labor-union delegates from all the states gather to discuss where their common pressure can be best exercised; Negro delegates seek one another out to make a common front. In the Democratic conventions, always, delegates of the Southern states rediscover their lost Confederacy and at these four-year reunions, recognizing how numerous they are again, they believe Dixie is to be reborn, and they develop an illusion of their own strength (as did the Johnson troops at Los Angeles) for several days until balloting begins.

Conventions and caucuses—like primaries—are uniquely American political institutions; had they not been invented 130 years ago, they would have to be invented now. Yet it is good that they happen only once in four years, for the strain and tension they engender, the bitterness and hates and ambitions they incubate, require months and years to soothe away. Nor can a nation bear to see the raw nerve ends of its political leaders so publicly exposed, their ambitions and pettiness so nakedly shown, more than once in four years. In France, under the much-maligned Fourth Republic, cabinet crises (which are the equivalent of American political conventions) took place on an average of three or four a year. The strain on the nervous system of France was so great that all the Fourth Republic's magnificent achievements of reconstruction, all its sweetly benevolent tolerance of human frailty and dignity, were obscured, and the French abolished the Fourth Republic in 1958 because they had had too much of conventioneering. Such strains and such spurting of ambitions operate constantly in every American national convention—only, at Chicago, more so.

In the past generation, conventions have, so say the veterans, slowly been changing. Partly it is because the ever-greater citizen participation in politics produces more and more citizen delegates and fewer and fewer of the sheeplike masses herded at will by delegate bosses. The Blackstone Hotel in Chicago still boasts of the famous "smoke-filled room" (Suite 408–409–410) in which the bosses chose Warren Gamaliel Harding to be President of the United States; but the "smoke-filled room" as political reality is now as dead as Prohibition. Conventions are now less bluntly controlled by bosses, and more sharply controlled by techniques and forces set in motion outside the convention city itself.

Partly, too, the change is due to the intrusion of television on the convention. The audience of the convention has now expanded from the 12,000 in the hall to the 100,000,000 Americans who witnessed on television all or part of both national conventions in 1960. Under the pressure of so huge a citizen audience, under the discipline of the camera, conventions are held more tightly to schedule, their times adjusted for maximum viewing opportunities, their procedure streamlined, not for the convenience or entertainment of the delegates, but for the convenience of the nation.

Thus, in the last week of July, 1960, as the Republican delegates met, they met as subdued and earnest men and women. If they did not experience the same jittered forebodings as the Democrats who had met in Los Angeles a fortnight earlier, it was because, perhaps, the giddy rocking of American diplomacy in the globe had finally steadied (the Polaris missile had been fired, giving the nation its most cheerful international headline in four months) and because the overwhelming majority of delegates assumed, as a matter of fact, they had come only to ratify a candidate, not to choose one.

There was surface color enough to satisfy all the TV cameras and boisterous Chicago gawkers. Eli, billing himself simply as "A Servant of the Lord," preached doom to the crowds outside the Conrad Hilton, handing out leaflets that told the delegates "You are so busy worshiping the almighty dollar and seducing each other that you do not see the handwriting on the wall: America Must Fall." A ghost of yesterday wandered through the press corps: Philip Willkie, son of the famous Wendell Willkie, who, believing he could single-handedly duplicate his father's feat in stampeding a convention, handed out press releases running himself for Vice-President with Mr. Nixon. (Mr. Willkie campaigned simultaneously in Chicago for election as Indiana State Superintendent of Public Instruction; among the cardinal points of his platform: to teach all children to read by the phonetic method and speak and understand a foreign language beginning in the primary grades.) Nixon girls dominated both hotels, some dressed in scarlet skirts with white blouses, others in pink-striped gingham. A Chicago jester, seeking exposure on the TV cameras, paraded his own candidacy by the twin hotels with a set of leggy, muscular beauties whose thighs, in skin-fitting black tights, were breathtaking. Rockefeller sound trucks blared their theme song, "For He's A Jolly Good Fellow," on one corner of Balbo, and Nixon trucks blared in answer "Merrily We Roll Along" from another. Yet the night-club owners growled that this was the most penny-pinching convention crowd they had ever known, and even at the Pump Room, at the height of the Convention, tables were always available for those who wanted them.

All this, as at Los Angeles, the TV cameras caught and showed the nation. Where the nation's vision of the Republican Convention broke down was where television, as a medium, could not show the essence of what was happening. For the clash and the drama at Chicago was not a clash of men; it was, strangely enough, a clash of ideas. It is rare in American politics that issues, of themselves, provide excitement. Yet it was so in Chicago, in 1960.

The issues that shaped the Republican Convention were those forced on it by Nelson A. Rockefeller. The fields of combat were, variously and simultaneously, the Platform Committee hearings at the Blackstone Hotel in Chicago, the apartment of Nelson A. Rockefeller in New York City and the Newport Naval Station in Rhode Island, where Dwight D. Eisenhower was summering.

For whether he meant to or not, Nelson Rockefeller was summoning the Republican Party to repudiate the administration and policies of Dwight D. Eisenhower before the Party faced the nation in November.

For a full year Nelson Rockefeller had been presenting his positions to the American public. In the last six weeks he had honed them to a cutting edge. They covered the span of all American problems. We shall return in a moment to those specifics of his position on which the Convention locked. But the philosophy behind all of them was one of urgency. All rested on the assumption that a great government must not only deal with situations-as-they-are but go on to change, by its own initiative, the frame of problems or the machinery to deal with them.

This native Rockefeller attitude is as different from that of Dwight D. Eisenhower as one can imagine; yet Eisenhower, too, eighteen months earlier, had decided something fresh must be done to change the Republican Party's posture to life; and this earlier Eisenhower initiative was now to tangle with the present Rockefeller initiative.

Dwight D. Eisenhower is a major citizen of America and full loyalist to whatever cause to which he gives his heart. Thus, after the Republican election disasters of 1958, he had called for a complete re-examination of Republican philosophy and program, because they were obviously not appealing to the American people. Eisenhower had, therefore, in 1959, set in motion a Committee on Program and Progress to examine the philosophy of Republicanism, and this committee had become the immediate responsibility of Richard M. Nixon. Mr. Nixon, in turn, chose an extraordinary young Republican businessman named Charles H. Percy, President of the Bell & Howell Company of Chicago, to lead this continuing committee of Republican philosophers through 1959 and the spring of 1960 and to develop a new credo for modern Republicans.

Mr. Percy—young (forty), intelligent, efficiently executive, blond, attractive, above all a man of good will—had taken his work seriously. "When Percy takes a drink of Dubonnet on the rocks," said one of those who worked most closely with him, "he thinks he's being one hell of a fellow and dissipating like mad." Percy had, through the months of 1959 and 1960, not been dissipating; he had been trying with all sincerity to weave, almost by himself, a Republican philosophy of modern government and stretch an ideological compromise over both wings of his party. This compromise[2] lay at the base of all early Republican platform drafting in the spring of 1960. Not only this effort but Percy's own remarkable personality, exercised as Chairman of the Platform Committee, combined to make the platform and program of the Republican Party for 1960 more important than it had ever been before.

The draft platform of Mr. Percy as it had developed in the weeks before the Republican Convention was a harmonious whole—at once laudatory of the administration of Dwight D. Eisenhower and forward-looking, as befits modern Republicanism. But Nelson Rockefeller believed that the nation was in peril, and the Eisenhower administration did not. Here was a conflict for which nothing in Mr. Percy's previous brilliant business experience had prepared him.

Early in July Mr. Percy had flown to New York to discuss this conflict with Nelson Rockefeller and his advisers on Fifty-fifth Street and to show them a copy of the draft platform, which the official public Platform Committee of the Republican Party would in a few weeks be invited to accept. The platform as drafted did not satisfy the Governor of New York. Mr. Rockefeller had a wide range of national concerns: care for the aged, rights for Negroes, stimulation of capital investment for growth of the national economy, foreign affairs; above all, the Governor of New York was worried about national defense; and one should pause, at least briefly, to examine the substance of the Governor's position on this issue most important to him.

America was entering the period of the Missile Gap, Rockefeller insisted. Our B-47s and B-52s operated from bases vulnerable to Soviet retaliation. Instant and constant alerts were required. At least three billion dollars more of effort, he felt, should go into the defense budget. The pace of construction on those missile bases already underway should be immediately speeded up; they must be made hard against Russian attack, at the fastest pace the American economy could command. Any Governor of New York, who must daily worry about the normal vulnerability of Megalopolis at the mouth of the Hudson and the complicated ganglia of its technology, should act, always, as if he were responsible for the shielding of this delicate system from all harm. Mr. Rockefeller was the first to behave as if this re-

[2] The full report of Mr. Percy's year-long labors is available in a booklet entitled *Decisions for a Better America*, published by Doubleday & Company, New York.

sponsibility were personal, and burdened most by threat of war. Yet as he insisted that the national defense be reorganized to protect his state and city, he was insisting at the same time that the Republican Party question publicly the direction of our defense by Dwight Eisenhower.

In essence, Mr. Rockefeller insisted that the platform on defense cry: Emergency!

But, in essence, the Republican administration of the country denied emergency.

Sorely perplexed, Percy left New York on July 6th to consult with the second party of the trio who were later to dominate the Republican Convention: Mr. Nixon. Nixon blessed Percy's efforts at compromise; and Percy had then gone back to Chicago to preside over the gathering platform drafters, who believed themselves to hold authority over Republican policy.

In the hard life of politics it is well known that no platform nor any program advanced by either major American party has any purpose beyond expressing emotion. Platforms are a ritual with a history of their own and, after being written, they are useful chiefly to scholars who dissect them as archeological political remains. The writing of a platform does indeed flatter many people, gives many pressure groups a chance to blow off steam in public, permits the leaders of such pressure groups to report back to their memberships of their valiant efforts to persuade. But in actual fact, all platforms are meaningless: the program of either party is what lies in the vision and conscience of the candidate the party chooses to lead it.

Nevertheless, since the American people have come to expect the ritual of a platform, both Republicans and Democrats provide platforms, although they manage the stagecraft of platform writing differently. The Democrats usually have one large gang session in which the whole platform is discussed, and then the Convention accepts the deliberative conclusions of the platform committee and approves what was written before the witnesses were heard. The Republicans usually break their platform sessions into subcommittees, each writing one plank of the whole (on foreign affairs, farm, education, science, defense, etc.). Then they, too, report to the Convention, and the Convention approves the draft that would have been written had no hearings been held at all. In the Republican Party, more than in the Democratic Party, the committees are actually allowed to play with phrases. But phrase making and editing are harmless exercises in both parties, and flatter all the people appointed to platform committees, or platform chairmanships, into the belief that they are important.

What happened at the Republican Convention was that platform writing became terribly important, not only in theory, but in tight, contentious practice, too.

The Republican Platform Committee is usually chosen by selecting two delegates from each state. These are then assigned to subcommittees for consideration of individual planks. Since the process of naming men and women for this relatively unimportant task is normally without significance, it is thus tossed over to the machinery controlled by the regulars. Thus, the Republican Platform Committee of 1960 consisted of 103 men and women overwhelmingly chosen from the "regular" or Taft-Hanna-Weed twin of the Party. Yet what they had to consider were matters most enormously important to the citizen wing of the Party, led by Rockefeller.

They began their labors a week before the Convention opened, on Monday, July 18th, in a general public session in the Crystal Ballroom of the Blackstone and then disappeared, as subcommittees, into smaller rooms and chambers on Wednesday, July 20th (into the Sheraton Room, the English Room, Regency Room, Ivy Room, French Room, etc.) to hear witnesses in their particular areas of interest.

There is always something touching about the effort of good citizens to improve the policies of their government; and some of the platform sessions were indeed fascinating. Of my memories of the Republican Convention, the one I like best is the placid colloquy (in the midst of general strife) between the education subcommittee and several witnesses on the problems of gifted children and the grave morning discussion as to whether gifted children are or are not better adjusted than normal children when they grow up to be responsible. (One of the witnesses, testifying from a Ford Foundation study, reported that whereas 14 per cent of all students grow up maladjusted, only 7 per cent of gifted children grow up maladjusted.) The subcommittee on national defense was, by contrast, flat; it held session only one morning, and heard only four witnesses, who wished to make their views known to the architects of policy of the then-governing party of America. (Two were Fortress America advocates; one, a Chamber of Commerce representative; one, a lady representing Shelters Anonymous of California.) Yet the subcommittee on national defense was to deadlock the Republican Convention on the most somber problem of the nation.

By Thursday, July 21st, the subcommittees had begun their final redraft and rewording of the planks that Percy and his staff had so carefully tried to stretch as a compromise over Rockefeller, Nixon and Eisenhower. But the drafts that were passed from the Blackstone Hotel to the Sheraton Towers Hotel (where Rockefellers' deputies made their headquarters) contained none of that sense of emergency with which Rockefeller viewed the American crisis. In substance they were not too far different from the Rockefeller views (except on civil rights for Negroes and on defense appropriations), but in phrasing they applauded all the works of the previous eight years while hopefully promising to better the performance. With this attitude the Rockefellers would not agree.

It was now a matter of testing of nerve. Desperately Mr. Percy, the compromiser, offered to let the Rockefeller people write the preamble, the conclusion and the running commentary of the film that would be used to explain the platform. Desperately, all through Thursday, the Rockefeller people dodged, playing hide-and-seek in hotel rooms from emissaries of Mr. Percy seeking compromise. Whatever their mixed motives—some hoping for a Convention draft of Rockefeller, some hoping simply for a showdown on Republican policy—the Rockefeller people knew their only leverage at the Convention was the power of their ideas and their sense of urgency. If they could keep the edge of their ideas sharp enough, if they could keep the difference of purpose between themselves and Mr. Nixon, despite all Mr. Percy's efforts at compromise—then they had a combat position that might, if necessary, be taken to the floor of the Convention itself. If they did not, if they were sucked into compromise wording, they had nothing.

On the one hand, theirs can be seen as an exercise in courage. Against them were arrayed the overwhelming strength of the outgoing administration, the mobilized forces of the Vice-President, the unyielding attitudes of the bedrock regulars—plus a revolt in their own New York State delegate ranks. Mr. Rockefeller and his men had observed the collapse of the dignity, importance and probable future career of Governor Edmund Brown of California when that man failed to control his California Democratic delegates at the Los Angeles Convention. Within their own New York State Republican delegation, Rockefeller leaders now knew a similar revolt to be simmering, stirred hour by hour by the shrewd Len Hall. Upstate New York Republicans have always, largely, been Taft-influenced; they distrusted the Governor's spending programs at Albany; they knew that Mr.

Nixon would be nominated; and, like all politicians, they sought to be with a winner. The New York State delegation was to caucus on Sunday afternoon—how long could its restive members be held in line? At any moment Len Hall could lift the phone in his suite on the third floor of the Blackstone and mobilize twenty, perhaps thirty, New York State delegates to denounce their own Governor. And if this happened, Rockefeller would return to New York discredited, made to appear a buffoon, as Governor Brown of California had been made so to appear a few weeks earlier. Thus courage and high ideals must join to brace each other.

On the other hand, enemies saw the Rockefeller operation as an open exercise in political blackmail. The Rockefeller forces had by Thursday night decided, if need be, to fight the draft platform in two main areas—national defense and civil rights. If they took the fight to the floor and denounced the national defense of the country, present and prospective, as being inadequate, they would be giving the Democrats such a club to beat the later Republican nominee as, in Jack Kennedy's skillful hands, would be murderous. And if the draft plank on civil rights (a moderately progressive one) was opposed by a Rockefeller plank on civil rights that offered to go all the way to please Negro leadership— how could a Republican nominee who rejected the Rockefeller plank have any hope of carrying the critical Negro vote in the vital Northeastern electoral states? From this point of view, the Rockefeller team had Messrs. Nixon, Percy and Eisenhower all with their backs to the wall.

Governor Rockefeller had left his command authority in Chicago with a strategy board in the Sheraton Towers by the lake. This strategy board of four men consisted of two tactical lieutenants (Malcolm Wilson, Lieutenant-Governor of New York, and L. Judson Morhouse, Republican State Chairman, both of them as shrewd and skillful political tacticians as the Empire State's Republican Party has known for a long time) and two principal strategists. The two strategists were Emmet Hughes and George L. Hinman, and there is something romantically dramatic about their alliance in Chicago. For this alliance of a youthful non-Republican ideologue, much traveled around the world, with a wise and gentle lawyer from a small upstate New York town decided in a Chicago hotel room to debate and contest all the ultimate problems of national defense, nuclear destruction, and American foreign policy with the President and Vice-President of the United States. Only in America could such a challenge be made.

By Thursday evening this strategy board had reviewed all the draft planks of the platform and found them wholly unsatisfactory—so unsatisfactory that they decided to recommend to their leader an open floor fight. From Albany came the Governor's assent. On Friday morning on the press bulletin boards of the Convention went up a simple statement: Governor Nelson Rockefeller had expressed from executive chambers in Albany his concern over the content of the platform being drafted. He found the draft platform "still seriously lacking in strength and specifics."

This was threat of open civil war on the Convention floor.

Within minutes the wire services had carried this threat to Washington, to Newport, to wherever politicians read wire tickers or listen to the radio.

And now the scene shifted to New York.

It was Mr. Nixon who shifted the action there. Within hours of receipt of the news on Friday of Rockefeller's open break with the platform drafters, he had telephoned to New York to Herbert Brownell, former Attorney-General, erstwhile strategist of both Eisenhower election victories, partner in all political enterprises with Thomas E. Dewey. Within minutes thereafter, Brownell in New York telephoned Nelson Rockefeller to announce that the Vice-President would like to come to New York immediately to talk with the Governor: no true division of opinion on either foreign policy, civil rights or national defense separated Governor and Vice-President, he said. Could they meet on neutral ground, say at Brownell's home?

The Governor delayed his answer until he had consulted his strategy board in Chicago. The strategy board, having taken its initial act of courage that morning, was now for being firm. Be tough, they urged, Nixon will cave in. And the terms they demanded for the meeting were almost those of surrender: that Nixon telephone Rockefeller personally with his request for a meeting; that they meet at the Rockefeller apartment, not at Brownell's house; that the meeting be secret and later be announced in a press release from the Governor, not Nixon; that the meeting be clearly announced as taking place at the Vice-President's request; that the statement of policy issuing from it be long, detailed, inclusive, not a summary communiqué. Briefly the Governor questioned the toughness of his advisers, then agreed to outface Nixon. Within an hour and a half Rockefeller was telephoning his strategy board again: Nixon had accepted all their terms and would fly to New York that evening; they were to stand by for action in Chicago that night and begin immediately drafting the terms to which Nixon would be summoned to agree.

The Vice-President arrived in New York, secretly, at 7:30 in the evening with his one aide, Major Donald Hughes, and drove directly to the triplex apartment of Nelson Rockefeller at 810 Fifth Avenue.

In Chicago, the Convention simmered and sputtered; the platform drafters, believing their work almost done, were beginning to relax; the press hammered out its dispatches in ignorance. And in equal ignorance of all that was happening, the Nixon entourage in Chicago went to sleep. Never, perhaps, has a principal political actor taken so momentous a decision alone, leaving his personal staff so entirely ignorant and exposed to error on a matter of such moment. When, in the dawn hours of Saturday, July 23rd, first rumors of such a New York meeting began to leak in Chicago, the Vice-President's chief press aide, Herbert Klein, was still denying that any such meeting had happened (which he believed) and was being denounced by newspapermen, who previously trusted him, as a liar.

In New York, Messrs. Nixon and Rockefeller proceeded about their work quietly and efficiently. They dined first; and for an hour and a half at the table Nixon tried to persuade Rockefeller to be his Vice-President. When, conclusively, Rockefeller had refused, they passed on to the substance of their differences about America's future. They talked about these matters until midnight, discussing the draft of a proposed statement hastily telephoned to them by the Rockefeller staff from Chicago.

By midnight they were ready to inform platform headquarters in Chicago of their agreements, and so a four-way telephone circuit was established, linking Percy at the Blackstone; a Rockefeller deputy nearby in Chicago; Nixon, who sat at the desk in Rockefeller's private study; and Rockefeller himself, who lounged, sitting, on his bed in the handsome room that looks out at night over the twinkling vista beyond Central Park. For more than three hours, the four-way long-distance telephone conversation continued between New York and Chicago, Nixon boggling now and again at some portion particularly difficult to swallow, Rockefeller, on advice of staff, insisting, and Nixon generally yielding.

What emerged, finally, was the famous Fourteen Point Compact of Fifth Avenue. Seven points concerned foreign policy and national defense (demanding in foreign affairs the formation of new friendly confederations of American diplomacy, and in national defense an accelerated program of hard bases, second-strike capacity and flexible forces for brush-fire wars, at whatever cost to the budget). In domestic affairs, the two agreed that the federal government be totally reorganized in its executive branch and that the Rockefeller theses on economic growth, medical care for the aged and civil rights prevail.

At 3:20 in the morning they had finished their agreed text, and Mr. Nixon left for LaGuardia Airport to return to Washington. From LaGuardia his aide, Donald Hughes, for the first time informed Nixon headquarters in Chicago what had happened. By five in the morning the Rockefeller statement, edited and mimeographed, was being released to the national press in New York, Chicago and Washington.[3]

Magisterially, it began, "The Vice-President and I met today at my home in New York City. The meeting took place at the Vice-President's request. The purpose of the meeting was to discuss the platform of the Republican Party. . . . The Vice-President and I reached agreement on the following specific and basic positions on foreign policy and national defense. . . ."

Two simultaneous explosions now occurred: one in Chicago, Illinois, at the Blackstone Hotel; the second at the Newport Naval Station, Rhode Island, where Dwight D. Eisenhower was vacationing.

The first and most vivid explosion was, of course, in Chicago, and came from the Platform Committee. No words of pain, outrage and fury can describe the reaction of the Republican Platform Committee. The 103 members of the Platform Committee had been chosen by the machinery of the Party—which, as we have noted, had chosen them naturally and predominantly from the regulars who make up the bony structure of the Party. They had been presented with Mr. Percy's spring labors in the draft platform and, after days of hearing witnesses, had been allowed to redraft and edit certain of the phrases of the platform to give them the illusion of participation. Even the moderate and compromise language of Mr. Percy had pressed these grass-roots conservatives as far as they could honestly go. They had been pushed hard, and they had stretched hard; one of the weary drafters who worked with them said, "Don't you see, in this Party you have to run as hard as possible to stay in the same place; getting them to approve what Eisenhower has already done is an achievement in itself." The Platform Committee

---

[3] See Appendix B for full text.

had nonetheless approved a platform fundamentally more cohesive and substantially more reasonable than the platform the Democrats had adopted in Los Angeles several weeks earlier. Few members of the committee could explain how this draft platform had come about. Its ideas had been imposed on them by Eastern liberals—but, over twenty years of national conventions, the regulars had learned to accept such ideological impositions by the citizen wing of the party and resigned themselves to the belief that some mysterious Eastern conspiracy was always and permanently at work to frustrate both them and the Party from an expression of true faith.

Now, on Saturday morning, their conspiratorial theory of history was not only proved—their pride was rubbed in it. Never had the quadrennial liberal swoop on the regulars been more nakedly dramatized than by this open Compact of Fifth Avenue. Whatever honor they might have been able to carry from their services on the Platform Committee had been wiped out. A single night's meeting of two men in a millionaire's triplex apartment in Babylon-by-the-Hudson, 830 miles away, was about to overrule them; they were exposed as clowns for all the world to see. It was too much.

Thus on Saturday morning, two days before the Republican Convention publicly convened, it knew chaos. The delegates stormed; they would not be dictated to. Senator Barry Goldwater of Arizona, leader of the Republican right, now raised his voice in bitterness at a press conference: he had spoken to Nixon by telephone in Washington the previous morning and been told nothing of the secret meeting; Goldwater styled the Compact of Fifth Avenue a "surrender," the "Munich of the Republican Party," the guarantee of "Republican defeat in November." By noon, not even all Mr. Percy's charm and good will could soothe the members of the Platform Committee to a semblance of order; and they suspended sessions, howling at their humiliation.

Another sound now joined their anguish: that of a muffled explosion in Newport, Rhode Island. There Dwight D. Eisenhower had finally read the text of the Compact of Fifth Avenue, and he was furious. He was furious, first, at what he considered the personal treachery of Nelson A. Rockefeller. It was Eisenhower himself who had first conceived the idea of reorganizing the executive arm of the American government so that a First Secretary of Cabinet would be established as Chief of Staff to free the President of administrative detail for policy making. It was Eisenhower who had invited Nelson Rockefeller to serve on the small committee that had elaborated this idea for the President's private planning. And it had been the President's fond dream that in his last message to Congress in January, 1961, when he should have become in the eyes of all men no longer a man of politics but the revered war hero and elder statesman, he could present this scheme of reorganization of government to the Eighty-seventh Congress as his legacy in history. Now, in the Compact of Fifth Avenue, Rockefeller had imposed the idea on Nixon and, through Nixon, on the platform makers; Rockefeller had made it a partisan, factional proposal. This was treachery; this was personal theft; this was idea stealing, credit hogging. Eisenhower blazed. Yet he could not fight the idea itself, for he devoutly believed in its necessity.

Eisenhower could, however, fight on another front: the national defense points of the Compact of Fifth Avenue. These amounted to little short of outright repudiation of his competence as Commander-in-Chief. Though Nixon, in the night session at Fifth Avenue, had softened the tone of earlier Rockefeller statements on defense (Nixon had, for example, chopped out the specific figure of an additional three billion dollars in defense appropriations, which Rockefeller had estimated was immediately necessary), the substance of Rockefeller's views remained intact and the tone of emergency was clear.

Thus in the course of Saturday afternoon was formed a curious alliance between regulars and Eisenhower men at Chicago against the Nixon-Rockefeller forces who had overnight become allies. Up to now the Rockefeller people had believed that if they imposed their ideas on Nixon, Nixon could impose these ideas on the platform and the Party. By Saturday evening this thesis had exploded. Under pressure from Newport, Thruston Morton, Chairman of the Republican National Committee and a deeply loyal Eisenhower man, ordered that all the planks so far drafted be mimeographed and released—he would have no part of the Compact of Fifth Avenue, he would let the full Platform Committee—now a runaway committee—decide whether these drafts should be altered to meet the terms of the Compact.

By Sunday the Republican Convention was thoroughly out of control. Overnight, planks had been published by the subcommittees on farm policy, on education, on national defense, before the Nixon Headquarters could choke them off for further consideration. On Sunday the chairman of the national defense subcommittee, Congressman Glenard P. Lipscomb of Southern California, held a press conference and proudly boasted that not one single word or phrase of his national defense plank had been altered from its original draft by the Nixon-Rockefeller agreement in New York. In Hubbard Room No. 1, on the second floor of the Blackstone, the 103 members of the Platform Committee now convened again, adamant in their refusal to accept dictation; and, from the suburbs of Chicago, demonstrators of the regular wing appeared with hastily scrawled hand-lettered placards to support the committee. PLATFORM COMMITTEE, YOU WRITE THE PLATFORM, NOT ROCKY read one outside the Hubbard Room. NO ROCKS IN OUR HEAD, HOW ABOUT YOURS read another.

What was happening, and who would pull order out of matters?

This was the scene of confusion in Chicago on Monday morning, July 25th, when Vice-President Richard M. Nixon arrived to take over.

It is necessary to see all the delicate and conflicting strategies that the Vice-President had held in mind all spring to understand how well he now performed.

All spring his tactical position and personal attitude had been that of a man in a trap. While Nelson A. Rockefeller, free of any Washington responsibility, could free-wheel about the country appealing to citizen Republicans and independents alike, Nixon, as Vice-President, was bound by the rules of politics to support the administration of Dwight D. Eisenhower. Whatever Nixon felt personally about administration handling of foreign policy in the unsteady spring months—and his aides colorfully reflected his disenchantment with the State Department—he must in public support it, praise it, minimize crisis. He was part of this administration, though not responsible for it; limited by the parsimonious budget of the Vice-Presidential office (less than $125,000 for all its ceremonial and official duties), he could not afford such a staff or Brain Trust as fueled Rockefeller and Kennedy with ideas. Even had he been able to organize a Brain Trust of volunteers, he knew that Mr. Eisenhower would resent it as a disloyal move; and he needed Eisenhower's support for whatever electoral campaign he planned to conduct in the fall.

Nevertheless, the confinement and subordination irked Nixon; he had the regular wing of the Party firmly with him; what he would need in the coming election were the citizens and the independents. Yet defending the Eisenhower political front, to which the President was indifferent, forced Nixon to take that narrow partisan position in which the Democrats so delighted in exaggerating him.

Thus Rockefeller's liberal assault on Nixon's right flank had not come entirely as tragedy. The principles Rockefeller chanted were neither entirely strange nor distasteful to Nixon; indeed, with many of the Rockefeller positions he privately and wholeheartedly agreed. In his own eyes, the Compact of Fifth Avenue was not necessarily the abject surrender it appeared to be in the press. The Compact permitted him to turn both to President Eisenhower, whom he could not offend directly, and to the regulars, who adored him, and say to both, in effect: this was a necessity for Party harmony; it was blackmail; I was forced to do it by threat of a floor fight; you know what Nelson is like.

Although deeply hurt and offended by their exclusion from the Vice-President's confidence on Friday night, all but one of the Nixon aides (Len Hall) accepted the announcement of the Compact with pleasure. "That guy," said one of them, referring to Rockefeller, "is taking high ground for us we could never have taken on our own."

Yet the high ground was not to be taken so easily. Now, over the week end, the convention had exploded from Nixon's control. Unless the Nixon men demonstrated to Rockefeller that they could deliver a platform in the spirit of the Compact of Fifth Avenue, Rockefeller could cry treachery and still take the fight to the floor. Yet if they rode roughshod over the platform committee, they would be exposed to the outriders of Barry Goldwater crying "Treason" or "Tyranny" from the right.

Mr. Nixon arrived, apparently undisturbed, from Washington shortly before noon on Monday, smiling boyishly and sunnily at the airport; held a press conference; made the necessary ceremonial calls at various caucuses; then settled down in his own second-floor suite of the Blackstone to operate.

Obviously he could not nakedly demand that the Convention submit to his discipline only in order to appease Nelson A. Rockefeller on all points. Yet Rockefeller had, somehow, to be appeased. With no apparent uncertainty, Mr. Nixon settled on one principal point raised in the Compact of Fifth Avenue and decided to offer fight on that as Rockefeller's ally, at whatever risk of offending all regulars: this was civil rights.

One should pause here in these hasty events of the long Monday-Tuesday ordeal of the Republican Convention to observe how the most profound and long-range problems of politics enter history first as tactical decisions. For the civil rights battle, into which Mr. Nixon now plunged, forecast what may become in the next ten years the greatest reorientation of American politics since the Civil War; on its resolution in the coming decade depends the future of both major American parties.

The problem of civil rights in America—which is another way of speaking of the relations of Negro Americans with white Americans—poses, for political strategists, the sharpest choices in national planning. Since the northward migration of the Negro from the South (see Chapter Eight for a fuller treatment), the Negro vote, in any close election, has become critical in carrying six of the eight most populous states of the union. To ignore the Negro vote and Negro insistence on civil rights must be either an act of absolute folly—or one of absolute calculation.

For twelve years now this problem of Negro vote and Negro rights has roweled the Democratic Party. Northern Democrats and Northern Negroes have agreed that in the area of civil rights the federal government should supersede state authority and intervene in state affairs. But Southern whites wish to deal with their race problem on their own; and the support of Northern Democrats for federal intervention in Southern race problems has shaken, perhaps permanently, the Democratic grip on its old Southern base. Concurrently has come the phenomenal growth of the Republican Party in the South, resting in large part on the recognition of growing millions of Southerners that the Regular Republicans, who seek to curb the powers of the federal government in general, are their natural allies in preserving state sovereignty in race relations, too.

The prospect for the Republican high command is thus tantalizing in the extreme. If they adopt a civil rights program only moderately more restrained than the Democrats', the South can be theirs for the asking; and with the South, if it comes permanently to Republican loyalties, could come such solid addition of electoral strength as would make Republicans again, as they were for half a century, the majority party of the nation and the semipermanent stewards of the national executive power. Furthermore, since the Northern Negro now votes habitually for the Democrats, by overwhelming margins (of 3 to 1 to 8 to 1), why seek to outbid the Democrats where they cannot be outbid? So argue conservative Republicans, and their philosophy can be summarized as one of trade: let us give the Northern Negro vote to the Democrats, and we shall take the Old South for ourselves.

Now, in Chicago, Richard M. Nixon found himself faced on the eve of a national campaign for the Presidency with precisely this strategic dilemma, shaped over the week end in tactical form. The original draft plank prepared by the Platform Committee was a moderate one: it avoided any outright declaration of support for Negro sit-in strikes at Southern lunch counters and omitted any promise of federal intervention to secure Negroes full job equality—both of which the Democrats, at Los Angeles, had promised. This plank, as written, would almost certainly have carried the Southern states for Nixon and, it seems in retrospect, might have given him victory. Barry Goldwater now insists that the original "moderate" Republican platform plank on civil rights would have guaranteed a 1960 Republican victory; and that the Rockefeller-Nixon rewrite of that plank cast victory away. On Monday, July 25th, it is almost certain, it lay in Nixon's power to reorient the Republican Party toward an axis of Northern-Southern conservatives. His alone was the choice.

Nixon made his choice, I believe, more out of conscience than out of strategy. But conscience is different from a personal code of history or a realization of the shape of great events. Nixon insisted that the platform committee substitute for the moderate position on civil rights (which probably would have won him the election) the advanced Rockefeller position on civil rights (which might also have won him the election in the North, had he understood the Rockefeller position). Later, under the strain of the election campaign, in September and October, the temptation of victory came so close that he apparently could not decide whether he was campaigning for Northern electoral votes or Southern electoral votes; he thus later completely befuzzed his original position in Chicago and succeeded, in the end, in alienating Northern Negro *and* Southern white, losing both along with the election. This is one of Nixon's characteristic and fatal flaws—that he presents too often a split image.

At Chicago, however, conscience and tactic both briefly urged Nixon in the same direction. His conscience believed in civil rights. He knew also that the Negro vote in the Northern cities was critical in the elections; he recognized further that Nelson Rockefeller, who governed New York and whose family had assumed obligation for Negro rights two generations before, would not compromise in this area; and Nixon acted masterfully. One by one, he summoned key members of the Platform Committee and their masters to his presence and insisted that the civil rights plank be rewritten to please Rockefeller and match the Democrats'. "We collected," said one of his aides, "every political IOU we held in the country that night."

On Tuesday, when the full 103-man Platform Committee had been assembled again, Nixon was ready; the pressure had been exercised, the IOUs collected. Percy yielded the chair to Mr. Melvin Laird of Wisconsin, an accomplished parliamentarian, and the rules of parliamentary procedure were applied in three successive votes with such strength that, on the final tally, the committee was voting 50 to 35 (plus abstentions) to give the Vice-President a hearing for the new, advanced plank on civil rights; which was then adopted. I spoke to a Southern lady from Louisiana a few minutes later. "Oh, I know," she said, "I know what you Northerners think. But we've lost Louisiana, I tell you, we've lost Louisiana. Lyndon Johnson's going to come across the border now and talk 'magnolia' to them and they'll vote Democratic and we could have had Louisiana, we could have had it." (The Republicans did lose Louisiana, too—John F. Kennedy was to carry it by 50.4 per cent of the popular vote, while Republicans and segregationists split the balance.)

Yet performance on civil rights alone could not satisfy the Rockefellers. For them, national defense was equally important; uncompromisingly, they insisted that Nixon support them in rewriting the national defense plank, too. This, however, was more difficult, for on national defense the original draft plank was supported not only by the regulars but by Dwight D. Eisenhower in Newport. At one point, after midnight on Monday, the Rockefeller team had to renew their threat of open floor fight before the Vice-President would yield. All through the overnight of Monday-Tuesday, therefore, Nixon aides negotiated with Newport by long-distance telephone, discussing phrases and compromises, before, on Tuesday morning, they were able to bring the Rockefellers a redraft of the original national defense plank that went as far as Newport would permit Nixon to move in appeasement of the New York Governor.

In a night session of hard negotiating, Newport had approved the change of some sixty-seven words in the original draft of the national defense program. The new plank called for "intensified" efforts, for mention of "submarine and ballistic" missiles, for "acceleration" and "production" of long-range missiles, for the provision of "any necessary increased expenditures to meet new situations." Would the Rockefeller people accept this compromise with the President?

They would. The same afternoon of Tuesday that saw the passage of the Rockefeller civil rights platform saw the passage of the new defense platform as approved by both Rockefeller and Eisenhower. Thereafter, Mr. Rockefeller withdrew his threat of floor fight and announced to his restive and turbulent New York State delegation that he was definitely withdrawing from the race for President.

One can look at the Rockefeller performance at Chicago either as absurdity or as courage. Yet either way he had withdrawn from the field of battle with honor, in full control of his own state political system and delegates, and with the knowledge that in the platform there were wordings of alert both on civil rights and national defense that would permit Richard M. Nixon to campaign on a forward Republican position if he so chose. But it was up to Mr. Nixon. And Mr. Nixon had not yet faced the campaign or the pressures that act on a man when the Presidency is close.

All this was over by Tuesday evening. The rest of the Convention was public. The keynote address was made by Congressman Walter Judd; since Nelson Rockefeller, who loves people, had not wished to make it, the Republican National Committee had chosen Judd, who is a master at arousing hate; and Judd made the rafters roar and the benches shake as he asked,

"Was it the Republicans who recognized the Soviet Union in 1933 . . . as if it were a respectable and dependable member thereof?

"Was it the Republicans who, at Teheran, against the urgent advice of Mr. Churchill, agreed to give the Russians a free hand in the Balkans? ["No," roared the crowd.]

"Was it the Republicans who secretly divided Poland and gave half of it to the Soviet Union? ["No."]

"Was it a Republican administration that divided Korea and gave North Korea to the Communists?" ["No."]

And so on. And at each question, the regulars rocked back and forth and roared "No." It is curious that at both Democratic and Republican Conventions the best technical orations, the responsive orations, came from Minnesota men, Eugene McCarthy and Walter Judd, as if both had inherited the old-fashioned Minnesota Populist knack of heating the political blood.

So, finally, on Wednesday evening, July 27th, Richard M. Nixon's name was placed in nomination for the Presidency of the United States. The Louisiana delegation offered the name of Barry Goldwater, who received ten votes on a final roll call of 1321 to 10; the Arizona delegation then moved to make the nomination unanimous; and at 11:13 in the evening Richard M. Nixon became the Republican nominee for President of the United States.

There ensued then the choice of a Vice-President, performed in a closely guarded room in the Blackstone Hotel to which Nixon had summoned thirty-six Republican leaders in the small hours of Thursday morning, July 28th. Richard M. Nixon had been chosen as Republican Vice-Presidential nominee at just such a meeting in 1952 in a room in the Conrad Hilton across the way—but Mr. Eisenhower had not participated personally in that meeting and had left the selection to his strategy board. In 1960, Nixon was present himself; he did not propose to leave the choice of Vice-President to the consensus of others. He had tentatively chosen Henry Cabot Lodge as his running mate months before, assuming Rockefeller would not accept the post; but he now gave every man a chance to speak. The question, as it divided, was whether the Republicans needed a man who could appeal more to the farmers of the Midwest (said Governor Stratton of Illinois: "You can say all you want to about foreign affairs, but what's really important is the price of hogs in Chicago and St. Louis"), or one who could appeal more to the generality of Americans across the board. Nixon declared, "If you ever let them [the Democrats] campaign only on domestic issues, they'll beat us—our only hope is to keep it on foreign policy." Twenty of those present agreed with him that Henry Cabot Lodge was the best man to lift Americans' imagination to the problems of foreign policy and, since this was already Mr. Nixon's prior decision, so it was to be.[4]

On Thursday evening, July 28th, Mr. Nixon thus strode onto the platform of the Stockyards Amphitheater, where Dwight D. Eisenhower had accepted his first nomination. He entered by the traditional back, or stockyard, route, was briefly interviewed by reporters at his most boyish form, and told them he had been reading "history, literature and philosophy" for two weeks to prepare for this speech; then he climbed to address his fellow partymen:

> To stand here before this great convention [he said], to hear your expression of affection for me, for Pat, for our daughters, for my mother . . . is, of course, the greatest moment in my life. . . .
> . . . I would like to discuss tonight some of the great problems which will confront the next President of the United States, and the policies I believe should be adopted to meet them. . . .

[4] I rely for this version of the Vice-Presidential selection on the excellent and exclusive reporting of Carleton Kent, in the Chicago *Sun-Times,* reporting acknowledged by those who were present to be authentic.

I serve notice here and now that whatever the political consequences, we are not going to try to outpromise our opponents in this campaign.

.   .   .   .   .

And in this campaign I make a prediction. I say that, just as in 1952 and 1956, millions of Democrats will join us not because they are deserting their party but because their party deserted them at Los Angeles two weeks ago....

And now I want to speak to you of another kind of aggression—aggression without war, for the aggressor comes not as a conqueror but as a champion of peace, of freedom, offering progress and plenty and hope to the unfortunates of the earth.

And I say tonight that the major problem—the biggest problem—confronting the next President of the United States will be to inform the people of the character of this kind of aggression, to arouse the people to the mortal danger it presents and inspire the people to meet the danger....

And this will be a difficult task. Difficult because at times our next President must tell the people not what they want to hear but what they need to hear. Why, for example, it may be just as essential to the national interest to build a dam in India as in California. It will be difficult, too, because we Americans have always been able to see and understand the danger presented by missiles and airplanes and bombs; but we have found it hard to recognize the even more deadly danger of the propaganda that warps the mind, the economic offensive that softens the nation, the subversion that destroys the will of a people to resist tyranny.

. . . When Mr. Khrushchev says our grandchildren will live under Communism, let us say his grandchildren will live in freedom.

When Mr. Khrushchev says the Monroe Doctrine is dead in the Americas, we say the doctrine of freedom applies everywhere in the world.

A hundred years ago, Abraham Lincoln was asked during the dark days of the tragic war between the states whether he thought God was on his side. His answer was, "My concern is not whether God is on our side but whether we are on God's side."

My fellow Americans, may that ever be our prayer for our country, and in that spirit with faith in America, with faith in her ideals and in her people, I accept your nomination for President of the United States.

So Mr. Nixon closed the Republican Convention, with a

pledge and a prayer, and prepared to face John F. Kennedy and the American people.

The climactic phase of the American electoral process was now about to begin.

PART
TWO

PROLOGUE

WITH the end of the nominating process, American politics leaves logic behind.

If the conventions have done their work well, as normally they do, then the American people are offered two men of exceptional ability. Now they must choose. And they must choose in a primitive and barbaric trial. Although the contest is bloodless, the choice that ends the contest is nonetheless as irrational as any of the murderous, or conspiratorial, choices of leadership made elsewhere in great states. Until Plato's republic of philosophers is established, leaders will always be chosen by other men, not out of reason, but out of instinct and trust. In America all citizens help choose.

It is to reach instinct and emotion that the great election campaigns are organized. Whatever issues are discussed, are discussed only secondarily, in an attempt to reach emotions. Logic has been dismissed with the conventions' end. Now other matters must be organized, on a different scale, by different men. Now registration drives must be mounted; now citizens must be fired with enthusiasm; now the explosive mechanisms of TV are wheeled into action. And all to the one point: so that the citizens—as they gather at rallies or read their newspapers or sit at home watching the candidates on TV—will be able to stew, mull, reflect and argue, until finally there simmers down in the mind and belly of each individual his own decision on choice of the national chieftain.

The shelves of our libraries sag with the weight of studies on the behavior of the American voter. This book makes no claim to scholarship in that field of academic exploration. But when all is read and summarized, all such studies can be boiled down to a single sentence of truth, beyond which we know not:

Every American election summons the individual voter to weigh the past against the future.

The past consists variously of the voter's ethnic stock, the way his father voted, the tales his mother told him, the prejudices he has accumulated on the way of life, the class

243

and status of society he has attained or inherited. And the future consists of his fears and dreams: if he is a farmer, his fear of being squeezed out; if he is a Negro, his aspiration for libertarian equality; if he is a businessman, hope and fear for his enterprise; if he is a pensioner, his dependence on the social security system; and for all, the future course of America in war and peace.

Each of the great tribal communities of American life is split between Republicans and Democrats in different proportions; but these different proportions are among the most enduring realities in our political system. They change slowly; the past holds imaginations, prejudices and dreams fixed. And what each candidate must do in the campaign is to chip away at this grip of the past within each subgroup by holding out some vision of a new future. Even in the most dramatic campaigns the change in these fixed proportions is more like a slow chipping away of voters' conviction than a sharp turning of their perception. It is generally held that 80 per cent of American voters vote by inheritance and have made up their minds by the time the conventions are over. The frantic exertion of all the millions involved in the campaign thereafter is only a battle for the remaining 20 per cent—and the split of the remaining 20 per cent is what creates landslides or squeakers.

And always, forever, at whatever level, the central exercise is the same—the setting of the future against the past.

It is well, then, to examine Americans as they were in the fall of 1960, as the past, both recent and remote, had shaped them, before one examines the assaults of the two candidates on this past and their analyses of how to stir it.

Chapter 8

RETROSPECT ON YESTERDAY'S FUTURE

One of the occupational hazards of reporting is that it takes so long for the reporter to recognize the importance of what he learns while he is learning it.

Thus now, long after the Wisconsin primary has passed into the morgue of time, it occurs to me that I failed entirely to understand the meaning of a long evening's conversation with an old friend during the winter and spring weeks of the contest there.

I had discovered, while calling on Wisconsin's Governor Gaylord Nelson, that an old comrade of mine from the East Coast now served on his staff. With the provincialism of New York, I wondered what had happened to make him leave the excitement of Washington and New York and transfer to the politics of Madison, Wisconsin.

We dined late that evening, my mind on the national importance of the primaries there and baffled by his apparent unconcern. After a few drinks we began to talk about what did concern him here and what the Govenor's office was trying to do.

Governor Nelson, it appeared, was having a tough time, particularly with taxes and budget. I said, idly, that I'd heard the state-tax story in New York and Massachusetts and Pennsylvania and it was always the same—the state governments wanted more, but so did the federal government, so did the municipal governments. Where was all the money going? Why were the states so rapacious?

The question must have piqued him.

"You talk about the population explosion, don't you?" he said sharply.

Sure, I said, everyone did, it was a cliché.

"No," said he, "it isn't a cliché. In the past ten years, the population of Wisconsin's gone from 3,400,000 to 4,000,000. Those are figures. But do you know where the jump has come? Seventy-four per cent of that jump is in kids under eighteen years of age, or old people over sixty-five. Do you know what that means? It means practically the same num-

245

ber of people in their working years have to take care of almost double the number of dependents—we've got eight more dependents for every two new taxpayers.

"It means schools. You've got to have more schools, and that means more state aid for schools. We've got a university and ten state colleges now, and every single year the kids, the college kids, increase, they increase at the rate of three thousand a year. That's equal to the entire enrollment of two new state colleges every year.

"It means we have to take care of the old people and put more money into the problems of aging. It means hospitals. We've always had a good program in Wisconsin for mentally retarded children. But those kids aren't dying now—not with the new drugs. Some of our mentally retarded children are now forty and fifty years old, and still under state care.

"And then park facilities. People want to get out of Milwaukee and Chicago for the week end and vacation. We've put through a forty-seven per cent increase in state camping facilities—and we need roads to get them there, they're all cramped, they're all desperate for outdoor recreation."

He swung now from the tax needs into the technicalities of the Governor's tax problems, and he made the technicalities seem important, giving a tone of desperation to the dreary arguments about sales tax versus income tax, excise tax, use tax, which weary men in Boise, Harrisburg, Albany and Boston. He was worried about Gaylord Nelson's chance for re-election.[1]

I said that it seemed simple enough to dramatize and one could make a fairly effective campaign out of it. He said no.

"Because," he continued, "You can't get attention. You can't get attention for schools, or for taxes, for problems of aging, or mentally retarded children. All you can get is attention for STAMP OUT WATERSKIERS."

"What's that?" I asked.

"The same population explosion," he said. "We've got wonderful lakes in Wisconsin, and lots of them. But they're getting crowded too. Some lakes ought to be for swimming, some for fishing, some for waterskiing. But the waterskiers and the power boats go roaring over the water ruining all the fun for

---

[1] It is noteworthy that the chief casualties in both parties in the fall elections later in 1960 were governors beset by such problems as these. There were twenty-seven governors of the union up for re-election in the Presidential year, and twelve governorships changed hands, largely because of grass-roots tax revolts. Gaylord Nelson squeaked through with 51.6 per cent. Of thirty-four Senate seats at stake last year, only two changed hands. It is obviously far more dangerous to be a Governor than a Senator.

fishermen, swimmers and old-fashioned loafers. Well, we've put in a proposal to zone some of the lakes against water-skiing. We've got nine front-page stories about the waterskiing controversy—that's the most attention paid to any one program so far."

"Any other interest?" I asked.

"Yes," he said. "We've got a lot of attention for our bill to control highway billboards. Those are the things the public understands and pays attention to. That's the way Ribicoff made his name in Connecticut—on highway safety. But try to get attention for anything else.

"A couple of weeks ago I went down to Whitewater with the Governor and we got a crowd of about two hundred people. Nelson was mad that night and he really laced at them. 'People say the state government produces nothing, why does it take all that money.' He took off after them. 'You name anything,' he said, 'that you can produce as important as educating a kid. Name anything as important as keeping water from being polluted. Name anything as important as conserving the open wild land.' He gave it to them. Well, after it was over this small storekeeper came over to us and said, 'My wife had to drag me here tonight, but I'm glad I came now, I learned something.' You can reach them one by one and make them understand. But how do you make them all understand?"

II

Every twenty years the election of an American President coincides in date with the great federal census. Nineteen sixty was such a year and so, as the candidates charged and countercharged about the broad land, the silver-gray spools of electronic tape on which the census records us all were spinning off the new decennial picture of the American life the candidates sought to shape. This picture of 1960 we must now examine.

Each census is an event; yet some censuses have acquired a dimension and importance all their own in American history and imagination. The census of 1890, for example, was the official farewell to the American frontier. That year the counters of the census announced that the Great Plains and the prairies had been so covered by settlement in the previous decade that no longer could anyone draw the line of frontier that had been the horizon of American life for two and a half centuries. It was from these figures of the census that three years later, after study, Frederick Jackson Turner arrived at his theories of the significance of the frontier in American life and gave the American historic imagination a new vision of the nation.

It was obvious from midsummer of 1960 on, as the 10,000 miles of electronic tape in the census warrens of Suitland, Maryland, began to spew out the new patterns of American life, that the census of 1960 was to be of importance and historic dimension equal to that of 1890.

Someone has said that there are no miracles in history, only the sudden recognition by many men of what up to then has been unclear to them. None of the measuring men who inhabit the austere offices of the Bureau of the Census had looked forward in January to the decennial head count expecting miracles; and in late spring, as the figures began to come in to be translated into electronic impulses on electronic scanners, no miracles, indeed, were there to astound them. Their attention over the decade had been too keen, their tools of analysis too sharp, to permit the census to surprise them. What was astonishing became astonishing only as one looked back and pressed the measure marks of 1960 against the measure marks of 1950 and 1940. For if these were not miracles that had happened, they were at least the visible turnings of history itself.

The greatest miracle was the raw total of growth. The United States had grown from 151,300,000 people in 1950 to 179,300,000 people on April 1st of 1960. The percentage jump—18 per cent—was the greatest for any decennial period in 50 years. The numerical jump amounted to 28,000,000 people—or almost as many as inhabited the United States at the outbreak of the Civil War a century before. Some 41,000,-000 Americans had been born in the decade (16,000,000 had died), the rest had come by migration. In a world swelling and bursting with people (its population expected to rise from 2,850,000,000 to 3,480,000,000 in another decade), the United States would keep pace, its population expected to rise to 210,000,000 or 215,000,000 people by 1970.

This was entirely predictable.

What was more exciting was the changing pattern of growth. For just as the census of 1890 announced the passing of the frontier, the census of 1960 announced the passing of the great city. For half a century the great urban centers had dominated American culture and politics. Decade by decade, as if by some irrevocable law of history, the great cities had steadily increased in size at every count.

But in 1960 the crest had passed, and they were dwindling. In all but one of the fifteen largest metropolitan areas of the United States (those with populations of approximately 1,500,-000 or more) the core city, the central municipality, had lost population. From New York through Baltimore, Washington, Buffalo, Cleveland, Chicago, Detroit, clear across to San Francisco, all had lost citizens in a sweep so broad as to define not an individual local crisis but a universal phenomenon. The sole exception to this sweep among the fifteen largest was Los Angeles, which had gained 24 per cent in population. Yet Los Angeles had never presented itself to history as a city in the classic sense, but rather as a collection of suburbs (and blight was already ravaging its central areas too). The chief loser, in percentile points, was Boston. Memory carries this writer back to the twenties, when he was a boy in Boston's public schools, and our teachers taught us to expect, as an article of faith, that Boston (then 750,000) would some day reach 1,000,000. Boston barely touched 800,000 in 1950. The 1960 count showed it had fallen to 697,000, a smaller population than when I was born. Only in the South, a generation behind American life, were cities—like Houston, Dallas, Atlanta, Birmingham—still growing. But the perspectives for them, too, were clear.

Not only had the great cities lost people. So had the countryside. Of the nation's 3,072 counties, more than half, or 1,536, had also lost population. Arkansas, West Virginia, and Mississippi had actually lost total population on a statewide basis. But nineteen other states (sweeping in a great arc from the South, through the Appalachian-Ozark hill country, through the North Central states, through the Rockies) numbered more counties that had lost population than had gained population. An emptying belt of flight and desertion seemed to be spreading across the heart of the country, with lesser spots of emptiness and abandonment in upper New England. One could see it in the figures, but one could also see it if one were out campaigning in the countryside. All through the spring in West Virginia it seemed to me as if the wild bloom —the buttercup and the white dogwood, the feathered dandelion and butter-and-egg, the new ash and thin buttonwood with its fuzz-brown pods—grew brightest in those patches of land where spindly second-growth hardwood was now rising to screen the weather-beaten abandoned shacks and outhouses of people who had lived in these hollows and left. At the height of the Convention frenzy in Los Angeles, as one of the critical caucuses of the Minnesota delegation searched its conscience between Kennedy and Stevenson, I remember one sturdy farmer delegate rising to speak his piece; and he said, "Two miles from Dalton, we have seventeen vacant farms. We can't afford to lose our small farms. I just want to call their attention to this."

Thus Americans were abandoning the city and deserting the countryside, said the 1960 census.

It also told where they were going: to the suburbs. Two thirds of the stupendous 28,000,000 growth of the nation had taken place in suburbia. From the census one had the impression of a strange new society being formed: a series of metropolitan centers growing and swelling in their suburban girdles until the girdles touched one another, border on border, stretching in giant population belts hundreds of miles long while wilderness rose again on the outside of the girdle (we now count more deer in the United States than when the settlers came) and rot blighted the inner urban cores.

From the air the changes were clearly visible. By day one could see the dust clouds rising in midsummer as the bulldozers tore away at the potato patches of Long Island to clear land for more developments on the East Coast girdle; and flying out of Los Angeles, one could see again the same dust clouds as the bulldozers tore away at the orange groves of the San Fernando Valley. Late in the fall, flying north from Florida to New York on the Kennedy press plane, I went up to the cockpit to talk to the pilot. It was night as we spoke. It used to be, said the veteran pilot, looking out on the carpet of twinkling cities (the red-green-blue neon lights knotting at all the crossroads far below), it used to be that you could fly visually on a clear night like this. You could pick up Norfolk from the air, then you could recognize Washington, then you could recognize Baltimore, and all the way up to Boston it was that way—one city, then the next. Now, he said, there was just a continuous belt of night light from Newport News north, and you couldn't locate yourself visually; you had to do it by instruments. "There's still a patch of open country you can pick up at night between Hartford and Boston, though," he said.

This change in the American pattern of living has already become the most overworked subject of humor, sociology and analysis in American intellectual discussion. Yet the change is so vast, so profound, so all-embracing, that the political exploration of the change, the political solutions to its problems, have not yet even begun.

This new pattern of American life has cast off old needs, created new needs and problems. American life no longer needs, for example, the railway structure of the past; and only 822,000 men regularly work on the nation's railroads today, where 1,464,000 found jobs in 1945. Suburbanites drive to work—and Jimmy Hoffa's teamsters in their trucks carry the supplies out to the new supermarkets. As the logistics of suburban living increasingly require rubber-wheeled transport, Hoffa's power over American life and the American economy grows with each year, until it rivals that of the railway barons of the 1870s and 1880s, who could similarly strangle those they disliked on whim, if not for other reasons. Other changes occur. The new nation, for example, no longer uses coal in its suburban split-levels or ranch-type houses. It uses oil and natural gas. (In the decade 1950–1960, the consumption of natural gas in the nation more than doubled. Coal has dwindled to a meager 23 per cent of the nation's energy supply; and so in West Virginia the number of coal miners is 35 per cent of what it was fourteen years ago, having dropped from a peak 116,421 in 1947 to 42,900 in 1960.)

From the figures of the census, as from a crossroads, a dozen highways of analysis led forth.

One avenue, for example, could lead to all the political implications of credit and credit controls (a deadly dreary subject for debate, and one both candidates decided, after some hesitant examination, to dodge). The suburbs, to state one of the gross facts of this new American life, rest upon credit. To build the vast girdle of suburbia since the war has required a national exertion greater than that of clearing the original wilderness. Housing and construction have become America's greatest single industry—employing 5 per cent of all Americans in 1960. One quarter of *all* the homes in which Americans today live have been built since 1950, a testimonial to the past decade's vigorous energy that no other nation can match. This has been the largest single capital investment in American life, and it has affected our entire credit structure. From the end of World War II until the beginning of the Presidential year, the great corporations had needed to dip into the outside credit facilities of American finance only to the extent of some $90,000,000,000 dollars to finance their expansion of production facilities; and to the extent of some $36,000,000,000 more for mortgages on factories, office buildings, and commercial structures. But suburban Americans had used up $116,000,000,000 of mortgage money to finance their new homes.

Suburbia is not only collectively mortgaged to the hilt, and thus a claim against the public future, but it is also a claim against the future of all the individuals who live in it. Americans, so the census reported in 1960, are among the marryingest people in the world; they marry now more youthfully than any other civilized people in the Western World. (Today, 29 per cent of our maidens marry by the age of nineteen; in their mother's generation in 1940, only 10 per cent married at so early an age.) These young marriages must be equipped and financed, not out of savings, but out of credit. Where before World War II only one dollar out of every fourteen in take-home pay was pledged against installment payments, to-day, it is estimated, one dollar out of every nine is obligated for the appliances, the tools, the cars that make possible comfortable living in the suburbs.

The growth of the nation, thus said the census, had come in suburbia, and other figures explained that suburbia rested upon credit.

There followed, then, the political implications. This flexible credit, magnificent in its application, had not just happened. It had its roots in the past and in the political policy of government—first the New Deal housing laws, then the New Deal credit laws, later the veterans laws. Just as the Republican homestead acts of the 1860s, by throwing the lands of the West open to free settlement, eventually, thirty years later, erased the frontier of 1890, so the legislation of the early 1930s had changed the appearance of the America mirrored in the census of 1960. In each case the wise and farseeing policies of one generation had succeeded—and in their success had posed an entirely new problem for the following generation.

Thus in the summer of 1960, out of suburbia, were to rise and sputter on the fringes of the Presidential campaign the intellectual arguments that accompanied it. What was to be done with this new form of civilization? How was it to be financed? Was American prosperity to gush in a torrent of self-indulgence (as many Democrats saw it gushing) to the ultimate ruin of moral fiber and purpose? Or was it to flow on, strong and hearty (as the Republicans liked to imagine it), proceeding under its own free-enterprise laws, to the greater expression of individual well-being and national strength?[2]

---

[2] At one point, carried away in devotion to his theme of free private enterprise as a force in national growth, Richard M. Nixon was to tell a Mississippi audience: ". . . I note the tremendous progress of this city. The mayor was telling me in the twelve years that he has been mayor you have had practically a doubling of population. Where has that progress come from? That progress has not come primarily from government, but it has come from the activities of hundreds of thousands of individual Mississippians given an opportunity to develop their own lives."

As the thinkers of both parties debated the problem above the level of public understanding, waiting for the phrase or moment of clarity, the problem came to be another of the campaign clichés: was the private good always the public good? Were two women, meeting at the meat counter of the supermarket and passing up the chuck roast for the sirloin cut, really more interested in the quality of the marbled meat than in the quality of the schools whose overcrowding they grumbled about? Were two men mowing the lawn on a Sunday really better served by the power mowers they had just bought on time—or would they be happier without power mowers, if only the clogged roads by which they drove to and from work could bring them home more quickly, more safely, with less strain? How were the roads, or the schools, or the hospitals, to be paid for in these new communities already mortgaged collectively and individually to the hilt?

How were American energies to be used? That was the question. By private enterprise or public plan? How were the new universities, the new labs, the new teachers, to be prepared in the short ten years before 1970 when the university population would double? What price good schools, good medicine, good roads, new bridges—at what sacrifice of good meats, louvered windows, new cars, new appliances?

All that the census had to say could be made endlessly fascinating.

For the figures talked not only in geographic terms as they described the coarse sprawling and contracting of the waves of population—they talked also of the kind of people Americans were becoming.

Above all, said the figures of 1960, America was becoming a nation of white-collar people. Some time between the year 1950 and the year 1960 (census scholars fix the date uncertainly at the year 1955), for the first time in American history, the number of white-collar Americans (professional, managerial, clerical, and sales people) had become greater than the number of those who held blue-collar jobs (productive or operative). By the summer of 1960 the margin between them was clear: 28,700,000 Americans were employed sitting at desks or selling at counters as white-collar workers; only 24,200,000 Americans made things with their hands or delivered things or produced things. (At the great Boeing aircraft plants, the ratio of white-collar to blue-collar workers has, in the past fifteen years, reversed itself from 3 to 1 for blue-collar worker over white-collar to 3 to 2 of white-collar over blue-collar.)

Exploring the changing occupational structure further, one

comes on a series of illuminations. The number of clerical workers in American life had incredibly increased (from 7,600,000 in 1950 to 9,800,000 in 1960). Professional workers had risen from 8 per cent of employed Americans to 10 per cent. Yet despite the enormous increase in volume of the American economy (from $360,000,000,000 gross product in 1950 to $500,000,000,000 gross national product in 1960), the percentage of sales workers had remained constant and, some analysts thought, was about to diminish. All across the older settled areas of the nation, from Massachusetts to Wisconsin, one could see the boarded-up windows of the little groceries and butcher shops wiped out by the spread of the supermarkets. In every major center of commerce the small jobbers, small distributors, small businessmen, were being gobbled up by larger ones. It had never occurred to me during the Wisconsin primary to regard Commission Row, which runs down North Broadway in Milwaukee, as significant. Yet there was a time twenty years ago, the old men there said, when four commission houses alone would, on a Monday morning, move to the little grocery stores between 200 and 250 carloads of merchandise, of berries, fruits and vegetables. Dawn traffic used to strangle Milwaukee's market area as it still does Les Halles in Paris. Now the streets are clear. Fifteen of the commission houses had withered in the past twenty years, two between the beginning of 1960 and the Wisconsin primary in April. It was the supermarkets that were doing it, said the old men, the great chains dealing directly with the great producers and buying directly in carload lots. Time was, twenty years ago, when Milwaukeeans who loved apples could have a choice of thirty varieties. Now the homogenization of American life, distribution and agriculture had cut commercially available varieties to four—all of them brighter than red. And where were the Baldwin and the Russet apples of yesteryear?

Most disturbing, perhaps, of all the fresh data of 1960 were the figures for self-employment—the people who, in America, work for themselves in their own small businesses and enterprises. In a decade of expanding American employment opportunity, in which the over-all number of employed had risen from 60,000,000 to 67,000,000, the number of people who worked without a boss and for themselves had remained constant or, perhaps, even marginally dwindled. In July of 1950, a decade before, 6,400,000 Americans had been masters of their own shops; in July of 1960 their number had fallen to 6,300,000. The census masters were quick to point out that so slight a difference might be a seasonal fluctuation

—but certainly, they said, the proportion of nonagricultural self-employed to total employed had sharply fallen to the lowest level in American history (from 11.6 per cent in 1950 to 10.4 per cent in 1960).

Americans thus worked more and more for other men, in larger and larger enterprises. The giants of American employment (like the Bell System, which increased its employees from 602,466 to 735,766 in the decade) were baronies in themselves, self-governments, huge, almost unbelievable bureaucracies—as large as the government bureaucracies, with which they clashed and warred in an effort to maintain their organizational independence. The image of the small businessman, of the small free private-enterpriser, whom both parties sought to coddle in the campaign of 1960 was that of the vanishing American—like the American farmer, whose numbers in the decade had dwindled from 4,393,000 to 2,780,000.

On and on ran the census reports, as they will continue to run for the next two years while the endless digits are resorted and resifted for new truths by the humming computers in the air-conditioned glass-walled enclosures.

Much of what the census freshly reported had already seeped through to the campaigners and their staffs; and as they stumped from end to end of the country, the candidates seemed to vie with each other over which could schedule more supermarket stops and which assemble more housewives there.

Yet what the census said of the year 1960 was of less importance to the candidates than what the census reflected of the more remote past. For the census also had much to say about the frozen past of America's roots and origins. And it was this remote past that most concerned the campaigners.

No subject is more intensely discussed in the privacy of any campaign headquarters, either state or national, than the ethnic origins of the American people and their bloc-voting habits. Men have made careers and politicians have won office by being (or claiming to be) experts on the Polish vote, the Jewish vote, the Irish vote, the Negro vote, the Scandinavian vote, the Italian vote, and what the rights, expectations, offices and dignities of each of those blocs are. In some Eastern states, where the "balanced ticket" has prevailed for generations, particular jobs are traditional claims of particular national groups against the community. In Boston, now an Irish-American city, the post of Director of the Boston Public Library is still gracefully reserved by tradition for a

Protestant of old colonial stock; in Connecticut both parties traditionally reserve the designation of Congressman-at-large for a Polish-American; in New York City the post of Police Commissioner is traditionally reserved for an Irish-American, and the Borough Presidency of Manhattan has now become a fief of the Negro community.

The balanced ticket is, of course, not without honor in American history—Abraham Lincoln was promoted to national fame only by such an old-fashioned balanced ticket when in 1858 the early Republican politicians of Illinois sought a Senatorial candidate of downstate Southern stock to run against Democrat Stephen Douglas; their state list, they felt, was too heavy with upstate candidates of Yankee stock. But, as practiced now in such a world center as New York (where in one election in the late forties, the bosses agreed to choose the triumvirate of top city officials by letting the Bronx machine pick the Jew, the Manhattan machine pick the Italian, the Brooklyn machine pick the Irishman), it is a mockery of that glorious mingling of cultures and stocks that is the noblest achievement of American civilization.

A national ticket for the Presidency is not chosen by this squalid method of racial and ethnic balancing. Yet once it is selected, its leaders too must concern themselves with all the delicate inheritances of the subordinate tribal communities of America and address themselves to the imposing task of convincing each little group that somewhere in the candidate's mind and affections they will find a reflection of their own concerns and aspirations. While speaking to the nation as a whole of its national future, the candidate can never forget that he speaks to each of these blocs in terms of its own past.

It is therefore important to understand this ethnic past, for in no area of American politics does student, writer, or politician enter into a realm of greater fancy, generalization, and speculation. What we know of our past origins consists of much romantic history; substantial but incomplete statistical fact; and an enormous component of conjecture.

Statistical history of immigration begins only in 1819, when the Congress of the United States first required that immigrants arriving on the Gulf and East Coasts of the United States be counted by the countries of their origin; in 1820 that count began.

We know, for the census tells us, that in 1820 America held 9,638,000 people, of whom almost 20 per cent were Negroes; and the rest are considered to have been the parent "colonial stock" of America—an overwhelmingly British stock, spiced lightly with adventurers from all northern

Europe. In the 140 years between then and June, 1960, so say the historical records, 43,177,000 immigrants arrived in this country, almost entirely from Europe and Canada.

We know something, too, of the rhythm and crests of this great migration, one of the most unbelievable and awesome folk movements in human history. The Irish were the first to arrive in numbers large enough to alarm the old colonials with the accent and brogue of an alien culture. In the eight years between 1847 and 1854, the Irish who came to this country numbered 1,186,000—or almost *7 per cent* of the white population of the nation at the time! The logistics of this mass movement on tiny sailing vessels under the hazards of that time boggle the imagination.

The Germans came almost simultaneously and in similar force—889,000 in the eight years between 1850 and 1857. And the Germans kept on coming in great waves—another 900,000 in the seven years after the Civil War; another 950,-000 in the five years of 1881–1885; another 300,000 in the five years of 1923–1928; a final 300,000 in a last three-year burst in 1950–1952—to make the German heritage in American life today the second largest component after the colonial heritage. (Politicians who divide people and stocks by party will point out that the Irish were Democrats from arrival, leading the Draft Riots in New York against the Republicans' Civil War in 1863; and that the Germans were Republicans from arrival, forming some of the sturdiest cadres of the Union Army.)

After the Civil War, while Germans and Irishmen continued to migrate to America, there followed a wave of Scandinavians in the eighties and nineties, when the migrations from the north and west of Europe peaked; and then, between 1890 and 1910, came the great migrations from eastern and southern Europe. Between 1900 and 1914 (the outbreak of World War I) Italy contributed no less than 3,035,000 of her sons and daughters to the migration; and eastern and central Europe in the same period contributed 6,500,000 people (fairly evenly divided, it is believed, between Slavs and Jews).

It was these late migrations from southern and eastern Europe that touched off the concern of the old colonial-stock Americans.

The political perspectives were already clearly written to see. The Irish had arrived in New York and Boston, to be treated like animals in the 1850s. Thirty years later, however, the sons of the Irish had moved the old-stock Tammany leaders out of power and taken over Tammany, and thus New York, for themselves. They met greater resistance from the political leadership of the old colonial stock of Boston (where, indeed, John F. Kennedy's grandfathers were chieftains of the Irish political challenge). In Boston the alarm was so great that Massachusetts provided the first clear voice calling for a choking off of immigration. The voice, curiously enough, was that of Henry Cabot Lodge—the first major Congressional leader in the fight to restrict immigration—grandfather of the Henry Cabot Lodge who as Republican Vice-Presidential nominee in 1960 had moved so far from his grandfather's position that he was considered by Republican strategists the most appealing and popular of their candidates with those same ethnic groups whose arrival his forebear had sought to choke off sixty years before.

The debates over immigration policy lasted twenty years after the turn of the century and reached their climax in 1924, when the open gates of America were finally closed. (It is amusing, again, to see how time reverses labels and attitudes. In the immigration debates of 1921 and 1924, it was the American Federation of Labor that insisted that immigration be halted and the National Association of Manufacturers that insisted that immigration be continued free and open to all.) These debates forced the first public examination of who the Americans were, what their origins were, how they fit together in the harmony of American culture. Congress demanded in its immigration acts that the inflow of migrants from Europe be so mixed in composition as to maintain the same racial and ethnic proportions as prevailed in the American population as a whole in 1920. Only 150,000 immigrants a year were to be admitted (as against the peak inflow of 1,285,000 in 1907); and these immigrants were to be broken down into national quotas, each quota proportionate to that nation's contribution to the American population of 1920.

It was here that bafflement set in. Congress charged a technical interdepartmental committee of State, Justice and Commerce to establish national origins from existing immigration and census statistics—but there were no records of migration to America before 1820. A remarkably complicated formula was worked out by the unhappy committee members, dividing every individual American into ethnic parts to make up quota units (i.e., one individual with four Irish grandparents or four individuals with one Irish grandparent both worked out to one American of Irish stock; fractionated Americans had their fractional grandparents assigned to other quotas); elaborate estimating went to fill in gaps in historic data, and the tedious calculations lasted for years. Not until 1929, when the National Origins Act of that year went into effect, were the calculations complete—and these calculations, despite refinements and exemptions made since, are still the basis of our immigration laws.

It is best to disregard this legal formula of American origins and, for a more realistic appraisal of the seed stocks of America, examine a much later study prepared in 1954. In that year, when the McCarran-Walter Immigration Act was being debated, the census was again asked to provide data on where Americans came from, and this time the census scholars prepared, but did not publish, what this reporter, with several large qualifying conditions, regards as still the best available breakdown of American roots.

This still-unpublished census study started with a base of 135,000,000 white citizens out of a total population of 151,-000,000 Americans in 1950. Of these, 126,000,000 Americans came from the quota countries of our European origins.

Americans of British descent (English, Scots, Welsh, Ulstermen) were, in this study, first—in all, some 52,000,000 men, women and children, one third of the whole. Next came Americans of German descent—some 21,000,000.[3] Then came an estimated 14,000,000 Americans of Irish descent. (This progression of stocks is teasingly but artificially reflected in the progression of the three names: Truman, Eisenhower, Kennedy.) There followed, fourth, Americans of Italian descent, with 7,000,000; fifth, Americans of Scandinavian descent, with 6,000,000; sixth, Americans of Polish descent with 5,000,000. All the other stocks of our country—French, Dutch, Canadian, Spanish, Czech, Swiss, Russian, Greek, Belgian, etc.—made up the balance. (Americans of Jewish descent, strained from the arbitrary European countries of origin, are estimated at 5,400,000.)

Any inquirer about these figures is immediately warned by the census scholars that they are in no way a perfect reflection of our country's origins.

First, it is pointed out, such figures are compiled from past immigration figures with a neat, mechanical extrapolation from decade to decade according to birth rates then prevalent. Thus each group is assumed to have grown in numbers at the same rate as every other group—High Episcopalians being assumed to have the same birth rate as Mormons, Scandinavians assumed to have the same birth rate as devout Italian Catholics. Government officials cannot permit their official calculations to be influenced by those observational realities that politicians know, vaguely, to be

---

[3] Nonwhite stock came to approximately 16,000,000 at this time.

true, but which cannot be statistically demonstrated. It is safe to assume, however, that the original overwhelmingly Protestant British stock of the nation has had a perceptibly lower birth rate than have later arrivals, and that its proportion of the whole, rather than being one third of the total, may be as low as one fourth.

Another and even greater caution is raised. These figures ignore one of the dominant facts of American civilization— that boys and girls in America for hundreds of years have been willing to fall in love, marry and raise families with mates of background, custom and parentage different from their own. English and French, Dutch and German, Italian and Irish and Scandinavian have mixed their blood, hope and seed in this country for so long and with such faith in America's common future that their progeny, bearing all the mixed genes of Europe in single individuals, is probably the largest single component of America's people. Yet no one can guess how many they are, or who they are, or what they are. The melting pot has been melting now for almost two hundred years; groups have melted at different rates into the common whole; and when asked to guess how many of which group have come down entirely closed in the tribal communities of pure ancestry, the men of the census throw up their hands. It is impossible.

It is this impossibility of exactitude that makes American politics such an art. How many Americans are so tied to their past that they cannot be summoned to face the American future? To how many of each group must a politician give insurance policies of protection and respect? How many of each group will be offended by a coarse appeal to their tribal origin that divides them from all other Americans? All, all, are Americans, for the harmony of America's origins is what gives America its symphonic vitality. Yet the politician, roughly cherishing this knowledge, also knows for sure that he cannot ignore the strength of kinship politics.

Thus the politician's map of America differs from the geographical map. For the political campaigners, the South, the border states, the farm states reaching up through the Dakotas (as well as patches of upper New England and upper New York) are areas of British stock, parent-stock country. Buffalo, Detroit, Chicago and some of the upper Midwest farm country bring to mind the Polish vote. Wisconsin, Minnesota, Montana, Washington suggest the Scandinavian vote. The Jewish vote registers on the politician's mind with overwhelming impact in New York City and its suburbs, and then again in Chicago, Philadelphia, Boston, Los Angeles and Miami. The voters of German stock are so broadly spread across the country that except in Wisconsin they cannot be treated separately. The Italian voters make themselves felt as a bloc with particular vigor in New York City, Connecticut, Rhode Island, northern New Jersey, Pittsburgh, and Ohio.

The Irish are a special case. For the Irish, as the earliest of the great migrant communities, have had the longest stretch of American experience, and the operation of the many influences of American culture has produced in them the greatest political diversity of any of the immigrant stocks except for the parent colonial stock. Until 1870 they were the largest foreign-born nationality group in America, to be replaced thereafter by the Germans. But their role as political pioneers for the other late-coming arrivals persisted long after they were outnumbered in the immigration tallies by other nationalities; and it is this role of pioneer that explains how that stock figure of jest, the "Irish politician" came to be born.

The "Irish politician" is worth pausing over in American political history; for whether he is described as a figure of honor or vilification, his role was absolutely essential in the shaping of modern American political life. On the urban frontier he was the builder and architect of a political system that lasted for almost sixty years.

His role is easy to explain. As the millions of European immigrants came off their boats in New York, Boston and Philadelphia, they found themselves, all of them, tongueless, hungry and despised in this strange land of their hope. They brought no understanding of the workings of democracy from the autocracies of old Europe, nor even the faintest concept of the working of Anglo-Saxon jurisprudence. They could all vote, just as soon as they had learned to read and write primitive English. But what they were voting for, or how the system of government that enfranchised them within five years of arrival worked, they did not know.

Among all these immigrant groups who shared the slums and tenements, who looked at the police with fear and trembling, who offered their untaught skills for whatever wages industry chose to offer, there stood out only one that could speak the tongue of the land: the Irish. Such words as "sheriff," "surrogate," "mayor," "alderman" were familiar in all the counties of Erin. The Irish, alone at first and for generations almost unchallenged by other immigrants, understood the instrumentation of government set up by the settlers of British tradition. Government to the immigrants was important: government was the policeman who could pinch or release a peddler, the judge who could jail or pardon a first offender, the school that could be pried open or remain barred to children. And so, in their need for government and in their alien tongueless wonder, the other groups accepted the Irish among them as leaders because the Irish understood, at once, the English language, the immigrant needs and the American government.

What political power the Irish won in the big cities of the North in the closing decades of the nineteenth century they hung on to with tenacity for years and years afterward in the command machinery of the Democratic Party.

It was only in the 1930s that two events shook the grip of the Irish Democratic leadership in the big cities. One was, of course, the New Deal in Washington, whose generosity in relief and jobs dwarfed anything the local Irish machines could provide for their clients. The New Deal freed the slum clients of the machines from utter dependence on the machine's sporadic generosity and favor. The second event, slower maturing, was simply the growth in education and dignity of the sons and grandsons of later immigrants who had arrived a generation or two after the Irish. English-speaking now, American-trained, American by instinct, they began to shove and push the Irish for leadership in American city life. Some groups made a lateral penetration, as did the Jews, through the professions or via Washington. Others, like the Italians, fought a jungle war of claw and fang with Irish leadership for their place in the sun. (It is noteworthy that in New York City, where the Italians constitute the largest single ethnic group of the population, it was not until 1932 that the Irish-led Tammany Hall permitted a single Italian district leader to sit in its councils—and that seat was won not by gentle persistence but in a bare-knuckled, head-cracking East Side fight.)

There are still, to be sure, many small-time politicians of Irish extraction in the big-city machines—but they are indistinguishable from their Italian, Jewish, Polish, Negro colleagues; they win no city or statewide leadership by right of inheritance or because there are no others to challenge them. There is, I believe, only one "Irish politician" left in the country who exercises anything like the old-fashioned backroom control over a statewide coalition of races. Where Irish names stand out in political leadership today, they stand out in the open—Daley of Chicago, Lawrence of Pennsylvania, Green of Philadelphia, Shelley of San Francisco are men who run openly for Congress, mayoralty, or governorship. Their political wars are conducted in the open and their victories are claimed at the polls, not in the back rooms. And beyond such men there is yet the third political wave of Irish descent—the young men and women of the fourth and fifth generation, educated at the great universities, who find their homes alike in the Democratic and Republican Parties, staffing the Stevensonians and the reformists, the Nixon and the Rockefeller organizations, with no sense of parochialism, entirely merged in the common American attitude to life.

Every national election takes account of these facts. Both National Committees analyze and reanalyze the ethnic groups every four years, knowing that the old colonial stock splits North and South into Republican and Democrat, that German and Scandinavian stock will split heavily for the Republicans, that Jews, Poles and Italians will break heavily for the Democrats, that the Irish are now unpredictable—and that a coalition must be made of all of them, so that the victorious candidate, when President, can claim the full loyalty of every group and, with this confidence, can summon them to their tasks and duties as Americans at home and abroad.

In the election of 1960, however, two other cleavages were to acquire an importance in electoral strategy greater than ever before in American political history.

These were the cleavages, first between white Americans and Negro Americans; and next between Protestant Americans and Catholic Americans. Here the weight of the past had the heaviest impact on the campaign.

The mingling of white and Negro Americans has been the most terrible problem of American politics since the Constitution makers first became embrangled in a hopeless search for its solution; out of their inability to find a humane solution came the Civil War; this mingling of white and Negro remains today, along with peace-and-war and the proper conduct of the economy, one of the three cardinal problems of American life.

It is not so much color that divides Negro and white Americans as the way the past has created different conditions of life and thus different social habits and mores.

The past begins with the abomination of slavery. Some historians believe that in the discovery and colonial eras more black than white persons were brought to the new hemisphere; estimates of the African transshipment run from a low of 6,000,000 to an unbelievable 15,000,000. Trapped in Africa (by their own kind), then manacled and sold to the white traders (who commerced in them), Negroes were exported as animal energy to the New World. The estimate of those Africans who were brought to what is now America runs from a generally accepted figure of 350,000 to 400,000 up to a million. So merciless were the conditions of life under which they were penned, however, that, by the time of America's own revolution a century and a half after the first Negroes arrived only an estimated 500,000 could be counted alive as slaves; and as slaves then, for another eighty-five years, they were worked, bred and beaten, like nonhumans, in one of those sins of mankind for which there can never be expiation. Divorced from all culture and refinements; denied, except rarely, the rights and sacraments of marriage; forbidden the opportunity of hope or education, they were freed in 1865 and cast hopelessly adrift in a Southern society that still used them on farm and field more as animals than as people. Until 1870, 80 per cent of all Negroes in America could neither read nor write. And until only twenty years ago, the Negro was an *object* of American political discussion— not a participant.

What has happened in the past decade is that Negro Americans insist on discussing their own fate with white Americans; in the campaign of 1960, this insistence, and the recognition of it by American politics, became an overriding consideration of both candidates.

The rise of this insistence, the power to enforce this insistence, comes from the greatest geographic migration in American life since the settlers took their covered wagons west—the movement of the Negro from the South to the North and West, and (in both South and North) from farm to city. There is little to be seen or photographed of this vast continuing migrant movement. One can stand any evening at midnight in the 63rd Street Station on Chicago's South Side as the Illinois Central Railroad brings its gleaming orange-and-brown special, "The City of New Orleans," up from its all-day run out of the lower Mississippi valley. There are usually no more than twenty, fifty, sometimes eighty Southern Negroes who step off the train, blinking in the station lights, some dressed in their best go-to-meeting clothes, others dressed in tattered work clothes, with all their possessions wrapped in a cloth sack. Relatives greet them and they disappear inconspicuously in the night. They are similarly inconspicuous as they climb out of the weather-beaten, flat-spring trucks that unload platoons of migrant labor each summer to work on the farms of New Jersey and New York; the trucks return south each fall, but they carry fewer Negroes back than they brought north. The Negro trickle is as unnoticed on arrival as was the daily but incessant trickle of white people that arrived at Castle Gardens in New York seventy years ago from Europe. Negroes, like other immigrants, become visible only when they clot in the big cities; only then is their migration measurable.

There is no specific count made of any group of Americans as they move about the country; in some years it is estimated the Negro migration from the South may be as low as 100,000, in other years as high as 200,000. Only in retrospect can the United States census measure what has happened. In 1910, 90 per cent of all American Negroes lived in the states of the Old South, left to the mercies of Southern custom, excluded totally from all American politics, working in the fields. By the 1960 census it was revealed that only 52 per cent of American Negroes still lived in the old Confederacy—almost half now lived in the North and West, and these Negroes gathered preponderantly in the great metropolitan centers of the North.[4]

The change, both North and South, has been dramatic. In the South no state any longer counts a majority of Negroes (as did Mississippi and South Carolina before the war). In the decade of the 1940s alone, the net migration from Mississippi of Negroes was nearly 260,000—approximately one fourth the total Negro population of the state in 1940; and the Negroes who left were the youngest and most vigorous— nearly one half of all Mississippi Negroes who reached the age of thirty in the 1940s fled that state.

In the North the result of the migration has not only been dramatic—but just short of explosive. In 1960 the city of Washington, D.C., the nation's capital, became the first major city of the world to count a Negro majority of population (54 per cent in 1960 as against 35 per cent in 1950). New York City has seen the number of its Negroes grow from 775,000 in 1950 (9.8 per cent of the total) to 1,087,000 in 1960 (14 per cent of the total). (In the Borough of Manhattan, with a population of 1,900,000, three quarters of all children in the public elementary schools are either Negro or Puerto Rican.) Philadelphia's population is set at 26 per cent Negro today and Detroit's at 29 per cent; the Negro population of Newark, New Jersey, has almost doubled in the past decade—going from 75,000 (or 17 per cent) in 1950 to 138,000 (or 35 per cent) in 1960. In 1940, Newark counted only 10 per cent Negroes. All the major cities of the Northeast have lost population in the past decade, says the census. The population they have lost has been white population; the population that has replaced them has been Negro. (New York has lost over 450,-

---

[4] Nationally, the census of 1960 recorded the number of Negroes at 18,871,000, or 10.5 per cent of the total American population. In 1950 it had been 15,048,000, or 10.0 per cent.

000 white people in this decade; its Negro population has grown by more than 300,000; Newark has lost 100,000 whites in this decade; it has gained 65,000 Negroes.)

This has resulted not only in the most violent problems of neighborhood adjustment in each Northern city. It has posed a political problem of the first magnitude.

Negroes vote in the North. And they vote predominantly in the big-city states, which carry the largest blocs of electoral votes in the nation. Among them, Illinois, Pennsylvania, New York and Michigan measure out to 132 electoral votes—or almost exactly half the number needed to elect the President. In these states, the queen city of each state harbors a Negro vote that may mean the difference between success or failure in a close national election.

Time was, forty years ago, when Negroes voted solidly Republican out of gratitude to Abraham Lincoln and emancipation. ("I remember," once said Roy Wilkins, Executive Secretary of the National Association for the Advancement of Colored People, "when I was young in Kansas City, the kids threw rocks at Negroes on our street who dared to vote Democratic.") But Franklin D. Roosevelt changed that. Under Roosevelt, government came to mean social security, relief, strong unions, unemployment compensation. ("Let Jesus lead me, and welfare feed me" was a Negro depression chant.) And, like a heaving-off of ancient habit, as the Negro moved north he moved on to the Democratic voting rolls.

Many of the most eminent Negro leaders in America today have personally lived through this political transition. "I was born in Dougherty County, Georgia," said Congressman William Dawson of Chicago, senior Negro in the American Congress, several years ago, "just one step this side of Hell. I stood guard with my father all one night to stop a lynching when I was fifteen. I hated the word Democrat when I came north. I saw them bring Negroes up from the South in World War I and stuff them in here, into four and a half miles of the Black Belt, until it was the most populated spot on the face of the globe. I saw them ripping basements out of stores and pushing people to live in rat-infested filth, until the Black Belt was the damnedest pesthole ever conceived by the mind of man."

But Roosevelt made Dawson switch from the Republican to the Democratic side. Roosevelt brought assistance and relief in the depression. "Negroes would have died like flies if he hadn't kept his hand on the money until it got to them," said Dawson. And so Dawson became, as he still is, a Democratic political boss in Chicago, at first only of the Negro wards, then in the senior council of Cook County.

Just how much the Democratic Party owed to men like Dawson and the Negro vote did not become apparent until 1948. But when in 1948 Harry Truman squeezed ahead of Thomas E. Dewey by 33,612 votes in Illinois, by 17,865 votes in California, by 7,107 votes in Ohio, no practicing politician could remain ignorant of how critical was the Negro vote in the Northern big city in a close election.

Since then, as the Negro migration from the South has quickened in pace and size, the importance of the Negro vote has grown to be almost obsessive with Northern political leaders. Running proportionately in some places (like New York) at 3 to 1 Democratic and in others (like Detroit) at 8 to 1 Democratic, the Negro industrial vote is one of the most solid political properties in Democratic custody. It represents power.

Nor can this huge power, this ability to swing half the electoral votes necessary to make a President in a close election, be hidden from Negro leaders themselves.

For as the great migration has moved north, other things have been happening to Negroes besides industrialization—most noteworthy among them, education. No measurable group in American life, one can learn from a special census report of 1959, has made so remarkable a stride in education and development over the past decade as the Negro. Today, only 7 per cent of Negroes are still illiterate. Between 1940 and 1959, the proportion of college graduates among young adult Negroes tripled. And the result has been the development among Negroes of a leadership across the nation of such brilliance, devotion and zeal as to be among the most significant triumphs of faith in democracy. Except that it is a leadership still locked in its subcommunity, still parochially devoted, and energized almost entirely and exclusively by Negro purposes, not yet willing (even if permitted) to lend its leadership to national purpose as a whole.

This Negro leadership now, in 1960, stood full of confidence and vigor after a six-year march from one triumph to another. Beginning in 1954, with the decision of the Supreme Court that all public schools in America must desegregate, this leadership had finally sensed itself backed by the might of the law. And with the law on its side, it moved year by year, issue by issue, state by state, battle by battle—from Autherine Lucy and the Montgomery bus strike of 1955 to the sit-ins of 1960—to use its leverage on the political system to win its demands of society. Never in any election before 1960 had any group, under leadership of such talent, presented its specific community demands in such blunt and forceful terms.

It would be so good and happy a thing if a political reporter could leave the Negro problem in the United States at the level of its superb political leadership; or at its bare political statistics; or at the net balance of justice, which certainly supports Negro leadership, as it did in 1960 with righteousness and justification.

But no political writer in the United States can adequately report the problem of white-Negro relations without presenting the full balance of the ledgers, or what disturbs the whites of the South and, increasingly, the whites of the big Northern cities.

For what has happened over the past twenty years, as Negro progress has come so swiftly, is that the gap between its own advanced leadership and the troops of its rear echelon has widened almost as fast as progress. If Negro education, Negro culture, Negro responsibilities have soared, so, sickeningly, has the heritage of a past now sampling life with an abandon once choked by Southern white cruelties. Perhaps the most dramatic and alarming of the figures attendant on the release of the Negro from his previous Southern punishments has been the rise in the proportion of illegitimate Negro births as the Negro has moved North. In 1940 (so records the census) 16.8 per cent of Negro children in the United States were born out of wedlock. (In that same year, the proportion of illegitimacy among American whites was 2.0 per cent.) By 1958 (the last year for which comparative figures are available) the figure for white illegitimacy was substantially the same: 2.1 per cent. The proportion of Negro illegitimacy had, however, swollen to 21.2 per cent. One fifth of the Negro children in the United States are born fatherless —and in some of the larger Northern cities, the proportion is estimated at one fourth or more.

Differing heritage and social customs produce these grim figures; in 1950, 21 per cent of the homes of nonwhite families with children under eighteen were broken homes; for white families the comparable figure was around 8 per cent. But attendant on those figures are all the figures of delinquency and street violence; and the political implications thereof.

Whether or not the present trend of violence and crime is a transitional crest in adjustment to city living among Negroes or whether it is more morbid, no one at the moment knows. Some years ago this reporter tried to investigate the dimensions of what was happening in the four Northern cities with the largest Negro populations. At that time the latest figures available for public inspection were those of 1955, a year of high prosperity, and they read thus: In Chicago (where Negroes were then estimated at 17 per cent of the total) Negroes accounted for 65 per cent of the jail population, 70 per cent of the occupants in public housing, 75 per cent of those on relief. In New York (Negroes at that time: 12 per cent) Negroes accounted for 38 per cent in public housing, 38 per cent on relief, and the jail figures were not publicly revealed. In Philadelphia (then 21 per cent Negro) Negroes made up 80 per cent of the jail population, 43 per cent of those in public housing, 50 per cent of those on relief. In Detroit (then 19 per cent Negro) Negroes made up 58 per cent of the jail population, 50 per cent of those in public housing, 69 per cent of those on relief.

Although these figures alarm, there appear also to be two counterweights to such figures.

The first was one I heard from a distinguished and heartful Negro member of the Philadelphia City Council with whom I discussed the situation. He said, "Do you remember reading Richard Wright's book about the colored boy in the slum, looking up at the airplane in the sky and muttering, 'Fly that plane white boy, fly that plane'? He just knew it was a white boy flying that plane and it could never be him, no matter how much he wanted. The Negro feels trapped. He feels he has to fight everybody. The police kick him around, social workers treat him not like people but like a 'case,' and a 'Negro case' at that. School authorities try to restrict him, teachers as soon as they get a little experience want to be transferred elsewhere. A white boy raises hell—the police bat him around and send him home. When a Negro boy raises hell, he's fingerprinted, arrested, mugged; from then on he's got a record, he's a target. Twenty-five years ago, only one in ten arrests in Philadelphia for dope involved a Negro; now it's the other way around. Dope lets him rise above the world, above discrimination, it's another form of escape. He lives in the slums and hates it, and nobody will let him live anywhere else."

The second counterweight comes from figures alone. Los Angeles is that city of the United States where the Negro probably receives the most decent treatment and has the best opportunity for decent housing. In Los Angeles, in 1955, Negroes constituted 11.3 per cent of the population—yet only 14 per cent of the jail population, 18 per cent of those in public housing, 18 per cent of those on relief. It is possible, if the Los Angeles figures are valid, that when Americans of any color are given full equality in jobs and in housing, they behave with full and equal responsibility too. It has not yet proved so in the big Northeastern cities. Other groups from Europe, adjusting in times past to American urban life, have done so with equal violence. Faith and history urge today's observer to hope that Negro violence will also slowly diminish.

Such statistics as these are generally of more interest to sociologists than to politicians. Yet politics are only sociology in action; and the abrasions and frictions of urban life in the Northern big cities have begun to rub off in politics. No Northern political boss has yet begun to make political capital of these frictions as race-blind Southern politicians have done for decades; yet more than one Northern big-city boss has privately considered the matter.

It is the ominous growth of friction in the streets that places so exquisite a problem of real leadership and responsibility on both white and Negro political leaders. In the past, white bosses have tried to find low-grade "Uncle Tom" leadership for their Negro wards, dull puppets who could be manipulated at white will. But the Negro community all across the nation is now in the process of repudiating such leadership and seeking new, positive men of its own stock. Yet the new positive men win votes in their wards only by the most unqualified denunciation of the white "power structure," and the poverty, desolation and overcrowding it imposes in Negro slums. It is as if all their energies and drives were directed outward against the white enemy, with none left for responsible guidance and attention to those patterns of Negro living and manners that so worry the white community. In the long reach for a social harmony in American life, responsibility for common standards must rest upon both leaderships—white leadership and Negro leadership alike. For, if it is politically impossible that Negro leaders ignore the demand of their community for better schooling, better housing, better job opportunities for its youth, so is it politically impossible for many white political leaders to ignore the demands of *their* communities for an orderly tranquility and urban peacefulness in the process of adjustment.

It is this growing political problem that creates the artificial and untrusting quality of dialogue between Negro leaders and white politicians in the North. White politicians in the North know the Negro vote to be vital. Negro leaders press publicly for equal rights, and white leaders verbally agree. But Negroes know that white leadership always, privately, holds back on the basis of concern that both refuse to discuss.

However these matters may add up in the long run of American history, the election of 1960 was indeed to prove a bench mark. Even more than the election of 1948, the outcome of 1960 was to be dependent on Negro votes. And the leadership of the Negroes, like the leadership of so many minorities in the great cities of the United States, was to exert its electoral strength. For the Northern cities of the United States, commanding the electoral votes necessary to make an American President, have for generations provided a leverage on American power to shape and alter the world itself. During the years of World War I, the Irish of the great Northern cities had provided the leverage to free Ireland from Britain; the Czechs of Pennsylvania had actually written the first Constitution of the Free Czechoslovak Republic in Pittsburgh in 1919. During and after World War II, the Jews of the great Northern cities had exercised their political leverage to win and guarantee the independence of Israel.

And so, in 1960, the Negroes of the Northern cities meant to exercise their leverage on the Presidential election, to compel equality for their kinfolk in the South. Deeply motivated, Negro leaders watched the electoral campaign begin in the summer of 1960; and, deeply concerned, both candidates wondered how in conscience and in tactic they could honorably harness these motivations to the conquest of the American Presidency.

There remains one last division of the past to be considered as the Americans moved to consider their candidates—the largest and most important division in American society, that between Protestants and Catholics.

America as a civilization began with religion. The first and earliest migrants from Europe, those who shaped America's culture, law, tradition and ethics, were those who came from England—and they came when English civilization was in torment over the manner in which Englishmen might worship Christ. All through the seventeenth century, as the settlers arrived from the downs, the moors, and the villages of England, they came scarred with the bitterness and intensity of the religious wars of that era, wars no less bloody and ferocious for the fact that they were fought between Protestant sects, Protestant against Protestant. The harshness of Cromwell, that somber figure, was a reflection of the harshness with which Protestants assailed each other, as well as Catholics, over sect and dogma.

It was with this remembered bitterness that the English

migrants began the building of a new society in a new world; and out of this bitterness they distilled, though not without a struggle, that first great landmark in America's unique civiliza- tion, that first of the creative American compromises that was to set America apart from the old world: freedom of worship, the decision that government should have no right to make inquiry into the faith of its citizens and that the state should remain forever divorced from any religious establishment. Never in civilization, since the earliest ziggurats and temples went up in the mud-walled villages of prehistoric Mesopo- tamia, had there been any state that left each individual to find his way to God without the guidance of the state. In retrospect, this is probably the greatest historic decision en- shrined in the American Constitution.

The Americans of the age were not an irreligious people; and the fact that they were Christian was very important, for the marks of Christianity lay all across the Constitution. Al- though Christianity has never been the *guarantee* of a demo- cratic state anywhere in the world, no democracy has ever thrived successfully for any period of time outside of Chris- tian influence; without the quality of mercy and forgiveness, there is only logic and reason to guide a state, and these guar- antee no freedom to any man. What the American Constitution did was to accept and code a working compromise that had been reached by men and women of English descent escaped from the fratricidal wars of religion in Europe and unwilling to transfer such wars to the new land. Each man would wor- ship in his own manner; and the state would limit itself to the affairs of Caesar. For the Protestants who created the American state, the very antithesis of these ideas was the code of the Church of Rome, which their forefathers had repudiated in England over two hundred years before.

Not until the 1850s did the Protestant civilization of Amer- ica begin to include a serious proportion of Catholics, and then (apart from the historic New Orleans community) it was a Catholicism confined to the few large cities of the Eastern seaboard, where the great Irish migration was beginning to arrive. And not until 1891 did the United States census his- torically begin to estimate, from Catholic sources, the num- ber of Catholics in the American population. In that year, estimates the census, there were in America 8,277,000 Cath- olics out of a total population of 64,361,000 in America—or 13 per cent. By 1928, the year an American Catholic, Alfred E. Smith, first ran for President, the proportion had grown to 16 per cent (or 19,689,000 out of 120,501,000). In 1957 the United States conducted a special census of religion in America, and in that year one has the choice of two divergent sets of figures. Following the old tables and accepting Catholic estimates of Catholic communicants, America held 34,564,000 Catholics out of an estimated total population of 171,229,000 citizens, or 20 per cent. Accepting instead the special census figure of 43,037,000 Catholics at that time, the Catholic proportion of Americans amounted to 26 per cent.

The huge difference between the official Catholic claim and the higher estimate of the Bureau of the Census—a difference of 8,600,000 in the year 1957—illustrates the trickiness of all figures on religion in the United States. Some groups—such as the Christian Scientists—refuse to offer any estimate of their numbers at all. Some Protestant groups, such as the Lutherans, count all members of their faith from the moment of baptism, as do the Catholics. Other (and most Protestant) groups count their communicants only from the age of thirteen or fourteen. For some years Jewish groups numbered only the male heads of household; now Jewish groups estimate their numbers on the basis of established congregations (it is estimated that there are 5,400,000 Jews in the United States today, the largest Jewish community since the Destruction of the Temple). All figures on religious breakdowns in the United States, either by state or nation, are thus guesses, subject to error of up to 20 per cent.

It is obvious, however, from the spread of the census figures since 1890 that the increasing percentage of Catholics has come first from the great south and central European migrations of the early 1900s (Italian, Polish, some Czech, some German Catholic); and has thereafter been amplified by the Catholic birth rate. Dr. Donald N. Barrett of the University of Notre Dame has estimated that in the years 1950–1959 the Catholic population of the United States increased by 35.8 per cent while the general population increased by 16.6 per cent. Or in other words, as he has said, "Forty-one per cent of the total United States growth in 1950–1959 was derived from the Catholic sector of the population."

Such a statistical development reflects, of course, a change in the composition of American life, of which American politics has been aware for generations. From the Eastern Seaboard all the way through to St. Paul, Minnesota (or Omaha, Nebraska) this change has for a full generation been the working problem of practicing politicians of both parties.

In general, and for reasons quite apart from faith, most Catholics have voted Democratic. They have voted Democratic because when they arrived as immigrants in the large industrial cities they found the national political machinery at the time of their arrival in the hands of Republicans who distrusted big cities; Catholic immigrants entered, naturally, into the party that sought and cultivated their votes, the Democratic. Not only did they enter—within a period of fifty years they had come to lead and possess the Democratic Party in a bloc of states that stretched from New England to Illinois. In New York State, for example, in a recent year, of sixty-two counties in the state, the Democratic County Committeemen in fifty-seven were Catholic. (Two of the other five were Jewish, three were Protestant.) In Massachusetts, Connecticut and Rhode Island so sharp is the cleavage between religions that the Democratic Party might almost be defined as the party of Catholics, the Republican Party as the party of Protestants. In Pennsylvania, Illinois, Ohio, Democratic leadership is largely Catholic, too. For thirty years, by tradition, the chairman of the Democratic National Committee has been a Catholic.

Yet in American politics no figures are ever certain or stable. Groups slowly move from party to party from generation to generation; as the Negroes over the past thirty years have passed from being predominantly Republican to being predominantly Democratic, so have millions of Catholics over the past thirty years, as they have prospered and moved forward in life, been slowly drifting away from the Democratic Party to the Republican. "Ah," said a mournful political leader to me once, "These guys whose grandfathers used to want to be captain of the ward now all want to be president of the country club.")

This drift of Catholics away from Democratic leadership was all through the 1950s the chief concern of Democratic Party leadership. Roosevelt, in his later elections, had begun to lose some of that 65–70 per cent margin of the Catholic vote that the Democrats had normally thought of as their own. Harry Truman in his 1948 election brought them back. But Adlai Stevenson, according to the findings of the major opinion analysts, lost Catholics to Republican Dwight D. Eisenhower in decisive proportions. In 1952, so estimates George Gallup, Stevenson retained only 56 per cent of the Catholic vote; in 1956 he barely managed to win a shadow margin of 51 per cent.

How to bring the Catholics back into the Democratic Party, how to repossess the base vote of an enormous group of Americans who were no longer immigrants, no longer dependent on political favor for progress, no longer clients of any one party, who now exercised freely their choice between the candidates of both parties—this had haunted Democrats ever since 1952. For, despite some Protestant judgments of Catholics, the Church committed itself to no narrow political loyalties; Church leadership in America has entered that stage of sophistication where it feels as much at home with Republicans as with Democrats. In many of the most important dioceses of the nation it was known in 1960 that if the Catholic Church had any silent inclination, it leaned to Richard M. Nixon rather than to John F. Kennedy.

Yet, though every man knew that the Church would remain scrupulously neutral in the coming campaign; and that millions of upper class Catholics had permanently passed into the Republican Party; and that, further, it was impossible for either major party to make an outright bid for Catholic votes *as* Catholic votes—it was still certain that Catholics, by and large, as well as every other group in the country, Jewish and Protestant, would have a natural gravitation to a candidate of their own faith. Between two Protestants, Catholics would vote impartially by personality, economics, instinct, aspiration or tradition; but if the choice lay between Protestant and Catholic candidates, the kinship issue would certainly be raised and thus cut both ways. That was the question: would a Catholic candidate gain more from his kinsmen's inclination to vote *their* past, or would he lose more from the Protestants' inclination to vote *their* past?

This question had been debated by Democratic Party leaders ever since 1924, usually in terms of Electoral College votes. In 1924 the Party had first seriously considered a Catholic, Alfred E. Smith, for its nomination; in 1928 it had given him the nomination; ever since, with the memory of his overwhelming defeat in mind, the Party leadership (even though substantially Catholic) had believed that a Catholic candidate, in any election, would lose far more than he might gain by his faith.

This was the hazard that John F. Kennedy faced in the summer of 1956 when he sought the Vice-Presidency and that, for four years thereafter, until 1960, was his greatest political handicap. His Party's Eastern leaders were incapable of discussing the matter in terms of doctrine, of American civilization, of tolerance. They would discuss the matter only in terms of practical election arithmetic, and so only in these terms could Kennedy hope to persuade a Democratic Convention to let him offer himself against the hazard.

The arithmetic used by the Kennedys is probably as reliable as anybody else's in the vague and tentative estimates one must make of religious affiliation in the United States. According to this arithmetic, there were at least fourteen vitally important states, states which normally swing back and forth in national elections, and in which the proportion of Catholics to total citizenry was large enough to count *for* Kennedy rather than *against* him. These states were:

> New York (Catholics, 40 per cent)
> Pennsylvania (Catholics, 29 per cent)
> Illinois (Catholics, 30 per cent)
> New Jersey (Catholics, 39 per cent)
> Massachusetts (Catholics, 50 per cent)
> Connecticut (Catholics, 49 per cent)
> Rhode Island (Catholics, 60 per cent)
> California (Catholics, 22 per cent)
> Michigan (Catholics, 24 per cent)
> Minnesota (Catholics, 4 per cent)
> Ohio (Catholics, 20 per cent)
> Wisconsin (Catholics, 31 per cent)
> Maryland (Catholics, 21 per cent)
> Montana (Catholics, 22 per cent)

These states amounted to 261 electoral votes—only eight short of the votes necessary to carry the national election. Not even this 1956 table (prepared by Ted Sorensen and John Bailey) could convince the big-city bosses of the East (mostly Catholic) that their kinsman-in-faith could master the profound religious division in American origins and go on to win. Not until Kennedy's spring exertions of 1960 in the cross-country primaries could he convince them and the leaders of other Democratic minorities that he might win.

Thus, when finally in the summer of 1960 John F. Kennedy turned to face the nation, he turned with a campaign split as few other campaigns by the contradiction of American voting. In word, speech and idea it reflected the candidate's innermost personal spirit, which was entirely addressed to the highest purposes of the American future. Yet it could not ignore its spectacular gamble about the American past: whether, for Catholic and Protestant, the past would outweigh the future.

So much depended on how this, the transcendent issue of religion, could be shaped—whether in practice the differing qualities of fear and bigotry could be separated. For bigotry, which is unreasoning, can be cured only by death. Yet fear, if honest, can be erased by truth.

In the folk memory of the dominant Protestant American community the Roman Catholic Church was known to have used the instruments of state in the past to impose its faith on countless communities by fear, force and pressure. But this was 1960, and the place was America. The institutional policy of any church, including the Roman Catholic Church, could be a legitimate, open and unbigoted subject of public discussion if it intruded itself in legislative matters (as later, indeed, it was to intrude violently in 1960 in the politics of an American Commonwealth, Puerto Rico). So could the attitude of any individual American seeking public office, if he sought thereby to carry into effect the policy of any church. The problem was not one of separation of church and state, a doctrine settled by the Constitution, but the attitude of an individual American to this founding doctrine—and that individual had to be judged as an individual, by the slow estimate of reasonable fellow Americans.

Yet there was no immediate American background for this kind of judgment. Few Americans had lived abroad long enough or widely enough to recognize how diverse are the attitudes and institutions of the Roman Catholic Church in the twentieth century—how vast, for example, is the gap between the benign and tolerant humanitarianism of the French Catholic Church and the narrow intolerance of the Spanish Catholic Church. Few Protestants realized how various are the attitudes of American Catholics (however loyal they may be in faith to their sacraments) to the role of their Church in public affairs. To persuade the dominant community of Protestant Americans that he was bound by no doctrine espoused by some obscure Pope at some other time in some other country but, rather, that he sought his authority only from their will and their free choice as citizens—this, then, became the first imperative of John F. Kennedy, who believed no other. In such a delicate exercise Richard M. Nixon (as Hubert Humphrey before him) could be only a witness and a bystander.

This was the past from which both candidates departed in August to stir the emotions of America—the immediate past of growth and change, of decaying cities and swelling suburbs, of technological change and work patterns changing with them, coupled with the remote past of mothers' songs and fathers' stories, of Negro humiliation and white fears, of hymns in church and martyrs forgotten—all to be weighed against the future the two candidates might describe for all, a future of war or peace, of outer space and ocean depth, of schools and medical care, of bounty or disaster.

And no logic anywhere to guide the two candidates except the stark figure of 269—the number of electoral votes needed to win the Presidency.

Chapter 9

KENNEDY FOR PRESIDENT: ROUND ONE

THE electoral exercise that now began and that was to continue from midsummer until the first snow flurries of November was, as all Presidential campaigns must be, an exercise in which no man could accurately separate the real from the unreal.

All through this period of confusion, as Americans sluggishly woke from summer to awareness of the struggle, the stage of politics rang with the blare of sound, the rustle of gossip, the boasts of partisanship—and no hard measure available for three months, until the last climax on November 8th, 1960. To chronicle these months is like packaging fog. Each witness and participant separates them into mood phases, divided into rounds of his own imagining or reconstruction. For each of the candidates there came, first, the opening round of the electoral campaign, as both felt their way around the country seeking theme and purpose; next, the great television debates of the midcampaign; and last, as a third round, their final all-out efforts to stir the emotions of the American people and bring the country to paroxysm.

For John F. Kennedy, Round One began in euphoria, sagged swiftly almost to despair, then rose to a point of cautious hope.

Kennedy had flown directly from Los Angeles and the Convention to Cape Cod and Hyannisport. There the sun shone through milk-blue skies, and the breeze whipped whitecaps off Nantucket Sound as it scrubbed the dunes clean. Home again with wife and child, the candidate could let his nerve fibers mend. He sailed with his wife, Jackie, and brother Bobby in the *Marlin*, his fifty-two-foot motorcruiser, he read aloud to his cruiser companions passages from press and magazine reports of the Convention; he browsed through Anthony Trollope's *The American Senator*. Outside the new stockade and the white-lattice fence that guarded the Kennedy compound the gawkers peered or, occasionally, tried to snatch as a souvenir one of the pink rambler roses that laced the picket fence. Within the compound the candidate and his brother Robert wandered back and forth across the lawn to each other's homes, or lounged, stripped to the waist, on beach chairs in the sun and slowly began to talk politics again —the new electoral politics.

In Chicago, the Republicans still rumbled away at their Convention, and the national attention focused there. But the Gallup Poll showed Kennedy as leading Nixon by 52 to 48 per cent across the nation, and all was well. So it was bliss for the candidate to be home to play with Caroline on the lawn; bliss to gorge on bowl after bowl of clam chowder; bliss to enjoy sun and beach; bliss to operate the machinery of the Party, for now the Party was his. Press a button—and the machinery responded. From Texas came Lyndon B. Johnson; from Michigan, "Soapy" Williams; from New York, Mayor Wagner; from Washington, "Scoop" Jackson, now Chairman of the Democratic National Committee; from far-off Carmel, interrupting his vacation, the Democrats' master TV-and-radio strategist, J. Leonard Reinsch; and, uninvited, labor leaders, special seekers, political traffickers, who wished to visit early and voice their say in the capture of the White House and the appointments that would follow.

All the ideas, all the reports, all the suggestions from great men and specialists, however, went into the same input machinery that had commanded the primary and Convention drive. As the old crowd gathered for its first session on the lawn outside Bobby's house, eight thickly padded green chaise longues were wheeled out, a telephone with an extended green cord was placed before them, and they were again together as they had been for months: the candidate and his brother Robert; Kenny O'Donnell and Larry O'Brien; brother-in-law Steve Smith, press chief Pierre Salinger, old-time pro John Bailey (still smoking his cigar, but persuaded to undo his necktie in the sun)—and the jaunty Jim Rowe, who, still bearing the wounds of his spring wars with the Kennedy clan, had nonetheless come to offer his help. A man whose national campaign experience goes back to the days of Franklin D. Roosevelt, Rowe had served in both Stevenson campaigns and had commanded the advance scheduling of the Stevenson campaign in 1956. He was now to be of counsel first to the Kennedys and then later in the national campaign to Johnson.

It is at this point that one should pause to consider the personality of Robert F. Kennedy.[1] Few observers during the

[1] Now Attorney-General of the United States.

campaign of 1956 had noted, as they followed the travels of Adlai E. Stevenson, a slim, tow-haired, baby-faced young man who journeyed in the back of the Democratic candidate's plane. Yet the young man—Robert F. Kennedy, then thirty years old, wide-eyed, curious, but ignored—was noting everything. As assistant to the late James Finnegan, the debonair campaign manager of the Democratic candidate of 1956, the young Kennedy had been assigned as liaison to the candidate's plane. "Nobody asked me anything, nobody wanted me to do anything, nobody consulted me," says Bobby Kennedy now, reminiscing about his blooding in Presidential politics. "So I had time to watch everything—I filled complete notebooks with notes on how a Presidential campaign should be run."

Thus in 1960 at Hyannisport, as he prepared to mobilize the Democratic Party for his brother's victory, he was in no sense a neophyte at national politics. Young as he was, he knew as a privileged witness, not only the inner personality of his brother Jack (whom he calls "Johnny" at serious moments, and whom he reveres), but also the mechanics of American electioneering. He had already studied and pondered deeply the scheduling of candidates, the use of speech writers, the habits of politicians, the priorities of organization.

To this knowledge he brought, moreover, the force of his singular personality—one that has baffled all political analysts who seek hidden sinuosities of theory or belief. For Robert F. Kennedy was, and is, above all a moralist, whose deepest-held beliefs might find expression in either party—or in the Y.M.C.A. For him all the vulgarities and weaknesses of the American manner—the crude violence of TV, the disgusting corruption he had found in his investigations of unions as Chief Counsel of the McClellan Committee, the physical weakness and seeming softness of American youth—are personally offensive. It is as a Boston Puritan, albeit of the Catholic faith, that Robert Kennedy should be seen.

Beyond that, he must be seen as a man in whom the motor reflexes are predominant. As a Puritan, Robert F. Kennedy believes that men should work hard, go to bed early, rise early, strive to the extent of their ability and be penalized ruthlessly when they fail in their responsibilities. It is his opinion that men play to win—whether in touch football or politics—with no quarter for friend or foe. All through the campaign that followed, this personal belief—that one gives one's all, both in effort and intelligence—inspired and moved all the Kennedy machinery. His relentless drive was to make him many enemies, and expose him to much sophisticated analysis by politicians and press alike. But essentially he is a simple man moved by great emotions; and these emotions, coupled with his great ability, must be seen in all the weeks that followed until election day as the motor moving the Kennedy campaign in the direction that his brother defined.

Almost all the key decisions that dominated the Kennedy campaign in the next ten weeks were taken at Hyannisport in early August; and in the execution of these decisions now taken on the lawn or in his house in the days that followed, one must always recognize Robert Kennedy as the chief propelling force.

§ First, the electoral strategy. Nine large states (New York, Pennsylvania, California, Michigan, Texas, Illinois, Ohio, New Jersey and Massachusetts) hold 237 of the 269 electoral votes necessary to elect a President. If these could be swept; and if another 60 or 70 electoral votes could be added by Lyndon B. Johnson in the Old South, and if a few more solid New England or Midwestern states could be counted in—then the election would be won handily. Thus, grand strategy: to concentrate the supreme Kennedy effort in the industrial Northeast, where seven states of the big nine clustered; Johnson would have to carry his native Texas; the candidate would give four of his personally numbered campaign days to California, and Adlai E. Stevenson would carry the rest of the freight there.

§ Next, the strategy of registration. Of the 107,000,000 Americans old enough to vote in 1960, approximately 40,000,000, it was estimated, had not bothered to register. Students of politics argue this figure both ways—the moralists saying that it is every man's civic duty to register and vote, the realists that those too indifferent or to ignorant to vote should be left undisturbed, for their vote is valueless. For the Kennedys, however, the compelling consideration was the generally accepted political guess that of the 40,000,000 unregistered voters, 70 per cent would vote Democratic if they could be pushed to the polls. Thus a massive registration drive would be mounted to bring 10,000,000 new names to the voting lists; if the new 10,000,000 broke as expected, it would mean 7,000,000 more Democratic votes. This drive was to be entrusted to a flamboyant and devoted Kennedy Congressman from Trenton, New Jersey, Frank "Topper" Thompson, a specialist in registration drives in his own district. (Within two months, Thompson was to be directing fifty state registration chairmen, two hundred key country registration chairmen and a paid staff of eight highly trained "leaders" headed by a thirty-three-year-old professor of English. In all, the Kennedy efforts combined with the counterpart Nixon drive were to jump the 1960 vote over the 1956 count by 6,800,000.)

§ Next, campaign scheduling. This was to be entrusted to Kenny O'Donnell. Campaign scheduling is an art in itself. Each day, each minute, of a candidate's time is counted, from the moment he launches his campaign until he goes to bed on election eve. To use that time most effectively, schedules have to be meshed and geared with political need, with the requirements of time and transportation, with the shepherding of a herd of newsmen and staffmen at the candidate's heels, with the feuds and sensitivities of all local political leaders. "Advance men"—the small teams of agents who arrange the tours of major candidates—are practitioners of one of the most complicated skills in American politics; a good advance man must combine in himself the qualities of a circus tout, a carnival organizer, an accomplished diplomat and a quartermaster-general. With a rough schedule in his pocket, O'Donnell departed immediately from Hyannisport to consult with political leaders around the country, bargaining with them about the days and hours of the candidate's personality he could meagerly dole out. In Washington, relying on his Massachusetts veterans, O'Donnell established a base scheduling and coordinating headquarters. O'Donnell, Maguire, Hartigan, Sullivan, O'Hare and O'Gorman—so read the roster of the scheduling staff in Washington as the Bostonians gathered, and one of them ruefully shook his head and muttered, "Wait till they read our names—Hibernian Hall all over again."

§ Ideas, next. From Harvard now the professors began to gather. Ever since 1952, individual professors of the Harvard faculty had been furnishing this most prominent of their living alumni with ideas, information and analysis, to shape his national thinking. He had over the years drawn them one by one into his closeness, until Harvard's faculty seemed his intellectual harem. In January of 1960 he had assembled his Brain Trust at the Harvard Club, on Boston's Commonwealth Avenue, and at dinner had bluntly told them they were now mobilized (permitting the Stevensonians among them to take leave if they so wished). Now, in July, they were to act. Professor Archibald Cox[2] of the Harvard Law School was to establish himself with a speech-writing detail in Washington; the professors were to think, winnow, analyze and prepare data on the substance of national policy, to channel from university to speech writers to Cox to Sorensen—and thus to the candidate.

§ Finally, organization. O'Brien was to emplane immediately for Washington, where he would become Director of Organization for the National Committee. Byron (Whizzer) White

[2] Now Solicitor-General of the United States.

would become National Director of a Kennedy-Johnson Volunteers Organization. Across the country, the O'Brien Manual would be impressed on the thousands and thousands of recruits for the new Kennedy-Johnson Volunteers. In each state, each of these volunteer organizations must be meshed with the existing political organization—a delicate task. Volunteers look with suspicion upon organized political machines. They distrust politicians, and politicians distrust them. Yet volunteer energies must be harnessed. Each state presents a different problem—an easy one if the state organization is one of citizen leadership (as in Minnesota, Wisconsin or Michigan); a manageable one if the organization is strong and confident enough to absorb and use citizen volunteers without fear (as in Illinois and Pennsylvania); but almost totally unmanageable where a fossilized, jealous machine is at daggers' points with citizen groups it sees as enemies (as in New York). Borrowing, unknowingly, from the practice of the ancient civil service of Mandarin China (which never appointed any individual to government position in his native province), O'Brien moved to set up "coordinators" brought from out of state to arbitrate between citizen and organization groups all across the nation. Eventually, before the campaign was over, O'Brien had forty-three such out-of-state emissaries established as provincial legates of his national authority.

Thus, impatiently, as August began, the candidate waited to start.

Primaries and Conventions lay behind.

Now there was Mr. Nixon—and after that the swollen and pressing forces of the outer world. Allen Dulles, Chief of the CIA, was sent once by President Eisenhower to brief the Democratic candidate on this outer world during these weeks. As the two left the Kennedy cottage, where they had talked alone, the candidate was heard to remark, "Haven't you got any good news in that black bag of yours?" And Mr. Dulles replied that, well, the situation in Iran looked a little bit better now.

Before the campaign could begin, however, the August doldrums must be survived—and in the following three weeks of August the Kennedy campaign sank to the miserable low of its long effort.

There was, first, the special session of Congress; and the special summer session of Congress had been planned, tailored and measured by Democratic leadership earlier in the summer, not to fit the Kennedy campaign, but the Johnson Presidency, now dead and buried. Trapped in the special session, seated uncomfortably in the rear row of the Senate hemicycle, peered at by summer tourists (on some days 40,000 tourists passed through the Capitol to watch a Senate that starred Kennedy, Nixon, Johnson, all at once), the candidate saw himself and his proposals mangled on the floor and in committee. The crisp and vibrant image of leadership he meant to offer was soiled by the long, droning sessions in which he was powerless to lead, powerless to impose his will. Very tidily, in the hot tedious weeks, Congress cleaned up its left-over spring housekeeping—a Treaty on Antarctica, a Foreign Aid Appropriations Bill, a Highway Bill, several other matters. Some of the Kennedy proposals squeaked through the Senate; but not a single item of all those matters that Kennedy himself sought to advance as avenues to the New Frontier survived the gauntlet in the House to become law: medical care for the aged under Social Security, aid for schools, the increase of minimum wages—all these died.

The Gallup Poll now announced another of its biweekly samplings—and the lead had switched. Now, said Dr. Gallup, Nixon was ahead by 53 to 47 per cent. If the Constitution follows the flag, it may be argued that modern-day polling reflects television exposure; and the television exposure of Mr. Nixon at Chicago had been impressive. Nixon had come to Chicago to find a Party in open civil war; in forty-eight hours he had, apparently, pulled it together; he had performed publicly as the Take-Over Man; and his closing acceptance speech at the Chicago Convention had been the best speech he was to make in the entire campaign. Nor was Mr. Nixon, that energetic campaigner, resting with his lead. Unbound by need of attendance at the daily Senate sessions, Nixon was raiding in the Deep South; and his flights to North Carolina, Alabama, Georgia were accompanied by demonstrations of such size and enthusiasm as to disturb Kennedy calculations. Pinned down at Washington by roll-call votes, the Democratic candidate could only watch his rival flip back and forth across the country from Hawaii to Washington to Detroit to the Deep South, and he ached to be going.

Over all, furthermore, was the general clanging of confusion. Bobby Kennedy, Larry O'Brien, Dick Donahue, Ralph Dungan and a dozen other personal Kennedy lieutenants had moved into the headquarters of the Democratic National Committee at 1001 Connecticut Avenue. There the crowded offices which, only a few months previously, had held sixty people now burst with two hundred scrambling for phones, secretarial help, desk space, attention. Suspiciously the old staff men of the National Committee and the new outdoorsmen of the Kennedy team eyed one another, caustically commenting on each others' practices. Across the country, in every state, new machinery was being installed—Kennedy-Johnson Volunteer Committees were being set up, State Coordinators were being chosen, special sections (Civil Rights, Registration, Religion, Farmers, Elder Citizens) were being staffed. But nothing was ready; and in the noise of hammering, carpentering and effort, tempers strained and frictions grew—friction between old and new in the National Committee, friction between Stevenson and Kennedy men in California, friction between reformers and Tammany in critical New York State, friction among the Negroes of the Civil Rights Committee, friction between the new Brain Trusters of the Cox speech-writing staff and the personal Brain Trusters of Kennedy's Senatorial staff, headed by Sorensen. The second-floor offices of the National Committee seemed to swell and swell again with more people—yet what was being accomplished? One afternoon I sat chatting with two old friends, veterans of the primary campaigns, when the door burst open and Bobby Kennedy, tieless and in shirt sleeves, exploded into the cramped cubicle. These were his own people, not old staffers, just sitting. "What are you doing?!" he cried. "What are we all doing? Let's get on the road! Let's get on the road tomorrow! I want us all on the road tomorrow!" And without waiting for a reply, he clapped the door shut and disappeared. The two shook their heads sadly and affectionately for they had been with Bobby for years now; sitting still in the cramped office was punishing him; he was an outdoor man, requiring action; now he must sit and plan. "You know what's happened to 'our smooth well-oiled machine'?" said Salinger gloomily one August evening at his home, quoting the phrase that had always distressed him. "It's diffusing. This country is just too big, there's too much of it."

Most of all, the spirit of the leader had percolated down through staff and machinery. And the leader was in bad temper. He had abused his speaking voice for months in the spring primaries; he had more than abused it in speeches to endless caucuses of the Los Angeles Convention. Not even the fortnight in the Hyannisport sun had completely erased the throat infection he had brought back from California; he was taking voice lessons from a speech professor in Boston, who was trying to teach him to speak from his chest, not his larynx —but he could not be sure whether his voice would last the campaign months ahead or fail him completely, as did Wendell Willkie's in mid-October, 1940. The staff frictions annoyed him, the regional disputes between citizen and organization groups bothered him. He was pinned in the Senate hemicycle, a target for Republican darts and shafts, watching warily each lure and maneuver on the floor for the hidden ambuscade that might trap him. Richard M. Nixon was already on the road; the reports from the South were bad; Baptist ministers had begun to preach against the Church of Rome and "its" candidate; the religious issue was swelling now, festering and ugly, and it must be lanced soon—but how could he do it from the floor of the Senate?

"He's in a bad mood," ran the word from the top to the bottom of the staff; thus their mood, too, was bad. It could not be changed except by a change of the candidate's mood, and that could not be changed so long as he sat in Washington. The session, he told his friends, was a complete washout, he had been kept from the people for a month and a half. "Out upon you," he would have cried with Cromwell if he could, as he contemplated the dreary session. "Out upon you, I say you are no Parliament." And so, finally, on September 1st, Democratic Congressional leadership managed to choke out the purposeless session, and at last the candidate was free.

He took off by chartered jet from Friendship Airport in Baltimore on Friday afternoon, September 2nd, as if he meant to swallow the country at a gulp. Friday evening he campaigned in Maine; by Saturday noon he was campaigning in San Francisco; Saturday night he flew to Alaska and then, with only four hours' sleep, turned the big jet back to the continent and urged it on all day to Detroit, where on Monday, Labor Day, he would officially open his campaign. There, in recent times, Democratic candidates for the Presidency have always opened their campaigns with an appearance at Cadillac Square before the union men of Detroit's assembly lines, who mass in thousands to hear the candidate make his traditional appeal for labor's support.

He arrived two hours late, at 10:15, on Sunday evening at Detroit International Airport, surveyed the scene—blue lights gleaming down the runway, police cars blinking their red flasher beacons to lead his procession, the crowd of 5,000 in shirt sleeves and house dresses holding their babies up to see him—proceeded to his hotel at eleven in the evening, attended a coffee reception at the Sheraton-Cadillac Hotel and then went to bed.

It is perhaps worth examining the first full day of campaigning in Detroit in some detail—for such days, for both candidates, were to succeed one another week after savage week

without stop until the choice of an American President seemed
to rest more on pure glands and physical vitality than on
qualities of statesmanship, reason or eloquence.

Kennedy had had four hours' sleep each of the two previous evenings, and now, in Detroit, he was allowed six and
a half hours' sleep before he was woken to the first of his
three breakfasts. The first breakfast at seven o'clock was
standard—the candidate's normal hearty meal of eggs, bacon,
orange juice and milk with his personal staff, O'Donnell, Salinger and Powers. The second breakfast, unannounced, was
brief: with John Swainson, the young and attractive Democratic candidate for Michigan's governorship—Swainson and
his young men would be taking over leadership from the older
Williams-Staebler group if elected, and Kennedy wanted to
know them. Then the third, public, breakfast at eight, with
Wayne County CIO leaders. Then, at nine o'clock, a full hour
of picture taking with all Congressional candidates, statewide
candidates and other dignitaries who must be flattered with
pictures of the Presidential candidate in conversation with
them; then another half hour of greeting and two-minute chats
with labor leaders and party leaders all of whom, forever after,
would be able to refer to their talk with "Jack." One half hour
of work revising his speech followed, and then out to Cadillac
Square in the brilliant sun to address the cheering mass; then
back, five minutes late, to honor Walter Reuther with a personal conversation; then a hasty meal with his own staff
(broiled chicken and two glasses of milk); then, as the cavalcade waited downstairs, picture taking again—a picture with
"Mudcat" Grant, Negro pitcher of the Cleveland Indians, to
please his Civil Rights Division; another picture with the Len-
non Sisters, several more pictures with various Detroit judges.
Then, since the elevators on his floor were being held for him,
a dash to the elevator, descent to the crowded lobby, and out
to the street only fifteen minutes late, to begin a motor tour
through Michigan.

The Michigan State Fair first, for five minutes; then the
Labor Day Picnic at Pontiac, Michigan (where he received a
ceremonial Indian headdress); then the long drive to Flint,
Michigan, and another Labor Day Picnic and another speech
(along the way he hastily read, then approved, a statement
blasting the State Department on the situation in the Congo);
then an airplane flight in the dusk (he had now switched to
his own Convair, the "Mother Ship" in which he was to remain for the rest of the campaign) to Muskegon airport; a
seven-mile drive through a defile of cheering people holiday-
ing on Labor Day to Pere Marquette Park, where he ad-

dressed another Labor Day Picnic, his voice hoarsening by now. Running about an hour behind schedule, he ate a rushed dinner alone in a hotel room (steak, salad, two more glasses of milk), found time for a telephone call to Hyannisport to speak to his wife, and then on to the Dew-Drop Inn of Muskegon to give the Democratic candidate of Michigan's Ninth Congressional District a lift. A short speech—mainly historical, intertwining Michigan's history with the history of the Democratic Party—and then out to the airport, taking off at eleven in the evening and arriving in Pocatello, Idaho, at two in the morning. (There would be five hours' sleep in Pocatello that night before he must rise for more breakfasts, more speeches, more flights, briefings on the situation in Idaho, in Tacoma, in Spokane, in Seattle.)

It was to be this way for both candidates from the first week in September until the day of voting—lunches, breakfasts, dinners, travel, speeches, with no moment of privacy or thought.

Beneath the plane or from the windows of the buses or trains the country passes by—the squat, flat buildings of the great assembly plants of Michigan; the second-growth forests of the lake country, cut over, once tilled, now abandoned again; the endless plains of the West, where the roads run straight to surveyors' lines, not twisting as they do in old New England; the rumpling of the mountain masses and the dry tawny uplands where they harvest western wheat; the echoing acres of the great naval-gun factory in Pocatello, Idaho, now empty, with no further use for the tools or the men that milled the guns that hammered Japan's fleet to destruction; a day later, as the train comes down the Bay of San Francisco, similar acres of rusting destroyers, dead heroes, all now useless in their moored ranks; the sudden, screaming beauty of the Cascade Mountains, where the bare interior slope of the continental incline crests and is suddenly clothed with the green of fir forest on the ocean side; the snow-capped cones of extinct volcanoes, the mountain-blue lakes in the hills, the sudden infinite sweep of the Pacific as you see it from the plane; and also the friendly shoreline—the pleasure craft dotting Puget Sound, the huge log rafts where timber waits to be sliced to plywood, the gray hulk of the Boeing Plant beside the airstrip. Then the lush green of the Willamette Valley as one flies south again, and that moment in California when one passes the land of green fir and pine and sees the first palm tree and enters the other civilization.

One wonders what the candidate sees or absorbs of all this. For the candidate's attention seems always caught, not by the sight or the sweep of the country he hopes to govern, but by the men who are telling him about it, the men who prepare drafts for his speeches, the men who know the political topography and must guide him in strange territory. What do you talk about in Michigan: unemployment? automation? minimum wage? aid to the aged? What do you talk about in Idaho: natural resources? farm supports? mining? What can be done about the big deserted gun plant at Pocatello? What do you talk about in Spokane? What do you talk about in Seattle: national defense for the Boeing workers? foreign policy for those who face the Pacific? or education, because Seattle takes education seriously?

Then, as one wonders and as the campaign goes on day after day, the elements of what is going on begin to separate and one can begin to weigh the three different audiences who attend the ordeal of a man seeking the Presidency of this vast land.

The first of the audiences, in size, is always the national audience. Two score newspapermen and reporters of the great national news media follow doggedly in his wake day after day. Twice a day, to please them, the candidate must choke out a statement or prepared speech to provide both afternoon and morning newspapers across the country with fresh copy, a fresh report of his doings. A thicket of microphones sprouts before him at each stop, recording what he says for rebroadcast later, in one- or two-minute snatches, on the national radio networks. TV cameras pursue him, seeking film clips for evening shows. Through all these, the candidate reaches the national audience, the many millions who idly watch the evening television news or hastily scan the morning newspapers. Not for days or weeks will the candidate know the effect of any speech or statement on the national mood or on the minority group to which it is specifically addressed.

There follows the second audience, the strategically calculated audience. The candidate has picked out individual states, counted their electoral votes, and now he works them one by one. In each state the local newspapers and weeklies, the local TV stations and radios, swoop on the arrival of the great man as Event. On either side of his path, and in a great circle about his every stop, spreading over the entire circulation area of the large newspaper or listening audience of the major radio station, the citizens of the state are aware of the presence and the visit. He lays a powder train of excitement wherever he goes. If the candidate makes a speech in St. Louis, it is only a paragraph in the newspapers of San Francisco or New York —but in St. Louis it is a front-page story, and the front page blooms with pictures. Impact has been made on the state directly; the leading local dignitaries have been met and ignited; the volunteer organizations have assembled and have been tuned up, their enthusiasm at this personal visit must now spread and kindle others.

Then comes the personal audience, so small in numbers as to be minuscule—yet more important than any other. These are the men in work shirts and sports shirts, the women in house dresses with babies in arms, the farmers observing silently, the students listening intently, the bobby-soxers yipping and squealing. These are the people who gather at whistle stops, at airports, at crossroads, in numbers so tiny that there is no point in expending the effort of formal speech writing or policy making to capture their attention. But these are the people who count most. For the candidate, whoever he is, sits at the center of a web of affairs so complex as to be dehumanized; his ideas, his phrases, his finances, his schedules, are all prepared for him by others; wherever he pauses to consult with staff, he must already make the detached executive decisions of a President. Thus only the personal audience, below the level of strategic calculation, can give him the one thing he needs most: the response of warmth or frost, of applause or indifference. Its laughter, its scowl, its silence, its cheers, its yearning, its measuring eyes, are the only clues in the mystic communication between the leader and the led, to tell truly whether he has reached those he seeks to lead. Becoming President is an utterly personal business between the man who offers himself as national leader and the Americans who judge him. The candidate must feel the beat of the people he hopes to lead; their heart is his target. And no public-opinion poll or analysis can tell him half so well whether he has reached that target as can the people themselves, giving him the beat of their response.

So, slowly, in the first ten days of his campaign, John F. Kennedy began to find both style and theme; and listening, as the reporters did, to the same five minute "all-purpose" speech six or eight times a day, hearing it change from state to state and city to city, they could see both the change in style and the development of theme that was to shape the Kennedy campaign and the election.

Kennedy began his first round taut and tense, his voice rapid and rushed, as if trying to make up for lost time; he appeared uncertain—or so it seemed to listeners—as to what was quite the proper manner and posture of a man who seeks the Presidency. Then, gradually, his little crossroads all-purpose speeches grew easier. Personal touches showed the change—like mention of the expected baby. Out of his sense of privacy, Kennedy had omitted mentioning his wife or her pregnant condition in the early days of his campaign—and a tribute to the wife is rigidly required in American political orthodoxy. Then, one noon in the warm sun in the little park behind the gleaming color-splashed courthouse of Eugene, Oregon, he impulsively offered the courteous excuse that his wife was absent because she was "otherwise committed." A friendly ripple of laughter followed. The next morning, in northern California, he had changed it to "My wife has other responsibilities," and a warmer laugh followed. By afternoon the phrase had become a forthright "My wife is going to have a baby." In the San Joaquin valley the next day it was "My wife is going to have a boy in November." It had become a certified gag; and that afternoon in Los Angeles, it became a press-conference question that ended a tense interchange of questions on religion. "How do you know it's going to be a boy?" asked the questioner. "My wife told me," said Kennedy,[3] and the conference ended with a laugh.

What was more important than the slow growth of ease was the development in the humble all-purpose speech of the grand theme that was to dominate and shape his campaign to the end: *America cannot stand still; her prestige fails in the world; this is a time of burdens and sacrifice; we must move.*

He began his first round with a loose collection of phrases and anecdotes that he jumbled into a pudding for the all-purpose speech: a collection of historical anecdotes, and then the standard phrases: "the importance of the Presidency"; "the world cannot exist half slave and half free"; "only the President can lead"; "farming is our number one domestic problem"; "automation can be a blessing or a curse"; "we must move"; "I ask your help."

Then, gradually, as applause told him where he had hit and indifference informed him where he talked beyond the audience, the pattern began to shape itself into a theme. It seemed to do so most clearly in a glorious two-day passage down the valleys of California, as his campaign train, full of politicians, soothed by wine, crowds and proximity to the great, rocked over the roadbed of the Southern Pacific.

The train had left Portland, Oregon, the previous evening, and the California interlude opened from its rear platform the next morning in Dunsmuir, California, a tiny hill station sunk in a glen of giant redwoods that rose as a silent audience above

[3] She was right.

the little knot of people who had risen at six in the morning to look at a Presidential candidate.

He spoke for three minutes from the platform, and his voice rang through the forest glade: ". . . I thank you very much for coming down. This is an important campaign because it is an important country, and because all of us are anxious to see the United States move ahead. I ask your help in this campaign. . . ."

He spoke at Red Bluff an hour later and the sun was higher, but he was still in forest country.

"I campaign for the office of Presidency in a very difficult and dangerous time in the life of our country, and I do not do so promising that if I am elected all of the problems of California and the United States and the free world will be solved. . . . But we must recognize the close relationships between the vitality of our own domestic economy and our position around the world. If we stand still here at home, we stand still around the world. . . ."

At Richmond, California, by later afternoon, he was in gut-Democratic territory, and he was embroidering.

"If you think we can provide better schools for our children and more help for the older, if you think we can develop this state and the resources of the West, if you think it is possible to strengthen the image and prestige of the United States around the world, then come with us. If you are tired and don't want to move, then stay with the Republicans. But I think we are ready to move [Applause]."

All the next day, as the train pushed its way down the San Joaquin valley, as the early-fall nip of the northern hills gave way to the permanent summer of mid-California, as the train stopped in its course and the citizens brought him the produce of their golden valley whenever he paused in raisin country, rose country, fig country—all day the all-purpose speech became stronger, and the candidate's car filled with the peaches, grapes, olives, pears, prunes and fruits of the all-giving valley. By the time he reached Los Angeles that evening, he was ready to discard, as he did, his prepared text on civil rights and religious and racial freedoms and swing out, high and clear, in a completely extemporaneous oration that brought the ten thousand in the hall to their feet, stamping and cheering,

. . . Governor Brown and I have been pushing a train all the way down from the Oregon border, since yesterday morning, and picking up olives, grapes, bananas, corn and one thing or another all the way down the rich state of

California. I am reminded somewhat of an expedition which Thomas Jefferson and James Madison took in the 1790s when they went on a botanical expedition up the Hudson River to find fish and flowers, and coming down the river they stopped in New York. They met Aaron Burr and the Knights of St. Tammany, and they formed a link between the rural United States and the cities of the United States, they formed the Democratic Party. I have come here three thousand miles and I am not chasing butterflies. I am here asking for your support [Applause]. . . .

. . . My chief argument with the Republican Party has been that they have not had faith in the free system. Where we would set before the American people the unfinished business of our society, this administration has set ceilings and has set limitations. I think the record of the two parties, and its promise for the future, can be told pretty well from its record of the past. Mr. Nixon and I, and the Republican and the Democratic Parties, are not suddenly frozen in ice or collected in amber since the two conventions. We are like two rivers which flow back through history, and you can judge the force, the power and the direction of the rivers by studying where they rose and where they ran throughout their long course. . . .

Everything that we do in the United States, every issue which we now discuss, every fight held in the last month of the Congress, all go to this question of our ability to survive in a difficult and dangerous world. . . . I am confident that the future belongs to those who believe in freedom. . . . I don't think the world is moving in the direction of Communism. I think in time it will move in the direction that we have followed. . . . All of you will, in a sense, in 1961 hold office in the great Republic; upon all of you in your own way and in your own life great responsibilities will be placed.[4]

Technically, the first ten days of the Kennedy campaign were flat and discouraging. The set speeches were ignored by the press and, when delivered, were delivered badly. The advance work, particularly in Washington and Oregon, was atrocious and resulted in humiliation for the candidate. In

---

[4] One of the graces of the Kennedy campaign was the nearly immediate availability of a stenotype transcript of what the candidate had said, whether in mine, factory, village square or New York Coliseum. A husky stenotypist and good companion of the road, "Chick" Reynolds, made this possible. Thus reporters were able to relax and enjoy the Kennedy oratory, knowing that in an hour they would have an accurate transcript. For reasons that will be described later, the Nixon campaigners did not make such a service available until much later in the campaign.

California, no other cold reading of the Kennedy trip could be made except in terms of failure—he had been badly scheduled, underexposed and badly advised in the great valley, and then booked (out of timidity) to speak in Los Angeles at the Shrine Auditorium, one of the smaller available gathering places for that second-greatest metropolis of the nation.

All this was true of the first few days of the campaign—technically.

But all could be balanced and overweighed by the fact that the candidate had found his voice, had sensed a mood, had struck an attitude to the future and to the onward movement of America that would shape the rest of the campaign. He had come clear to himself and his audience. The sharpness of this single theme was to grow and grow, then communicate itself with the strength of simplicity.

One more high point marks the first round of the Kennedy campaign.

If the first swing (ten days; 17,000 miles) of campaigning had given the candidate his note for the future, it had not yet prepared him to address the past. That was now to come. In Washington, a gathering of some of the most respected Protestant churchmen of the nation gathered under the leadership of the Reverend Norman Vincent Peale, the most widely read Protestant minister in the nation, to question the loyalty of any Catholic candidate for the Presidency and the wisdom of choosing any man of that faith for the high office. In the South, in the border states, in the farm states the issue was not the future but the past—could a Catholic give true soul and full faith to the doctrines of the Constitution? To this Kennedy must address himself before the first round closed.

The Kennedy camp had picked up the first murmurings and rumblings of religious strife as soon as the Convention ended. Months before, in the West Virginia primary, they had hoped to settle the religious question for good; in retrospect, they now knew themselves to have been naive; the intertwining of religion and politics laced all through the history and traditions of America, and it must be openly recognized once more. Now, in September, the old echo of fear was slowly being amplified—not only in the border states of Tennessee and Kentucky, but in downstate Indiana and Illinois, in the farm belt, above all in the South. No politician as sensitive or as well-informed as Kennedy, traveling through California's Central Valley, where lived transplanted Oklahomans, Texans, Arkansans, needed to be told that these gut-Democrats were

disturbed by this candidate of Roman Catholic faith; and if
they were, so were millions of others.

There was, as the Kennedys had learned in West Virginia,
only one way to separate the bigots from the honestly fearful:
and that was to face the issue of religion frankly and in the
open, stripping it of the darkness, incense and strange rituals
that so many Protestants feared. The question, tactically, was
when. Originally the Kennedy strategy had been to wait, to
hope that the question could be addressed some time late in
October, close to the election, when it could be most effectively dealt with. But decisions in a campaign are forced on
one by timing of emotions over which no one has control.
The prestige of the Reverend Norman Vincent Peale had
now, in early September, given respectable leadership to ancient fear and prejudice. If the emotions of millions of Americans were left to crystallize under such leadership, positions
might be fixed so rigidly that nothing later could shake them.
And now, as he was moving swiftly about the country from
Maine to Alaska to Michigan to Idaho to California, decision
happened in Kennedy's mind: to accept an invitation from the
Greater Houston Ministerial Association to discuss his religion, on September 12th, at Houston, Texas. He would make
an opening statement, then submit himself, live, to any question they might choose to ask. Thus, all the while he was finding his way to the future as he traveled the Pacific Coast, his
mind focused on the past. Together at the Ambassador Hotel
in Los Angeles over the week end, he and Ted Sorensen—
Unitarian—shaped the draft of what he must say. "We can
win or lose the election right there in Houston on Monday
night," said Sorensen to a friend during the Los Angeles
week end.

The ministers had assembled in the pink-and-green-carpeted
ballroom of the Rice Hotel in Houston by 8:30, 300 strong,
with 300 spectators. At five minutes of nine, the youthful
Democratic candidate, dressed in dark suit and white shirt,
sat down beside the chairman, the Reverend Herbert Meza
(Presbyterian), and faced them. Kennedy had been barnstorming since early morning that day across Texas—from El
Paso through Lubbock through San Antonio. But if he was
tired, it showed only in the thumbs working nervously over
his clasped hands and in the occasional rubbing of his lips
with his fists.

His speech was short and in his best clipped style.

. . . I believe in an America where the separation of Church and State is absolute—where no Catholic prelate would tell the President (should he be a Catholic) how to act, and no Protestant minister would tell his parishioners for whom to vote—where no church or church school is granted any public funds or political preference—and where no man is denied public office merely because his religion differs from the President who might appoint him or the people who might elect him. . . .

. . . That is the kind of America in which I believe. And it represents the kind of Presidency in which I believe—a great office that must be neither humbled by making it the instrument of any religious group, nor tarnished by arbitrarily withholding its occupancy from the members of any religious group. I believe in a President whose views on religion are his own private affairs, neither imposed upon him by the nation or imposed upon him as a condition to holding that office . . .[5]

The questions followed, reflecting all the areas of Protestant concern over Catholic policy:

Why had he not, twelve years before, attended the consecration of an interfaith chapel in Philadelphia—did his religion forbid it, would it so forbid a President? Kennedy cleared the record: he had been invited on that occasion, not as a Congressman, nor as an American, but as a spokesman of the Catholic faith. This role he could not accept; but if it were a question, said he, of "whether I, as Senator or President, could attend a function in your service connected with my position of office, then I could and would attend."

What would he feel as President about the persecution of Protestant missionaries in Roman Catholic countries of South America? He replied, "I would use my influence as President of the United States . . . to encourage the development of freedom all over the world. . . . One of the rights I consider to be important is the right of free religious practice, and I would hope that the President would stand for these rights all around the globe without regard to geography, religion, or . . ." (Before he had finished, the audience broke out in applause.)

He was asked whether he would ask his hierarchical superior, Cardinal Cushing of Boston, to forward his endorsement of separation of church and state to the Vatican. He replied sternly, "May I just say that as I do not accept the right of any, as I said, ecclesiastical official to tell me what I

---

[5] For full text of the Kennedy statement, see Appendix C.

shall do in the sphere of my public responsibility . . . I do not propose also to ask Cardinal Cushing to ask the Vatican to take some action. I do not propose to interfere with their free right to do exactly what they want."

Would he accept Church direction in public life? He spoke deliberately in answer. "If my church attempted to influence me in a way which was improper or which affected adversely my responsibilities as a public servant, sworn to uphold the Constitution, then I would reply to them that this was an improper action on their part, that it was one to which I could not subscribe, that I was opposed to it, and that it would be an unfortunate breech—an interference with the American political system. I am confident there would be no such interference."

In short, he said, if he found any conflict between his conscience and the responsibility of the Presidency, he would resign that office.

When he had finished, he had not only closed Round One of his election campaign—he had for the first time more fully and explicitly than any other thinker of his faith defined the personal doctrine of a modern Catholic in a democratic society.

How much effect he had that evening no one could tell. He had addressed a sullen, almost hostile audience when he began. He had won the applause of many and the personal sympathies of more; the meeting had closed in respect and friendship. But how far the victory in this hall would extend its glow no one could measure. The national TV networks were to broadcast his performance the next day in fragments around the nation. Kennedy Volunteers were to use the filmed record over and over again in both Catholic and Protestant areas of the country for the next seven weeks; it was to be their basic document; no measure is available of how many millions saw the film played and replayed, still less is there a measure available of its effect.

Nevertheless the candidate, always happiest as a man when confronting crisis with action, felt better. As if miraculously, his cracking voice began to clear; in a few weeks, he could dispense entirely with the constant attendance of the voice coach who had hitherto accompanied him.

The next day he barnstormed to growing crowds under the patronage of Lyndon B. Johnson and Sam Rayburn; the following day to crowds in St. Louis; and then he was off to New Jersey and New York and ever greater throngs in the industrial Northeast, where he meant to win.

Chapter 10

NIXON FOR PRESIDENT: ROUND ONE

"I HAVE been asked by the newsmen sitting on my right and my left all week long, 'When is this campaign going to begin, Mr. Vice-President?' And this is my answer: This campaign begins tonight, here and now, and it goes on. And this campaign will continue from now until November eighth without any letup. . . .

"And I've also been asked by my friends in the press on either side here, they say, 'Mr. Vice-President, where are you going to concentrate? What states are you going to visit?' And this is my answer: In this campaign we are going to take no states for granted and we aren't going to concede any states to the opposition.

"And I announce to you tonight and I pledge to you that I, personally, will carry this campaign into every one of the fifty states between now and November eighth. . . ."

Thus on the evening of July 28th, 1960, to the cheers of the Republican National Convention as he accepted their nomination, did Richard M. Nixon describe the campaign he was about to wage.

Nor did he even for a moment hesitate in his pledge. No uncertainty or indecision seemed to mark his take-off. In a streak across the skies he was off from Chicago—to Rhode Island, to confer with President Eisenhower at Newport; back across the Midwest to a brief touchdown in Nevada (his wife's birth state); another brief touchdown in Southern California (his own birth state); a fling across the ocean to Hawaii (the newest state); a return across the Pacific via Seattle; and then back to the nation's capital. Within ten days of his nomination, he had campaigned in Illinois, Rhode Island, Nevada, California, Hawaii and Washington State. Behind him a wake of newspaper headlines marked his vigor and pressed his activity on public attention. The barometer of the Gallup Poll reversed itself and projected him, for the first time since January, into a lead against Kennedy of 53 to 47. As spirits in the Kennedy camp plunged, spirits in the Nixon camp soared. The Vice-President was off and running—and in the lead. His strategists settled down to consider the long course.

There had been no lack of earlier consideration of this strategy, and it is worth examining this staff strategy even though it was never later implemented—for it reflected what some of the ablest minds in the Republican Party saw as the way to make a President.

As early as May friends of the Vice-President and members of the Republican National Committee had begun to plan a Nixon campaign on the assumption that the Vice-President would certainly be nominated. They had planned an early take-off in August, then an intense nine-week schedule starting on September 12th. They had winnowed all the hundreds of invitations offered the Vice-President, pondering the proper engagements in the priority states, meshing them with trips, flights, logistics. All state chairmen had been requested to fill out questionnaires on key issues they wished Nixon to stress in their individual states and to have them ready for screening at the Chicago Convention. Regional TV, they decided, would be used extensively; the suburbs would be hit hard, scheduling would be buttoned down before September 12th, both for travel and for TV, with only the last two weeks left flexibly open.

Further, there was to be set up in Washington a Plans Board that would have all authority over detail and timing once the Vice-President had set policy and principles. The Vice-President would make no commitments independently of his Plans Board, and he agreed to meet with them once a week. On the Plans Board would sit the Campaign Chairman (Leonard W. Hall), the Campaign Director (Robert Finch), the Planning Director (James Bassett), the National Chairman (Thruston B. Morton), the National Committee's veteran Publicity Director (L. Richard Guylay), the Director of TV Operations (Carroll Newton) and a liaison man from Eisenhower's White House staff (Robert Merriam). These men would operate the nationwide machinery of the Republican Party in support of the candidate and feed into the master plan of the campaign such personalities as Eisenhower, Rockefeller, Goldwater, Dewey, Percy, Lodge, Mitchell and Judd wherever such names would do most good.

Several of the conceptions of these men are still fascinating in retrospect and two at least should be noted for the record.

The first can be called the Len Hall–Jim Shepley strategy, an ideological theme that pictured the bridge between the past and future that Nixon, later, was never to make clear. This early Hall-Shepley strategy proposed a theme reflecting contentment with the immediate past: the country was prosperous, the wars had ended, Eisenhower had given the new nominee a magnificent base of departure—Peace and Prosperity. The candidate should take his theme of departure from this base, yet add to it the theme of America's future in this world of science and change. Now that Eisenhower had pacified the world and set the economy on an even keel, Nixon should evoke all those wonders of science and technology that are about to come upon our lives, presenting himself as an experienced man, yet a new man who could develop all these wonders for the greater bounty of America and mankind. Nixon has more than a passing interest in the development of American science, and his years in Washington have given him sound competence in its discussion. It is interesting to muse over what might have happened had Nixon adopted this as his forward, positive line in the fall campaign, as his close advisers believed he would.

Another concept offered early in the campaign can be called the Newton-Rogers concept. Carroll Newton of New York (one of the most fertile and imaginative minds in the use of modern television), and Ted Rogers (Nixon's personal TV adviser, one of the most skilled and experienced practitioners of political TV), loyal Republicans both, insisted that television must in 1960 be used more creatively than in the past. They insisted that the Vice-President should not, in the old style, face the camera directly and talk in his ad-lib, wide-roving manner of hard political matters. Instead they suggested a program of five big shows—a TV show called "Khrushchev As I Know Him," with film clips and visualizations of Nixon abroad and in conflict with Khrushchev; another called "You and Your Family in 1960," in which Nixon might take himself out of the context of politician and present himself as a family man with family problems; another would be a beginning show of Nixon's first crosscountry week of campaigning, which would be followed up by a closing show of film clips of the highlights of the campaign; the planners offered also the concept of a well-planned telethon at the end of the campaign, and several other ideas for TV, such as an ingenious pictorial analysis of the dreary Democratic failure in the summer Congressional session, to be conducted either by Eisenhower or Nixon, and various regional TV shows that would hammer home the Vice-President's concern with deep but localized problems in key electoral areas. The Vice-President suspended judgment on these matters, and his advisers waited for his directives.

For slowly it became clear in August and September that the

strategy of the Nixon campaign would be whatever the Vice-President himself personally determined.

There were, to be sure, elements in the Vice-President's personal planning obviously parallel with the hard elements of Kennedy planning. Where the Kennedys identified nine states as the chief battleground, Nixon identified a big seven (California, New York, Illinois, Ohio, Pennsylvania, Texas, Michigan). Where the Kennedys worried about the suburban vote and the Protestant vote, Nixon worried about the farm vote and the Catholic vote. Nixon also moved immediately to the creation of a massive Citizens for Nixon-Lodge organization across the country; and, untroubled by the feuds that divided Party machine from restive reformers on the Democratic side, he mobilized in the end a citizen movement as effective as the classic Eisenhower citizen mobilization of 1952.

Where the Nixon strategy departed from the Kennedy strategy was in style—in an intuitive difference in appreciation of the rhythm and mystique of American electioneering.

There was, first, and governing the entire Republican campaign, the Nixon theory of "pace." Where the Kennedy clan believes in starting early and running flat out all the way, the Nixon theory is that there is a rhythm and natural tide in any great campaign. A campaign, according to the Nixon theory, has its ebbs and surges; and it is essential not to "peak" a campaign too early, essential not to "weary" the public, essential to change mood and pace at the appropriate moment.

Specifically, then, the Nixon campaign would be paced this way: it would open in a bland low key of quiet confidence and optimism. "We have to erase the image of pugnacity first" was the way the Nixon campaigners in Round One phrased it, or as Nixon is reported to have replied in early October when he was already under attack from Republican regulars for his "kid-glove" campaign, "I have to erase the Herblock image first."[1] Gradually as October wore on he would take off the

[1] Herblock (Herbert Block) is the cartoonist of the Washington *Post-Times Herald* whose cartoons of Nixon with heavy black beard, dark eyes, hanging jowls and ski-jump nose were printed nationwide. Nixon, an extraordinarily sensitive man, suffered under the constant pounding of the Herblock cartoons more than anyone outside his inner circle ever recognized. He would not let the Washington *Post-Times Herald* be delivered to his home for the entirely understandable reason that his children might see the Herblock cartoons. Desiring above all to be liked and accepted by the Eastern world which had always seemed so strange to him, he could make no behavior or speech of the "new Nixon" acceptable to the liberals. "The trouble with Dick," said one of his friends, "is that he's been brainwashed by the Eastern liberals. If he lives to be a hundred, he'll never forget that Herblock cartoon of the welcoming committee, and him climbing out of the sewer to greet it, all covered with that stubbly beard of his."

kid gloves and step up the pace of the attack. Finally in the last three weeks of the campaign he would unload, with every "control element" of TV and media advertising the Republican National Committee could finance, and let Kennedy have it.

The corollary of the theory of "peak and pacing" was "flexibility."

"We have to keep control," said one of Nixon's planners in August, "of our own timing. We can't freeze on schedule too early. We can't let him get caught in a situation where he loses his flexibility." Thus while the Kennedy campaign was frozen as early as Labor Day in trip schedule and concentration of personal effort (only two days were left open on the Kennedy schedule to strike at geographic targets of opportunity), the Nixon campaign kept its datings and movements open well into October to permit the candidate to choose his targets of opportunity as they rose.

Paradoxically, however, along with this insistence on "flexibility" the candidate rigidly froze himself to his original convention pledge of a "fifty-state" campaign. Nixon had first expressed the desire to do an every-state campaign in the 1956 election—but he had been overruled at that time, for it seemed unwise to Republican strategists of 1956 that the husky and vigorous young Vice-President make such a demonstration of vitality when Eisenhower, only barely recovered from heart attack and ileitis, could not match the performance. Now that he, Nixon, was on his own he meant to revive the 1956 idea; it seemed to him a dramatic demonstration of the "national image" he meant to create. All through the campaign, as the race narrowed and it became obvious that it would be won or lost in the teetering industrial Northeastern states, Nixon was cramped by his public pledge—so that on the last week end of the campaign, as Kennedy barnstormed through populous Illinois, New Jersey, New York and New England, Nixon found himself committed to fly all the way north to Alaska, which offered only three electoral votes.

There came next the strategy of the "national image," a matter discussed consciously and in detail by the Nixon thinkers.

It would be impossible, they concluded, to try to match or assemble a coalition strategy similar to that of the Democrats. The Democrats are a party of coalition, as we have seen, a gathering of minorities that yields its leadership from generation to generation to one or another of its elements. The only sound Republican strategy—so ran Nixon thinking at the outset—was to run as an across-the-board "national" candidate who rested his appeal on the issues of "Experience" and the Eisenhower record of "Peace and Prosperity." Nixon did not want to speak to parochial Puerto Rican, Negro, Jewish or minority groups. If there was to be any special seeking among ethnic groups, that would be left to Henry Cabot Lodge, whose record in the General Assembly of the United Nations had made him a hero to all those minority groups in America who see American foreign policy as the shield of their kinfolk left behind in the Old Countries.

Precisely how this "national image" was to be presented would be left to the candidate himself; for Richard M. Nixon alone was running for President, and it was his instinct as solitary leader that governed his campaign from beginning to end.

If the Kennedy campaign opened in gloom, the Nixon campaign opened in a burst of jubilation—in the Old South.

Indeed, for any reporter who followed Richard M. Nixon in his early raids into the South in August it was difficult to deny him this sense of euphoria—or later to wonder how much this initial intoxicating good fortune affected the "flexible" campaign of the man who carried his entire strategy in his head. For even now, months later, it is difficult for me, despite all the later excitement, demonstrations and outpourings of the September–October weeks of the campaign, to erase the memory of what happened at Peachtree Street and Hurt Park in Atlanta, Georgia, on August 26th, 1960. It is equally difficult for me to make that day's unbelievable welcome of Nixon by the Atlantans correspond to the historic fact that these same Georgians were, in November, to give John F. Kennedy a greater margin over Richard M. Nixon (62.5 per cent to 37.4 per cent) than any other state of the union except one, Rhode Island in his native New England.

The Vice-President, leaving John F. Kennedy trapped in the Congressional session, had slipped out of Washington early that Friday morning, had spoken to enthusiastic audiences in Alabama and in midafternoon, on the way home to the capital, stopped off at Atlanta. The drive from Atlanta's airport in campaign-cavalcade formation over the new throughway was a carefully slow one, and gradually the outline of the city grew on the ridge—the gold dome of the State House glittering, handsome modern buildings appearing on the crest, chunky towers rising from their midst—strikingly Northern in profile. The Vice-President had already enjoyed a strenuous welcome in Greensboro, North Carolina, nine days before and a hearty reception in Alabama that morning; but Georgia was the most solidly Democratic state of the Union, and how would it be here?

The moment the procession climbed the incline to turn on to Peachtree Street, the gossip of politics and whispering of hope became substance in a clap. The Atlantans were there, not in the twos and threes of ordinary, orderly political demonstration, but here, in midafternoon, they had gathered in ranks five deep, six deep, eight deep that blotted the sidewalks and then, as one approached the center of the city, choked the streets themselves. From the windows above a storm of confetti, of paper streamers, of torn scrap, of red, blue, gold spangles rained down, thickening to a blizzard more spectacular than anything Wall Street was later to offer the two candidates when they paraded through downtown New York. The Atlantans waved their banners, shouted, screamed, crowded thicker and thicker until the procession slowed to an ooze, and then at Atlanta's famous Five Points, where Peachtree turns left to Edgewood to descend to Hurt Park, they burst out of control to overwhelm him completely. From then on down to Hurt Park there was no order to the procession as the white-helmeted police, the middle-aged ladies, the sober young men, all trotted after him as if he were magic. Screaming and chanting, they galloped along as happily as the herd of young girls in white skirts and red-white-blue hats who jiggled and hip-wriggled and trotted after him all the way to the park. At Hurt Park there were two or three acres of people, crowding over the limestone parapet above, sitting on the ledges of the swimming pool, yodeling and yipping rebel yells, yearning to listen to him, waiting to be taken. It was, Dick Nixon was later to remark, the most impressive demonstration he had seen in fourteen years of campaigning; he was to make that remark, of course, a full score times in the later campaign to different audiences, but that day he meant it, and he was at his best.

I remember chiefly that on that day he spoke with a clear, round and mellow voice—confidently and slowly. (Later in the campaign one of the odd developments was that as the heat grew, Nixon's delivery became ever more hasty and melancholy, while Kennedy's, which had started in a hoarse rapid-fire pace, became slower and slower and more resonant.) I remember the speech also because the elements of this first campaign speech were to be repeated several hundred more times across the country in the next ten weeks; and although items were subtracted here and added there, Nixon ended the campaign as he began it, with this same all-purpose talk. In it, as in the Kennedy all-purpose speech, were cast his basic themes and thoughts for 1960, more sharply than in any formal oratory or prepared presentation.

It began with a folksy, "regular-fellow" note that linked him personally to this Georgia audience. The Vice-President said that at Duke Law School he had roomed with a Georgia boy who had graduated first in their class, who was now a "real success; he's the Vice-President of Ethyl Corporation in New York—making a lot more money than I am [Applause]! And since I roomed with Bill Perdue for three years at Duke University Law School, I learned much of the tradition, the culture, and the intelligence of the people of this state; and so I know you better than you might think I would. . . ."

Having identified himself with his local audience, as he was to do everywhere in this manner, he moved deftly on to politics.

"Before I came down here on this trip, there are those who said: 'Why are you going to Georgia?' They said: 'After all, Dwight Eisenhower, who was the most popular man ever to be President or run for President in this century, he won by nine million votes in 1956, if he couldn't carry Georgia, why should any Republican candidate for the Presidency ever bother coming here?' And so I did a little checking in history and you know what I found? In the last quarter of a century there hasn't been a Democratic candidate for President that has bothered to campaign in the State of Georgia. . . . I don't think that's a good thing, a good situation. . . . What I believe is this: I think it's time for a change. I think it's time for the Democratic candidates for the Presidency to quit taking Georgia and the South for granted. . . . I think it's time for the Republican candidates to quit conceding the South to the Democratic candidates and to come down here, too. Because the people of this state, the people of all our country, should have a choice . . . in selecting the man who is going to lead this nation and the free world in the next four years."

He then spoke of the choice in terms of man and party.

"Don't make that choice on the basis of the age of the candidates, on the basis of their religion, on the basis of their personality; don't make that choice on the basis of the party labels they wear, but make it on where they stand on the great issues, and if they stand closer to you—regardless of the party label—vote the man who agrees with you more than the other man. This is the way to make the choice [Applause].

". . . May I turn now to what I believe is the overriding issue confronting us in this election campaign. You know what it is. Look at those boys sitting around that pool. We want those boys to grow up in a world of Peace without Surrender [Applause]. Because we can have the best social security program and the best health program and the best job that anybody can possibly imagine and it isn't going to make any difference if we're not around to enjoy it. . . . I say to you today there is no man in the world who has had more experience and who has shown more ability to deal with the Communist leaders across the conference table than the man that I trust will be the next Vice-President, Henry Cabot Lodge, our representative at the U.N. . . ."

One must imagine oneself hearing this talk given in a sunny square, slowly, warmly, almost conversationally, with friendship—and punctuated by applause at almost every sentence, with enormous peaks of applause at the phrase "Peace without Surrender" and the name "Henry Cabot Lodge." From Peace without Surrender Nixon made a quick transition to another of his standard themes, the conduct of our leaders when facing Russians across a table—and the collapse of the summit conference. There were some, explained Nixon, who said that Eisenhower should have snapped back at Khrushchev across the table. But "I've had a little experience in talking with Mr. Khrushchev, even if it was just in the kitchen," and losing one's temper in such a situation could lead to "nuclear disaster." On the other hand, he said, should the President have apologized? ("No," roared the crowd.) Of course not, "may the time never come when a President, Democrat or Republican, feels that it is necessary to apologize or express regrets for defending the United States against surprise attack from a potential enemy." (A stormy crescendo of applause here.)

The second theme was the domestic one. There were plenty of problems in this country and they had to be solved, we all wanted a better life. "I want a life, as my Dad used to tell me when we were growing up, that is better for my children than I've had myself." But who was going to pay the bill for all the promises the Democrats were making? The Federal Government? No! They were. As for his Party—Republicans didn't want any money to be sent to Washington that they, in the audience, felt they knew how to spend better right in their own state. Should all problems be sent to Washington for solution? No. Our 180 years of history proved that this is the wrong way, just having one man solve everything.

Thus to an invocation of the theme of states' rights and federal rights and the declaration that it is the Republican Party that stands for true Jeffersonian principles and the Democratic platform that denies them. This was why in November, he said, millions of Southerners would vote the Republican ticket—not because they were deserting the Democratic Party but because the Democratic Party had deserted them.

The close, as it was always to be later, was on a spiritual note: a reminder of the faith other peoples all around the world have in America, what America means in the hearts of people everywhere. Then, finally, ". . . I ask you only . . . to do this one thing. Consider what I have said, consider what my opponents and others may say, and on election day don't just vote a party label . . . but cast a vote for America, and if it's in the best interests of America it will be in the best interests of Georgia and of all the people in this great audience."

The crowd cheered again, yipped, yodeled, whistled and shrieked, and Mr. Nixon had had a Roman triumph. Overhead two airplanes carried streamers proclaiming IT'S NIXON DAY IN ATLANTA. The 150,000 who had gathered to hear him broke up slowly while thousands clustered outside the auditorium where a reception was being held for him. He held, or so it seemed, the citizens of Atlanta in the palm of his hand. "This has been the greatest thing in Atlanta," said Ralph McGill, one of the wise men of the modern South, "since the premiere of *Gone With the Wind*."

That evening on the press plane returning from the South the reporters tried to weigh and measure what had happened —for demonstrations can, indeed, be manufactured, but not this kind of wild enthusiasm. What did the Nixon trip mean to the South? Could the South be moved? Then one of the reporters, who was closer to Nixon than any other, said, "That's not the question at all. The question is not what effect this kind of trip has on the South—it's what the effect of this trip is going to have on Nixon. I can see him now up there in the other plane, belting down a couple of Scotches, unwinding, and picking the day apart detail by detail. It's what he thinks of it more than what they think of him that counts."

The observation was, I believe, a perceptive and powerful one. For in his August forays into three Southern states, Nixon had discovered that boiling discontent of the Southern states which has for twenty years been seeking new leadership. He had scheduled his first darting foray into North Carolina, as one of his aides explained it, only "to disturb Jack Kennedy's rear, to worry him and make him spend some of his time down there." The trips to Alabama and Georgia had been scheduled as a result of his first triumph in North Carolina and had been even more successful—so successful that no electoral strategist could ignore the potential.

Nixon had already, in Chicago, weighed the strategy of the election; he had considered then the alternatives of an advanced civil rights program that could win the Negro vote in the key Northeastern industrial states as against a program that by moderation could win the votes of the Southern whites and thus carry the states of the Old Confederacy. By opting for the advanced civil rights plank of Rockefeller in Chicago, Mr. Nixon had already made his key decision and aimed at the Negro vote in the North. Now, however, the excitement of such demonstrations as he had seen in Atlanta could not help tantalizing him. Might the South also be had? It was a conundrum, and all through the following weeks of the campaign Mr. Nixon, like Mr. Kennedy, wrestled with the conundrum: how could one win the suffrage of both Southern white and Northern Negro? If one could do so, then the national election was won. But how? Both candidates, as we shall see, were to answer it in different ways before election day came round. But for Mr. Nixon, who believed in a "flexible" approach to matters, the temptation was particularly acute and unsettling.

There was always an element of sadness about the Nixon campaign, from beginning to end, and a sequence of episodes that wrung sympathy for him even from his most embittered opponents. Of all the episodes, however, the very worst was his illness. He had struck his kneecap on the door of a car on his trip to Greensboro, North Carolina. It had become infected. Two days after his triumph in Atlanta he was informed by his doctors that this was no ordinary infection but one caused by hemolytic staphylococcus aureus, an infection of such virulence that unless he were immediately hospitalized and the knee immobilized, the cartilage of the joint would be permanently destroyed—or worse. It was a doctors' order that no sane person could ignore, and so from August 29th to September 9th he lay ill at Walter Reed Hospital—his leg held in traction by a five-pound weight, fuming and impatient to be out and on the road, as John F. Kennedy had been impatient a few weeks before.

From this impatience and from this anger were to rise a series of decisions whose full importance would not be apparent until he faced the TV cameras in late September. In essence, though, the hospital stay meant that Nixon would lose two full weeks of campaigning; and if he were to campaign in all fifty states, as was his determination, he would have to make up for those two weeks by an overexertion in scheduling that would drain his vitality and health to the utmost. Thus, out of impatient impulse, and against the advice of his closest associates, Mr. Nixon proceeded to schedule himself from the hospital bed as if he must make up for lost time by starting the marathon with a sprint. The concrete result of such impulse could be traced in a single day's events, five days after he had left his hospital bed, in the thirty-six-hour period that stretched from the evening of Wednesday, September 14th, to the night of Thursday, September 15th.

Released from his hospital on Friday evening, September 9th, he had scheduled the formal opening of his campaign for Monday, September 12th. On that Monday morning he had flown by jet from a rainy send-off at Baltimore's Friendship Airport to a fine demonstration in Indianapolis in the morning, to a wild demonstration in Dallas in the afternoon, to a husky demonstration in San Francisco late that night.

After night conferences in San Francisco, and with only six hours' sleep, he had risen to address a press conference on Tuesday in San Francisco and then worked Vancouver, Washington; Portland, Oregon; and Boise, Idaho, all in the same day. He had flown on Wednesday from Boise, Idaho, to Grand Forks, North Dakota, to Peoria, Illinois, meeting Party officials, greeting dignitaries, addressing rallies and working in the back of his plane on two major pronouncements of policy: a labor speech and a major farm-policy speech at the same time. The farm-policy speech had been in preparation for some time in his Washington research offices, but the labor-policy speech was of intense emotional interest to him. For as he had lain fretting with impatience in his hospital bed, he had scheduled his labor speech to be given at St. Louis on the morning of Thursday, the 15th—and had scheduled it over the protest of his staff, who felt that on such a day as Thursday, before his farm speech, no more exertion could be crowded in. Yet Mr. Nixon had insisted from his hospital bed in Washington and now, on the road, faced his Thursday.

He had on Wednesday, five days out of his hospital bed, already caught a cold in the flight from Grand Forks, North Dakota, to Peoria, Illinois. Now at eleven o'clock at night, as he was leaving Peoria, he must fly back 250 miles south to St. Louis. Still nursing his cold, he arrived in St. Louis shortly after midnight in a drizzly rain and then worked in his hotel room until three in the morning on his labor speech, to be given the following morning to the International Association of Machinists. At three he tried to sleep, could not, called an aide who came and sat with him briefly, finally fell asleep and then, three hours later, rose to address the Machinists. A cold audience gave him courteous applause (John F. Kennedy had addressed them the day before and had been in good form). From St. Louis now he flew 900 miles across the continent to Atlantic City, New Jersey, to address a club of Republican women. His voice now was scratchy, but the accompanying press was told he was suffering from hay fever. Having finished his address to the Republican ladies in New Jersey shortly before four o'clock in the afternoon, he now found himself scheduled for the South—to Roanoke, Virginia. He arrived at Roanoke at about 7:30 and was driven to the Roanoke stadium, where in the chill mountain air he shivered as he spoke (he now had a fever) and observed, almost through unseeing eyes, one of those American pageants of high-school bands, tasseled musicians, and drum majorettes in scarlet, white and gold that make up the splendor of color that should enliven every Presidential campaign. He quit Roanoke, Virginia, at about 10:30 and then, mounting to his plane, flew back all the way to the midcontinent—to Omaha, Nebraska, where he arrived after two in the morning, only 350 miles west of where he had started.

Not only did a sequence of such days as this exhaust the candidate's own vitality and perceptions. It exhausted his staff. Moreover, it exhausted the press—and this was important, too. To inform the American people, the press must itself first be informed and understand. When a matter as complicated as farm surplus is to be explained by a major candidate in a major policy statement, his thinking and proposals should be made clear to the press. If not, though reporters do the best they can, they can give only a mechanical summary. Mr. Nixon had worked intently, with his best advisory brains, on his farm speech for two full days, under strain and occasionally with fever. But no one had explained it in advance to the accompanying correspondents. As the press plane followed Mr. Nixon's plane off into the night from Roanoke, Virginia, the tired reporters—only slightly less tired than the candidate—were given the text to be delivered the next day, which they must immediately translate into a simple, readable news report. The correspondents labored over the complicated proposal for disposal of the farm surpluses that Mr. Nixon felt was of the essence in solving the farm problem. They wrote their dispatches as well as they could.

Then having done their duty, they began frivolously to write imaginary dispatches of what they felt would be a more accurate transcription of their private understanding. I reproduce here a few leads of such dispatches as illustrations of what happens when the press feels itself abused.

"GUTHRIE CENTER, Iowa [read one]—Vice-President Nixon said today farmers should eat their way out of the surplus problem. . . ."

"GUTHRIE CENTER, Iowa [began another]—Vice-President Nixon said today that farmers are too blankety-blank greedy. He suggested they get what he called 'honest jobs' in urban industries. . . ."

"GUTHRIE CENTER, Iowa [another]—Vice-President Nixon admitted today that the farm problem was too big for the Republican Party to handle. He said that if elected President, he would appoint Senator Hubert H. Humphrey as Secretary of Agriculture and let him wrestle with the problem. . . ."

"GUTHRIE CENTER, Iowa [another]—Vice-President Nixon today called on Pope John XXIII for guidance in finding a solution to the troublesome farm problems which have plagued Catholic, Jew and Protestant alike. . . ."

If there was malice in such private amusements in the press plane, it was kept scrupulously out of public press dispatches; yet if there were roots to the malice, they lay up ahead in the plane carrying the candidate and his staff. The candidate and his staff had decided very early in the year that the press was their enemy and that they could reach the American people by direct emotion only via television. How both of these decisions were to work out we shall see later.

These private woes of the Republican candidate were, however, effectively concealed both from the press and the public. The antibiotic treatment for his infected knee had exhausted him; he had lost eight pounds in weight; later he was to start drinking three or four chocolate malteds a day to regain the lost weight; yet in public, in this first phase of the campaign, he appeared enormously impressive. One noticed as one followed, however, strange things about the image of the man, all the more curious in one so interested in "imagery."

One noticed, for example, the harshness of the television eye and the electronic cruelty of the camera to his countenance. Sitting one evening in the press ranks a few feet from the candidate in Union Square in San Francisco as he spoke, I noticed that one of the local correspondents had brought a portable television set with him, so that one could observe him at once in person and on the screen. The man on the stand before me in person was a handsome young American—only recently out of the hospital, he was attractively slim, as lithe as Kennedy, a fine and healthy American, almost an athlete. His face as he spoke to this friendly audience was a smiling one—and Nixon has a broad, almost sunny smile when he is with friends. His is a broad open face and the deep eye wells, the heavy brows, the broad forehead give it a clean, masculine quality. Yet on television, the deep eye wells and the heavy brows cast shadow on the face and it glowered on the screen darkly; when he became rhetorically indignant, the television showed ferocity; when he turned, his apparently thick brush of hair showed in a glimmering balding widow's peak; when he smiled and his fine white teeth showed, it was the smile made meaningless by the grin of all the commercial announcers who appear with similar white teeth showing.

Another thing one noticed was the volatility of the man's moods. When he was in a hostile or unfriendly territory, or speaking to indifferent audiences, he would be either sad or harshly strident. But in friendly audiences he could become warm and radiant and glowing.

Just as with Kennedy, the first few days of his opening round were Nixon's attempt to feel out the heart of an audience and develop his themes. He had performed excellently on his first day's flight across the country from Baltimore through Indianapolis through Dallas through San Francisco. He continued in high in the Northwest and Midwest, sagged badly on his Black Thursday, awoke on Friday in Omaha and appeared at his breakfast meeting in Omaha's Civic Auditorium (at eight, after four hours' sleep) still pale and haggard. A rousing reception from the Republican stalwarts of Omaha (6,648 Nebraskans had paid one dollar each to attend this breakfast) cheered him; and then he crossed the great Missouri River from Omaha to Council Bluffs in Iowa; the sun was out—and he was free in home country, loved and adored by the crowds that greeted him, and one could see his spirits visibly soar and his energy come back in a single day.

One could learn much from a day like the day that followed as the Nixon cavalcade crossed into Iowa.

All day, from morning until late evening, the cavalcade moved across the plains toward the Mississippi—from Council Bluffs to Red Oak to Atlantic to Guthrie Center to Dalles Center to Des Moines, and the cornland was approaching harvest. As soon as one crossed the Missouri the corn greeted the eye, two weeks from ripening, darkening from the top down. The tassels had already browned, and the leaves were yellowing but still rich green as the stalk reached to the earth. Corn as far as the eye could see rolled and billowed on the ripples of Iowa's rich earth, swelling and falling in waves of green, tossing a foam of brown cornsilk. After a while the eye grew tired of corn and began to notice what was not corn—occasional stands of umber sorghum heads; dark ivy-green patches of soybeans; the upsweep of a slope on which the cubes of baled hay lay dotted like yellow dominoes on the green of meadowland; the glistening yellow or red or green of farm machinery in the fields; a copse of trees that marked the line of a brook or river running through a flat. But as the afternoon wore on to dusk, the corn was still there, and the eye realized that it had been seeing only corn all day long, 125 miles of corn from the Missouri to Des Moines, and beyond Des Moines lay 150 more miles of nothing but corn; the immensity of it overpowered one. For this was the greatest food-producing civilization in history, and Iowa, in the summer of 1960, had planted more acres to corn than ever before in its history and would harvest 740,590,000 bushels in the next two weeks; the aluminum bins and towers that one saw everywhere were already full of surplus grain, but they must hold more; and this immense productivity was a blessing for which all the rest of the world yearned, while here in Iowa the plenty was almost a curse. All of it had been produced under no government plan, with no compulsion, by these sturdy, handsome people; and with these people, in these small towns, in the sun, Richard M. Nixon was thoroughly at home.

One had to see Nixon entering a small Iowa village—the streets lined with schoolchildren, all waving American flags until it seemed as if the cavalcade were entering a defile lined by fluttering, peppermint-striped little banners—then see him stop at a Harvest Festival (in Red Oaks)—where on the festival tables lay the ripened ears of field corn, already husked to show the mottled jeweling of the many-colored kernels—to see him at his best. For in such small towns he found an echo. These people were his natural constituency, his idiom their idiom. All the little anecdotes, the phrases ("Incidentally, now . . . Just listen to me now . . . You have to think of the other fellow . . .") made him one of them. He was a small-town boy and he understood them. There were only rare moments of real eloquence in the Nixon campaign; no other effort matched his acceptance of the Republican nomination. Nixon hated to speak from a prepared text, preferred spontaneous ad-lib delivery; nor could he ever summon passion when he spoke, or draw a natural laugh, or bring a choke in the throat, as Kennedy could at his best. Nixon's style was a simple earthy one and could only be appreciated in the little groups in such towns as Red Oaks, where each of his pretested punch lines drew its spatter of applause in a cadence that led from "Peace without Surrender" to "My partner, Henry Cabot Lodge" to "It's not his money he wants to spend, it's yours" to the final evocation of "The Spiritual Values of America." Iowa was to give Nixon 56.7 per cent of its votes; all the farm states of the cornland were to follow suit (Kansas, 60.4; Nebraska, 62.1; North Dakota, 55.4; South Dakota, 58.3), making all together the most solid and decisive expression of will of any of the major regions of the United States (see Chapter Fourteen).

Analysts were later to ascribe this farm-belt Nixon victory to the influence of religion and bigotry; while this was certainly true in other states of the union, it seemed to this writer that in the farm belt it was not religion that operated, but much more the culture of the small town. These were Nixon's people, by nature and upbringing, by speech and culture; he spoke for them. The cadence and Harvard prose of John F. Kennedy, the meticulous grammar and elegance of the Democrat's style, were to such people alien and suspect.

Even in Iowa, though, as his spirit revived in the sun and the cornfields, the volatility of Nixon's moods was conspicuous. He had spent an inspiring morning traveling through the small towns; had lunched on a box lunch (fried chicken and ham sandwiches) at Atlantic, Iowa, in Sunnyside Park by the Memorial of the Grand Army of the Republic; and had then proceeded to the crown piece of the day—his farm-policy speech at Guthrie Center, where the State Plowing Contest was being held. The speech went badly—the farmers and their wives sat on the slopes of a hill in the sun and listened to his proposal for disposition of surplus stolidly, indifferently, as if they were alienated from both parties of American politics, as if no one, not even Nixon, could reach them. Flustered, he telescoped his prepared remarks as much as he could, then made a transit to the issue of peace and war. "Peace without Surrender" found him on solid ground again with his certified punch lines, and he left to take to the road once more. On the move again, he was excellent, joshing the children who gathered to greet him in the late afternoon ("Imagine coming to see me in the afternoon, when they aren't even letting you out of school for it"), and he entered Des Moines just before dark at peak form.

Round One of the Nixon campaign could not help but please him. He had done magnificently well on his Southern appearances; and as he moved through the Midwest, he had found resonance wherever he went. He was moving according to plan and pace; some of his advisers grumbled that his speeches were too "defensive," but he told them that he had

several weeks to go before he would erase the image of pugnacity. He was, to be sure, overstraining himself physically with
travel and speech making; but there was not to be another
Black Thursday, and as he attempted to cut down on his
flexible schedule, his health began to mend and some of the
weight to come back.

So Nixon (like Kennedy) approached the second round of
the campaign and the hazards of television in an episode not
only new to this campaign but entirely fresh in the sweep
of American political history.

Chapter 11

ROUND TWO:
THE TELEVISION DEBATES

At 8:30 p.m., Chicago time, on the evening of September 26th, 1960, the voice and shadow of the previous show faded from the screen; in a few seconds it was followed by another voice and by a visual clip extolling the virtues of Liggett and Myers cigarettes; fifteen seconds were then devoted to Maybelline, the mascara "devoted exclusively to eye beauty, velvety soft and smooth." Then a deep voice regretfully announced that the viewers who turned to this channel would tonight be denied the privilege of viewing the Andy Griffith Show—and the screen dissolved to three men who were about to confirm a revolution in American Presidential politics.

This revolution had been made by no one of the three men on screen—John F. Kennedy, Richard M. Nixon or Howard K. Smith, the moderator. It was a revolution born of the ceaseless American genius in technology; its sole agent and organizer had been the common American television set. Tonight it was to permit the simultaneous gathering of all the tribes of America to ponder their choice between two chieftains in the largest political convocation in the history of man.

Again, it is the census that best describes this revolution. Ten years earlier (in 1950) of America's then 40,000,000 families only 11 per cent (or 4,400,000) enjoyed the pleasures of a television set. By 1960 the number of American families had grown to 44,000,000, and of these *no less than 88 per cent, or 40,000,000, possessed a television set*. The installation of this equipment had in some years of the previous decade partaken of the quality of stampede—and in the peak stampede years of 1954–1955–1956 no fewer than 10,000 American homes had each been installing a new television set for the first time *every single day of the year*. The change that came about with this stampede is almost immeasurable. By the summer of 1960 the average use of the television set in the American home was four or five hours out of the twenty-four in each day. The best judgment on what television had done to America comes from the research departments of the large television networks. According to them, it is now possible for the first time to answer an inquiring foreign visitor as to what Americans do in the evening. The answer is clear: *they watch television.* Within a single decade the medium has exploded to a dimension in shaping the American mind that rivals that of America's schools and churches.

The blast effect of this explosion on American culture in the single decade of television's passage from commercial experiment to social menace will remain a subject of independent study and controversy for years.

What concerns us here is politics and power; and the power of television to shape the American mind, concentrated, as it is, decisively in three commercial network offices in Manhattan, New York, has long perplexed the American Congress and its agent, the Federal Communications Commission. What perplexes Congress, fundamentally, is whether the hallowed doctrine of freedom of the press can responsibly be applied to the modern reality of American broadcasting. If, as Walter Lippmann has pointed out, there were only three printing presses available to publish the written word for the entire country, then the concern of the nation with the management of those printing presses would probably transcend "freedom of the press" too. Thus, Congress and the FCC, down into the summer of 1960, had monotonously repeated their respect for television's freedom of expression, yet persistently restricted the power of the proprietors of TV to express this freedom politically. In essence, the regulations over our new communications system have permitted its proprietors any freedom of vulgarity, squalor or commercial profit—but little or no freedom of political expression.

These restrictions had, for years before 1960, irked the men who control and direct the great television and radio networks. However much they might be compelled to operate their companies as profit-making enterprises, they, too, were not only infected with the responsibility of American press tradition but also tantalized by the fantastic opportunities television offers for informing, educating and shaping the American mind. At its worst—which is common—television is one of the most squalid expressions of American culture; at its best—which is rare—it can achieve a breath-taking magnificence. Like most normal human beings, those who direct television yearned to show their best once their worst had made them rich.

In 1960 this yearning of the television networks to show their best was particularly acute. For the men who direct television are sensitive to public criticism; they wince and weep in public like adolescents at the slightest touch of hostility in print—and in 1959 they had suffered the worst round of public criticism and contempt since their industry was founded. The shock of the "payola" scandals of 1959; the Congressional hearings on these scandals; the editorial indignation in the "Gutenberg" media not only at these scandals but at the drenching of the air by violence, vulgarity and horse opera— all these had not only given the masters of television an inferiority complex but also frightened them with the prospect that the franchise on the air given to them so freely in return for their legal obligation of "public service" might be withdrawn, curtailed or abolished. It was a time for the "upgrading" of television; and the Presidential campaign of 1960 seemed to offer a fine opportunity for public service—if only Congress would relax those regulations and laws that had manacled and *prevented* television from doing its best.

Thus in the winter and spring of 1960 the networks, led by NBC and CBS, had pleaded with Congress that they be allowed to do their best, and had fastened, in public hearing and testimony, on the abolition of a technical passage of communications law called Section 315. Section 315, more generally known as the "equal time" rule, is that section of the law that requires every radio and television station when offering "free" time to any candidate to offer similar "free and equal" time to every other candidate for the same office. But as interpreted by the FCC (and particularly in the Lar Daly decision of 1959), it required broadcasting stations to offer equal time not only to candidates of the two major parties but to *every candidate of every party competing for the same office*. For 1960 it meant, in effect, that not only must the television networks offer time to the Republican and Democratic candidates but also to each of the tiny splinter parties that have always operated on the American scene. (In 1960 there were actually fourteen other candidates for the Presidency besides John F. Kennedy and Richard M. Nixon.[1]) The Lar Daly decision not only curtailed the offer of direct free time to candidates

[1] C. Benton Coiner (Conservative Party of Virginia), Merritt Curtis (Constitution Party), Lar Daly (Tax Cut Party), Dr. R. L. Decker (Prohibition Party), Farrell Dobbs (Socialist Workers Party, Farmer Labor Party of Iowa, Socialist Workers and Farmers Party, Utah), Orval E. Faubus (National States Rights Party), Symon Gould (American Vegetarian Party), Eric Hass (Socialist Labor Party, Industrial Government Party, Minn.), Clennon King (Afro-American Unity Party), Henry Krajewski (American Third Party), J. Bracken Lee (Conservative Party of N.J.), Whitney Harp Slocomb (Greenback Party), William Lloyd Smith (American Beat Consensus), Charles Sullivan (Constitution Party of Texas). This listing is taken from a statement of Frank Stanton, President of CBS, before the Senate Subcommittee on Communications on January 31, 1961.

of the two major parties, but also sternly diminished television's previous freedom to offer the public reportorial coverage, press conferences, or discussions and visits with anybody acknowledged to be a candidate. Hearings on the public plea of the broadcasting networks to abolish such restrictions were held in the spring; by May, bills were offered in Congress permitting a temporary suspension of Section 315 for the campaign of 1960 alone; on June 27th, Section 315 was officially suspended and the leash slipped on television's power of political participation.

It is important to understand why the debates of 1960 were to be different from previous political use of the medium.

Television had already demonstrated its primitive power in politics from, at least, the fall of 1952, when, in one broadcast, it had transformed Richard M. Nixon from a negative Vice-Presidential candidate, under attack, into a martyr and an asset to Dwight D. Eisenhower's Presidential campaign. But from 1952 until 1960 television could be used only as an expensive partisan instrument; its time had to be bought and paid for by political parties for their own candidates. The audiences such partisan broadcasts assembled, like the audiences at political rallies, were audiences of the convinced—of convinced Republicans for Republican candidates, of convinced Democrats for Democratic candidates. Generally, the most effective political broadcast could assemble hardly more than half the audience of the commercial show that it replaced. This was why so many candidates and their television advisers sought two-minute or five-minute spots tacked on to the major programs that engaged the nation's fancy: the general audience would not tune out a hostile candidate if he appeared for only two or three minutes, and thus a candidate using TV "spots" had a much better chance of reaching the members of the opposition party and the "independents," whom he must lure to listen to and then vote for him. The 1960 idea of a "debate," in which both major candidates would appear simultaneously, thus promised to bring both Democrats and Republicans together in the same viewing audience for the first time. Some optimists thought the debates would at least double the exposure of both candidates. How much more they would do than "double" the exposure no one, in the summer of 1960, dreamed.

The future was thus still obscure when the representatives of the two candidates and the spokesmen for the broadcasting networks first met at the Waldorf-Astoria Hotel in New York in September to discuss the conditions and circumstances of the meetings. By this time each of the two major networks had offered eight hours of free time to the campaign, and the third had offered three hours, for a total of nineteen hours of nationwide broadcasting, worth about $2,000,000; they had also made it clear to the candidates that this was not "gift" time but time over which they, the networks, meant to exercise an editorial control to insure maximum viewing interest. Slowly, in discussion, the shape and form of the debates emerged—a controlled panel of four press interlocutors; no notes; dignity to be safeguarded; opening statements of eight minutes by each candidate in the first and last debates; two-and-one-half minute responses to questions. The Nixon negotiators fought to restrict the number of debates—their man, they felt, was the master of the form and one "sudden-death" debate could eliminate Kennedy with a roundhouse swing. They viewed the insistence of the Kennedy negotiators on the maximum possible number of debates as weakness. ("If they weren't scared," said one Nixon staffman, "why shouldn't they be willing to pin everything on one show?") The Kennedy negotiators insisted on at least five debates, then let themselves be whittled to four. ("Every time we get those two fellows on the screen side by side," said J. Leonard Reinsch, Kennedy's TV maestro, "we're going to gain and he's going to lose.")

By mid-September all had been arranged. There would be four debates—on September 26th, October 7th, October 13th and October 21st. The first would be produced by CBS out of Chicago, the second by NBC out of Washington, the third by ABC out of New York and Los Angeles and the fourth, again by ABC, out of New York.

In the event, when all was over, the audience exceeded the wildest fancies and claims of the television networks. Each individual broadcast averaged an audience set at a low of 65,000,000 and a high of 70,000,000. The greatest previous audience in television history had been for the climactic game of the 1959 World Series, when an estimated 90,000,000 Americans had tuned in to watch the White Sox play the Dodgers. When, finally, figures were assembled for all four debates, the total audience for the television debates on the Presidency exceeded even this figure.

All this, of course, was far in the future when, on Sunday, September 25th, 1960, John F. Kennedy arrived in Chicago from Cleveland, Ohio, to stay at the Ambassador East Hotel, and Richard M. Nixon came from Washington, D.C., to stop at the Pick-Congress Hotel, to prepare, each in his own way, for their confrontation.

Kennedy's preparation was marked by his typical attention to organization and his air of casual self-possession; the man behaves, in any crisis, as if it consisted only of a sequence of necessary things to be done that will become complicated if emotions intrude. His personal Brain Trust of three had arrived and assembled at the Knickerbocker Hotel in Chicago on Sunday, the day before. The chief of these three was, of course, Ted Sorensen; with Sorensen was Richard Goodwin, a twenty-eight-year-old lawyer, an elongated elfin man with a capacity for fact and reasoning that had made him Number One man only two years before at the Harvard Law School; and Mike Feldman, a burly and impressive man, a one-time instructor of law at the University of Pennsylvania, later a highly successful businessman, who had abandoned business to follow Kennedy's star as Chief of the Senator's Legislative Research.[2] With them, they had brought the portable Kennedy campaign research library—a Sears, Roebuck foot locker of documents—and now, for a twenty-four-hour session at the Knickerbocker Hotel, stretching around the clock, they operated like young men at college cramming for an exam. When they had finished, they had prepared fifteen pages of copy boiling down into twelve or thirteen subject areas the relevant facts and probable questions they thought the correspondents on the panel, or Mr. Nixon, might raise. All three had worked with Kennedy closely for years. They knew that as a member of the House and the Senate Committees on Labor he was fully familiar with all the issues that might arise on domestic policy (the subject of the first debate) and that it was necessary to fix in his mind, not the issues or understanding, but only the latest data.

Early on Monday they met the candidate in his suite for a morning session of questions and answers. The candidate read

[2] These three young men today still remain Kennedy's "personal" Brain Trust, as distinct from his "academic" Brain Trust (Schlesinger, Galbraith, Bundy, Rostow), or his "political" Brain Trust (O'Donnell, O'Brien, Donahue and Dungan). Although somewhat aloof with outsiders, this trio has a fey, intellectual quality that is quite captivating. They like to amuse themselves with double-dome guessing games too complicated to be readily described. On election day, for example, they tried for the first time the standard Question Game and found it quite easy. The Question Game is that game in which one person offers a phrase or a statement and the other players are summoned to imagine the question to which the statement replies. On their drive from Boston to Hyannisport on election day the trio played the game intensely and the best Answer-Question of their contest was "Nine-W." To what question is "Nine-W" the best response? Question? According to the trio, the best question to the answer, "Nine-W," is, "Do you spell your name with a V, Mr. Vagner?"

their suggestions for his opening eight-minute statement, disagreed, tossed their suggestions out, called his secretary, dictated another of his own; and then for four hours Kennedy and the Brain Trust considered together the Nixon position and the Kennedy position, with the accent constantly on fact: What was the latest rate of unemployment? What was steel production rate? What was the Nixon stand on this or that particular? The conversation, according to those present, was not only easy but rather comic and rambling, covering a vast number of issues entirely irrelevant to the debate. Shortly before one o'clock Goodwin and Feldman disappeared to a basement office in the Ambassador East to answer new questions the candidate had raised, and the candidate then had a gay lunch with Ted Sorensen, his brother Robert and public-opinion analyst Louis Harris. The candidate left shortly thereafter for a quick address to the United Brotherhood of Carpenters and Joiners of America (which Nixon had addressed in the morning) and came back to his hotel room for a nap. About five o'clock he rose from his nap, quite refreshed, and assembled brother Robert, Sorensen, Harris, Goodwin and Feldman for another Harvard tutorial skull session.

Several who were present remember the performance as vividly as those who were present at the Hyannisport meeting in October, 1959. The candidate lay on his bed in a white, open-necked T shirt and army suntan pants, and fired questions at his intimates. He held in his hand the fact cards that Goodwin and Feldman had prepared for him during the afternoon, and as he finished each, he sent it spinning off the bed to the floor. Finally, at about 6:30, he rose from his bed and decided to have dinner. He ate what is called "a splendid dinner" all by himself in his room, then emerged in a white shirt and dark-gray suit, called for a stop watch and proceeded to the old converted sports arena that is now CBS Station WBBM at McClurg Court in Chicago, to face his rival for the Presidency of the United States.

Richard M. Nixon had preceded him to the studio. Nixon had spent the day in solitude without companions in the loneliness of his room at the Pick-Congress. The Vice-President was tired; the drive of campaigning in the previous two weeks had caused him to lose another five pounds since he had left the hospital; his TV advisers had urged that he arrive in Chicago on Saturday and have a full day of rest before he went on the air on Monday, but they had been unable to get through to him, and had not even been able to reach his press secretary, Herbert Klein. Mr. Nixon thus arrived in Chicago late on Sunday evening, unbriefed on the magnitude of the trial he was approaching; on Monday he spoke during the morning to the United Brotherhood of Carpenters and Joiners, an appearance his TV advisers considered a misfortune—the Brotherhood was a hostile union audience, whose negative reaction, they knew, would psychologically disturb their contender.

When Nixon returned to his hotel from the Brotherhood appearance at 12:30, he became incommunicado while his frantic TV technicians tried to reach him or brief him on the setting of the debate, the staging, the problems he might encounter. The Vice-President received one visitor for five minutes that afternoon in his suite, and he received one long telephone call—from Henry Cabot Lodge, who, reportedly, urged him to be careful to erase the "assassin image" when he went on the air. For the rest, the Vice-President was alone, in consultation with no one. Finally, as he emerged from the hotel to drive through Chicago traffic to the studio, one TV adviser was permitted to ride with him and hastily brief him in the ten-minute drive. The adviser urged that the Vice-President come out swinging—that this was a contest, a fight, and that Kennedy must be jolted at the first exchange. The Vice-President was of another mind, however—and wondered whether the suggestion had originated with his adviser or with someone else, like Frank Stanton, President of CBS, who, said the Vice-President, only wanted a good show. Thus they arrived at the studio; as Nixon got out, he struck his knee again —a nasty crack—on the edge of the automobile door, just as he had on his first accident to the knee at Greensboro, North Carolina. An observer reports that his face went all "white and pasty" but that he quickly recovered and entered the studio.

Both candidates had had representatives in the CBS studio from 8:30 in the morning of the day of the debate.

Mr. Nixon's advisers and representatives, understandably nervous since they could not communicate with their principal, had made the best preparation they could. They had earlier requested that both candidates talk from a lectern, standing— and Kennedy had agreed. They had asked several days earlier that the two candidates be seated farther apart from each other than originally planned—and that had been agreed on too. Now, on the day of the debate, they paid meticulous attention to each detail. They were worried about the deep eye shadows in Nixon's face and they requested and adjusted two tiny spotlights ("inkies" in television parlance) to shine directly into his eye wells and illuminate the darkness there; they asked that a table be placed in front of the moderator, and this was agreed to also; they requested that no shots be taken of Nixon's left profile during the debate, and this was also agreed to.

The Kennedy advisers had no requests; they seemed as cocky and confident as their chief.

Nixon entered the studio about an hour before air time and inspected the setting, let himself be televised on an interior camera briefly for the inspection of his advisers, then paced moodily about in the back of the studio. He beckoned the producer to him at one point as he paced and asked as a personal favor that he not be on camera if he happened to be mopping sweat from his face. (That night, contrary to most reports, Nixon was wearing no theatrical make-up. In order to tone down his dark beard stubble on the screen, an adviser had applied only a light coating of "Lazy Shave," a pancake make-up with which a man who has heavy afternoon beard growth may powder his face to conceal the growth.)

Senator Kennedy arrived about fifteen minutes after the Vice-President; he inspected the set; sat for the camera; and his advisers inspected him, then declared they were satisfied. The producer made a remark about the glare of the Senator's white shirt, and Kennedy sent an aide back to his hotel to bring back a blue one, into which he changed just before air time. The men took their seats, the tally lights on the cameras blinked red to show they were live now.

"Good evening," said Howard K. Smith, the gray and handsome moderator. "The television and radio stations of the United States . . . are proud to provide for a discussion of issues in the current political campaign by the two major candidates for the Presidency. The candidates need no introduction. . . ."

And they were on air, before seventy million Americans.

Rereading now the text of the first of the great debates (and of the following three also), one can find only a blurred echo of the emotions that rose from the performance, and the intense, immediate and dramatic impact of the debate on the fortunes of the two candidates.

This, the first of the debates, was committed to a discussion of domestic issues—an area in which the Democrats, by their philosophy and record, make larger promises and offer a more aggressive attitude to the future than the Republicans. Kennedy, opening, declared that the world could not endure half-slave and half-free, and that the posture of America in the world rested fundamentally on its posture at home—how we behaved to each other, what we did to move American society forward at home, this affected not only us, but the world too: "Can freedom be maintained under the most severe attack it has ever known? I think it can be. And I think in the final analysis it depends upon what we do here. I think it's time America started moving again."

Nixon's opening statement, as it reads now in print, was one of good-willed difference: he agreed with Kennedy in all the goals Kennedy had outlined. He differed with Kennedy only in the methods to reach those goals. He lauded the progress made under the seven and a half years of the Eisenhower administration—hospitals, highways, electric power, gross national product, growth rate, were all moving at a rate, he said, never matched before in any administration.

The clue to what was happening can be remembered only in rereading the penultimate passage of Mr. Nixon's opening remarks: "The final point that I would like to make is this: Senator Kennedy has suggested in his speeches that we lack compassion for the poor, for the old, and for others that are unfortunate. . . . I know what it means to be poor . . . I know that Senator Kennedy feels as deeply about these problems as I do, but our disagreement is not about the goals for America but only about the means to reach those goals."

For Mr. Nixon was debating with Mr. Kennedy as if a board of judges were scoring points; he rebutted and refuted, as he went, the inconsistencies or errors of his opponent. Nixon was addressing himself to Kennedy—but Kennedy was addressing himself to the audience that was the nation. In these debates, before this audience, there could be no appeal to the past or to the origins of any ethnic group—there could only be an appeal, across the board, to all Americans and to the future. This across-the-board appeal to all Americans had been Mr. Nixon's basic strategy from the very beginning—a generalized pressure that would fragment the minorities coalition of the Democrats. Yet here, before the largest audience of Americans in history, Nixon was not addressing himself to his central theme; he was offering no vision of the future that the Republican Party might offer Americans—he was concerned with the cool and undisturbed man who sat across the platform from him, with the personal adversary in the studio, not with the mind of America.

Ten questions followed from the panel of television reporters who sat before the debaters: on the importance of a candidate's age; on the quality of decision in Presidential affairs; on farms; on taxes; on schools; on Congressional politics; on subversion; and on schools again. In each pair of answers, the same contrast repeated itself: the Senator from Massachusetts, ignoring the direct inquiry when it suited him, used each question as a springboard for an appeal to the mind and the imagination of the audience assembled before the countless sets. But the Vice-President's mind and attention were fixed there in the studio. As one rereads the text, one finds him, over and over again, scoring excellently against the personal adversary in the hall beside him, yet forgetful of the need to score on the mind of the nation he hoped to lead.

The defensive quality of Mr. Nixon's performance (evident from his first enunciation: "The things that Senator Kennedy has said many of us can agree with. . . . I can subscribe completely to the spirit that Senator Kennedy has expressed tonight, the spirit that the United States should move ahead. . . .") can still be reconstructed from the texts. What cannot be reconstructed is the visual impact of the first debate.

For it was the sight of the two men side by side that carried the punch.

There was, first and above all, the crude, overwhelming impression that side by side the two seemed evenly matched—and this even matching in the popular imagination was for Kennedy a major victory. Until the cameras opened on the Senator and the Vice-President, Kennedy had been the boy under assault and attack by the Vice-President as immature, young, inexperienced. Now, obviously, in flesh and behavior he was the Vice-President's equal.

Not only that, but the contrast of the two faces was astounding. Normally and in private, Kennedy under tension flutters his hands—he adjusts his necktie, slaps his knee, strokes his face. Tonight he was calm and nerveless in appearance. The Vice-President, by contrast, was tense, almost frightened, at turns glowering and, occasionally, haggard-looking to the point of sickness. Probably no picture in American politics tells a better story of crisis and episode than that famous shot of the camera on the Vice-President as he half slouched, his "Lazy Shave" powder faintly streaked with sweat, his eyes exaggerated hollows of blackness, his jaw, jowls, and face drooping with strain.

It is impossible to look again at the still photographs of Nixon in his ordeal and to recollect the circumstances without utmost sympathy. For everything that could have gone wrong that night went wrong. The Vice-President, to begin with, suffers from a handicap that is serious only on television—his is a light, naturally transparent skin. On a visual camera that takes pictures by optical projection this transparent skin photographs cleanly and well. But a television camera projects electronically, by an image-orthicon tube, which is a cousin of the x-ray tube; it seems to go beneath the skin, almost as the x-ray photograph does. On television, the camera on Nixon is usually held away from him, for in close-up his transparent skin shows the tinest hair growing in the skin follicles beneath the surface, even after he has just shaved. And for the night of the first debate, CBS, understandably zealous, had equipped its cameras with brand-new tubes for the most perfect projection possible—a perfection of projection that could only be harmful to the Vice-President. (In the later debates, Nixon was persuaded to wear theatrical make-up to repair the ravage TV's electronic tube makes of his countenance; but for this first debate he wore only "Lazy Shave.")

The scene of the debate, the studio of WBBM, had, further, been tense all day long, as furniture, desks, lecterns, background, had been rearranged and then rearranged again for best effect. Nixon's TV advisers had been told that the background would be gray-scale five, a relatively dark tone; therefore they had urged their principal to dress in a light-gray suit for contrast. Yet the backdrop, when they saw it, was so markedly lighter than they had anticipated that they insisted, rightly, it be repainted. Several times that day it was repainted —but each time the gray tone dried light. (The background indeed was still tacky to the touch when the two candidates went on the air.) Against this light background Nixon, in his light suit, faded into a fuzzed outline, while Kennedy in his dark suit had the crisp picture edge of contrast. The Nixon advisers had, further, adjusted all lighting to a master lighting scheme for their candidate before he went on the air; but in the last few minutes before the debate a horde of still photographers from newspapers and magazines were permitted on the set, and as they milled for their still pictures, they kicked over wires and displaced lights and television cameras from their marked positions.

There was, lastly, the fact that the Vice-President had still not recovered from his illness, and was unrested from the exertions of his first two weeks of intense campaigning. His normal shirt hung loosely about his neck, and his recent weight loss made him appear scrawny. And, most of all, psychologically, his advisers now insist, he lacked the energy to project—for Nixon does best on television when he projects, when he can distract the attention of the viewer from his passive countenance to the theme or the message he wants to give forth, as in his famous "Checkers" appearance on television in 1952.

All this, however, was unknown then to the national audience. Those who heard the debates on radio, according to sample surveys, believed that the two candidates came off almost equal. Yet every survey of those who watched the debates on television indicated that the Vice-President had come off poorly and, in the opinion of many, very poorly. It was the picture image that had done it—and in 1960 television had won the nation away from sound to images, and that was that.

The Vice-President was later to recover from the impression he made in this first debate. But this first debate, the beginning of the contest, was, as in so many human affairs, half the whole. The second debate concerned itself with foreign policy and ranged from Cuba's Castro through the U-2 and espionage to the matter of America's declining prestige, and closed on the first sharp clash of the series—the defense of Quemoy and Matsu.

The third debate resumed, like a needle stuck in a phonograph groove, with the subject of Quemoy and Matsu, hung there almost indefinitely, then broke away with Nixon's stern disapproval of President Truman's bad language, and went on to other matters such as bigotry, labor unions and gold outflow. This, according to all sample surveys, was Nixon's best performance in terms of its impact on the audience. This was the debate in which Nixon spoke from Los Angeles while Kennedy spoke from New York, and it was as if, separated by a continent from the personal presence of his adversary, Nixon were more at ease and could speak directly to the nation that lay between them.

The fourth debate was the dreariest—both candidates had by now almost nothing new left to say, and they repeated themselves on all the matters they had covered in the three previous debates. Curiously enough, the audience which had been highest for the first debate and dropped off slightly for the second and third, returned on the last debate to almost match the total of the first.

No accurate political measurement or reasonable judgment is yet possible on a matter as vast as the TV debates of 1960. When they began, Nixon was generally viewed as being the probable winner of the election contest and Kennedy as fighting an uphill battle; when they were over, the positions of the two contestants were reversed.

No reporter can claim any accuracy in charting the magic and mysterious flow of public opinion between the time a campaign starts and the ultimate tally of feelings at the polls; and so opinion seesawed back and forth for weeks, as it still seesaws back and forth now, long after the debates are over,

330 THE MAKING OF THE PRESIDENT 1960

as to what, specifically, the debates achieved in shaping the campaign and American opinion.

There were fragmentary and episodic achievements that no one could deny.

Any reporter who followed the Kennedy campaign remembers still the quantum jump in the size of crowds that greeted the campaigning Senator from the morrow of the first debate, the morning of Tuesday, September 27th, when he began to campaign in northern Ohio. His crowds had been growing for a full seven days before the debates, but now, overnight, they seethed with enthusiasm and multiplied in numbers, as if the sight of him, in their homes on the video box, had given him a "star quality" reserved only for television and movie idols.

Equally visible was the gloom that descended on Republican leaders around the country; they were angry with their own candidate, angry at his performance, angry most of all at his "me-too" debating style. At Nixon headquarters in Washington, the telephones rang incessantly, demanding that someone get to this "new Nixon" and convince him that only the "old Nixon" could win.

There were other measurable hard political results. On the evening of the first debate, the Democratic governors of the Southern states were gathered for one of their annual conferences at Hot Springs, Arkansas. Except for Governor Luther Hodges[3] of North Carolina, they had until then viewed Kennedy with a range of emotions that ran from resigned apathy to whispered hostility. Watching him on TV that night, they too were suddenly impressed. We do not know whose idea it was to send Kennedy the telegram of congratulations which ten of the eleven signed that evening—but the enthusiasm and excitement of the telegram was not only genuine but a tidemark in the campaign. The Southern governors were with him now; and if they were with him, it meant that the machinery of their political organizations would be with him, too.

It is much more difficult to measure the debates in terms of issues, of education of the American people to the tasks and problems before them. For there certainly were real differences of philosophy and ideas between John F. Kennedy and Richard M. Nixon—yet rarely in American history has there been a political campaign that discussed issues less or clarified them less.

The TV debates, in retrospect, were the greatest opportunity

[3] Now Secretary of Commerce.

ever for such discussion, but it was an opportunity missed. It is difficult to blame the form of the debates for this entirely; yet the form and the compulsions of the medium must certainly have been contributory. The nature of both TV and radio is that they abhor silence and "dead time." All TV and radio discussion programs are compelled to snap question and answer back and forth as if the contestants were adversaries in an intellectual tennis match. Although every experienced newspaperman and inquirer knows that the most thoughtful and responsive answers to any difficult question come after long pause, and that the longer the pause the more illuminating the thought that follows it, nonetheless the electronic media cannot bear to suffer a pause of more than five seconds; a pause of thirty seconds of dead time on air seems interminable. Thus, snapping their two-and-a-half-minute answers back and forth, both candidates could only react for the cameras and the people, they could not think. And, since two and a half minutes permit only a snatch of naked thought and a spatter of raw facts, both candidates, whenever caught out on a limb with a thought too heavy for two-minute exploration, a thought seemingly too bold or fresh to be accepted by the conditioned American mind, hastily scuttled back toward center as soon as they had enunciated the thought. Thus Kennedy's response to the first question on Quemoy and Matsu was probably one of the sharpest and clearest responses to any question of the debates; in that response, actually, Kennedy was tentatively fingering at one of the supreme problems of American statecraft, our relation with the revolution in Asia. Yet he was out too far with such a thought for a two-minute response[4] and, in succeeding debates, in reply to succeeding questions, he fuzzed the distinction between his position and Nixon's until it was almost impossible to tell them apart.

If there was to be any forum for issues, the TV debates should have provided such a forum. Yet they did not; every conceivable problem was raised by the probing imagination of the veteran correspondents who questioned the candidates. But all problems were answered in two-minute snatches, either with certain facts or with safe convictions. Neither man could pause to indulge in the slow reflection and rumination, the

[4] For a full development of this two-minute answer, one had to wait for days, until Kennedy's extraordinarily lucid half-hour speech on Quemoy and Matsu in New York on Columbus Day, October 12th. That speech was heard only by a local audience, and its full text was reprinted, so far as I know, in only three newspapers in the country. It was as fine a campaign discussion of an issue of national importance as this correspondent can remember—yet its impact on the nation was nil.

slow questioning of alternatives before decision, that is the inner quality of leadership.

If, then, the TV debates did little to advance the reasonable discussion of issues that is the dream of unblooded political scientists, what did they do?

What they did best was to give the voters of a great democracy a living portrait of two men under stress and let the voters decide, by instinct and emotion, which style and pattern of behavior under stress they preferred in their leader. The political roots of this tribal sense of the whole go as far back as the Roman Senate, or the beer-blown assemblies of the Teutonic tribes that Tacitus describes in his chronicles. This sense of personal choice of leader has been missing for centuries from modern civilization—or else limited to such conclaves of deputized spokesmen of the whole as a meeting of Tammany Hall captains, a gathering of Communist barons in the Kremlin or the dinners of leaders of the English Establishment in the clubs of London. What the TV debates did was to generalize this tribal sense of participation, this emotional judgment of the leader, from the few to the multitude— for the salient fact of the great TV debates is not what the two candidates said, nor how they behaved, but how many of the candidates' fellow Americans gave up their evening hours to ponder the choice between the two.

There are many measures of the numbers of Americans who viewed the debates. The low measure is that of Dr. George Gallup, America's most experienced pollster, who sets the figure of Americans who viewed one or all of the debates at 85,000,000. The two most extensive surveys of audience were those made by NBC and CBS, the two great television networks. Their independent measures of the audience are so close that they must be taken seriously: NBC has estimated from its surveys that 115,000,000 Americans viewed one or all of the great debates; CBS has estimated the number at 120,000,000. With or without issues, no larger assembly of human beings, their minds focused on one problem, has ever happened in history.

Even more significant than the numbers who viewed the debates was the penetration upon them of the personalities of the candidates; and on the effect of this penetration the public-opinion samplers were unanimous.

There are any number of such surveys. The best localized survey (and that most respected by Nixon's television advisers) was performed in New York by a research-testing firm called Schwerin Research Corporation. The Schwerin Research Corporation, which operates a studio on Manhattan's West Side with scientifically selected audiences of three to four hundred people from the New York metropolitan area, is considered by some Madison Avenue experts as the best television-testing operation in the entire range of consumer-goods advertising. Testing each debate in turn before its audiences, the Schwerin analysts reported that Kennedy outscored Nixon by 39 to 23 (balance undecided) in the first debate; by 44 to 28 in the second debate; lost to Nixon by 42 to 39 in the third debate (in which the contestants were separated physically by the space of the continent); and came back to win by 52 to 27 in the last debate.

The measurements of Dr. George Gallup coincide. After the first debate, 43 per cent of his respondents considered Kennedy to have been the best man, 23 per cent Nixon, 29 per cent considered them to have come off even, and 5 per cent were undecided. After the last debate Kennedy was held by 42 per cent to have won, Nixon to have won by 30 per cent, while 23 per cent considered the men even and 5 per cent were undecided.

There is, finally, the most extensive survey, that conducted for CBS by Dr. Elmo Roper. Sampling across the country, Dr. Roper estimated for CBS that 57 per cent of those who voted believed that the TV debates had influenced their decisions. Another 6 per cent, or over 4,000,000 voters (by this sample), ascribed their final decision on voting to the debates alone. Of these 4,000,000 voters, 26 per cent (or 1,000,000) voted for Nixon, and 72 per cent (or almost 3,000,000) voted for Kennedy. If these extrapolations are true, then 2,000,000 of the Kennedy margin came from television's impact on the American mind—and since Kennedy won by only 112,000 votes, he was entirely justified in stating on the Monday following election, November 12th: "It was TV more than anything else that turned the tide."

There is a politicians' rule of thumb, particularly hallowed by Democratic politicians, that no election campaign starts until the World Series is over. A campaign, according to them, begins only when the men at the bar stop arguing about the pitchers and batters and start arguing about the candidates. It was 3:45 in the afternoon of Friday, October 13th, 1960, when Bill Mazeroski, second baseman for the Pittsburgh Pirates, in the last half of the ninth swung deep and low into the second pitch and slammed it over the left-field fence for a home run, ending the game with a 10-to-9 win and the series with a 4-to-3 victory for the Pirates—their first World Series pennant since 1925.

Mazeroski had clubbed his homer at 3:45. At 6:45, the television cameras told of Mr. Khrushchev's farewell to America and the United Nations and showed him pounding his shoe in anger on the table. For twenty-five days the rotund chief of the Russians had made camp on New York's Park Avenue and had made sport at the United Nations. He had chuffed and puffed, hustled and bustled, and succeeded in distracting a disproportionate amount of American attention from the serious business of choosing a President to his own meaningless but threatening presence. Now, as he announced that he was leaving in the evening, Khrushchev let it be known without bluster that he was suspending his colloquy with America over the destiny of the human race until the Americans should have chosen a new leader. Whether or not he had watched the two rivals for America's leadership during their great debates, no one knows.

At 7:30, Eastern Daylight Time, that same day, the cohorts, flaks, servants and press corps of John F. Kennedy gathered in the barnlike studios of ABC in New York while those of Richard M. Nixon gathered in the Hollywood studios of the same company for their third debate. When they had finished at 8:30, with Kennedy proceeding to Illinois and Nixon staying to campaign in California, the last round of the campaign was about to begin. There was only one more debate to go—on the 21st. But now, finally, there were no other distractions—neither the World Series nor Mr. Khrushchev nor Mr. Castro—to divert the American mind from choice of the man who should lead them.

There were but three and a half weeks more to election day. It was up to Mr. Nixon now, who knew himself to be behind (the Gallup Poll read: 49 per cent Kennedy, 46 per cent Nixon and 5 per cent undecided) to bring his campaign to "peak," to prove what he could do.

Chapter 12

NIXON FOR PRESIDENT: ROUND THREE

FOR Nixon, the television debates had been disaster. Even though by the end of the series he had perceptibly recovered from the initial debacle, nonetheless a vital intangible had been wiped out: the illusion of separation between himself and his opponent, that psychological distinction between himself as the "experienced" heir to Eisenhower and his junior rival as an "inexperienced" youth. One hundred twenty million Americans had seen the debates; and though Republicans and Democrats might vehemently disagree on which candidate was better, no Republican could insist with a straight face that a "mature" Nixon had exposed Kennedy as a frightened stripling. If Nixon could match Khrushchev in debate, then Kennedy had proved he could match Nixon.

For Nixon, thus, the period of the debates was an ordeal he must simply endure to the end, and his normally volatile spirit plunged into gloom as he waited for its end, when he might move his campaign into its third, or final phase, "peaking" it for impact on the week end before election when, he hoped, the drive of his rival would have faded.

Even before the debates were over, on Sunday, October 16th, the high command of the Nixon staff had already gathered in Hartford, Connecticut, for an emergency planning session. Such men as Hall, Shepley, Finch and Newton had always sought to pin the candidate down for a good long staff session, in which they might all discuss the battle order and perspectives that the candidate carried in his head. Now, at the Statler Hotel in Hartford on a rainy, dreary Sunday morning, five days before the last TV debate, they settled down to consider what should come next.

There were many matters to discuss with the two candidates, for Henry Cabot Lodge, Nixon's running mate, joined them at this meeting. Lodge, and his entourage, had already provoked the most intense anger of the Nixon staff by a pledge to the Negroes of East Harlem in New York that Nixon, if elected, would name a Negro to the Cabinet of the United States. This was a pledge that, if allowed to stand, committed

Nixon—a pledge from which he could hope to gain few additional votes in the North, but which might cost him millions in the South. ("Whoever recommended that Harlem speech," said one Virginia Republican, "should have been thrown out of an airplane at 25,000 feet.") Lodge had to be disciplined and his enthusiastic cultivation of minority groups across the country moderated.

Next the high command had to discuss whether the fifty-state pledge should be honored or not. It was obvious that in the twenty remaining days of the campaign there was too much to be done in the critical big states to spend time anywhere but on the major battlefield of the Big Seven. For weeks his advisers had beseeched Nixon to consider the two-week hospitalization in September as an honorable release from his Convention pledge. Yet Nixon held firm; he would campaign in every one of the states, cost what it might in energy and exertion.

The religious problem was once again discussed with great intensity and deliberation. Pressure had long been building up in the Republican high command, from Republican Catholics as well as Protestants, that Nixon, too, address himself to the religious issue. Although Kennedy personally was scrupulously refraining from any further (i.e., after Houston) discussion of that issue, his lieutenants, particularly in the South and in the labor unions, were discussing not religion but "tolerance" with such intensity that Nixon, like Humphrey before him, was almost strangled for an effective answer. Such Protestant laymen as Arthur Flemming (Secretary of Health, Education and Welfare) and Fred Seaton (Secretary of the Interior), both prominent in Nixon's council of advisers, were of a mind to offer a Protestant-to-Catholic countercall for equal tolerance. The issue was explosive. Flatly, Nixon refused to let them raise it—in any manner.

Again, his advisers pressed him for a more dynamic, harder-hitting campaign—a bit more of the "Old Nixon" manner in advocacy of the "New Nixon" positions. They pressed him to attack Kennedy's poor attendance record in the Senate and at his committees for Disarmament and African Affairs. Nixon refused. He was about to launch his own hard-hitting finale, and he would do it in his own way, proving that the old punch was still there. There was some discussion of rescheduling for the final weeks, with particular attention to New Jersey. All agreed that Nixon should hit and hit hard on the high-cost-of-living theme ("Jack Kennedy is going to raise the price of everything you buy in the stores by twenty-five per cent"); and there was some discussion of the final ten days on nationwide TV, when all the "control elements" of the final drive would be brought into play.

It was not a very happy conference that broke up on Sunday evening, and the rest of that week was even gloomier, perhaps the gloomiest of the entire Nixon campaign. Mr. Nixon flew, exhausting himself further, from Hartford to Bridgeport to Buffalo and Niagara to Jacksonville to Miami to Tampa to Wilmington and on to New York, all in the space of two days. He arrived in New York to read the morning newspaper reports of the orgiastic welcome New York had given John F. Kennedy the previous day in a demonstration that had assembled an estimated 1,250,000 people. Nixon sat Wednesday, Thursday, Friday, in the Presidential suite on the thirty-fifth floor of the Waldorf Towers, emerging for only one major appearance, at the Alfred E. Smith Memorial Dinner. The Alfred E. Smith Dinner, a tribute to the late New York Governor, is usually presided over each year by the senior prelate of the Catholic Church in New York, in 1960, Cardinal Spellman. Nixon, sharing the dais with his opponent, heard the Democrat in one of his most sparkling campaign addresses.[1]

---

[1] Kennedy was in high form that evening, and since Kennedy exerts over Nixon the same charm that a snake charmer exerts over a snake, the effect was doubly harmful to Nixon's ego. Kennedy originally, in August, had ben reluctant to accept the invitation to this strictly Catholic affair; he felt it would accentuate the religious issue. Evidently he decided finally to speak with a light touch, and for two days before the engagement his aides had been circulating through the press, asking, "Do you know any jokes?" Kennedy began his remarks thus:

> I am glad to be here at this notable dinner once again and I am glad that Mr. Nixon is here also [Applause]. Now that Cardinal Spellman has demonstrated the proper spirit, I assume that shortly I will be invited to a Quaker dinner honoring Herbert Hoover [Laughter]. Cardinal Spellman is the only man so widely respected in American politics that he could bring together amicably, at the same banquet table, for the first time in this campaign, two political leaders who are increasingly apprehensive about the November election—who have long eyed each other suspiciously and who have disagreed so strongly, both publicly and privately— Vice-President Nixon and Governor Rockefeller [Laughter].
>
> Mr. Nixon, like the rest of us, has had his troubles in this campaign. At one point even the *Wall Street Journal* was criticizing his tactics. That is like the *Osservatore Romano* criticizing the Pope.
>
> But I think the worst news for the Republicans this week was that Casey Stengel has been fired [Laughter]. It must show that perhaps experience does not count [Laughter and applause].
>
> On this matter of experience, I had announced earlier this year that if successful I would not consider campaign contributions as a substitute for experience in appointing ambassadors. Ever since I made that statement, I have not received one single cent from my father.
>
> One of the inspiring notes that was struck in the last debate was

Nixon conferred at the Waldorf-Astoria with Herbert Hoover, Roy Howard, Thomas E. Dewey and other *genro* of the Republican Party; rested himself, gloomed more; sent his press chief downstairs to open a press conference in Peacock Alley that began, dourly, with the remark, "I hear some doubts are growing up about Vice-President Nixon's election, and I want to give you some figures. . . ." Then, on Friday, at ten o'clock (EDT), both candidates were whisked to the Sixty-seventh Street studios of the American Broadcasting Company in New York and jousted for the last time before camera in the dullest of their debates—and the TV ordeal was over. There were now eighteen days left to the campaign, and Mr. Nixon was free to take the gloves off and "peak" in his own manner.

Nixon stumped through Pennsylvania on Sunday, spoke in Pittsburgh on Sunday night, and then, as the campaign train rocked over the rails south and west from Pittsburgh in the night, he was over the slope of the Appalachians. By morning he was in Ohio, father country, in the state where his father had been born, in the culture and the small towns that had shaped his thinking, and the seaboard had been left behind. (He was not, as it turned out, to carry a single state between the Atlantic and the Appalachians except for the rock-ribbed trio of Maine, New Hampshire and Vermont, plus Virginia and Florida.) The touch of the home country on him was a revival to his spirit, and·day by day from then on to the end of the campaign (except for one last disastrous day in New

---

struck by the Vice-President in his very moving warning to the children of the nation and the candidates against the use of profanity by Presidents and ex-Presidents when they are on the stump. And I know after fourteen years in the Congress with the Vice-President that he was very sincere ·in his views about the use of profanity. But I am told that a prominent Republican said to him yesterday in Jacksonville, Florida, "Mr. President, that was a damn fine speech" [Laughter]. And the Vice-President said, "I appreciate the compliment but not the language." And the Republican went on, "Yes sir, I liked it so much that I contributed a thousand dollars to your campaign." And Mr. Nixon replied, "The hell you say." [Laughter and applause].

However, I would not want to give the impression that I am taking former President Truman's use of language lightly. I have sent him the following note: "Dear Mr. President: I have noted with interest your suggestion as to where those who vote for my opponent should go. While I understand and sympathize with your deep motivation, I think it is important that our side try to refrain from raising the religious issue." [Laughter and applause].

Such speeches always ·disturbed Mr. Nixon, whose light touch is never publicly evident and whose private touch is sprinkled with normal profanity. Besides, Nixon liked Kennedy, which was not reciprocally true.

York City, always a nest of enemies for him) his campaign built to a crescendo. It was in this last stage that Richard Nixon began to come clear to me.

I had observed him by this time for many months, and he had persisted as a puzzle to my mind and understanding from my first glimpse and sound of him.[2] Now I decided that rather than being the hard, cruel, vengeful man as constantly described in the liberal press, Nixon was above all a friend seeker, almost pathetic in his eagerness to be liked. He wanted to identify with people and have a connection with them. And this effort to communicate, to evoke warmth and sympathy, was his greatest problem. I do not know whether Nixon can speak well on a high level of eloquence, although I suspect he can. Yet where Kennedy always, in talking to the public, reached for the highest flight of discourse and communication, Nixon seemed obsessed with appearing "just plain folks"; his press releases, like Kennedy's, were standard political prose; but when he was talking freely to his admirers, it seemed that Nixon sought above all to reach the "regular fellow."

His prose reflected the effort. He woke in Marietta, Ohio, on Monday, October 25th, to begin his last "peak" effort, and it was clear from his first speech of the day that he was at one with his audience as he had not been since he had passed through the corn fields of Iowa in the first week of the campaign. A sign outside the courthouse of Marietta, Ohio, read: HIGH SCHOOL DEBATERS GREET WORLD DEBATER—the sign was apropos and of the essence of this last trip as he revived. For he *was* a high-school debater, the boy who had, some thirty years before, won a Los Angeles *Times* prize for his high-school oration on the Constitution. He was seeking not so much to score home a message as to win the hearts of his little audiences; his style was homestyle and during the next two weeks told much about him.

"Now let me tell you why," he would say as he closed for his hitting lines. He would point his finger at the audience, the

[2] This writer should offer the reader the information that, throughout the campaign, for him as for most other correspondents, it was impossible, despite repeated and persistent effort, to meet or talk with Mr. Nixon privately or discuss his campaign with him. I offer the fact only because the interpretation offered throughout this book—despite the most generous confidence and extreme courtesy of most of Mr. Nixon's staff advisers and friends—is that of an observer who, for weeks, followed a personality with whom he was forbidden personal contact. However long one may travel with a man, and however close personal proximity, an interpretation distilled from such observation is subject to normal human error of understanding.

way the man in a white smock selling an analgesic does on the television screen. He would ramble on about his opponent in "team-spirit" metaphors, accusing Kennedy of criticizing the "team" and America just because he could not run it. "Do you want that guy to be captain?" asked Mr. Nixon. He had a penchant for the conjunction "incidentally"; when he began a passage with "incidentally," it usually foretold a needle or a dig into the Kennedy record: "Incidentally, in that connection." "But, seriously now, if I may say" he would use at the turnings of his discourses when he wanted to assure the folks that he was serious. He would use the word "listen" in a rhetoric that comes from kitchen argument, as for example: "Listen—I grew up in a family where it mattered whether you had a job or not." He also used the "sick-and-tired" idiom, as at Parkersburg, West Virginia: "I'm tired of hearing our opponents not only run down West Virginia but run down the United States of America—I say we've had enough of it, and we've got to stop it."

His public statements and infrequent formal speeches continued, in these last few days, to come off flawlessly—if unread —under the editorial ministrations of James Shepley and Gabriel Hauge, who handle words so well. But the naked, unadorned personal flavor of the candidate was much more interesting.

As he came over the ridge that separates the alien and sophisticated East from this father country, he sensed these people with him, as they still are, and he indulged in public privacy. He told them how he had wanted to be an engineer—but it hadn't worked out. At another stop he mourned that he had never made the football team back in Whittier, California. At another stop, how he had wanted to be a piano player—but that had not worked out either. As Nixon worked his way up from Pennsylvania (where he told how his father had died at seventy-seven, leaving medical bills of $3,000 and this was why he was *not,* as Democrats charged, against helping older people who need medical care), through Ohio (where he told how he had always wanted a toy train set but had never had one) and into Michigan, the man began to etch his own silhouette. His resentments were real— yet he expressed them too easily. In Michigan, on the day's campaigning, he had been the target for five eggs and three tomatoes thrown at him,[3] and Mrs. Nixon had been the target for vile and evil language. At the end of his Michigan day

---

[3] There is a rough rule-of-thumb in American politics, never verified, that the man at whom the crowd throws eggs or tomatoes is usually marked as the loser.

his temper snapped (Kennedy never permitted his temper to snap in public all year long). They were heckling him—and he crackled, "I would also suggest, while I am talking about manners, incidentally, that I have been heckled by experts. So don't try anything on me or we'll take care of you. All you do is to show your own bad manners when you do that. Now, boys [to the hecklers], go on around. I didn't hire you. So stay right out of here. O.K.?"

He had great capacity for self-pity. The next day at Danville, Illinois, he told of his mother: "I remember our mother used to get up at five o'clock every morning in our little country grocery store to bake pies so that I and my five brothers could get the education my father didn't have. My father came from Ohio, and his mother died when he was quite young. Consequently, he went to work and he only got a sixth-grade education. But, incidentally, that didn't hurt him. He was still quite a fellow. But I was going to say this: my mother and my father had this devotion: the thing they lived for was the five of us—they wanted us to have a better chance than they had. That's what they wanted. So they got up early in the morning and she baked pies, while my dad was going over to the market to get vegetables and put them in the store."

Late that afternoon at Centralia, Illinois, he topped this with another story: "I remember that when we were growing up my older brother for one year very desperately wanted a pony. My father could have bought it for about seventy-five dollars. And my brother, who died when I was quite young, kept saying, 'Oh, I want this pony more than anything in the world.' Now, being the oldest son, he was kind of a favorite, as you can imagine, with my mother and my father, and they wanted more than anything else to give him what he wanted. It would have been easy for them to say, 'Look, you can have the pony.' But, you know what happened? My mother and father had a little family council and they came in and they said, 'Now, look, if we buy this pony we're not going to have enough money to pay the grocery bill; we're not going to have enough money to pay the clothing bill; we're not going to be able to get the shoes for your younger brother.' It was an awfully hard decision for my mother and father but it was the right thing."

The reporters debated whether to call that day "Maudlin Friday" or "The Day the Pony Died."

The refrain might grow dull to those who followed him; yet it must have been impossible, seeing him just once at a railway station, not to want to comfort or to help this man who, like so many of his listeners, was one of life's losers.

For there were two things that seemed quite clear about this last effort of Mr. Nixon's, taking whistle-stop pronouncements and major statements alike, the pause in the small town as well as the massive gathering in Herald Square on the threshold of Macy's in New York.

The first was that Mr. Nixon was tired. It came out most clearly in his speech, which was now so much more rapid than the clear, measured, healthy cadence of the earlier weeks. It came out in the drawn, almost wasted face of Mrs. Nixon, who followed her husband everywhere and whose quiet charm, never ruffled, bore his exertions with a stoic weariness and tired sweetness that, to some who followed her, was close to tear-provoking. It came out mostly in that increasing fluffing of phrase that is the telltale mark of the tired mind. He spoke in these last few days of his policy of "Peace *and* Surrender" when he meant, of course, "Peace without Surrender"; or: "We are going to make far more progress in education in the next four years than we did under the past administration" (which was his own); or: "I will say this of my opponent, no man has done a better job of fighting Communism in the UN than Henry Cabot Lodge"; or, attempting to identify himself very late in the campaign with Eisenhower, whose public ambiguity on Nixon's decision-making experience had become a minor issue: "I have sat with the President as he made those lonely decisions."

The second was the odd sense that came to those who followed him that he was frightened, that he scared easily. It was difficult to accept this slowly developing thought for anyone who had for years thought of Nixon as a hate-slash-cut, bare-knuckled alley fighter. Yet it could not be denied, even in this last phase of the campaign, that Mr. Nixon was on the defensive—that his "gloves-off round" was not really a strategic offensive, but rather the snarling response of a frightened man backed into a corner.

This thought first came to me on a disheartening day of following Mr. Nixon through New York's Borough of Queens. He had made a superlatively good impression at a morning forum in Manhattan before a thoroughly Republican gathering of magazine publishers, and—as when he found himself with any friendly group—he had lived up to their expectations in tone, performance and style. Then he had been miserably scheduled down the apartment-walled stretches of Queens Boulevard. Where he had expected thousands to greet him, he found little knots of several hundred housewives trapped in police barricades, listening in suspicious silence. His manner changed, as it usually does when he hits unfriendliness. "What I resent most," I suddenly heard him saying, "is when they call us the party that doesn't care. We *do* care," he insisted to them. Later in the afternoon, stopping in front of a department store in Queens, he declaimed, "The United States needs more roads, more schools, more hospitals. This is what our opponent says. But we can do it better—because they want to send the job to Washington and do it by massive spending, and we want all the people to participate in keeping the country moving forward."

As the campaign wore on to its end, one could note more and more of the Kennedy phraseology creeping into the Nixon discourses, far deeper in his consciousness than the moving-forward theme, on which he belatedly now echoed his opponent. He, too, began to accept Kennedy's New Frontier as an issue. "This country has always been full of the great spirit of conquering new frontiers." Or, in extenso, like this (Marietta, Ohio):

So I say, yes, there are new frontiers, new frontiers here in America, new frontiers all over the universe in which we live, but the way to cross those new frontiers is not through weakening Americans, but to remember how we crossed the old frontiers and who did it. You remember? Pioneers, with individual spirit, with faith in themselves, not thinking that they were a second-rate, second-class people, but thinking that they were the best in the world and that's what we are today and I'm tired of hearing our opponents downgrade the United States and letting our enemies abroad have the benefit of it by what they say.

The hard line, the "gloves-off" final, hard-hitting phase of the Nixon campaign, which the press and the Republican high command had long expected, boiled down then, not to an assault, not to a ringing, forward invocation of the future the Republican Party offered America or a devastating personal dissection of his opponent. It was the counterpunching of a man parrying, jabbing, pushing the opponent away, not pushing the opponent back.

In tone, it sounded like this (Syracuse, New York):

He said, and I quote—he said, "The Republicans have always opposed Social Security." He knows that's a barefaced lie and I say it right here today [Cheers and applause]. . . . He knows that Social Security has never had a better friend than the Eisenhower Administration, and it will never have a better friend than the Nixon Administration in the next four years as well. You can be sure of that [Cheers and applause]. . . .

And to hold up to the people of this country on Social Security this specter that we oppose it and, therefore, would take it away—this is irresponsible, this is despicable, and the American people are going to show what they think of it on election day, as this kind of lie is nailed, as it should be, where it was made right here in this city of Syracuse [Cheers and applause].

In content, the elements of the great Nixon counterattack could be boiled down to these themes:

1. That John F. Kennedy, by declaring that American prestige was at an all-time low, was "running America down and giving us an inferiority complex."

2. That the Democratic platform, if put into effect, would raise the price of everything the housewife buys by 25 per cent.

3. That the times were too grave for America to try inexperienced leadership ("Incidentally, I have talked with Khrushchev") and that Kennedy was a bad citizen running the team down since he could not be captain himself.

A sample of the full-dress counterassault might be these excerpts from his rally in front of Macy's Department Store at Herald Square in New York City, after his own ticker-tape parade up Broadway on November 2nd, six days before the election. It contained all the elements of defensive counterassault, sympathy and regular-fellowship.

So, my friends, the reason why the American people are going to reject our opponents and are going to elect us is that we fight for the truth, and the people know the truth, because the people live the truth, and it——[Cheers and applause]

. . . And then there's one other thing I want to set straight: I'm getting sick and tired of hearing this constant whimpering and yammering and wringing of the towel with regard to the poor United States. Oh, under Eisenhower, they say, everything's gone to pot. Our education is now second. Our science is second. We're second in space. We're running down in our economy and are going to be second there. Our military strength is being frittered away, and over across the way, the great Soviet Union, as Mr. Stevenson said recently—and I quote from *Pravda* which quoted him—and over across the way the Communist world looking more dynamic than the American world. Listen, my friends, I have been to Russia, and I have seen it; I have been to the United States, and I have seen it, and there is no reason for a second-rate psychology on the part of any American [Cheers and applause].

Yes, by all means, one of the things that makes America great is that we do criticize our faults, and we improve. One of the things that makes America great is that in any campaign we hit hard; we discuss the issues, but, my friends, I say to you that the people who are asking for the opportunity to cross new frontiers should not be talking about giving up the frontiers we've already got around the world. . . . [Cheers and applause]

[He changed here to an identification with his audience before he got onto his "price theme" and talked about Macy's.]

. . . I remember when I came back from overseas and we were stationed in New York for about four months, one of the most exciting times we ever had. We had a little apartment over on West Ninety-third Street, and every night we used what little savings we had to go to a show. We sat in the balcony, you know, incidentally, pretty close seats up there in that Metropolitan, I can assure you. We saw the shows, we did everything, but also we saw these great stores and, you know, you can buy anything in Macy's, as you know. I want to tell you what Macy's has to do with the President, a candidate for the Presidency, and a candidate for the Vice-Presidency. . . .

[He transferred out of this by a discussion of prices and their relationship to government spending, and went on.]

How much is going to be spent? And this I concede: my opponent will spend more, fifteen billion a year more. Now, what does that have to do with Macy's, the price of groceries, the price of clothing in Macy's, the price of furniture in Macy's? I will tell you what it has to do. If you spend to keep the promises that have been made in my opponent's platform and in this campaign, the prices of everything that Americans will buy are going to go up and up and up. . . .

My friends, do we want a twenty-five-per-cent increase in our grocery bills? [Cries of No!]

Do we want to pay off these promises and pay it in higher prices and higher taxes? [Cries of No!]

Well, there's a way to do it, and that's to go with Nixon and Lodge [Cheers and applause].

The speech was not only interesting in itself. The manner of its setting and staging was morbidly fascinating as a demonstration of the barbarism of American electioneering. For three months now this handsome American of forty-seven

years had been flung back and forth across the country, denied
privacy, denied rest, denied the normal recuperation any
serious illness requires. At the age of forty-seven, no man is
a boy; body and spirit both require refreshment and repose
before they can function at maximum efficiency. The campaign had taken both candidates and flung them, by senseless
ritual and tradition, into such a physical exertion day after
day, night after night, as would sap the energies of a trained
athlete. The newspapers, agencies and broadcasting networks
recognized this, and the correspondents assigned to the never-
resting candidates were replaced and rotated from week to
week lest they break down; yet the principals themselves, on
whom fell the burden of combat and the heat of leadership,
were never spared, never rested, were never permitted those
moments of quiet thought that, somehow, should accompany
an attempt at so great and responsible an office.

One could listen to such a speech as Mr. Nixon gave in
Herald Square and quibble and pick at its phraseology; but one
could not look at the man who sat on the dais and deny that
he had given all that was in him to this effort at the Presidency; and, looking at him, one could only sorrow both for
the man and his wife.

Richard M. Nixon sat on the right of Dwight D. Eisenhower, President of the United States, on a dais that mounted
not only the President but also the Governor of New York,
Nelson A. Rockefeller, both United States Senators from
New York (Jacob K. Javits and Kenneth B. Keating) and his
running mate, Henry Cabot Lodge. The President, twenty-
three years older than his putative successor, sat, cherubic
and ruddy, in the cold day. The Governor of New York was
pale and drawn from his own exhausting supporting schedule
of speeches. And the Vice-President, Richard M. Nixon, sat
as the others spoke, with a face of unmasked bleakness. He
stared at the overcast sky, and his mind seemed several thousand miles away from this introductory oratory he had heard
so often in so many places; his mouth fell half open, his jaw
was almost slack and he panted visibly as he sat; he mused in
some private place of his thoughts and suddenly was aware
that Nelson Rockefeller had begun to clap at an applause
point in someone else's speech, and he hastily began to clap,
too. When called upon to make his own speech, the mask of
vacancy suddenly disappeared, he waved, smiled, spoke in a
loud, if rushed, delivery, and then sat down again to give way
to Dwight D. Eisenhower. It was interesting to watch him
while the President of the United States spoke. The carry-over
of physical alertness that had marked his own speech persisted

for a few minutes. Nixon frowned with attention as he cocked his head to one side and listened to the President; then the frown faded, but he was still intent; then, slowly, his head seemed to sag with exhaustion; the mouth half opened in tired slackness again; and he was away once more in his own thoughts.

That afternoon he must still journey to Yonkers, New York, to address another rally, return to New York for a national telecast from the Coliseum, speak once more at an open-air rally; then fly that night to South Carolina and Texas; then on to Los Angeles; then on across the ocean to Alaska (the fiftieth state on his schedule); then to Madison, Wisconsin; then to Detroit, Michigan; then back to Chicago, to Los Angeles and voting day.

When, as in 1960, 68,832,818 people vote freely and secretly for their leader, there is no way of measuring or identifying the surges of emotion or the exact episodes that influenced them in their decision. One knows intuitively and realistically that one or another episode has had a critical effect on the final tally—yet one is never able to measure that effect precisely in the final result.

It is the almost unanimous opinion of all those concerned with the election of 1960—either as participants, observers or directors of action—that the last ten days of the 1960 campaign produced a surge for Nixon, against Kennedy, which brought the Vice-President within a percentile of carrying the popular vote of the American people. A shade more pressure behind the surge, so runs the theory, and Richard M. Nixon would now be President of the United States; a shade less pressure, and John F. Kennedy would have won by a solid, historic margin.

We shall come back to this surge later in this book. But in telling the story of Nixon's third and last round, at least two episodes of major dimensions must be recorded, however divergent may be the significance men later assign to them. These episodes were, to be specific, the intervention of Dwight D. Eisenhower in the campaign, and the final all-out Republican TV effort. Political scientists will debate the weight of these episodes against the final hair-thin margin of popular result for decades, but neither they nor we will ever be able to measure them except as matters of speculation.

The most interesting of the episodes for speculation is, perhaps, the intervention of Dwight D. Eisenhower in the last ten days of the campaign.

From the very beginning it had been Eisenhower's decision

that he would let "Dick" Nixon run his own campaign in his own way. As early as 1956 he had offered Nixon the choice either of a cabinet post or reappointment to the Vice-Presidency; Nixon chose the Vice-Presidency, but it remained Eisenhower's shrewd opinion that Nixon could have made a better run for the Presidency from the Cabinet than from the Vice-Presidency. Down into the last month of the 1960 campaign Eisenhower still averred to intimates of his staff that Nixon would have had a better base for campaigning as either Secretary of Defense or Secretary of State, with a record of his own behind him.

At the Chicago Convention Eisenhower had not remained after his own appearance to see Nixon nominated but had, almost tartly, congratulated him on being now "at last free to speak freely and frankly in expressing your views."

The two had met next to discuss the campaign—in one of those rare strategic meetings in the Nixon effort—at Newport, Rhode Island, four days after the Republican Convention closed. There the President had made it clear to Nixon that he would do all and everything that Nixon asked of him—but that Nixon was free to manage his own campaign however he saw fit. The Presidential counselors at Newport thus carried away the impression that a clear division had been worked out between the outgoing and prospective Presidents: Nixon would concentrate on the solid Republican vote, and the President would address himself to the millions of independents and the "discerning Democrats" (as Eisenhower liked to call them) who helped him to office in 1952 and 1956. Eisenhower agreed to make three national television appearances for Nixon—one on closed-circuit TV on September the 29th in Chicago, to raise funds for the Party; one in early November; one on election eve. Beyond that he would make various "nonpolitical" appearances around the country, so as to impress the theme of Peace and Prosperity on the nation. This was all that was asked at Newport and all that was offered. But, said one member of Eisenhower's staff, "All of us expected the President would get into the campaign one hell of a lot more than he actually did."

The fact that Eisenhower did not, the fact that the President wanted to do much more, the fact that Eisenhower, with his magic name, sat waiting for a call to participation that never came, still rankles bitterly among Eisenhower men and, probably, in the memory of the ex-President himself.

But the Nixon people and Nixon himself, who had been treated like boys for so many years by the Eisenhower people, now apparently itched to operate on their own, to direct the

Republican Party as they had yearned so long to do. "All we want out of Ike," said one of the Nixon inner group to this writer in the early euphoric stages of Round One, "is for him to handle Khrushchev at the UN and not let things blow up there. That's *all*"—and he stressed the word "all."

As the weeks wore on, the irritation of President Eisenhower, according to the then White House staff, grew. The President was unhappy with the Nixon directorate that had permitted the first TV debate to be scheduled on the very same evening, September 26th, that he, Eisenhower, was going to appear on nationwide TV addressing the banquet of the critically important Catholic Charities in New York—the President was thus to be blanketed from public attention. The President was further irritated as the bite of Kennedy's attack on the administration, on sagging American prestige, on the mishandling of defense sharpened. He expected Nixon to counter these charges immediately; or, if Nixon—then in the mollifying Round One, or "New Nixon" phase, of his campaign—did not do so, Eisenhower expected Nixon to invite him, the President, to counter.

It was not until Saturday, October 29th, that a White House aide (visiting Chicago to support a local Republican Congressman) heard accidentally from a Nixon aide that Nixon now intended to call heavily on the President for the last week's campaigning. The White House aide pointed out that the President was not only eager but anxious to help—but he could not be commandeered, he must be informed and requested to help. Hastily on Monday, October 31st, a White House lunch was arranged for senior members of the President's and Presidential nominee's staffs to work out details. Those present remember that the squab hash was delicious—and that Mr. Nixon was at the point of utter exhaustion, so "beat," says one of those present that "he couldn't think either clearly or quickly, and the conversation at the table was completely irrelevant." At this lunch the President consented to appear personally in Pittsburgh and in Cleveland and to devote a full day to barnstorming the New York suburbs and Manhattan itself.

The Eisenhower intervention in these last eight days is remembered by all who followed the campaign as crisp, fresh and dramatic. Eisenhower has, and retains, a magic in American politics that is peculiarly his: he makes people happy. No cavalcade I have followed in the entourage of any other political figure in this country has ever left so many smiling, glowing people behind as an Eisenhower tour. Americans watch Eisenhower—and they are happy. Nor is he, despite all the sharp dissection of his political qualities by sophisticates, a naive campaigner; he conducts politics in his own way, personally and effectively.

Republican leaders still debate whether or not Eisenhower should have been used more in the campaign—and whether his efforts in the last week were best used. His performance was unstinting and wholehearted; but the handling and scheduling of his performance remains one of the major ifs in the myriad ifs that followed the election: If Eisenhower had been used that last week in Chicago, in a state that was on edge as the election approached, rather than in New York, in a state conceded as lost, would it not have been wiser? If he had been used in Michigan rather than Ohio, might it not have switched the 35,000 necessary votes to win? And what if Eisenhower had been allowed to barnstorm all through October (as he was so obviously willing to barnstorm) defending the administration from John F. Kennedy and freeing Nixon for the advance or forward-future program—would that not have been wiser?

None of these ifs can ever be adequately answered. I assume, as do most other observers, that the force of Eisenhower in the last ten days of the campaign was one of the great support bursts in the Nixon surge. And I like to remember Eisenhower as I last saw him as President—on the evening of November 2nd, outside the Coliseum in New York. The President had then just finished a formal address inside the Coliseum, as had the Vice-President. They had both had an unpleasant day of exertion at supermarkets, suburban shopping centers and at outdoor rallies where there were too many conspicuous signs saying WE LIKE IKE BUT WE BACK JACK. Now an overflow crowd gathered around the gates of the Coliseum in the chilly evening, and the spotlights played on the bunting and the American flag, and the old soldier stood there, arms locked behind him, his cherubic face pink in the glare, his tuft of thin white hair glistening in the light, and he gave them two minutes of his good spirit. He waved their cheers silent and said that it seemed to him he knew what they were trying to say, they were saying that all of them, along with their government, had been responsible for some great achievements in these past few years; and he wanted to thank them; and if he could, he wanted to add a personal note; that all these years people had been yelling "We Like Ike"—it meant a lot to him, it had kept him going sometimes when things were very difficult and when he was very tired. So he thanked them and blessed them; and they adored him with a yearning burst of cheers so different from those they had just given Richard M. Nixon, and the band struck up "God Bless America"; and he passed off into the night having said farewell to New York as its President—Eisenhower had carried New York by 1,597,562 votes in 1956, a greater margin than any man has ever won in the Empire State; Nixon was to lose it by 383,666.

If the weight of the Eisenhower intervention in the last days of the campaign must remain a subject of political speculation, the weight of the final Republican television burst is more subject to reasonable measurement. No figures have yet been released by the Republican National Committee on its television expenditures in the last twelve days of the campaign because such figures always require imaginative reconsideration before publication. Legally, neither of the two national committees is permitted to spend more than $3,000,000 in the election of a President, whereas the actual cost of electing a President is, minimally, at least four times that sum. The Democrats admit to having spent $2,600,000 in the last eighteen days of the campaign, mostly for broadcasting; but their figures, like the Republicans', have not yet been distributed legally over the books and ledgers to meet the laws. It is a safe guess that Republican expenditures were substantially more.

The Republicans began their final assault on the American mind with a national telecast of a Nixon rally in Cincinnati on October 25th; followed it with an Eisenhower telecast out of Pittsburgh on Saturday, October 29th; offered another national rally on television with Eisenhower, Nixon and Lodge out of New York on November 2nd; followed this every night of the last week with a live Nixon television show of fifteen minutes at seven o'clock in the evening. And then, on Monday, November 7th, the day before the election, they let the purse strings pop in what was certainly the most expensive and probably the most effective burst of television electioneering since the medium invaded American culture. On Monday afternoon, November 7th, at a cost that Republicans estimated at $200,000 (and Democrats insisted was $400,000), Nixon held national attention on the ABC network from Detroit in a four-hour telethon that mixed schmaltz and substance in equal proportions, showing the Republican candidate at his best (talking of peace) and at his worst (discussing the high cost of living with Ginger Rogers, who said she too had to live on a salary). It is estimated that one out of five American homes entertained the Vice-President at some time during that afternoon. And although the audience was largely one of housewives who flicked the candidate on and off as they received the children back from school, prepared supper and waited for the breadwinner to come home, there can be no doubt that millions of them must have caught him in his good moments and have been influenced by him. Nixon was followed at 6:30 (EST) for fifteen minutes by Governor Thomas E. Dewey, at an estimated cost of $35,000 to $40,000. A three-way half-hour hookup between Nixon, Eisenhower and Lodge at eleven in the evening probably cost between $50,000 and $70,000, and its repeat over ABC and NBC from 11:30 to midnight probably cost the Republicans another $45,000 for each network. All in all, Monday before election saw half a million dollars spent on the Republican television effort; and when to this are added the previous week's expenditures and the local expenditures of Republican regional and Congressional campaigners over local or independent stations, the total figure is somewhere in the neighborhood of $2,000,000 spent in the last ten days in the greatest electronic effort ever made to move men's minds.

How much it did indeed move men's minds on that final week end no one can say; it is this writer's opinion, which he cannot substantiate, that it was vastly important and contributed mightily to the last Nixon surge.

The Republican television effort in the last ten days of the campaign is equally interesting for the inner light it throws on the Nixon campaign.

It had been Nixon's original theory that he would carry his message to the American people by the most imaginative use of television ever displayed in a national campaign. On the assumption that they would be allowed to experiment in novel use of the medium, his television advisers had prepared a basket of tricks and special shows designed to use the medium as it had never been used before (see Chapter Ten). Yet Nixon could not bring himself either to approve or disapprove the plans of his television advisers. He feared the tag of "Madison Avenue"—therefore his television advisers in New York, volunteers of the finest brains of New York's advertising agencies, had to install themselves in an unmarked office on Vanderbilt Avenue in New York, one block *east* of Madison Avenue, to avoid the label. From these offices his television advisers watched the progress of the campaign and gradually realized that they were being ignored. From July 25th—the night of Nixon's acceptance speech in Chicago—until October 25th, three months went by in which Nixon not once appeared in a national television broadcast under his own control of circumstances. The opportunity to attack the Democrats for their record in the summer session of Congress was ignored by Nixon, despite the pleading of his advisers. When he did speak on television, he spoke in the old-fashioned manner—face full to the camera, trying to cram his all-purpose speech into a little talk. He discarded at the beginning of the campaign the idea of a well-planned October telethon—and then, when at the end of the campaign he felt urgent measures were necessary, reversed himself. It was one o'clock in the afternoon of Saturday before election when the television staff in New York found they were supposed to have ready a complete telethon set-up, to go on air within forty-nine hours—whereupon, in a frenzy, the staff had over the week end to rouse the broadcasting networks and rout out the executives of American Telephone & Telegraph to set up the long lines necessary for the elaborate performance. What was achieved by television in support of Nixon was thus achieved, not by imagination, but simply by the sheer impact of time and exposure.

The discontent of the television staff was reflected at every echelon of Republican campaign organization.

The elaborate campaign plan blueprinted in June and July (see Chapter Ten) died a still death. The planning group met sporadically in four sessions, and then, in mid-September, the candidate abandoned them. The Republican National Committee headquarters in Washington waited on its leader—and waited. "You could have," said one of its most important directors, "taken the key to the Republican National Committee, locked the door, thrown the key into the Potomac, shipped all hundred and seventy-five employees off to the Virgin Islands and saved money—for all that he ever listened to us." One member of the planning board said, "Ah, we used to meet for strategy sessions at the University Club—and we were like ten guys in a house of mirrors entrancing each other. We satisfied each other with how smart we were—but nobody could get through to Dick."

By the end of the campaign, disaffection from the candidate had become general. Nixon's top-level planners and volunteers were men of high talent, many of them absentees on leave from impressively important jobs in American enterprise; yet they could receive no hearing from their political chief, and their efforts to reach him degenerated into both the bizarre and the humiliating as they tried to penetrate through his inner court to his attention. Those who found themselves received by the Republican candidate found themselves almost always so burdened with messages from other people that they could scarcely get their own message across. One of his television advisers reports that on coming out of the Waldorf-Astoria suite of the candidate during Nixon's October stay in New York, he was greeted by an envious, anxiety-ridden Nixon speech writer who asked him, "So you saw him—how's the meanest man in the world this morning?"

There was never any absence of great political ability—at any level—in the men who made up the Republican command staff during the campaign; and what infuriated these men of ability, said one of them, was that "he reduced us all to clerks."

It is with the final proposal of Nixon's campaign that one should leave the picture of the Republican candidate. On Sunday, November 6th, from Los Angeles, the Vice-President announced his last proposal to buttress the grand theme of Peace without Surrender: that ex-Presidents Hoover, Truman and Eisenhower be sent to visit Eastern Europe and organize freedom's underground against Communism there—with Nikita Khrushchev's permission.

It was a good-hearted proposal, and probably sincerely advanced. Yet it did not fit the picture of the world as it was; it did not make sense to hope that Khrushchev would peacefully invite America to liquidate his Eastern empire. The proposal was absolutely specific; yet the philosophy behind it incomprehensible.

And this, finally, was the only summary one could make of the campaign that Richard M. Nixon had so valiantly waged, under such personal suffering: that there was neither philosophy nor structure to it, no whole picture either of the man or of the future he offered. One could perceive neither in this last climactic proposal nor in his prepared speeches nor in his personal discourses any shape of history, any sense of the stream of time or flow of forces by which America had come to this point in history and might move on. Nixon's skills in politics were enormous, his courage unquestioned, his endurance substantial. But they were the skills, courage and endurance of the sailor who knows the winds and can brave the storm and recognizes the tide. There was missing in him always the direction of the navigator, the man who knows the stars and is guided by the stars and who, when blown from course by storm, waits for the stars and sun to come out again and returns to course observing them.

From this weakness of philosophy comes that apparent volatility that has plagued Nixon throughout his career—and that meanest, unmerited epithet, "Tricky Dick." There have been few tricks in Nixon's career, and none by the light of his conscience—only the sharpest veerings as the winds have blown him. If Nixon won his first major campaign (against Helen Gahagan Douglas) as a Red-baiter, it was because that was the ethos of the time and place where he campaigned. If, as in 1954, he declared that the election of a Democratic Congress would "swing [America] down the leftward road to socialism," it was because in all sincerity he believed this. It is doubtful whether there ever was an Old Nixon or a New Nixon. The young Congressman from Southern California who voted on the extreme conservative wing of his Party fourteen years ago did not hold his positions deeply. He was easily educated out of them in Washington to another set of new beliefs. With no inner philosophical contradiction he could become the most positive advocate of advanced foreign aid, after Paul G. Hoffman, in his entire Party.

It was this lack of an over-all structure of thought, of a personal vision of the world that a major statesman must possess, that explained so many of those instances of the campaign when he broke under pressure.

It was thus when he flew to New York from Washington during the Republican Convention. It was scarcely believable to the fearful yet courageous Rockefeller staff that they could press Nixon that night and keep pressing him and see him yield, point by point, all the way down the line. Yet Nixon did yield, for his mind considered the Compact of Fifth Avenue a system of points, while Rockefeller's saw it as a structure.

Of much more pointed political relevance was his indecision on the vast subject of civil rights. Though he had thrown his weight in Chicago for a platform designed to challenge the Democrats for the Negro vote in the North, he had been swayed by his early Southern visits to the hope that he might win the Southern white vote, too.

Thus it is impossible to distinguish, from his campaign performance, what Nixon's personal political attitude was to the arrest of Martin Luther King when the hero figure of American Negroes was arrested in the last days of the campaign. John F. Kennedy's attitude was instantly clear (see Chapter Thirteen); Richard Nixon's was not. On the afternoon of the sentencing of Martin Luther King to four months of hard labor in Georgia, the Department of Justice—at the suggestion of a wise yet shrewd Republican Deputy Attorney-General (Judge Lawrence E. Walsh)—composed a draft statement to support the application for release of the imprisoned Negro minister. Two copies of the draft were sent out immediately for approval—one to the White House, one to Mr. Nixon's traveling headquarters (on that day in Ohio). No one has yet revealed who killed this draft statement that was so critically important in the tense politics of civil rights. Either President Eisenhower or Vice-President Nixon could have acted—yet neither did. However obscure Eisenhower's motivations were, Nixon's are more perplexing, for he was the candidate. He had made the political decision at Chicago (see Chapter Seven) to court the Negro vote in the North; only now, apparently, he felt it quite possible that Texas, South Carolina and Louisiana might all be won to him by the white vote and he did not wish to offend that vote. So he did not act—there was no whole philosophy of politics to instruct him.

There could never be any doubt of the Vice-President's pugnacity or innate courage; yet it was a pugnacity and courage committed without a framing strategy to make them effective.

Whether this uncertainty of philosophy explained his solitary nature or whether his solitary nature explained the uncertainty, no one can say—but certainly he was one of the most solitary and lonesome men in politics. His personal office in the Capitol was Room P53—he alone worked there. His personal secretary worked two floors below, in T6. His administrative staff operated apart from him in a corner suite of the Old Senate Office Building. Many of those he trusted most in his personal cabinet were people who had served him for less than two years; some were individuals of only a few months' association. Only Rose Mary Woods, his devoted and efficient private secretary, had been with him for any long period of service and confidence (eight years).

The bitterness of those of his advisers who were Republicans first and Nixon men second is understandable and explains much of what went wrong in the campaign.

But the perplexity of those members of his kitchen cabinet who felt themselves closer to this man than to their Party is more revealing of the personality involved. "You must remember," said one of the ablest of his kitchen-staff members, "this terrible emotional frustration of his as the result of being Vice-President for so long; he wanted all the decisions in his own hands, all of them—the fifty-state decision, the use of Eisenhower, the approach to the debates. His attitude was the result of his own introspection, his own brooding—my role was only to implement them the best way I knew how."

A White House aide who tried to bridge the gap between Nixon and Eisenhower put it this way: "You must start with a basic psychological fact—that Nixon is an introspective man. He just can't *ask* anybody for help. He could have had our help any time he wanted. He could have had help from Baruch or Sulzberger[4] or MacArthur. But Nixon couldn't bring himself to ask help of anybody."

Another man who had been as close to Nixon as anyone during the campaign said to me, "Don't ask me what went wrong. I really don't know. I thought I was close to him, I thought I was in communication. I kept urging him to make major speeches. But he was so good at ad-libbing, at milking his punch lines, that you couldn't pin him down to a major policy statement. He was always more interested in the thirty thousand people in front of him than in the hundred and eighty million people in the U.S.A. The mistakes he made were personal—but then you'd have to get into such areas of privacy to understand it that you just have to leave it there."

The Vice-President, since his first entry into the Senate of the United States, had been a man under pressure and constant attack. Yet all exercises in power are conducted under pressure, and the idiot physical ordeal and demands of the campaign of 1960 finally imposed more pressure on Nixon than he could bear. It was difficult to be generous in judgment even for those who loved him most. "Dick didn't lose this election," said one of the few who had been with him for more than two years. "Dick blew this election." Among older Republicans, the judgment was sometimes phrased even more harshly. "Maybe," said one member of the Planning Board, "Dick was never cut out to be top banana from the very beginning."

So, at midnight on November 7th by Eastern Standard Time (eleven o'clock Chicago time), Richard M. Nixon took off from Chicago's International Airport. His press agents had already released the extent of his campaign in a statement: he had flown 65,500 miles, appeared in 188 cities at least once, made over 150 major speeches, and, they estimated, had been seen by 10,000,000 people in the flesh.

He was tired but confident. A few days before he had released his own estimates to the press. It would be close. But of the big seven states he had marked as critical he felt he

---

[4] The thought here is probably unreal. There is a belief among some highly placed Republicans that Arthur Hays Sulzberger, publisher of *The New York Times*, is at heart a Republican, while his wife, Iphigene, is a secret Democrat. The corollary of this belief is that policy of *The New York Times*, the greatest newspaper in America, is hammered out in family argument. According to this belief, a Nixon overture to Mr. Sulzberger would have stiffened him against Mrs. Sulzberger and brought the great newspaper to a Republican endorsement of the Vice-President. I cannot accept this theory myself.

would carry five: Illinois, Pennsylvania, Texas, Ohio, California. Michigan, he felt was a toss-up (50 to 50). Only in New York did he feel he would certainly lose. He felt hopeful of carrying South Carolina, Louisiana, Minnesota and Delaware.

But for him as for Jack Kennedy it was too late now to worry more. It was all done. His big jet arrived at the Ontario International Airport, east of Los Angeles, at four o'clock Eastern Standard Time (one o'clock Pacific Coast Time) on Tuesday morning of election day. He had been traveling now to the extreme end of all effort. He had had less than three hours of sleep since he had left Los Angeles on Sunday afternoon for the final 7,170-mile jet trip to Alaska, Wisconsin, Michigan and Chicago. A black Cadillac carried him from the airport eighteen miles to the Ambassador Hotel on Wilshire Boulevard in Los Angeles. At the Ambassador, he was to be installed in the "Royal Suite," on the fifth floor. The Royal Suite, decorated in reds, pinks, purple, blues and violet, is considered to be Oriental in décor, and is furnished with bronze furniture, said to be of Siamese motif, to heighten the effect. His mother was domiciled on the floor below. The next morning he would drive the thirty-odd miles to East Whittier, California, to vote in Precinct 33 in the town where he had been raised. But that too had changed.

We must see him in this Oriental splendor, at a Schine hotel, ending this campaign as he had begun—as a guest. He had begun the campaign as a guest under the palms at the home of a friend in Key Biscayne, Florida. He was to end it as a guest in a hotel.

His campaign had been based on home talk. But he had no real home except where his wife was; he was a stranger, even here in California, seeking home and friendship.

Chapter 13

KENNEDY FOR PRESIDENT: ROUND THREE

No GREATER contrast in moods can be imagined than that between the roving encampments of John F. Kennedy and Richard M. Nixon. In retrospect, the remembered moods of both headquarters underline the political axiom that the worst seat for judging a campaign is one closest to the candidate himself.

I had made my last extended trip with the Nixon campaigners in the final week in October—from Pittsburgh through West Virginia through southern and central Ohio. Despondency hung like a cloud over the candidate's entourage, and through the gloom at every stop dripped Nixon's words of melancholy and self-pity. One evening on the Nixon campaign train I found myself astounded as two of his personal aides began to discuss whom *Kennedy* would probably choose as his Secretary of State and Secretary of the Treasury. One of them —a Nixon speech writer—turned to a correspondent in our conversational knot and matter-of-factly inquired if he thought it was true that Kennedy, when elected, would name Professor Kenneth Galbraith of Harvard as Secretary of the Treasury; the Nixon speech writer was told that Kennedy yielded few leaks of this kind, but that the Galbraith appointment seemed unlikely; the Nixon man shook his head sadly at the dreadful thought nonetheless.

I had been with the Kennedy forces the week before this Nixon trip and rejoined the Kennedy camp again as election day drew near. The contrast was stunning. At the Kennedys', confidence had swollen to overpowering certainty. The debates were over now and Lou Harris' polling indicated that Kennedy had scored through during the debates, not only in personality, but on themes—the issue of slipping American prestige had become the dominant one of the campaign and Kennedy had (according to Harris) scored 62 to 38 per cent with the viewers on this issue. The Gallup Poll confirmed Harris. In early September Nixon had been ahead 47 to 46 (with 7 per cent undecided); after the first debate, Kennedy had moved ahead 49 to 46 (with 5 per cent undecided); after the late debate, said Gallup, the margin had moved up to 51 to 45 (with only 4 per cent undecided). Kennedy staffmen were laying bets; one of the most seasoned of them was offering even money that no one could name six states all of which Nixon would carry for sure. Yet this Kennedy cockiness was to prove as misleading as the Nixon gloom.

There were warnings, of course. In Washington, at the Democratic National Committee, insulated from the jubilation of the road team, trusting only the reports of the co-ordinators, Larry O'Brien insisted it was still terribly close, a tossup either way. From New York, studying his poll results, Harris warned that the Democratic candidate must prepare for a last-minute Republican TV blitz, the entry of Eisenhower into the campaign—and, above all, a last-minute surge of religious sentiment as the image and thus the impact of the clean-cut young Democrat faded after the last of the TV debates; whereupon, felt Harris, the weight of the past, with all the past's fears, might reclaim its own. Harris urged that Kennedy face the religious issue frontally again—in a nationwide television show. Bobby Kennedy lashed and flogged his organization, lest it relax from overconfidence. (Later Bobby Kennedy, who believes that Nixon's theory of "peaks" and "rhythms" in a campaign is nonsense, was to say, "We simply had to run and fight and scramble for ten weeks all the way, and then we would win. We got on top with the debates, we fought to stay on top, and we did win. And if we'd done one bit less of anything, then we might have lost.")

Yet as the debates ended and the Kennedy campaign entered its third and last round, whoever traveled with the Democratic candidate became dazzled, then blinded, with the radiance of approaching victory. Warnings might come from rear-echelon headquarters, but for those who traveled the combat front with the combat element of John F. Kennedy, it seemed impossible there could be danger still. For in the six weeks since mid-September, this campaign, and the campaigners with it, had changed: decisions now came with snap and confidence; the machinery purred; the candidate's style seemed to top itself with each day's touring; and the response, there before one's eyes, overwhelmed judgment.

The decisions that framed this last round of the Kennedy campaign spanned the range from the most technical to the most profound. Only a handful, in retrospect, are interesting in a study of the reach for America's internal loyalties.

One set of decisions—entirely professional—had been reached at Hyannisport in the only Saturday of rest Kennedy allowed himself from the beginning of October to the end of the campaign. There, at a five-hour conference on October 1st, the candidate had gathered his inner circle (his brother Robert and his father, Joseph Kennedy, Ted Sorensen, O'Donnell and O'Brien, Pierre Salinger, Lou Harris and John Bailey, along with Clark Clifford, who was now in charge of post-electoral planning) to take a reading on the first debate and draw plans for the campaign's last weeks. They decided that the Nixon performance in the first debate had erased whatever advantage the "experience vs. youth" issue had originally given the Vice-President; that they must expect now, certainly, an Eisenhower rescue operation—but that Kennedy should not assail Eisenhower directly, only ignore him; they decided also that Nixon should be prevented from his obvious attempt (made in the first debate) to describe Republicans and Democrats as alike in goals, differing only in method; Kennedy must make clear that the two parties were wholly different in goals and pin the Republican label on Nixon as tightly as possible, hammering him as the spiritual descendant of Mc-Kinley, Harding, Hoover, Landon and Dewey.

Another set of decisions, quite routine, worked out between O'Donnell and the candidate, confirmed the original scheduling of the campaign as planned in August. The last three weeks of the campaign would be devoted, they confirmed now, to the most intense stumping of the populous Northeastern states, where the big electoral vote lay—with driving emphasis on the suburbs around Chicago, Philadelphia and New York. California would have its allotted two days of the candidate's time—one and a half days for Southern California, half a day for northern California. It was decided to add Oklahoma to the candidate's original schedule in what proved a vain attempt to hold that border state, so long Democratic but so suspicious of Catholics, in its traditional column.

The most interesting and precise of the decisions of this period, however, was one made by the candidate himself—particularly as it contrasted with the simultaneous Nixon decision on the same problem. This concerned the Martin Luther King affair—an episode that tangled conscience with the most delicate balancing of the Northern Negro–Southern white vote.

Martin Luther King is one of the genuine heroes of the tumultuous Negro struggle for authentic equality in American life; a luminous man, he speaks responsibly for the best there is in his community. On Wednesday, October 19th—at about the same time of day that John Kennedy and Richard Nixon were addressing the American Legion in Miami on the national defense—Martin Luther King was arrested with fifty-two other Negroes in Rich's Department Store in Atlanta for refusing to leave a table in its Magnolia Room restaurant. On the following Monday, all other "sit-ins" arrested in this episode were released; King alone was held in jail and, worse, sentenced on a technicality to four months' hard labor and thereupon whisked away secretly to the State Penitentiary. This was no ordinary arrest—no Negro in America has more deservedly earned greater warmth and adoration from his fellow Negroes, North or South, than Martin Luther King; but no Negro menaces the traditional prerogatives of Southern whites more importantly. It was not beyond possibility that he would never emerge alive from the Reidsville (Georgia) State Prison, deep in "cracker" country, where he had been taken; nor did anyone believe more in the prospect of his lynching than his wife, then six months pregnant. Had King been lynched, the violence that would have resulted would have overmatched the violence later shown by the American Negro community over the lynching of Patrice Lumumba in Africa, in inverse proportion to the distance between Georgia and Katanga. The American Negro community girded; so did the Southern whites; during the previous few weeks, even before the arrest, no less than three Southern governors had informed Kennedy headquarters directly that if he intruded in Southern affairs to support or endorse Martin Luther King, then the South could be given up as lost to the Democratic ticket. Now Kennedy must choose. This was a crisis.

The crisis was instantly recognized by all concerned with the Kennedy campaign. On the night of Tuesday, October 25th, the suggestion for meeting it was born to one of those remarkably competent young men that the Kennedy organization had brought into politics to direct the Civil Rights Section of their campaign, a Notre Dame law professor named Harris Wofford. Wofford's idea was as simple as it was human—that the candidate telephone directly to Mrs. King in Georgia to express his concern. Desperately Wofford tried to reach his own chief, Sargent Shriver, head of the Civil Rights Section of the Kennedy campaign, so that Shriver might break through to the candidate barnstorming somewhere in the Middle West. Early Wednesday morning, Wofford was able to locate Shriver, the gentlest and warmest of the Kennedy clan (he had married Eunice Kennedy, the candidate's favorite sister) in Chicago—and Shriver enthusiastically agreed. Moving fast, Shriver reached the candidate at O'Hare Inn at Chicago's International Airport as the latter was preparing to leave for a day of barnstorming in Michigan.

The candidate's reaction to Wofford's suggestion of participation was impulsive, direct and immediate. From his room at the Inn, without consulting anyone, he placed a long-distance telephone call to Mrs. Martin Luther King, assured her of his interest and concern in her suffering and, if necessary, his intervention.

Mrs. King, elated yet still upset, informed a few of her closest friends. Through channels of Negro leadership, the word swiftly sped north from Atlanta, and thus to the press, that Kennedy had intervened to protect the imprisoned Negro leader. And Bobby Kennedy, informed in the course of the day of the command decision, proceeded even further and the next morning telephoned a plea for King's release from New York to the Georgian judge who had set the sentence; on Thursday King was released from Reidsville prison on bail, pending appeal—safe and sound.

The entire episode received only casual notice from the generality of American citizens in the heat of the last three weeks of the Presidential campaign. But in the Negro community the Kennedy intervention rang like a carillon. The father of Martin Luther King, a Baptist minister himself, who had come out for Nixon a few weeks earlier on religious grounds, now switched. "Because this man," said the Reverend Mr. King, Senior, "was willing to wipe the tears from my daughter[-in-law]'s eyes, I've got a suitcase of votes, and I'm going to take them to Mr. Kennedy and dump them in his lap." Across the country scores of Negro leaders, deeply Protestant but even more deeply impressed by Kennedy's action, followed suit. And where command decision had been made, the Kennedy organization could by now follow through. Under Wofford's direction a million pamphlets describing the episode were printed across the country, half a million in Chicago alone, whence they were shipped by Greyhound bus. On the Sunday before election, these pamphlets were distributed outside Negro churches all across the country. One cannot identify in the narrowness of American voting of 1960 any one particular episode or decision as being more important than any other in the final tallies: yet when one reflects that Illinois was carried by only 9,000 votes and that 250,000 Negroes are estimated to have voted for Kennedy; that Michigan was carried by 67,000 votes and that an estimated 250,000 Negroes voted for Kennedy; that South Carolina was carried by 10,000 votes and that an estimated 40,000 Negroes there voted for

Kennedy, the candidate's instinctive decision must be ranked among the most crucial of the last few weeks.[1]

Decisions now not only followed crisply and unfalteringly in sequence, but where decision pointed, the organization followed—and the various parts of the organization had all passed through their break-in period, had been road-tested, and purred in the comforting hum of human machinery intermeshing with the same complete efficiency that one remembers of the American bomber crews flying out of Tinian and Saipan against Japan in the concluding July and August weeks of the Pacific war.

The machinery purred across the country in the operational exercises of the O'Donnell-O'Brien combination; it purred in the forty-two states with special coordinators; it purred in New York where artist William Walton held high-minded Democratic reformers and low-minded Tammany clubbers working in uneasy harness; it stuttered a bit in California; but purred silkily south of the Mason-Dixon line, where Lyndon B. Johnson oiled it with essence of magnolia.

It purred at the high level of words and ideas; and purred at the low level of buses, hotel reservations, baggage pickup and receptions, which the advance men had now mastered.

There were virtuoso performances now, for as the campaign stepped up and the World Series was over, Americans had more attention to pay to the choice of their leader. Americans wanted to read more about the election now; thus both Nixon and Kennedy had to provide more copy each day, though there remained less and less new to say; and as news demands grew and content dropped, the efforts to keep up the appearance of novelty were prodigious.[2] The intellectual performance I like best to remember was a two-day exertion of the Sorensen-Goodwin team, stretched out over forty-eight hours and three states—as illustrative as any other episode of the weight and impact of ideas on an American Presidential campaign.

Ideas, which are very important to John F. Kennedy, are nevertheless all too frequently deputized and subcontracted by him to other men. Kennedy had had one failure in organizing the intellectual "feed" to his campaign: his academic team of speech writers, headed by Professor Archibald Cox, had proved unable to establish authority over the hurly-burly of

[1] See p. 355 for Nixon's parallel reaction.
[2] The normal news file from correspondents with the Kennedy camp transmitted by the attendant Western Union service staff grew from an average of 60,000 words a day to an average of 90,000 words a day in the closing week.

the roving campaign from its offices at 1737 L Street. Two of the ablest journalists in America had joined Kennedy on the road, however (John Bartlow Martin of the *Saturday Evening Post* and Joseph Kraft, author of *The Struggle for Algeria*), to provide something that, in Martin's term, was called "editorial advance." These two preceded the candidate as he traveled, scouring the local scene with the savvy of veteran newsmen for background and material for Kennedy's crossroads remarks. Yet for high affairs and high pronouncements Kennedy relied only on his original Sorensen-Goodwin tandem, and the episode I remember is one that shows the effort leadership can evoke from able men when all are going flat out.

All Sunday afternoon, October 16th, in Washington, D.C., Goodwin had worked preparing, and then briefing the candidate on, questions he might be asked on a "Meet The Press" television show, scheduled for six o'clock. Simultaneously, Sorensen had worked on a speech, tentatively entitled "Ethics In Government," to be delivered at Wittenberg College in Springfield, Ohio, the following day. Both Brain Trusters had finished their labors in Washington almost at the same time and, immediately "Meet The Press" was over, had joined the Kennedy campaign squadron of planes flying off from Washington to Ohio that evening. Then they leapfrogged. On Monday, the Senator proceeded to campaign by road through Franklin and Hamilton counties in Ohio to Wittenberg College for his ethics speech, accompanied by Sorensen. While the Senator and Sorensen traveled, Goodwin remained at a hotel in Middletown, Ohio, with the portable Kennedy campaign research library, working on a speech to be delivered in Tampa, Florida, the next day—on Latin American affairs. When at 4:30 Goodwin had to leave Middletown, local Democratic headquarters raced him to the airport at Columbus, Ohio, where the campaign flight would depart for Florida. There he met Sorensen, totally exhausted at this point, who had already received from the Cox office in Washington the raw speech material on national defense and had begun to hammer it into shape. Both men then joined the candidate, also exhausted, on the night flight to the south. And while Kennedy read the Latin American pronunciamento that Goodwin had drafted in the Manchester Hotel in Middletown, and revised it, Goodwin discussed the national-defense speech that Sorensen had begun to draft on the road, and prepared to help on that. Thus two major pronouncements on American policy worked through their collective minds, until they arrived at the airport motel in Miami, Florida, at two in the morning, where the candidate slept for five hours.

His two exhausted Brain Trusters, however, were still burdened with the final drafting of the national-defense speech; they decided to work in shifts. Goodwin went to bed while Sorensen labored with a secretary until five A.M. When Sorensen went to bed at five, his secretary woke Goodwin, after his three hours of sleep, to give him the Sorensen draft. Goodwin worked on that draft until eight, when he woke the Senator to present it to him. But now the Senator wanted substantial changes—to include nonmilitary aspects of the cold war as well as the purely military. At 8:30 Goodwin began the last draft, pushing his sheets to the mimeograph machine as he wrote; meanwhile secretaries packed their bags to catch the plane that would depart Miami at two.

So, during the morning, as the candidate barnstormed and spoke at supermarkets and crossroads, the speech writers once more rearranged his words and ideas. Goodwin hailed a taxi when they had finished and sped out to intercept the campaign caravan and present the candidate with a finished text of his ideas on national defense; he intercepted the candidate at a toll gate on the Miami causeway, where he flagged the campaign caravan to a halt, delivering the final version to the candidate forty-five minutes before he was to adopt it as the defense posture of the next President of the United States. Then the two ideologues could take a cat nap; but that afternoon, as Kennedy delivered their Latin America speech at Tampa, they were up again, preparing quips and jokes to be used at the Alfred E. Smith Dinner in New York the following evening.

It is doubtful whether any historian should find it worthwhile to reproduce the speeches on ethics in government at Wittenberg University, on national defense at Miami, on Latin American affairs at Tampa. All such speeches passed through the dutiful typewriters of the press corps who followed the campaign; all were dutifully reproduced in the press across the nation; yet by that time specifics and issues had all but ceased to matter; only "style" was important. For the Kennedy "style" in the last few weeks had evolved as much as his organization and, for those who have an affection for American political performance, it was a thing of beauty.

Saturday, October 1st, at Hyannisport had been Kennedy's last day of rest. From then until election day, his hours grew longer, his sleep less frequent (in the last four days of the campaign, he averaged only four hours a night). Yet his voice grew stronger and slower. Earlier in the campaign, when he feared his voice might not last the weeks ahead, he had communicated with his staff on the plane by scrawling conversational answers on yellow pads as they talked with him. Now he wanted to stay up on the plane and talk—sometimes for hours, about all manner of things. It was as if second wind were coming to a long-distance runner; and, as his manner of delivery grew slower, his public language grew more elegant. His style, finally, began to capture even the newsmen who had heard all he had to say long before, but continued to listen, as one continues to return to a favorite movie.

Most of all, he seemed to be enjoying himself as the mobs stimulated adrenalin in his arteries; and the crispest edge of his enjoyment seemed to be the taunting of Nixon. This was supposed to be the all-out slash-and-hack last phase of the Nixon attack on Kennedy. But it was as if Nixon were wielding a club while Kennedy pinked him with a rapier. Kennedy particularly liked the phrase, borrowed from the Spanish bullfight ring, of *mano a mano*, or hand-to-hand combat; this was *mano a mano*, and he liked it.

Nixon called him a "barefaced liar" in New York; and Kennedy replied (in New Mexico): "Two days ago the Republican candidate, Mr. Nixon, quoted me as having said that the Republicans had always opposed Social Security, and in that wonderful choice of words which distinguishes him as a great national leader, he asserted that this was a barefaced lie. Having seen him four times close up in this campaign, and made-up, I would not accuse Mr. Nixon of being barefaced—but I think the American people next Tuesday can determine who is telling the truth."

In Arizona, Barry Goldwater's state (while Nixon was in the East trying for the last time to salvage New York's vote with the aid of Eisenhower, Rockefeller and Lodge), Kennedy chortled: "Actually, I came down here because I thought it was very unfair of Dick Nixon to take Governor Rockefeller, Henry Cabot Lodge and the President to New York without taking Barry Goldwater. If they can just get Barry out of that Confederate uniform that he has been using in the South . . . and get him up North, so they could see him up there . . ."

He chose the farm country of Wisconsin as the place to reply to Mr. Nixon's charges that Democrats would raise food prices by 25 per cent: "Mr. Nixon went to New Jersey the other day, and in one of those speeches for which he has become so famous, he said that the proposal that I put forward for increasing farm income would increase food prices by 25 per cent. Then he comes out here to La Crosse and says that my farm plan would not mean a thing for the farmers. He should make up his mind. He should say the same thing in La Crosse as he does in New Jersey. The fact is, he should say the same thing in the North that he says in the South, the same thing in the East that he says in the West."

Each of the blows struck at him by Nixon seemed to offer Kennedy opportunity for an artful parry; yet over and over again he would return to his central themes: that the country must move, that American prestige was slipping, and that the Republican Party was responsible. He seemed determined to fix Mr. Nixon in the mold he had made for him, the mold his midcampaign Hyannisport conference had carved. In Illinois he declared:

"Mr. Nixon, as you know, ordinarily runs as a rather ambiguous figure who is not really attached to any party because parties have no significance these days. But the other day . . . Senator Barry Goldwater got him in a room in Arizona and said, 'Dick, you are a Republican and you have to admit it.' So Nixon came out of the room rather shame-facedly and said, 'Yes, I am a Republican and I endorse every Republican candidate from top to bottom with great pride.' *I* have been saying that I am a Democrat for the past fourteen years because I believe the Democratic Party is associated with progress. . . . And I do not need Barry Goldwater or anyone else to remind me that parties are important." [3]

---

[3] The speech to which Kennedy referred had been delivered on October 15th at Phoenix, Arizona, at the Thunderbird Room of the Westward-Ho Hotel. Mr. Nixon had just been in session with Senator Goldwater, who felt that Mr. Nixon was not running as a good party man, that Nixon was too soft. Mr. Nixon's confidence had not been greatly bolstered by a Goldwater statement of a few days earlier that if Nixon lost in 1960, he, Goldwater, would try for the Presidential nomination in 1964. Goldwater is a very forceful personality, one respected enough by Kennedy to be called by him "civilized." Mr. Nixon had, up to then, in his campaign been pleading with voters to forget party labels and vote for the man, not the party. Now, under Goldwater's stern pressure, he said (verbatim), in a good sample of his prose style:

All of you are the people who make the party go, as Barry said, and he told me as we came in . . .
    . . . every opportunity I have I like to come before a group of the key party workers, be they precinct workers or chairmen or officials as the case might be. . . . We often forget that as far as a Presidential election is concerned, and its aftermath, that it's going to be tremendously important not only to win this election at the national level, which we're hoping to do, but also to elect as many Congressmen and Senators as we can, and also to build the Republican Party after this election and build it into a party which we know we can if we work, and that's why I want all of

In the South, where Nixon had been preaching the doctrine that he, not Democrat Kennedy, was the true heir of Thomas Jefferson, Kennedy parried with a quotation from one of Jefferson's contemporaries on the great Virginian,

" 'He [said the contemporary of Jefferson] is a gentleman of thirty-two who can plot an eclipse, survey a field, plan an edifice, break a horse, play the violin, dance the minuet.' Now what," Kennedy would challenge the Southern audience, "has *he* got in common with Mr. Nixon?"—and the audience would roar back: "Nothing."

Kennedy had learned, too, by the end of the campaign a technique that Nixon had long since mastered—except that in Kennedy's fresh hands it came alive. This was the technique of involving the audience with "yes" and "no," summoning them to respond and participate. Political audiences love to participate; they love to yell; the great orator is the one who can make them feel they are partners with him in whatever he is doing, that they have a role as well as he. And now Kennedy began to milk his punch lines as well as Nixon—except that he could add to the nos and the yeses the quality of laughter, too.

Some of his stories had by the end of the campaign become famous, and audiences would wait for him to do the bit as one waits for a performer like Sophie Tucker to do "Some of These Days." His favorite perhaps in the last days of the

---

you to know that I pledge to you that the Republican Party all over the nation, whenever the opportunity presents itself, I like to talk to groups like this because we have to strengthen our party. We have to strengthen it every place.

. . . I traveled the country in '58. It was not a very pleasant job, I can assure you, because when the campaign goes against you and when you go into state after state, where the party organization is on its back, when you go into state after state where you know you're going to lose, and yet you have to stand up there and go down the line for the candidates and the organization and the like, it certainly was not the most easy job I have undertaken and particularly when I was not a candidate myself. I think, however, there was a responsibility, and there is always a responsibility, on the nationally elected officials of the party to attempt to help out the party whenever we can, and that's true of bad times as well as good times.

. . . Frankly, if the time ever comes when I'm not proud of my party and proud of the candidates I'm running with, then, of course, the thing for me to do is to get out of the party. So I can only say, since I don't intend that, I'm going to continue to support every Republican candidate in this state, and also in the nation, and do it proudly, because we simply have to develop a spirit, a spirit which you already have in this state, a spirit which also can be developed in other states as well, a spirit that will rebuild our strength, and it is coming back.

campaign was his arabesque on "Nixon Day in New York." On November 2nd, as we have seen, Nixon had come to New York with President Eisenhower, Governor Rockefeller and Vice-Presidential Candidate Henry Cabot Lodge, the fullest assembly of top Republican power ever put together for the campaign. Kennedy had first taunted Nixon for being afraid to travel on his own, then declared that Nixon was only a trailer for Eisenhower's fame, then (at the suggestion of Adlai Stevenson) had begun to compare the Eisenhower-Rockefeller-Lodge-Nixon parade to the circus-elephant routine.

I last heard him do this sequence at midnight in New York on November 5th to a street-corner audience in the rain, and he ended it:

"You have seen those elephants in the circus [Laughter]. They have their heads of ivory, thick skin, no vision, long memory, and when they move around the ring in the circus, they grab the tail of the elephant in front of them [Cheers]. Well, Dick grabbed that tail in 1952 and 1956, but in 1960, he is running, not the President— . . . I stand tonight where Woodrow Wilson stood, and Franklin Roosevelt stood, and Harry Truman stood [Cheers]. Dick Nixon stands where Mc-Kinley stood and Taft—listen to those candidates [Laughter] —Harding [Groans from the audience], Coolidge [Groans from the audience], Landon [Groans from the audience], Dewey [Groans from the audience]. Where do they get those candidates? [Laughter] . . ."

But the responses were more than vocal.

For the crowds that erupted to greet Kennedy in the streets and squares of the Northeast in the last few weeks of the campaign were, and remain, unbelievable. Crowds are part of politics—and not the pleasantest part. In other countries, in other times and still today, crowds have shaped politics. The crowds that have stormed over the Place de la Concorde have changed French history; so, too, have the crowds on the Kurfuerstendamm and at the Brandenburger Tor changed German history; the crowds in Leopoldville today, the crowds in Delhi and Bombay in the thirties and forties, the crowds in Peking thirty-five years ago—such crowds have forced their way into decisions that were none of their business and thus warped reason and order. Underneath any crowd is a quality of violence, because a crowd bears within itself always the quality of a mob, which is a beast. In other countries, and particularly new countries, this beast quality of the crowd is the most unsettling factor in their politics; in mature countries, experienced and fearful of their own histories, like France and

Germany, crowds and demonstrations are strictly limited in size, in place, in convocation. In America, crowds are permitted regularly to gather every four years to yell and shove and scream, and it is tradition, more than anything else, that disciplines them. For four years Americans are tamped down, their politics running like invisible streams underground; then comes the quadrennial, and like the dry arroyos of the West in spring, the channels of politics come to torrent visibly in the streets.

Yet, discounting even for these quadrennial bursts, the Kennedy crowds were spectacular. It was not the numbers that made them spectacular (Kennedy's top crowd in his Broadway parade in New York on October 19th probably came to no more than 1,250,000, a figure that could be matched by an Eisenhower peak in the Eisenhower campaigns) but their frenzied quality.

One remembers being in a Kennedy crowd and suddenly sensing far off on the edge of it a ripple of pressure beginning, and the ripple, which always started at the back, would grow like a wave, surging forward as it gathered strength, until it would squeeze the front rank of the crowd against the wooden barricade, and the barricade would begin to splinter; then the police would rush to reinforce the barricade, shove back, start a counterripple, and thousands of bodies would, helplessly but ecstatically, be locked in the rhythmic back-and-forth rocking. One remembers the groans and the moans; and a frowzy woman muttering hoarsely as if to herself, "Oh, Jack I love yuh, Jack, I love yuh, Jack—Jack, Jack, I love yuh"; or the harsh-faced woman peering over one's shoulder glowering, "You a newspaperman?—You better write nice things about him, or you watch out" (and she meant it). One remembers the crude signs—hand-lettered, crayoned by school children, chalked on tarpaulin by workmen constructing new buildings, carried on staves by families (in the Bronx: "The home of the *knishes* thinks Jack is delicious" and "The home of the *bagel* thinks Big Jack is Able"). And the noise, and the clamor.

One remembers the motorcades and the people along the road—confetti pouring down at some stops until, when the convertible's door would open to release the candidate, the confetti would pour out like water from a tank. One remembers groups along the road waving, the women unbinding kerchiefs from their heads to wave; the grizzled workingmen and union men, too embarrassed to show emotion publicly, toughness written all over their hard faces, suddenly holding out their hands and waving at him *after* he had gone by—and the hand stretched out as in a Roman salute of farewell for full

seconds after the candidate had passed, and then slowly drop-
ping, of itself. One remembers the grabbers, bursting through
police lines, trying to touch him or reach him, and the squeez-
ers who grasped his hand and, to prove their affection,
squeezed extra hard until, one day in Pennsylvania, even the
candidate's calloused hand burst with blood.

One remembers, of course, the jumpers. The jumpers made
their appearance shortly after the first TV debate when from
a politician Kennedy had become, in the mind of the bobby-
sox platoons, a "thing" combining, as one Southern Senator
said, "The best qualities of Elvis Presley and Franklin D.
Roosevelt." The jumpers were, in the beginning, teen-age girls
who would bounce, jounce and jump as the cavalcade passed,
squealing, "I seen him, I seen him." Gradually over the days
their jumping seemed to grow more rhythmic, giving a jack-
in-the-box effect of ups and downs in a thoroughly sexy oscil-
lation. Then, as the press began to comment on the phenomenon, thus stimulating more artistic jumping, the middle-aged
ladies began to jump up and down too, until, in the press bus
following the candidate, one would note only the oddities: the
lady, say, in her bathrobe, jumping back and forth; the heavily
pregnant mother, jumping; the mother with a child in her
arms, jumping; the row of nuns, all jiggling under their black
robes, almost (but not quite) daring to jump; and the double-
jumpers—teenagers who, as the cavalcade passed, would turn
to face each other and, in ecstasy, place hands on each others'
shoulders and jump up and down together as a partnership.
The most endearing jumping I saw on the long campaign occurred in Florida—in Miami. One of the schools had trooped
its children out onto the lawn to see the Presidential cavalcade
go by, as was the custom in most communities for both candidates. By some misjudgment of logistics, the school authorities had put the older children—the seventh- and eighth-
graders—in the front row while the tiny kindergartners and
first-graders were drawn up several paces behind the big ones
on the grass. The big girls jumped, of course, as was to be
expected. But one could see behind them two files of little
ones in their gay-colored jumpers and smocks, jumping up
and down in their ranks as if they were colored balls being
bounced by an unseen hand. The little ones could see nothing
at all over the shoulders of the seventh- and eighth-graders,
but they were jumping nonetheless.

For whatever scientific value in crowd study, I herewith
offer my own observation on jumping: timing the processions,
I found that the candidate provoked the most vigorous,
rhythmic jumping when the cavalcade moved at a route speed

of about twenty miles an hour. Anything slower than that did not stimulate the best performance; and anything over twenty-five miles seemed to whizz by too fast to excite the glands.

Jumping was only one form of response; so was noise; so was frenzy; so were sheer numbers. All reports of Kennedy response were authentic; what was wrong was that all predictions of a Kennedy sweep based on crowd response ignored an enormous political truth: that quiet people vote, too.

"Crowdsmanship," or the measuring and estimating of crowds, was a game that politicians and press played continuously from the opening of the Nixon campaign in Atlanta (or the Kennedy campaign in Cadillac Square in Detroit) to the end of the trail. The same crowd might be estimated by the hostile eye as 30,000 and by the friendly eye as 60,000. The same crowd (if for Nixon) might be estimated in New York as 600,000 by Democratic leaders and 2,000,000 by Republican Governor Nelson A. Rockefeller. But crowds, in the end, proved to mean little. After many thousands of miles I can offer only this sterile observation: the absence of a crowd is, indeed, a bad omen. (A bleak day of emptiness, as Kennedy's in Seattle or Nixon's in Queens, signaled almost certain disaster.) But a big crowd, however huge or enthusiastic, means nothing at all—no greater demonstrations occurred than for Kennedy in Ohio, or for Nixon in Georgia; yet both of them lost those two roaring states stunningly.

During the campaign all this was still obscure. It was response that the press watched, and the response to Nixon and the response to Kennedy were entirely different. It was true indeed that Nixon commanded large crowds and several wild crowds—notably in Atlanta, in Philadelphia, in Texas. But the wildest of the Nixon demonstrations always seemed to be indoor demonstrations where, one guessed, chiefly the Party faithful were assembled. In Cincinnati, Ohio; in Peoria, Illinois; in the New York Coliseum, the Republican leadership could mobilize its devoted ones, and they would shout and roar loud enough to match any band of Democrats. Yet out of doors the Nixon crowds were incomparably more subdued than the Kennedy crowds. Kennedy evoked an excitement, a response to personality. Nixon held his crowds earnestly together in a sober, intent frowning mass. I remember within an interval of nine days making precisely the same journey with both candidates through southern Ohio from Middletown through Dayton through Columbus and watching them perform in the same places. Measuring space and distance with my eye at the Dayton Court House Square and the Columbus State House Plaza, I could see that both candidates had filled the spaces with almost the same number of people (in Dayton, Kennedy had spoken on a brilliant sunny morning, while Nixon spoke in a drizzle, so the equality of numbers probably was a score for Nixon); yet the reactions to the two men were so different that I could not help but chalk up Ohio as a certain Kennedy victory, thereby agreeing with all other newspapermen and the professional pollsters. My eye could see a banner in the Nixon crowd reading CHRISTIAN DEMOCRATS WILL CAST THEIR BALLOT FOR FREEDOM OF WORSHIP, but I felt I could safely ignore the sign, for this sober crowd seemed scarcely ruffled by any emotion, even at the candidate's peak eloquence. In the event, Ohio was to go for Nixon by 273,000 votes, or 53.3 per cent of its total, in the greatest upset of the election; but the crowd response for Kennedy had obscured reality.

This miscalculation was true for the vast preponderance of both the political analysts and political reporters who traveled with the two candidates. But the miscalculation was more serious for the press. For the reporting that came from such miscalculations glowed with Kennedy enthusiasm and prediction of a sweep. It was inaccurate in prediction. And since Vice-President Nixon and his staff have so seriously charged the American press with prejudice and bad reporting because of this contagious enthusiasm, one should pause and examine the charge as it reflects the condition of political reporting in America.

One must begin any reflection on the press reporting of the 1960 campaign by dissolving the word "press" from mind and replacing it with the picture of forty or fifty men, all veterans of their craft, all proud of their integrity and their calling, most of them having won the right to report the campaign after long careers of merit in their newspapers, magazines, or radio networks—and all of them individuals.

One must see these forty or fifty men, generally middle-aged, rocking groggily off a plane at between one and two in the morning ("Where are we now?" "Do we get our baggage here?" "Hey, where are we sleeping tonight?" "Are they feeding us here or not, do you know?"), then wearily listening to the worn remarks of the candidate as he greets the greeters, then piling into the bus to be driven half an hour to the hotel (watching for local color as they go), dashing upstairs to the hastily arranged press room ("Are there coffee and sandwiches there?") and getting the story off. Then to sleep between two and three, to be woken by the hotel clerk (who has been instructed by the advance man that all baggage must be in the lobby at six in the morning); downstairs to fight with the advance men, the staff, the other correspondents for eggs and coffee, before dashing off to hear the breakfast rally. (And, for the ninety-sixth time, from Mr. Nixon: "May the time never come when any President of the United States, be he Democrat or Republican, feels it necessary to apologize for trying to protect the United States from surprise attack," or from Mr. Kennedy for the ninety-sixth time: "This is a great country. But I think it can be greater. I think we can do better. I think we can make this country move again.")

Then to the morning rally, fighting with the police while charging the police lines to be close to the candidate; then back again on the bus. ("He had ten thousand there, I figure." "Ten thousand! You're crazy. If he had ten thousand here, then he had forty thousand in Nashville." "I heard five thousand— from the chief of police." "That bastard's a Democrat, if it were Kennedy he would have said twenty thousand." "All right—call it eight thousand, how's that?") Back again on the plane. ("Where are we going? New Jersey?" "No, Newark's later on tonight—we're going to Pittsburgh first." "No—not Pittsburgh." "Hey, let's get a revised schedule.")

On the plane there may or may not be sandwiches; there are never cigarettes—if you forget to get cigarettes at dawn, you won't be able to break from the campaign circus and find cigarettes until after midnight; but there is always liquor (and by October everyone is drinking before lunch). The press secretaries hand out the advance of the A.M. release (on conservation, on farmers, on unemployment, on old age, on Castro or on nuclear disarmament) and the typewriters peck the dispatch and the plane is down ("Where? Where are we now?") and one goes to the rally (ninety-seventh time: "May the day never come when any President of the United States . . ." or ninety-seventh time: "I think we can do better. I think this country is ready to move again"); and back on the plane; and the noon rally at the Shopping Center ("May the time never come when . . ." "I think we can do better . . ."). No time for lunch—maybe there'll be sandwiches on the plane. But the afternoon trek is by motorbus without sandwiches (will the baggage on the plane get to the hotel safely?); and the mob at the next city is wild ("I'd say fifty thousand at least." "How the hell can you tell, it's dark, you can't see." "But the Chief of Police said . . .").

Now on board the plane again, tired—the airline *is*, after all, serving dinner; you drink, eat, type, and you talk. At the airport of arrival, the short speech ("May the time never come . . ." "I think we can do better . . ."); and the good

Democratic ladies (or the good Republican ladies) have been told by the advance man to have box dinners ready for the press to eat on the bus. Second dinner today. In town, the local newspaper has lavishly spread itself to offer the visiting press a spectacular cold buffet. Third dinner today. And then the candidate has thrown away his advance speech on education. He's going to talk about Quemoy-Matsu instead ("For God's sake, where's the Western Union man, I've got to stop the story I wrote . . ."); you have a moment in your hotel and telephone your wife while the candidate talks on local TV. But baggage has to be in the lobby at midnight because the plane is taking off tonight for Albuquerque ("No! Salt Lake City." "No! Denver." "No! Minneapolis").

And at one in the morning the candidate stands in the lights of the plane while several local newspapermen buttonhole him, and the high-school editor asks him what is the best way of making peace with the Russians. The tired campaign press has missed his answer ("What did he say?" "Did you hear him?" "Who asked the question?"); and the local photographers pin the candidate down once more for one more picture with his comrade on the PT boat during the war ("Another one? My God, Kennedy must have had enough guys on that PT boat to man a battleship. What's this one's name?") or to take a picture with the Indian in feathered headdress ("It's a Sioux Indian, that's what the local reporters say." "No, it's a Winnebago Indian, can't you tell?" "Hey, someone told me Nixon is part Indian himself." "No. You're crazy"); and the candidate turns to the stairs, and the local radio station puts a mike before him ("Just this one tape recording, it won't take a minute") and the candidate says, "Think of the overriding issue—Peace without Surrender. May the time never come when any President of the United States, be he . . ." Or "This is an important state. This is an important election. I think this is a great country. But I think we can do better. . . ." And so up into the plane at 1:30 in the morning, to unwind and relax and worry about baggage and what to write of the day's events—and to talk.

Above all, to talk. The talk of the corps of correspondents who follow the candidates is not simply gossip; gossip is only its surface form. It is consensus—it is the tired, emotional measuring of judgments among men whom the weeks on the road have made into a brotherhood that only they understand. And the judgment of the brotherhood influences and colors, beyond any individual resistance to prejudice or individual devotion to fact, all of what they write. For by now they have come to trust only each other. The men assigned to cover a

Presidential campaign are, normally, the finest in the profession of American journalism—men of seniority and experience, some of them men of deep scholarship and wisdom, all of them full of dignity and a sense of their own importance. Yet for weeks and months they must live like tramps—shaken, rushed, fighting with police at police lines, dirty and unbathed for days on end, herded into buses like schoolboys. Physical care and handling of the correspondents were much alike in both revolving headquarters—the same instantaneous telegraphic and telephonic communications, the same box lunches, the same baggage-laundry-feeding-hotel arrangements. But none of this meticulous, logistic care could erase the turbulent reality of reporting, the insane jet-flight quality of the 1960 campaign—or protect the simple individual dignity of men who had to combine the qualities of roustabouts and philosophers under circumstances that inexorably deprived them of the last shreds of dignity.

What happened, I believe, in the press reporting of the campaign of 1960 was that the sense of dignity of these men, their craftsmen's pride in their calling, was abused by Mr. Nixon and his staff—and not by accident, but by decision. The brotherhood of the press was considered by Mr. Nixon and his press staff, not a brotherhood, but a conspiracy, and a hostile conspiracy at that; it was as if he accepted them permanently in their uncomfortable and unpleasant campaign role—as vagabonds.

The decision that the press was a conspiracy had been taken long before Mr. Nixon was actually nominated. One of his aides declared to me in June in flat words, "*Stuff* the bastards. They're all against Dick anyway. Make them work—we aren't going to hand out prepared remarks; let them get their pencils out and listen and take notes." This philosophy was expressed, not only to me, but to any number of members of the brotherhood. It was implemented early in the campaign by a punishment policy of withholding transcripts of the Vice-President's speeches from the press that followed him; only late in the campaign, when Kennedy's instant-transcript policy had shown its effectiveness, did the Nixon staff offer similar complete help to the harassed reporters.

Nor was the hostility between press and the Nixon campaign simply a fruit of this trivial disdain. Predominantly Democratic in orientation, the reporters who followed Nixon were, nonetheless, for the sake of their own careers, anxious to write as well, as vividly, as substantively as possible about him. Yet he held himself aloof; erratically, he would sometimes permit reporters to ride his personal plane and at other times forbid it (Kennedy would as soon have dismissed his copilot as have dismissed the rotating trio of pool reporters who rode his personal plane everywhere); what he thought, what he planned, what he wished to express, Nixon kept to himself, believing (until too late in the campaign) that he could reach the American people over the heads of the press via television, or conscript press support from the publishers, who are proprietors of the press. (Mr. Nixon did, indeed, win the editorial support of 78 per cent of all newspapers whose publishers endorsed a candidate in 1960, along with the editorial support of all mass circulation magazines whose publishers chose sides.) What Mr. Nixon really felt, what he wished truly to clarify, he made no effort to communicate to the reporters, who were his amplifiers.

Nixon's personal distrust of the press colored the attitude of his press staff, too. His press secretary, Herbert Klein of San Diego, was an honest and kindly man—yet elusive, uninformative, colorless and withdrawn; he, too, appeared to be talking to the press with a sense of deep suspicion. Indeed, it was more difficult to elicit information from Klein than from John F. Kennedy himself. As much as any man, Klein was responsible for Nixon's bad press. To understand the inner Nixon, one had to reach Finch (the source of almost all the warm and positive information about the Vice-President) or Nixon's exceptionally able Planning Director, James Bassett (then assistant managing editor of the Los Angeles *Mirror*), who was, unfortunately, left behind in Washington throughout the campaign. At the beginning of the campaign the reporters assigned to Mr. Nixon were probably split down the middle between those friendly and those hostile to him; by the end of the campaign he had succeeded in making them predominantly into that which he had feared from the outset—hostile.

To be transferred from the Nixon campaign tour to the Kennedy campaign tour meant no lightening of exertion or weariness for any newspaperman—but it was as if one were transformed in role from leper and outcast to friend and battle companion.

The difference in attitudes to the press corps that one found on the Kennedy side reflected the attitude of its principal, too. For Kennedy, who enjoys words and reading, is a Pulitzer Prize winner himself and a one-time reporter; he has an enormous respect for those who work with words and those who write clean prose. He likes newspapermen and likes their company. Kennedy would, even in the course of the campaign, read the press dispatches, and if he particularly liked a passage, would tell the reporter or columnist that he had—and then quote from its phrases, in an amazing performance of memory and attention. Occasionally, early in the campaign, he would play a rather gay trick; one of his favorite stories was the story of a Colonel Davenport of Hartford, and Colonel Davenport's role in the writing of the Connecticut Constitution—he had told the story so many times that he knew he had drugged his following newsmen to inattention with its repetition. Therefore, now and then, he would substitute the name of one of the newspapermen for Colonel Davenport's name and refer, say, to a Colonel Bradlee, then cock his head to see if the correspondent mentioned had caught the change. He would ask advice of newspapermen—which, though he rarely followed it, flattered them nonetheless. Most of all he was available for quick exchanges of conversation—whether getting on his plane, or in his plane, or by the side of the road where he would stop to drink a Coca-Cola and then chat with the correspondents who clustered round. When presented, say, with a box of apples, he might fling one of them in an underarm pitch to a correspondent, to test whether the man was on his toes. He would borrow combs and pencils from the press—or accept chocolate bars (early in the primary campaigns) when his meal schedule also went awry.

The attitude of the candidate controlled his staff. His advisers rode the press buses and yielded a constant flow of information; his press staff of Pierre Salinger, Don Wilson[4] and Andrew Hatcher[5] gave off a sense of joy when they greeted a correspondent joining or rejoining the circuit, as if they had waited for him, and him alone, to arrive—and then whispered to him a little nugget of color or some anecdote that his particular magazine or newspaper would especially want. It was not only that they respected the press, but somehow as if they were part of the press—half hankering to be writing the dispatches and claiming the by-lines themselves.

There is no doubt that this kindliness, respect and cultivation of the press colored all the reporting that came from the Kennedy campaign, and the contrast colored adversely the reporting of the Nixon campaign. By the last weeks of the campaign, those forty or fifty national correspondents who had followed Kennedy since the beginning of his electoral exertions into the November days had become more than a press corps—they had become his friends and, some of them, his most devoted admirers. When the bus or the plane rolled or flew through the night, they sang songs of their own composi-

[4] Now Deputy Director of the United States Information Agency.
[5] Now Associate Press Secretary to the President.

tion about Mr. Nixon and the Republicans in chorus with the Kennedy staff and felt that they, too, were marching like soldiers of the Lord to the New Frontier.

Yet if it was so, it was difficult to deny credit to the Democratic candidate for what he had achieved—or commiserate with Mr. Nixon for the distance he had made between himself and the men who sought to explain him.

It was 12:30 in the morning of Sunday, November 6th, when John F. Kennedy finally returned home to New England for the last effort of his campaign.[6]

For many years John Bailey of Connecticut had been waiting for this day—it was he (with Governor Ribicoff) who four years before had first proposed the Kennedy name for national office; all year Bailey, as a Kennedy lieutenant, had been on the road, dealing with the brokers of politics in every state of the Union, raiding, wheedling, persuading the support that Kennedy must have. He and Ribicoff had assured Kennedy that their state, Connecticut, was going to be safe—but they wanted their one day of show, too.

Now, after midnight, in the rain at the Bridgeport airport their day began; a high-school band blared through the night with its brass and its drums, the drum majorettes twirled their batons in the arc lights. From the airport to Waterbury, where Kennedy was to rest that night, is only twenty-seven miles; yet it was to take two hours to drive that twenty-seven miles. Every child, every man, every woman, every grandmother and grandfather on whom Bailey and his organization had a string of loyalty, was there in the damp to greet the returning hero. Up the Naugatuck Valley's old Route 8 they went—through Shelton, Derby, Ansonia, Seymour, Beacon Falls, Naugatuck, Union City, through all the craftsmens' villages of this seed bed of American technology. There at every crossroads, at midnight and at one and at two in the morning, they were waiting with torchlights and red flares to cheer and yell "We love you, Jack." Outside every fire station on the route, the Bailey men had lined the fire engines, their red beacons and red winkers flashing and revolving in salute in the night. Down from the bridges and overpasses hung the signs, the placards, the banners. Everywhere he must stop and make the speech.

[6] The previous, last week of the campaign his schedule, on an average of four hours' sleep, had run like this: Sunday, Philadelphia suburbs; Monday, again Philadelphia suburbs; Tuesday, Los Angeles; Wednesday, San Francisco and the Bay area; Thursday, Phoenix, Albuquerque, Amarillo, Wichita Falls, Oklahoma City; Friday, Virginia, Ohio, Chicago; Saturday, New York and its suburbs.

("This is an important election. Connecticut is important. This is a great country but it can be greater. This country must move again.") And back in the buses, the correspondents and the staff, too tired to care any longer, slept or sang, and waited to be at the hotel.

He arrived at the Roger Smith Hotel in Waterbury, Connecticut, at three o'clock in the morning, and 30,000 people waited on the old New England green before the hotel to yell for him. He was tired; it was three o'clock in the morning; but they wanted him. So he climbed out on the balcony of the hotel, with the spotlights illuminating him from below, and from high on the balcony he spoke over the crowded green:

My name is Kennedy and I have come to ask for your support [Cheers].

Back in 1956, when I was a candidate for the Vice-Presidential nomination, my name was placed in nomination by your distinguished Governor, and the first state support that I received was Connecticut four years ago [Cheers]. And the first public official in the United States to support my campaign for the Presidency was Governor Abe Ribicoff. . . .

This campaign really is fought over one issue, and it is an issue which I believe importantly affects the welfare of this country. Mr. Nixon has chosen to go to the people of this country in the year 1960, saying at home our prosperity has never been greater, that we never had it so good, and saying abroad that our prestige has never been higher [Groans]. I run as a candidate for the Presidency with a view that this is a great country but it must be greater [Cheers]. I want to see us build here in this country a strong and vital and progressive society that will serve as an inspiration to all those people who desire to follow the road that we have followed [Cheers].

At the time of the American Revolution, Thomas Paine said the cause of America is the cause of all mankind. Now in 1960 the cause of all mankind is the cause of America [Cheers]. We defend freedom. If we succeed here, then the cause of freedom is strengthened. If we fail here, if we drift, if we lie at anchor, if we don't provide an example of what freedom can do in the 1960s, then we have betrayed, not only ourselves and our destiny, but all those who desire to be free and are not free.

Franklin D. Roosevelt in 1936, accepting his second Presidential nomination, said, "Governments can err, Presidents do make mistakes, but the immortal Dante tells us that Divine Justice weighs the sins of the cold-blooded and the sins of the warm-hearted on a different scale. Better the occasional faults of a government living in the spirit of charity, than the consistent omissions of a government frozen in the ice of its own indifference." We don't want that [Cheers].

He told them it was now well after three o'clock in the morning and that they must go to bed. He said he had promised their Mayor he would send them all home before three o'clock, and the crowd groaned "No, Jack, no, Jack." He let the Governor of Connecticut speak for a few minutes, but they demanded he come back, and again, silhouetted by the stark white lights on the balcony high above the throng, he returned and said:

> I will close by telling you of a letter which Lincoln wrote in a campaign very much like this, one hundred years ago, when the issues were the same. He wrote to a friend, "I know there is a God, and I know he hates injustice. I see the storm coming and I know His hand is in it. But if He has a place and a part for me, I believe that I am ready." Now, a hundred years later, when the issue is still freedom or slavery, we know there is a God, and we know He hates injustice. We see the storm coming, and we know His hand is in it. But if He has a place and a part for me, I believe that *we* are ready. Thank you.

They cheered; they lingered on the green, calling him back until almost four in the morning, but he had to rest, for there were only forty-eight more hours on the road to election day and the Presidency, and he must have his three hours' sleep.

The next forty-eight hours are a great blur of noise and color and ending and departures and turbulence and a mixing of past and present and future history—for New England is the place to see past, present and future mix.

The candidate had once been musing over America with several correspondents, and I had asked him what part of the country, of which he had seen so much in campaigning, he thought was most beautiful. He thought for a moment and then, like most Americans, chose home—the hills of New England, when the leaves are turning in their fall rhapsody of color, were, he thought, the most beautiful sight of all the beauties of America's vastness. Now, however, in the last two days before election, he had come back to New England two weeks too late for the crest of the burst of color. On the hills now as he traveled,[7] the trees were beginning to fade to the

---

[7] All the last Sunday and Monday of the Kennedy campaign were spent in New England except for four hours touching down at rallies in Long Island and the northern New Jersey slums. The schedule, to

ghostly gray of winter, with only the round fan of a red maple still showing scarlet against the coming cold. In the gray web lacing of tree branches on the hills one could distinguish second-growth timber from third-growth timber, and one could recognize (as one cannot in snow or in summer green) where generations of New Englanders had worked these farms—and when they had left; for the fields of New England hold fewer people today than they have for a century.

The strange sense of American history, overlapping in the sequence of its times, weighed heavily on us all. Here, in the Waterbury-Springfield-Torrington-Hartford quadrangle of New England had happened one of those episodes in man's history similar to the episode of Athens in its age of splendor. In this little quadrangle, a century and a quarter ago, an outburst of Yankee genius had invented the technology of America and the modern world—all the arcane secrets of machine tools, precision machinery, interchangeable parts, mass production, alloys and tolerances had been worked out here first, later to be generalized over America's mighty industrial system and then across Europe and Russia. All things that lie at the root of America's industrial might—the bearings of Torrington, the rifles of Springfield, the clocks and brass of Waterbury, Sam Colt's pistols and the first machine guns, Eli Whitney's cotton gin and its interchangeable parts—all had been born in this tiny enclave of New England hills. Yet this genius had brought strange results—and cobbled streets were inhabited now by short-statured men and shawled women. Some New England towns still strove to adjust their genius to a changed America —an old red-brick factory proclaimed (in faded letters) that it made firearms and (in fresher paint) that it also made lawn mowers for suburbia. Some towns were entirely barren, the russet, gray and red fall leaves rustling through their gutters inches deep, their factories dead, the fields abandoned. Other towns throve—one passed the great jet engine plant of Hartford's Pratt & Whitney and thrilled at the thought that the jet engines of old New England now flew man at speeds faster than his senses could apprehend. Or one could pass the silently turning cobweb saucers of radar outside each large New England city, know they were guarding America from devastation, know they had come from the magic of New England's new

be precise, read over the forty-eight hour period: Waterbury, Wallingford, New Haven, Bridgeport, Suffolk County, Teaneck, Jersey City, Newark, Lewiston (Maine), Providence (Rhode Island), Springfield (Massachusetts), Hartford (Connecticut), Burlington (Vermont), Manchester (New Hampshire), and Boston (Massachusetts).

electronic industry and the RADLAB of Boston's MIT—and be frightened of the future.

The jangle of noise was continual; the shrieks, screams, jumpers and sheer blast of sound overpowered and angered one. Tempers frayed. Salinger, normally a jovial man, began to snarl and bite at correspondents who, like him, had been without sleep for days. Even Larry O'Brien (who had joined the circus for the New England homecoming) now for the first time lost his temper. John Bailey was left behind in Connecticut—to make sure that the Connecticut machine worked on voting day. The important correspondents, whom the great newspapers had sent to accompany Kennedy for months, now, one by one, began to slip away—to Detroit, to Chicago, to New York, to their home cities, in order to catch one night's sleep, regain their composure, cease vagabondage and be ready on election night to write the front-page story for their own newspaper of what this election meant. One said farewell to companions in the noise, and one rocked along with the caravan.

So we came back to Boston, that fascinating city, the candidate's home town, the town he had been born in when his parents had been among the first of the Irish to move the Protestants out of their Brookline enclave, into which (since) the Jews had followed the Irish. One came finally back to Boston late on the eve of election, having watched exhaustion, here on native ground, overtake the candidate for President of the United States.

In Boston, past and present history overwhelmed one. The weary candidate arrived in Boston to meet the screamers at the airport; he had hoped for an hour of rest in a Statler Hotel in Boston (where Statler and Sheraton Hotels now dominate the older independent hostelries); but the procession could not roll; it inched and crept all the way from the airport to the hotel through the screaming throng that loved its native son, so that before one reached the hotel it was already time to go on to the Boston Garden.

So the cavalcade oozed through the crowd down the narrow lane of Washington Street of Boston, everyone acutely aware that everything was behind schedule and the candidate must address the nation from old Faneuil Hall at eleven o'clock on national television. One oozed down the street behind a man who might possibly become President of the United States, and one passed all the landmarks of American history—the old Massachusetts State House, where John Hancock and John Adams and Samuel Adams had all debated the quality of representative government in a democracy before pressing those ideas on the American Constitution; they and the Virginians together had written the rules of the game under which John F. Kennedy hoped to win the Presidency. One passed again the marble plaque that marks the site of the Boston Massacre. Except that one knew now, in 1960, if one had to write of this first massacre of American independence, that it had been an "integrated" massacre—of the five Bostonians slain by the British musketeers in 1770, four had been white Bostonians and one, Crispus Atticus, a Negro Bostonian. The last cavalcade proceeded at inch-per-minute pace down the narrow lane of Washington Street while the solid mass of cheering citizens in the street refused to give way, hammered on the sides of the car, grabbed at the candidate and screamed, men and women alike, "I love yuh, Jack." So the cavalcade came to the old North End where, on "the eighteenth of April, seventy-five," lanterns ("one if by land and two if by sea") had been hung out on the night of Paul Revere's ride to warn the settlers that the British were coming; and we entered the Garden where wrestlers, boxers and hockey players now make their living; here Kennedy was to speak for the last time in public as a candidate.

The arena speech was a bad performance. The candidate for President was surrounded on the dais by a covey of the puffy, pink-faced, predatory-lipped politicians who had so dominated Massachusetts politics before he had taken over. The candidate for President was exhausted beyond the margin of normal exhaustion—as exhausted finally as his Republican rival, who was that night in Chicago, about to go home (to Los Angeles) himself. They yelled in the Garden before he could speak, so badly that the eardrums winced to bursting. Finally the local politician stopped trying to introduce him above the noise, and with a forlorn flip of his hand, the introducer beckoned to the candidate to speak. What he said that night before his election is not at all memorable. I remember only the remark of Richard Donahue, one of the candidate's Praetorian Guard, who listened to him and then pointed out to me the envious faces of the local politicians watching the candidate as he spoke. "You know," said Donahue, "they can't understand this. They think he has a trick. They're listening to him because they think if they learn the trick they can be President, too."

The candidate spoke briefly. Then he proceeded to Faneuil Hall, still surmounted by the gold weathercock that Paul Revere fashioned; then, with five minutes of briefing by his TV advisers, and a change of shirt, he came down in that hall where the Sons of Liberty had 190 years before gathered to plot the Boston Tea Party. He spoke to the television cameras and the waiting nation (his Nielsen rating that night was 17.7) of both past and future. Then he went back to the Statler Hotel, to snatch a few hours' sleep, wait for his wife, and be quit of the campaign.

One remembers of that last day in New England the beating of noise—from Providence through Springfield (where the first snow fell) through Hartford through Burlington through Manchester through Boston. Until midnight it was all noise, the gulf of tumult. At that point, as he went to bed on the fourteenth floor of the Statler Hotel, the hush fell. This might be a President.

Tomorrow would be Tuesday, and election day.

Chapter 14

·TO WAKE AS PRESIDENT

THERE is no ceremony more splendid than the inauguration of an American President. Yet Inauguration is a ceremony of state, of the visible majesty of power. And though the powers of the office are unique, even more spectacular and novel in the sight of history is the method of transfer of those powers—the free choice by a free people, one by one, in secrecy, of a single national leader.

Whether Americans have chosen this leader well or badly is of the most immense importance not only to them but to the destiny of the human race. Yet, well or bady done, no bells ring at any given hour across the nation when the voting is over, nor do any purple-robed priests wait that night to anoint the man who will soon be the most powerful individual in the free world. The power passes invisibly in the night as election day ends; the national vigil includes all citizens; and when consensus is reached, the successful candidate must accept the decision in the same rough, ragged, and turbulent fashion in which he has conducted the campaign that has brought him to power. He is still half-man, half-President, not yet separated from the companions of campaign who have helped make him great, nor walled off from the throngs he has caused to crowd and touch him over the many months. So there were no ceremonies on the night of November 8th–9th of 1960.

The candidate had gone to sleep at four o'clock on election night,[1] after waking his wife to tell her that it seemed all right, it looked as if it would be all right. But he did not know. Across the lawn, the operators of the control room in Bobby Kennedy's cottage packed their brief cases; they, too, must sleep, and so they filed into the bus that waited to carry them to the hotel, the same parade of men who had been with him all the way from the year before in this same house: Kenny O'Donnell and his wife, Larry O'Brien and his wife, Dick Donahue and his wife, Lou Harris, several others; grimfaced,

---

[1] See Chapter One for the story of election day.

somber, half-sullen they were driven to their hotel, silent. Alone in the now empty command post, until dawn, there remained only Bobby Kennedy. ("We had too much going for us to be worried, something must break our way," said Bobby a few hours later, when asked how he had spent the dawn watch and whether he had been worried.) California, Michigan, Illinois, Minnesota were all still out and uncertain when the candidate had left his brother to go to bed, and even though there was no further action to be powered by the motor of Bobby Kennedy, Bobby kept telephoning, calling, checking around the nation. (The long-distance telephone bill at the command post for the single election night was estimated at $10,000.)

Now in the night, as Bobby alone stayed awake, with no precision of hour or minute, the power was passing.

Across the land, in California, where Richard Nixon slept, his command half-heartedly waited for reprieve from what seemed obvious; they waited on two states—Pennsylvania and Michigan. Well before the Republican candidate woke (at 6:30 in the morning, Pacific Coast Time; 9:30 in the morning, Eastern Standard Time) they had been informed, first, by Hugh Scott of Pennsylvania, that the Kennedy lead in that state was now too powerful for any last-minute surge of the farms and suburbs to overtake; next, a telephone call from Michigan reported that the best Republican judgment in Michigan was that, however slim the margin might be in the automobile state (67,000 votes), it was a Kennedy margin and solid; so now Richard Nixon could not be elected, no matter how Illinois or California went.

It was Michigan, in fact, that marked the passage of power from one party to the other in what little official ceremony election night offered. All night, in his Washington home, the Chief of the Secret Service, Urbanus E. Baughman, a lean, graying, slow-spoken man, had sat watching the television screen, no better informed than any other citizen, yet burdened by law with the duty of guarding and protecting the body of the President-elect of the United States as soon as his identity should be known. Two direct long-distance wires linked him telephonically to Los Angeles and Hyannisport and to the two platoons (sixteen men each) of Secret Service men waiting for his word, at both centers, to move to protect a President—or not to move. In Hyannisport, at the Holiday Heath Inn, Inspector Burrell Petersen, watching his television set too, began to itch for the move at 2:35 in the morning when the television screen showed Kennedy at 261 electoral votes. Over the telephone, Chief Baughman instructed him to wait—Kennedy was still eight votes short. At 4:15 A.M., with Kennedy at 265 votes and still four short, Petersen called once more—and again was instructed to wait. At 5:35, Chief Baughman in Washington noted that television had given Michigan's 20 votes to Kennedy, to make a tentative 285 and a tentative majority. It was now too late to wonder or doubt any longer, for his responsibility was clear, and at 5:45 Baughman telephoned Petersen with instructions to move to establish security. The candidate and his staff still slept as the sixteen agents in their borrowed cars set out in the night for the compound by the beach; by seven in the morning, security had been established and the President-elect was walled off, as he would be for four or eight years to come, from all other citizens and ordinary mortals. The members of the Kennedy staff still remember with amazement the silent efficiency of these operatives. As each of the staff group arrived at the compound in the morning, the Secret Service agents recognized his face and name, knew his function, importance, responsibility; they had done all the homework necessary to protect the Chief Executive and distinguish his servants from the strangers.

Sorensen was the first to arrive, to be invited upstairs at 9:30 to the candidate's second-story bedroom, where he found the President-to-be in white pajamas sitting on the bed. It was Sorensen who told the President that California had definitely been carried and that he, John F. Kennedy, was now the next President. A few minutes later Pierre Salinger arrived with the same news, and for a few minutes all three, with little excitement, discussed the late flashes and reports of returns from across the country. It was still too early to claim victory publicly, although now all three were convinced it had happened; they would wait, the President-to-be decided, until Richard M. Nixon in California chose to yield. When his aides had left, the candidate strolled to the window, saw a fine, bright New England day and a knot of photographers and cameramen on the lawn below; he waved to them, smiling, then withdrew; he shaved (with a straight razor), dressed, and then went down to have his normal breakfast with his wife and child.

He came out after breakfast, shortly after ten—suntanned, windblown, smiling, a bit more tired than he had looked six months before, yet now revived from the exhaustion of the previous twenty-four hours. He was leading his daughter, Caroline, by the hand; he piggy-backed her for a few minutes at her insistent pleading, then invited his younger brother, Edward, to go for a walk along the beach. Several other Kennedys and Ted Sorensen now materialized, and they crossed the bluff and dune grass to the sands of the beach, followed carefully by Secret Service men, and walked until almost eleven, when they returned to Bobby Kennedy's cottage. There, Salinger had been informed by James Hagerty, Eisenhower's press secretary, from Washington, that a congratulatory message would soon be arriving from Dwight D. Eisenhower; Nixon's formal concession would also be coming momentarily. All sat down in front of the television set, and as the figure of Herbert Klein, Nixon's press secretary, appeared on screen, a dead hush fell over the group; for a moment the new President twitted Salinger on his appearance contrasted with Klein's, then all were silent. Someone cleared his throat as if to speak and the President-to-be said sharply, "I want to hear this," and leaned forward. When Klein had finished, the campaign was thoroughly over, and the new President said, "All right, let's go."

There followed a bustle of almost an hour. "Where's Jackie?" said the President-elect as he rose from his armchair. She was on the beach, walking by herself, and the President-elect went personally to fetch her, bringing her back as he found her, dressed in a faded raincoat, wearing flat-heeled beach shoes, a scarf wound around her head. Now all must dress; all must have their pictures taken in the living room of his father's house; all must be ready for the cavalcade to the Hyannis Armory, where press and television waited. The cavalcade formed outside the home of Joseph P. Kennedy and lingered; the President had dashed from the car as if propelled by an afterthought and ran again into the house. He had decided he would not yield to his father's year-long insistence on obscurity—his father must come with him now in this moment of victory, to be part of the public ceremony. While he waited for his father to dress, and the cavalcade waited for him, and the television cameras and the nation waited for all of them, the President tossed a football he had found on the lawn back and forth with one of his father's houseguests.

Then, finally, they were ready. Forty-eight hours earlier, in the heat of the campaign, such a cavalcade would have been considered a disaster—so few people lined to streets to watch him come; not until the procession reached the Armory was there any real mass of welcome sound and people. But there was no problem with this cluster. The Secret Service were used to protecting Presidents—they cleared the way, fanning from their practiced lope alongside his white Lincoln Continental into a wedge that opened his path. And there in the Armory they were all there lining the way to the platform—Sorensen and O'Donnell and O'Brien and Salinger and Reinsch and Dave Powers and Donahue and Dungan and Goodwin and Feldman and all the others. One or two of those closest to him as he climbed the platform insist that his eyes teared over and he could not speak when he shook hands with his aides before he mounted the steps; but this may have been imagination. When he finally spoke before the microphones and to the press and to the nation, he spoke evenly, with no tremor in his voice—only his hands holding the yellow telegraph forms and the white sheets of his replies shook and trembled, but they were below camera range. He read the congratulations he had received from both Eisenhower and Nixon, read his replies, answered a few questions and then again made his way out of the Armory, in a slow five-minute procession to the door as he shook hands with the reporters who had followed him; he paused to say a personal word to each that he could see.

Lunch followed at his father's house, full family present along with Sorensen and Walton. It was a laughing lunch as they discussed the returns, as they vaunted over who had performed best in what state, and needled those responsible for lost states.

In the afternoon family and friends went out to the lawn to play touch football, and in the midst of the game the President himself came running across the lawn to join them. The President became quarterback of one team, his brother Bobby quarterback of the other team, and the Secret Service men watching from the dune grass looked on in horror as his sisters screamed and clawed, as they bumped into one another, as players tangled and men fell to the ground and the President of the United States (whom they were sworn to defend) rose and fell with them. The game was over before five (Bobby's team had won by a single touchdown), and the President went back to his own cottage.

That night he dined with artist Walton again and with Mr. and Mrs. Benjamin Bradlee, all old friends. They talked of politics and personalities, among others of J. Edgar Hoover and Allen W. Dulles.[2] They also discussed quite warily and seriously the first note of congratulations from Mr. Khrushchev. At this point Joseph P. Kennedy arrived to invite them

[2] The next day he was to announce the names of these two men, Hoover and Dulles, as the first of his appointments to office. It was his reasoning that both of these offices are too sensitive to be headed by partisan appointments, and it was his hope to establish them henceforward, in any change of administration, as nonpolitical posts.

all to watch movies at his house. The movies began with an action picture with John Wayne and, since that satisfied no one, they interrupted it and began another movie, *Butterfield 8*. The President lingered for only a few minutes—the screen could not keep his attention, and he slipped out of the room. He asked no one to come with him nor did anyone offer to follow.

It was important for him to be alone. He had run all the way, and brilliantly. Yet the margin of voices that proclaimed him President was so thin as to be almost an accident of counting. One could read no meaning from the numbers—only from the shape and structure of the numbers. It was as if for a year he had been operating in a room full of dark, colliding forces; one could sense the outline of the forces; but there had been no light available to define the forces until election day itself. Then, like a high-speed stroboscopic camera in a photo flash of light, the election tally had stopped all motion and captured a momentary, yet precise, picture of the moods, the wills, the past and the future of all the communities that made America whole.

It is well to examine the picture of the voting of November 8, 1960—for the future of American politics and of American history would rest on what John F. Kennedy saw in it.

Men will examine the figures of the 1960 vote for decades, and as yet we cannot tell whether they will examine them as they did those of 1860, which closed an era of American history, or as they examine the figures of 1932, which opened one. Whether the vote says hail or farewell to one era or another depends on how President Kennedy now acts. But however the chroniclers will read the vote, they, too, as we, must start with the bare bones of tabulation.

John F. Kennedy was elected President on November 8, 1960, by 303 electoral votes, drawn from 23 states, to 219 votes for Richard M. Nixon, drawn from 26 states. One state, Mississippi, was carried by a slate of eight independent electors who, with seven other Southerners (from Oklahoma and Alabama) voted for Senator Harry F. Byrd of Virginia. The margin of this electoral vote, so apparently substantial, is however a tribute not to the victor but to the wisdom of the Constitutional Fathers who, in their foresight, invented the device of the Electoral College, which, while preserving free citizen choice, prevents it from degenerating into the violence that can accompany the narrow act of head-counting. On the same day the American people returned to Congress a Senate of sixty-four Democrats and thirty-six Republicans and a House of Representatives of 262 Democrats and 175 Republicans, a gain for the Republicans of two Senate seats and twenty-one House seats.

In the head-counting of the popular vote, 68,832,818 Americans voted for President, or 64.5 per cent of the 107,000,000 Americans old enough and eligible to vote by census estimate. This participation (which ranged from a high of 80.7 per cent in Idaho to a low of 25.6 per cent in Mississippi) was the highest recorded participation in numbers and percentage of any American national election.

John F. Kennedy received 34,221,463 of these votes (49.7 per cent), or 112,881 votes (one tenth of one per cent of the whole) more than Richard M. Nixon, who drew 34,108,582 (49.6 per cent of the total). Thirteen minority-party candidates divided the remaining 502,773 (0.7 per cent) votes of this total.[3] This margin of popular vote is so thin as to be, in all reality, nonexistent. If only 4,500 voters in Illinois and 28,000 voters in Texas had changed their minds, the sum of their 32,500 votes would have moved both those states, with their combined fifty-one electoral votes, into the Nixon column. Thus giving him an electoral majority of two, these 32,500 votes would have made Richard M. Nixon President of the United States.

Analysis of the meaning of the national vote must begin, then, by separation, proceeding from the gross figures, which can be established with hard accuracy, to the finer and more delicate speculations on the subdivisions of the vote, which attempt to illuminate the privacy of American minds.

Only when one begins to cluster the individual states into natural groups does the blur and confusion first dissolve into a rough pattern. Dividing America into its eight major regions, one finds that of the eight fairly distinct geographical communities in the nation, Richard M. Nixon carried five and John F. Kennedy but three.

One learns much by scanning the separate totals of these areas—for here there are true margins, thin but real.

The most decisive single expression of will for Richard M. Nixon came from the block of five predominantly farm states (Iowa, North Dakota, Kansas, South Dakota, Nebraska). Here, in the culture of the small town and the old America, in the Protestant homesteads of traditional Republican allegiance, Nixon led by a margin of 598,362 votes out of a total

[3] See Appendix A for a breakdown of the national vote by individual states. I have used here the final official figures as reported by the Associated Press.

of 3,395,088 (with 58.8 per cent of the whole). He scored well in the block of eight states that sprawl across the Rocky Mountains (Montana, Idaho, Colorado, Utah, Wyoming, Nevada, Arizona, New Mexico), where he led Kennedy by 192,313 votes out of 2,641,593 cast, or 53.6 per cent of the whole. The margin thinned somewhat in the five border states (Kentucky, Missouri, Oklahoma, Tennessee, West Virginia), which provided Nixon with a margin of 263,033 votes out of 5,837,945 cast, or 52.2 per cent. Here, in these traditionally Democratic yet Bible-loving and Protestant regions, religion played a heavy role—in only six states in the Union did Nixon outrun the Eisenhower percentages of 1956, and two of these were in border country (Tennessee and Oklahoma; the other four were in the Deep South: Georgia, Alabama, Mississippi, South Carolina). His lead was pared yet further in the six industrial Midwestern states that ring the lakes (Illinois, Michigan, Indiana, Minnesota, Wisconsin, Ohio), where Nixon led by 462,778 out of 17,607,696 cast (with 51.3 per cent of the whole). This, the industrial heartland of the country, still remains the greatest single base of Republican strength. Finally, the five Pacific states (California, Oregon, Washington, Hawaii, Alaska) provided his thinnest margin—107,461 votes out of 8,733,361, or 50.6 per cent.

These five geographic regions of the land, sweeping in a huge lopsided crescent from the shores of the Pacific to the Appalachians, together gave Mr. Nixon a margin of 1,623,967 votes. That these were not enough to affect the delicate amplification of the Electoral College was simply because Mr. Kennedy has *his* margin where it counted—in the populous Northeast and the Old South.

Of the three regions that Kennedy claimed, New England, as expected, performed best. In the six states (Maine, New Hampshire, Vermont, Massachusetts, Rhode Island, Connecticut) of this, the most heavily Catholic section of the country, and his native ground, Kennedy ran up a margin of 603,587 votes out of 4,977,169 cast, or 56.0 per cent of the total—almost, but not quite, as good as Nixon's margin in the five farm states. Ten states of the Old South (Alabama, Arkansas, Florida, Georgia, Louisiana, Mississippi, North Carolina, South Carolina, Texas and Virginia), came next in expression of loyalty—yielding a plurality of 530,693 votes out of 8,865,501 cast, or 52.9 per cent. Here, as we will see later, came the greatest and most significant Republican gains in the national election, a gain which, by proper strategic planning, might have been amplified enough to give Nixon victory and revolutionize American politics. Finally (the fruit of Kennedy's own determined strategy) came the great block of five Middle-Atlantic states (New York, New Jersey, Pennsylvania, Maryland and Delaware), which gave him a lead of 601,570 votes out of 16,372,790 cast, or 51.5 per cent—a thin lead in percentiles, but large enough in size and distribution to give him all 105 electoral votes of the region. Altogether, these three Kennedy regions provided a margin of 1,735,851 votes, or just enough votes in just the right places to give him victory—as he had planned it.

For never was planning and decision of greater importance in any campaign than in that of 1960—for supreme planning calculates both underlying force and vagrant accident, and provides enough underlying force to take advantage of or protect against accident; which is what the Kennedy planning, in essence, achieved; and which is why afterwards no Republican candidate in recent years, not even Thomas Dewey, has been more bitterly, if privately, denounced by his closest associates of campaign and headquarters than Richard M. Nixon. For unforeseen accidents happened on both sides; yet the Nixon strategy—or lack of it—made the Republican most vulnerable.

The election of 1960 can, if one wills, be seen as an interlocking set of ifs: if Nixon had made up his mind which he wanted, the Northern Negro or Southern white vote; if the Puerto Rican Catholic bishops had made their intolerant intervention into Puerto Rican politics earlier and if Nixon had taken advantage of it; if the hysterical States-Righters of Dallas had not roughed up Lyndon and Lady Bird Johnson in the hotel lobby; if Eisenhower had been used earlier; if Nixon had moved as forthrightly as did John F. Kennedy and Robert Kennedy in the Martin Luther King arrest; if only the citizen Democrats of California and the new coagulating boss groups of California had been able to work together in harness, as they could not; if Nixon had clung to his original television strategy and not panicked; if Nixon had clung to the original Forward theme of Hall and Shepley—an interminable series of ifs can be strung together to account for, reverse or multiply the tiny margin of 112,000 popular votes by which Kennedy led Nixon. Yet when all these ifs are strung together, they are only the froth and the foam in the wake of the strategies of the two candidates who sought to lead the American people.

The first of the Kennedy strategies had been a regional one, decided by the candidate alone, on the night of his nomination, by his choice of Vice-President. He felt he had New England locked up; that he must campaign personally for the big Northeastern industrial states; that Lyndon B. Johnson must be his

Lord Constable for the Old South. These grand calculations worked. Of the nine big states, Kennedy carried seven: New York, Pennsylvania, Michigan, Illinois, Texas, New Jersey, Massachusetts. Nixon carried only two: Ohio and California. It was in these big states that Kennedy invested the greatest part of his time and personal effort, while Nixon sought to spread himself over all fifty states of the Union. New England proved indeed to be in the bag; and Lyndon Johnson proved indeed able to captain the Southern electoral drive. Had Kennedy carried only one other state except those envisioned in this strategy (and he did carry Minnesota, Missouri, Nevada, New Mexico, West Virginia and Hawaii), this strategy would still have given him a majority of the Electoral College.

Within this larger regional strategy of voting, a subordinate but nonetheless major calculation must be signaled. This was Kennedy's October decision to hammer away at the great suburban belts in the large states—suburbs that in the past decade have been traditionally Republican. He left it to his big-city bosses to firm up the traditionally Democratic ethnic blocs inside the big cities, into which Eisenhower had previously cut so heavily. He himself hammered at the suburbs around Chicago, Philadelphia, New York and Baltimore, appealing to the younger voters in the developments, as he had learned to do in his native Massachusetts. A Lou Harris survey early in the campaign had come up with the oddly interesting fact that while fewer than 30 per cent of American families *now* send their children to college or junior college, no less than 80 per cent hope in the future to send children to college. In the suburbs, early and late, Kennedy hammered at educational themes within the broader theme of We Must Move, and the "young marrieds," worried about their children, must have hearkened. In the suburbs of the top fourteen Northeastern metropolitan areas he was able to increase the Democratic percentage in these naturally Republican girdles from the 38 per cent netted by Adlai Stevenson in 1956 to 49 per cent in 1960. On the East Coast, his gains in the Protestant suburbs of Baltimore and Buffalo were of the same order as his gains in the heavily Catholic suburbs of New York and Boston. (His record as the vote moved West was definitely not as good: moderate in the suburbs of Chicago and disastrous in the suburban outer fringe of Los Angeles; in Los Angeles a clear amount of the fall-off was due to mismanagement of the California campaign, where Kennedy ran farther behind his Democratic ticket mates than in any major state of the Union.)

The most precise response of result to strategy lay, however, in the Negro vote. And this was overwhelmingly for

Kennedy. It must be remembered that as Kennedy entered the Democratic Convention in Los Angeles, he was the *least* popular among Negroes of all Democratic candidates; many Northern Negro politicians preferred even Lyndon Johnson to Kennedy. Hard work (chiefly by the Civil Rights Section, led by the able Sargent Shriver and Harris Wofford) and the master stroke of intervention in the Martin Luther King arrest, not only reversed this Negro indifference to him, but gave him a larger share of the Negro vote than Stevenson had received in 1956 (although not quite as large a share as Stevenson had had in 1952). In analyzing the Negro vote, almost all dissections agree that seven out of ten Negroes voted for Kennedy for President—the Gallup Poll estimating 70 per cent, the IBM calculations estimating 68 per cent. In Detroit, Negro percentages ran at 8 to 1 or better; in the five Negro wards of Chicago's swollen South Side, the percentage ran approximately 4 to 1. And not only did the Northern Negro vote Democratic—so did the Southern Negro, in a complete reversal of form. In Memphis, Tennessee, Ward Thirty-five, a typical Negro ward, switched from 36 per cent Democratic in 1956 to 67 per cent Democratic in 1960; similar staggering switches occurred in South Carolina, in Georgia and in Texas. Some Negro political leaders claim that in no less than eleven states (Illinois, New Jersey, Michigan, South Carolina, Texas, Delaware, Maryland, Missouri, North Carolina, Pennsylvania, Nevada), with 169 electoral votes, it was the Negro community that provided the Kennedy margin of victory. This statement is interesting only as an example of wind in the sails of men who propose to move fast; it bears no relation to reality. Yet it is difficult to see how Illinois, New Jersey, Michigan, South Carolina or Delaware (with 74 electoral votes) could have been won had the Republican-Democratic split of the Negro wards and precincts remained as it was, unchanged from the Eisenhower charm of 1956. Nor can one avoid the observation that as October stretched on to November, and the economic downturn of the winter began to be felt, unemployment began to bite, as it always does, most sharply on Negro unskilled workers. ("Mister," said a Chicago Negro discussing his vote with me in 1960, "they could put a dog at the head of that ticket and if they called him Democratic I'd vote for him. This hollarium about civil rights doesn't mean anything to me—it's the man that puts money into my pocket that counts.")

There remains, then, in examining the vote, the most controversial of all areas of reflection: the Catholic-Protestant cleavage in American life. For these is little room to argue about how American Catholics and Protestants voted in 1960 —only about what the generally accepted (and valid) figures mean.

American Catholics voted preponderantly for John F. Kennedy. They had, indeed, voted preponderantly Democratic ever since the Irish first arrived in New York and Boston a century ago. But during the 1950s they had voted so heavily for the Republicans (or Dwight D. Eisenhower) that their return to the old pattern of voting at about 3 or 4 to 1 Democratic provokes the perplexing question of whether they were voting by faith, by political conviction or by resumption of interrupted habit. The extremes of research of Catholic voting in 1960 are those of Dr. George Gallup (who held that 78 per cent of all Catholics voted for Kennedy, in social breaks that ranged from 65 per cent for college-educated, prosperous Catholics to 83 per cent for poorer, grade-school-educated Catholics) to that of the IBM data computers that held that only 61 per cent of all Catholics voted for Kennedy. Not all Catholics, it should be noted, voted alike—for them, too, the past has many threads and sometimes the threads tangle. Italian Catholics (most analysts agree) voted about 70 per cent for Kennedy, Polish Catholics about 68 per cent. There is controversy about the margin by which Kennedy held or won back his Irish-Catholic fellows—the IBM data computers insist that about 68 per cent of definable Irish-Catholic voting units went for Kennedy, whereas the Kennedy staff grieves that in many areas (as in Hudson County, New Jersey) the expected Irish-Catholic vote fell so far below anticipation as to jeopardize election in close states.

The most interesting performance of the minor communities in the Catholic subcommunity of America was that of the German-Catholic-Americans. Where their vote can be isolated, it is estimated that it was 50 per cent Kennedy, 50 per cent Nixon. Here, in the German-Catholic-American vote, one sees two different kinds of past straining and tugging at the voter: an American of German ancestry must see a Democrat as one who belongs to the party that has twice led this country into war against the old fatherland; as an American Catholic, he must see a Catholic candidate as one, like himself, of a minority hitherto excluded. The two pressures of the past clash.

Perhaps the best demonstration of how this clash worked out in voting practice in 1960 happened in Wisconsin. In Wisconsin, political reporters talk of the "ten Catholic counties"— meaning those ten Wisconsin counties that, alone, voted both for Alfred E. Smith for President in 1928 and for state aid for parochial-school buses in 1938. These counties are populated largely by German and Irish Catholics. In the spring primary between Humphrey and Kennedy, these ten counties voted overwhelmingly *for* Kennedy *against* Humphrey, as if to prove that, between two Democrats, they preferred their co-religionist. But in the November election, when a Republican (Protestant) and a Democrat (Catholic) stood before them, and religion was confused with politics, they split—five for Nixon, five for Kennedy.

There is no doubt that millions of Americans, Protestant and Catholic, voted in 1960 primordially out of instinct, kinship and past.

One cannot examine the structure of the voting returns in Oklahoma, Tennessee, Utah, Florida, Kentucky, Oregon, Indiana, Ohio or Wisconsin without finding transparent evidence in precise counties and precincts that millions of Protestants could not tolerate the thought of a Catholic sitting in the White House. Equally, one cannot examine returns from New York, Illinois, Pennsylvania, and New England without recognizing that millions of Americans, equally blind, voted *for* Kennedy only because he *was* a Catholic. One has, for example, that marvelously clear pattern of interlocking bigotries of such a county as Nelson County, Kentucky. There, four predominantly Baptist precincts gave Kennedy only 599 votes (35 per cent) and Nixon 1,095 votes (65 per cent); yet in the same county, five predominantly Catholic precincts gave Kennedy 1,285 (88 per cent) and Nixon 174 votes (12 per cent). One has the pattern (if one wishes to analyze patterns further) of the three predominantly Irish precincts of Philadelphia with a permanent registration of 53 per cent Republican—which in 1960 went for Kennedy by 70 per cent. And the contrasting pattern, if one wishes, of the town of New Amsterdam in Montana, which had voted *for* Democrat Lee Metcalf, a Protestant, for Congressman in 1958, by 287 to 34; yet which in 1960, when he ran for United States Senator and was denounced by the local opinion makers as the candidate of the "Catholic Party," voted *against* him by 260 to 40.

Over all, there can be no doubt that the great majority of Catholics voted for Kennedy; and, situated as they were by history in the Northeast, they cast their votes in the big states, which counted most. All other matters but this were planned and mobilized by Kennedy—the concentration of campaigning in the Northeast, the emphasis on civil rights and protection of the Negroes, the cultivation of suburbia and the advocacy of a new important program of federally aided education. The Catholic vote, it is true, was counted in all Kennedy calculations as being committed to him in advance; yet this vote alone was *not* planned, nor was it mobilized. For even when the Catholic vote is added to the Negro vote, the Jewish vote and the suburban vote, one still has no true picture of what happened in the election of 1960 nor how its totals came about. For John F. Kennedy, as other Democrats before him, was not elected only by a federation of American minorities —nor does his Presidency rest on that fact, nor did his campaign at its highest and most important level plan that kind of victory.

In the long sight of history, John F. Kennedy cast his appeal, *above all*, to the overwhelmingly Protestant majority of the American people, and ran uphill to convince them that whatever differing pasts and heritages they brought to 1960, they shared a common future and common conviction for the years ahead.

It was this, indeed, that was the greatest success of Kennedy planning.

For the addition of minorities in no way explains the Kennedy total of triumph. No estimate or analysis of the final vote denies that in the final Kennedy constituency of 34,000,000 votes, the number of Protestants who voted for him materially outweighed the number of Catholics and Jews combined. The high estimate (IBM) is that 46 per cent of all American Protestants voted for John F. Kennedy, or 22,-500,000—making almost two thirds of his total. The low estimate (Dr. George Gallup) is that only 38 per cent of all American Protestants voted for John F. Kennedy—which still comes to some 18,600,000 of his 34,000,000 constituency, or critically more than half of his majority. If the exact percentage of Protestants who voted for Kennedy is forever indefinable, the truth must nevertheless lie somewhere between the low and high estimates; thus the Kennedy victory is a triumph of many facets—a triumph first of American tolerance and of the enlightened leadership of contemporary Protestant churchmen, a triumph next of the planning of the man who became President, a triumph finally of the American spirit, which is unafraid. Which invites us once more, in the afterlight of the election totals, to examine the strategies of the two candidates.

If Nixon were to win, he had need only to move forward from the Eisenhower base of Peace and Prosperity; the country was indeed at peace and, until the late fall downturn, more prosperous than ever before in history. To urge it forward, he need only have been bold, been strong, and offered visions. The past, both immediate and remote, weighed in his favor, and to this pressure of the past he need only add a minimum sense of future in which all could hope for more. Instead he tangled in words, locked himself on issues thrust at him by his rival, defending and retaliating when he should have been leading. He offered no vision of a greater future to any minority—Catholic or otherwise—within a moving, broadening American future that might win them from their past; and to the great majority Protestant stock of the country he offered, with utmost honor, no fear of religion—yet nothing to offset the emotions Kennedy sought to arouse in order to tug them, by hope, from their instinct and fear.

For Kennedy, the problem was equally clear, if different as in a mirror image. It was to stir the nation with a sense of anticipation strong enough to overcome the hidden and unspoken reluctance of millions of Americans to abandon their past—and not only the past of religion, but the pride of the Anglo-American peoples who had fought the Civil War, who had built America's industry, had cleared its plains, who found themselves still unable to recognize in the third or fourth generation of the immigrant hordes those leadership qualities that run in the tradition of Lincoln, Roosevelt, Adams, Hay, Wilson, Roosevelt, Stimson.

It was seventy years ago that Senator George F. Hoare (Rep.) of Massachusetts, replying to a European inquirer, declared, "The men who do the work of piety and charity in our churches, the men who administer our school system, the men who own and till their own farms, the men who perform skilled labor in the shops, the soldiers, the men who went to war and stayed all through, the men who paid the debt and kept the currency sound and saved the nation's honor, the men who saved the country in war and have made it worth living in peace, commonly and as a rule, by the natural law of their being find their places in the Republican party. While the old slave-owner and slave-driver, the saloon keeper, the ballot box stuffer, the Ku Klux Klan, the criminal class of the great cities, the men who cannot read or write, commonly and as a rule, by the natural law of their being, find their congenial place in the Democratic party."

One has only to travel through the Midwest or upper New York and New England today to find the echo of this generations-old statement. If Joseph P. Kennedy had become an apostate Catholic and baptized his son an Episcopalian at birth in Trinity Church, Copley Square, Boston, John F. Kennedy would, nonetheless, have had to run against the same sense of the past and the same unease that the American people felt when they considered putting their destiny into new hands. Consciously or unconsciously, therefore, in all his elegant quotations from Franklin and Jefferson, from Lincoln and Roosevelt, from Thoreau and from Emerson, Kennedy sought to identify himself with this past. (At times, indeed, following him about the country was like attending a peripatetic and anecdotal course in American history.) And out of this past he attempted to urge all Americans to move forward with him to a common future.

The fact that he succeeded at all is, in retrospect, more startling than the narrowness of his margin. He had, of course, the entire future to himself—no other Republican candidate has ever so willfully conceded so vast an area to a Democratic opponent without struggle. But his problem was fantastic nonetheless. For politics is the slow public application of reason to the governing of mass emotion. And it is rare that reason can reach an entire people without clarification by disaster—such as the disaster of the depression in America in 1932, or defeat in battle of the Germans in 1945. Kennedy spoke to a peaceful and prosperous people in the year 1960, a people for whom the crises of swelling problems lay still unclear years ahead. He insisted that they must move to meet those obscure crises—which he did not define—and urged them to give into his untested hands the greatest of all crises, war and peace, without ever telling them how he meant to meet it. It was on this above all that he won—a sense of purpose, in a year of malaise; a sense of confidence, in a future that darkened.

Several other observations must be made of the forces we can discern in the election of 1960—forces that will shape the Presidency of John F. Kennedy and our time.

The most startling, in strictly political terms, was in the Southern revolt.

There, in the Old Confederacy, Richard M. Nixon made his greatest gains. It was felt by Democrats, hopefully, in 1952 and 1956 that only the glamor and fame of Eisenhower—coupled with the true affection he has in American hearts—carried the South from its traditional loyalties to the Republican column in his two elections. Yet Nixon managed to *increase* the Republican vote and *outrun* Eisenhower in no less than four states of the Deep South—Alabama, Georgia, Mississippi, and South Carolina (all of which he lost)—and carry two others (Virginia and Florida) by margins almost equal to that of the war hero. All in all, in the eleven states of the Old Confederacy he polled 4,723,981 votes as against 5,179,550 votes for Kennedy, to score 47.7 per cent; in 1952,

Eisenhower had polled only 4,113,525, or 48.1 per cent; and in 1956, 4,218,468, or 50.5 per cent. (In 1948, Thomas E. Dewey had drawn only 1,361,742 votes, or 26.8 per cent for the Republicans.)

One can argue that this was a matter of style—that Nixon appealed more to the small towns of the Old South, with their homespun folksiness, than did Kennedy with his Eastern manners. Yet the sharpest bulge in the Nixon-Republican total was chalked up in the bustling, modern cities of the New South: in Dallas, in Houston, in Birmingham, in Atlanta, and in their suburbs. Nixon's successes in these areas in 1960 cannot be seen as episodes—they must be seen as a trend that poses the most acute problem, not only for the Republican and Democratic high commands, but for all American domestic tranquility.

For there are at least two forces in the South, generating pressures that, over the past twelve years, have combined to loosen its ties with the old Democratic coalition. One is the genuine and welcome regional expression of the nationwide citizen revolt against machine politics; in the South, where big cities are racked by small-town political machines, the citizen revolt carries thousands of decent citizens naturally into the Republican Party to protest. But the second is the pressure of race tension—for the Southern white knows himself bound to a Democratic Party that, in the North, is increasingly responsive to Negro pressure for intervention in domestic Southern affairs.

Either one of these two pressures offers a major strategic opportunity to the Republican Party such as it has not had since before the Roosevelt revolution. It is an opportunity that must insistently knock on Republican thinking; and only a man so sublimely uninterested in partisan politics as Dwight D. Eisenhower could have let this opportunity pass, or failed to take the practical measures to organize a true southern Republican Party out of his electors.

The Nixon success in the South proves the Republican opportunity is permanent, the most unsettled problem in American domestic politics.

Yet the Republican Party's opportunity is teased with contrary temptations. For the South can be organized to Republican loyalty by taking advantage of either one or the other pressure. It can be organized, at its highest level, within the new cities of the South, by creating leadership out of the white-collar suburbanites and businessmen; or it can be organized generally out of racial fear, by a forthright Republican abandonment of all seeking of Negro votes in the North.

This second course can only envision a new and triple alliance between the Midwest farm belt, the racists of the Old South and those political forces in the Northern suburbs that more and more seek to exclude Negroes from their neighborhoods and segregate them in the old core cities.

On the strategic decision of Republican leadership in the next four years may hang America's domestic peace; and one can be sure that, as the Goldwater and Rockefeller wings of the Republican Party clash in their approach to 1964, this will lie, as much as anything else, at the heart of their quarrel.

The counterpart of the Republican opportunity is the problem of the new President. For he cannot, in any of the accepted ways, meet the pressure of Northern Negroes for government intervention in the South without losing the marginal but essential victory he won in the Old Confederacy in 1960. Unless, indeed, as the master politician of the United States, he can find ways to enlighten the leadership of Southern Democrats while simultaneously strengthening the best responsible leadership of Northern Negroes, and then bring them both to discuss reasonably the problems of race and integration—unless he does this, so portend the election results of 1960, he will be dramatically vulnerable to Republican counterattack in 1964.

An almost similar impression of Kennedy's vulnerability comes from a contrast in the structure of the vote for the Presidency and the vote for the two parties as expressed in Congressional and local races.

For when these two votes are separated and contrasted, any analyst must admit that the Republican Party, as a party, despite the least inspiring candidate since Alfred M. Landon in 1936, not only held its own but gained. The gross national figures on Congressional voting read that the Democratic Congressional tickets captured 55 per cent of the national vote and Republican Congressional tickets 45 per cent. Yet if one subtracts the states of the Old South, where few Republican Congressional candidates campaign at all, and examines the vote of the rest of the nation—then the Republicans amassed 48.8 per cent of the major party vote in the rest of the country. All across the country, wherever a break in vote structure can be detected, the break favored the Republicans. At the grass roots they wrenched away from Democrats complete control over both houses of no less than seven state legislatures and added control of one or another house of legislature in six additional states. They added two Senators. And, most importantly, they added twenty-one Congressmen to the number of seats they hold in the House of Representatives.

It is the Congressional results that most perplex political prediction. For it is in the character of new Congressmen, elected for the first time, that one normally detects ground-swells of American political movement—and in the first testing of the sixty-three freshmen Congressmen elected in 1960 (in the fight over the enlargement of the all-powerful House Rules Committee) Kennedy was later (in February of 1961) to observe that these new Congressmen voted against him by 44 to 19. If the American people chose in 1960 a man impatient to move his country forward, they also chose, to accompany him to Washington, the most conservative Congress in six years. For the apparent Democratic majority of 262 Representatives in the House includes 101 Democrats from the Old South—of whom more than half are permanent allies of the Republicans on most domestic matters. The Americans had chosen, in fact, to send to Washington a Congress that fell permanently short by twelve to twenty votes of giving John F. Kennedy a natural working majority.

The control of Congress by a President carries us into another realm of politics. Yet one cannot help but note how differently this problem of Congressional control presents itself to a Democratic and a Republican administration. For deep down there are enduring differences of philosophy between the two great American parties, differences so simple that the Americans accept them too casually.

The Democratic philosophy, usually unspoken but quite clear nonetheless, is that government is there to be used as an instrument of action. This philosophy has gathered together over the past half-century a varied assembly of Democratic loyalists—citizen groups who wish to use government for new departures, minority groups who want from government protection and advancement, labor groups and farmers in trouble who wish to influence or extend government's leverage on the national economy; it has also held to the Democratic Party the largest of its old components, the Southerners, who know by memory of defeat and occupation how powerful an instrument of action is the American federal government and who seek to retain a veto power always within it.

The Republican philosophy is entirely different, clearer in metaphysical terms yet murkier in political expression. It is the belief, deep down, that each citizen bears a responsibility in private life and in community life as great or greater than the responsibility of government to shape that life and community. Part of the Republican tragedy in recent years has been the inability of its thinkers to articulate this philosophy clearly enough to draw political conclusions and programs from it. Though this philosophy might, under certain circumstances, produce a President of enormous drive and visions, it has not done so in modern times. A Republican President, like Dwight D. Eisenhower, could easily sit in the White House with a Congress hostile to him for six years, and if, by lack of control of that Congress, no great federal matters moved forward, it abused neither his personality nor his philosophy.

For a Democratic President, however—like John F. Kennedy who, both by temperament and political philosophy, believes that the government he commands must act—the sense of inaction is galling, and the Congressional elections of 1960 are bitter to the taste. He cannot act freely or boldly, but must bargain for half a dozen or a dozen votes at each proposal and each movement forward until, finally, his directions and leadership become clear enough to the people at large to force Congress to follow—or give him a new Congress of his own in 1962.

Behind the raw figures of votes, both popular and electoral, and the catalogue of Senatorial, Congressional and state-house seats won or lost by both parties are other realities, more obscure, which make it difficult to determine whether the voting of 1960 was the beginning or close of an era.

Many observers held, in the afterflush of the election, that John F. Kennedy had succeeded in re-establishing the old Roosevelt electoral coalition of Southern white-big city-big labor-ethnic minority votes. Yet a closer examination makes it difficult to support this thesis—and raises the question whether the old Roosevelt coalition exists any longer even in potential.

Two great disruptive forces seem, from this election, to be permanently at work in the old coalition.

One is, as we have seen, the growing disaffection of the Southern element of the Democratic coalition, the growing yearning of many Southerners for a new home in a states'-rights Republican Party, their repudiation of the general purposes of the Democratic Party that expresses itself in the profound alienation of Southern Congressmen from the artificial Democratic majority in the House of Representatives.

The second is that huge but still unstable element of citizen participation, the heritage of the Stevenson years of leadership in the Democratic Party—for Stevenson changed the Democratic Party almost as much as did Franklin D. Roosevelt, by trumpeting to its service scores of thousands of emancipated middle-class Americans who fit into no neat category of occupations, traditions or pressure blocs. In Los Angeles County, for example, where Stevenson Democratic strength is so powerful, Kennedy ran 200,000 votes behind the local Democratic candidates for the State Assembly—not, local politicians insist, because of his religion, but because the citizen elements of the Democratic Party were indifferent to his appeal or embittered by his local alliances and so cut him. (In all of California, as a matter of fact, Kennedy ran 1,000,000 votes behind the Democratic registration there.) Where Kennedy ran ahead of his Party—as in New York, Minnesota or Michigan —he ran best where his citizen support was strongest and best meshed with his campaign.

In short, the old Democratic coalition of Roosevelt days can express itself only in the apparent majorities of Congressional representation. In the separate and individual local Congressional races each regional or minority group can support local Democratic candidates out of a conviction that government must act in their interests; but when these Democrats come together in Washington to act as special spokesmen on Capitol Hill, pressing the federal government to action or delaying it, they cannot agree on a common course. And when, finally, all the elements of the Democratic coalition must gather publicly to vote on a single man as national leader the weakness of the coalition becomes entirely clear. Not since 1944 has any Democratic candidate (Franklin D. Roosevelt) received a majority of the popular vote (51.7 per cent). Harry Truman in 1948 could win but 49.5 per cent of the American popular vote, and John F. Kennedy in 1960 but 49.9 per cent. To become a true majority President, John F. Kennedy must again recreate a majority party—a task that is not easy.

The Democratic Party over which Kennedy presides today puckers with problems, regional and national. In Massachusetts, his home state, he has so gutted the party machinery of its finest young talent for his national campaign and administration that Republicans carried both Senate and Governor's seats in the teeth of his enormous 1960 plurality. In New Jersey his no-quarter war against the forces of Governor Robert Meyner during the nominating campaign has split the party in two. In California his necessary spring alliances against the Stevenson forces to win the nomination has required of him a loyalty to men and groups that could easily undo the Democratic victories of 1958. In New York he presides over a Democratic Party whose disasters are not of his architecture[4] but whose misfortunes are his responsibility.

If the Democratic Party at best, in 1960, held even with the Republicans and at worst suffered a defeat, only one lasting conclusion can be drawn therefrom: that the election of 1960 was a personal victory for John F. Kennedy, not for his Party. When one strips off the Old South, where American politics are distorted by the race problem, John F. Kennedy in the states of his most important victories ran ahead of his Party or even with his Party—not behind. And whether his Party grows or dwindles in his incumbency, whether a new coalition of forces can be formed behind his leadership or the old coalition can be firmed up, will also be his personal responsibility.

But it has always been this way in American politics. So great is the power of the American Presidency that the President, whoever he is, sets the rules by himself. He creates the issues for each new departure in American politics by his actions and by his perceptions of what is right and wrong. Were one to accept the results of the voting of 1960 as static and final, one could easily see them as the end of the Roosevelt era that began in 1932, a testimonial to Eisenhower, an augury of Republican good fortune in 1964.

Yet the President of the United States has power to educate the people of America, to draw new battle lines. This book has been concerned with the system of American domestic politics. It has been thus concerned because no President can turn to the outer world and exercise the power of America abroad unless he is instinctively sure that at home he understands and can call on the full internal political loyalty of the American people. Franklin D. Roosevelt, more than any other President, could exert America's influence on the great outer world because he knew how to mobilize the internal politics of Amer-

---

[4] The plight of the New York Democratic Party is the legacy of Averell Harriman, and, as his legacy, is one of the most interesting studies in American political power. Over a period of fifteen years, no American proved more capable of exercising the end form of American power around the globe than Averell Harriman. In the sublime expression of American authority to such men as Churchill, Stalin, DeGaulle, Adenauer and Douglas MacArthur, Averell Harriman's instinct was as true and perfect as in his choice of early deputies for the operation of American foreign policy—men such as David Bruce, Charles Bohlen, William Foster, Milton Katz. Yet brought face to face with the domestic system of American power, no man proved more incapable of understanding it; and his performance of 1958 in directing the Democratic Party in New York not only destroyed the pride and honor of both machine and citizen elements of that Party but probably rendered the Party incapable of governing New York effectively again for years.

ica to support America's purpose. Woodrow Wilson, by contrast, whose perception of foreign affairs was as fine as Adlai Stevenson's, failed in the end to make lasting peace because he could not cause the American political system to follow him. Somehow, between the proper use of America's arsenal of nuclear bombs and the distribution of patronage, judgeships, honors and exemptions from prosecution lies the personal role and testing of the American President. At every time, in every place, those who understood their country's problems best at home could exercise their country's power best abroad—a rule that runs in time from Caesar to Clemenceau and in geography from Churchill to Mao Tze-tung.

The forces that run in American politics in our age are many and varied; they run in strange ways in our times of general education—they run in the meeting of white and black; in the nagging, daily concern for war and peace; in automation and unemployment. Yet one man must make them all clear enough for American people to vote and express their desire.

He is the President.

It is an entirely personal office. What the President of today decides becomes the issue of tomorrow. He calls the dance.

Having won a personal victory, John F. Kennedy must personally draw the rules for the next round of American politics—and perhaps for the entire world.

Chapter 15

THE VIEW FROM
THE WHITE HOUSE

SHORTLY before he died in 1950, the great Henry L. Stimson was asked which of the many Presidents of his acquaintance had been the best. Stimson, according to the man from whom I heard the tale, reflected a minute or two, for his career stretched over half a century of American history. He had known intimately or served importantly more Presidents, Democratic and Republican, than any other citizen of his age—from Theodore Roosevelt through Taft, Wilson, Coolidge and Hoover to Franklin D. Roosevelt and Harry S. Truman. After reflection, Stimson replied to his friend:

If, by the phrase "best President," the friend meant who had been the most efficient President—why, of course, the answer would be William Howard Taft. Under Taft, the Cabinet met in order, affairs marched to the agenda of the meeting, responsibility was clearly deputized, and when each man rose from the Cabinet table, he knew exactly what he was to do and to whom he was to report. Yes, Taft certainly was the most efficient. If, however, continued Stimson, by the "best President" one meant the "greatest President," then the answer must be different. The name would, without doubt, be Roosevelt—but he was not sure whether the first name was Theodore or Franklin. For both of these gentlemen, you see, not only understood the *use* of power; they knew the *enjoyment* of power, too. And that was the important thing.

Whether a man is burdened by power or enjoys power; whether he is trapped by responsibility or made free by it; whether he is moved by other people and outer forces or moves them—this is of the essence of leadership.

John F. Kennedy had known much of the quality of leadership in American life long before he became President in 1960—the legends, delights, songs, deals and reach of power in all its American forms had been talk in his family since childhood. From parents and grandparents he had learned of leadership and power in the Boston wards and Massachusetts districts, in City Hall and on Capitol Hill, in the upper reaches of American finance and American diplomacy. To this he had added his own experience and savor of power in academies of learning and manipulation of public communications—as well as in the leading and commanding of men under enemy fire. All this he had known before 1960, and in that year he added to his knowledge the experience of direct acquisition of power as he dealt with, then mastered, all the power brokers and power forms that stir American internal politics. To this had further been added his growing intellectual conviction that the greatest leadership and most sublime form of power is that of the Presidency of the United States. No candidate in modern times has so urgently yearned for the power of the Presidency—or more eloquently or precisely declaimed what that power is to the people he sought to lead. From the earliest primaries in the snows of spring he had chanted "the Presidency is the key office"—and he had meant it.

Yet to him, as to any other man, the Presidency could come in 1961 only as entirely new experience. For there is no apprenticeship a man can serve for the Presidency, no book nor any guide to the creative powers of the individual who leads the greatest of the world's free people, no instructive analysis of an office bound and defined not so much by law as by the nature of men and the pressures of history.

A one-time personal aide of President Truman once put the matter to me in this way: "The most startling thing a new President discovers is that his world is *not* monolithic. In the world of the Presidency, giving an order does not *end* the matter. You can pound your fist on the table or you can get mad or you can blow it all and go out to the golf course. But nothing gets done except by endless follow-up, endless kissing and coaxing, endless threatening and compelling. There are all those thousands of people in Washington working for you in the government—and every one is watching you, waiting, trying to guess what you mean, trying to get your number. Can they fool you? Can they outwait you? Will you be mad when you hear it isn't done yet? And Congress keeps shoving more and more power into the President's lap—the Formosa resolution gives the President power to declare war all by himself; and Congress keeps setting up new regulatory agencies, and you have to hire and fire the men who run them. And they're all testing you. How much can they get away with? How much authority can they take? How much authority do *you* want them to have? And once you choose your men—you have to keep them; which means the endless attrition of *your* will against *their* will, because some of them will be damned good men. You can't run this government unless you run the Pentagon, because that takes forty billion dollars out of the whole eighty billion in the budget; but you can't control *that* unless you control your generals *and* your Joint Chiefs-of-Staff *and* your National Security Council. But you can't do anything in defense unless you talk it over with your Secretary of State—and he'll have ideas, too. And then your Secretary of the Treasury will fight with you for days over a quarter-per-cent rise in the interest rate because it's important to him—but it's important to you, too. And those goddam bureaucrats—controlling *them!* Those regulatory agencies are so important now that they really control the whole economy. But who controls them unless you do? And a President gets out of those agencies only what he puts into them with his own energy."

The powers of the American Presidency, constitutionally and pragmatically, have been a subject of endless fascination to American political scientists.[1] By now the simple catalogue of Presidential duties is booklength. The President is Commander-in-Chief of all our armed forces, with power to promote, demote, reward and punish 2,500,000 soldiers, sailors, airmen in uniform; he deploys them, launches them, lets them lie idle. He is also chief architect of national legislation, and polices Congress with his veto. His is the power of pardon and reprieve over 22,500 prisoners in federal penitentiaries. He appoints all 361 judges of the federal judiciary, from Chief Justice of the Supreme Court down; he sets the rules and tasks of 2,400,000 federal civil servants; he is chief appointive officer for forty major commissions and agencies outside the departments of his Cabinet, for which he names 200 members with Senate approval, and 200 other responsible policy-making members on his own. He is chief diplomatic officer, designer of our foreign policy, and must recognize the names of chiefs of state and the chief American diplomatic representatives in 138 states abroad with full claim or aspiring pretensions to sovereignty, as well as a dozen-odd international bodies such as the United Nations and NATO. He is responsible for supervision of our economy, for the rate of its credit, the peace and harmony of its industrial relations, the throb of its commerce, and the interlocking of this commerce with world trade. He is high ceremonial officer for all public occasions of state. And he alone must, by law, decide when and how the nuclear weapons of America's cataclysmic arsenal

---

[1] It is almost impossible to list all the major books on the Presidency and its powers published recently. Among the best, however, one should note: Sydney B. Hyman, *The American President;* Professor Herman Finer, *The Presidency: Crisis and Regeneration;* Clinton Rossiter, *The American Presidency;* and Richard E. Neustadt, *Presidential Power.*

will be used if the death of the world becomes preferable to slow surrender.

On and on, endlessly, runs the catalogue of Presidential duties and powers defined either in law or by custom. And for each of them a vast battery of human instruments has grown up, an instrumentation so complex that even if a President spent all his years in office studying them, he would never learn how they function in detail.

These instruments of American government are, by and large, superb. So many and so able are the President's advisers of the permanent services of Defense, State, Treasury, Agriculture, that when crisis happens all necessary information is instantly available, all alternate courses already plotted. Only rarely is there danger of major, irrevocable stupidity. Yet for this, too, if it happens, he is responsible.

What separates the major from the minor Presidents is, however, not stupidity, blunder or crisis—it is something else. It is a President's ability, unaided, to see beyond the instruments and beyond his scouts; it is his ability to perceive and seize initiative.

For the laws of Congress cannot define, nor can custom anticipate, the unknown—and this is where the great Presidents must live, observant of the law yet beyond the law, Chief Executive and High Priest of American life at once.

This power of the will, this intellectual energy to imagine and perceive, this imposition of his own design on the living instruments of government and the customs of American politics—it is these qualities, *the expression of his initiative,* that cause a President to be remembered or forgotten.

No law permitted Thomas Jefferson to double the territory of the United States by the irresistible opportunity offered in the Louisiana Purchase; he acted on his own initiative. No law or passage of the Constitution defined what a President must do in the spring of 1861 when citizens of individual states, declaring themselves independent of the Constitution, seized those few post offices and forts in the Southern states that made concrete the authority of the then-primitive federal government. Yet Lincoln perceived that this was an act of war, accepted it as war, and made war. The antitrust laws of the 1890s had lain dead on the books for more than a decade when Theodore Roosevelt became President—it was he alone who made them come alive and thus he who reshaped the system of American enterprise. It was the initiative of Harry Truman that distilled new perspectives out of a Mediterranean crisis in the spring of 1947—an act of imagination that, departing from the troubles of Greece and Turkey, became in

execution, first the Marshall Plan, which saved freedom in
Europe, and then evolved into NATO, which armored and
defended that freedom. And when Dwight D. Eisenhower is
remembered as President twenty years hence, it is probable
his administration will be remembered, not—as it was lately
championed—for "Peace and Prosperity," but chiefly for the
major initiatives within it—the highway program that is
changing Amerca's face, and the solid-fuel missiles that are
changing her strategy.

Yet the initiative of imagination and execution, the touch-
stone of greatness in leaders, is, for the American Presidency,
particularly complex.

For the President of the United States is not only all the
many men listed in the official catalogue of his powers—he
is also the nation's chief educator, the nation's chief persuader,
the nation's master politician. Where he leads, his party, his
instruments, above all his reluctant people, must be persuaded
to follow.

In other systems it is not so; and one need only examine the
performance of great executives in other times and other
places to see how forbiddingly complicated is the job of the
American Presidency. I can recall, for example, out of all
the many superlative performances of American legates about
the globe after the war, the performance of Lucius D. Clay,
Military Governor, then High Commissioner, of Occupied
Germany. There, in Germany, within the five years 1945–
1949, he performed prodigies of statecraft. All German lay
gutted before him, its traditions, will and pride destroyed with
its vile armies. But under Clay's captaincy, a brilliant burst
of American genius shaped a new constitution for Germany,
reorganized its industry, set its people to work again, established a new press in decency, rewrote the textbooks of
its schools, refashioned its laws and courts. It was and remains
a dazzling performance, and Lucius Clay, even more than
Konrad Adenauer, must be recognized as the architect of the
New Germany. Yet the executive performance of Clay in those
five years, brilliant, initiatory and imaginative as it was, was
not, in the American sense, a *political* performance. For
General Clay commanded the American Army of Occupation;
his divisions and constabulary policed a nation forbidden free
expression of its will. By decree, as conqueror and military
dictator, he could abolish one currency and replace it with
another; he could imprison, condemn or reprieve without
restraint of court; a new idea that occurred to any member of
his staff and found approval at his desk could be imposed—no
voice in Germany could protest, no legislature stay his govern-

ment of the land. General Clay could command events—he need not persuade.

But a President governing the United States can move events only if he can first persuade. Each Presidency is unique, for each President must face in his own time an area of new unknowns, where both answers and questions are fresh, where only his instinct can produce those initiatives that the nation unknowingly and unwillingly requires, where only his skill can persuade the nation to follow. This art of persuasion is politics —yet entirely different from the kind of politics that brings a man to the White House.

For the winning of the President's power lies in noise and clangor, the flogging of the emotions and the appeal to all the tribal pasts of America.

But the exercise of the President's power must be framed by reason, by the analysis of reality as it can only be seen from the President's desk—and by leading other men to see this reality as he alone perceives it.

A hush, an entirely personal hush, surrounds this kind of power, and the hush is deepest in the Oval Office of the West Wing of the White House, where the President, however many his advisers, must sit alone.

The Oval Office, thirty-five feet long by twenty-eight feet, four inches wide, is almost too peaceful and luminous a place to echo to the ominous concerns that weigh upon the man who occupies it. Its great French windows, eleven and a half feet high, flood it with light, so that even on somber days it is never dark. From the south windows the President can, in leafless winter, see through the trees all the way to the Washington Monument and beyond; he can, by craning, see west to the Memorial where Lincoln broods. The three windows on the east open out on the lawn, on the rose garden and the brilliance of flowers in spring and summer; when he chooses, the President can enter or leave the Oval Office by one of these east windows, which opens as a door, going to or from his private dwelling place in the heart of the White House.

The tones of the room are as perfect as its proportions. The gray-green expanse of carpeting, into which is woven the Great Seal of the United States, is keyed to the same pastel tonality as the cream-beige walls and the beige draperies. The room changes somewhat from President to President, as it has changed from Eisenhower to Kennedy. Where in Eisenhower's time the room possessed an uncluttered, almost overpowering openness as one approached the seven-foot, four-inch dark walnut desk at which Eisenhower (as all other Presidents since 1902) sat, it has been softened now with two new curving cream-white sofas before the fireplace that invite the visitor to a respectful closeness with the President. Where the walls, in Eisenhower's time, were gay with the meadow-and-mountain colors of the landscape paintings he liked, they are now hung with the gentler faded grays and blues of old naval paintings and naval prints that reflect the taste of the new, more maritime, President. Yet the flags behind the new President's desk—an oaken shipboard desk made of the timbers of the old USS *Resolute*—are the same, the flag of the Union behind him and to his right, the personal purple-and-gold Presidential flag behind him and to his left. And the hush, too, is the same—for the room is all but soundless. When the windows are closed, the sound of Washington traffic, which hums as it passes by outside, is entirely locked out, and one is reminded that these windows are three inches thick of laminated glass, thick enough to stop an assassin's rifle bullet from beyond the grounds—if the assassin gets time enough to sight.

There is no power here that one can see or touch, there is no haste or noise or any manifest pounding of pressure.

But on his desk is the telephone console, and one who sits with the President is frequently mesmerized by the telephone —for in the technology of modern American politics the telephone has the symbolism of the sword or the mace in the politics of the middle ages. Politicians at every level of power in the United States talk of the telephone as if it were the knight's lance. I once asked a small politician why that amiable and much-abused man, Robert Wagner, wanted to go on being Mayor of New York. "Ah," said my respondent, "you've got to understand what it means being Mayor. Suppose its raining outside when he wakes up in the morning and he lays there in bed and he feels lousy, so suddenly the idea comes to him that he's going to name old Joe McBlank's son as magistrate. So he lifts the telephone by his bed and he says that's how it's going to be and all of a sudden he feels good again. You've got to understand the power a mayor has." The telephone is similarly an obsession with governors. Over and over again in talks with governors (which are held best when the men have already lost their legal powers), the memory that cuts most sharply on their emotions is that of sitting beside a telephone at night while a criminal is being readied for execution; only the governor's voice from his mansion to the execution chamber can reprieve or pardon the condemned. No governor I have ever spoken to, however mean some of them were, took such a moment lightly—life and death of an individual depended on *his* voice over the telephone.[2]

At the other end of the White House telephone system lies not only life and death, reprieve or pardon, of individuals—but life and death of the human race. In the armories of the American people lie the bombs and bomb material for thirty-five kilomegatons (the rough equivalent of thirty-five billion tons of TNT) of thermonuclear blast. This figure is meaningless except as projected against that scientific shorthand abbreviation of destruction called "DOE." "DOE" means "Death on Earth"—a rough calculation of how much thermonuclear blast it would take to wipe out every living thing on earth by polluting the atmosphere with nuclear poisons. By the end of 1960, America's thirty-five kilomegatons of fission-fusion explosives were one eighth of the quantity needed to bring DOE—more than enough to wipe out two thirds of Russia's population and bring the retaliation that would wipe out two thirds of ours.[3]

All this lies at the end of the telephone system that surfaces on the desk of the President in the Oval Office. Neither the commanding general of the Strategic Air Command at Omaha nor the Commanding General of NATO in his headquarters at Rocquencourt, France, can release any part of America's nuclear power against any adversary except by word from this desk. At any moment of the day or night an undisclosed number of America's bombers are in the air, their bomb bays filled with enough nuclear weapons to wipe out at least half a dozen of Russia's largest cities and invite the wiping out of half a dozen of ours. These American planes are in the air now; they drone around the clock; they are armed and ready; yet they cannot proceed beyond certain undisclosed parallels on the approaches to the North Pole without direct word from this desk, in this quiet room.

Nor can the President ever escape from this responsibility. Two systems of communication bring their webs together on his eighteen-button telephone console. One is, of course, the civilian web staffed by the White House operators, who are trained at any moment of day or night to track down any man the President wants to reach, who possess access to all secret and unlisted numbers, who must know the habits, movements,

---

[2] General de Gaulle of France, who operates in another tradition of power, will permit no telephone at all in his private office.
[3] The best contemporary discussion that I know of of America's destructive power and of arms control is *The Nation's Safety and Arms Control* by Arthur T. Hadley, published by the Viking Press.

and personal hideaway of any individual to whom the President's attention turns.

The other web is that of the U.S. Army's Signal Corps—distinguished on the console only by two colored buttons, an amber button and a red. The amber controls a direct line to an army switchboard that links the President's desk instantaneously to the desk of various Cabinet members and directors of critical agencies and a few select members of his personal White House staff. The red button is the "maximum security" button, a special line that scrambles the President's voice electronically so that no one without a similar button on his desk can unscramble or make sense of what the voice says. Both amber and red buttons on the President's desk, when he wishes, are linked instantaneously to yet another switchboard in the war room at the Pentagon—and from there, the reach of his voice is global. Sixteen "red lines" (so it is said; the actual number is impossible to report) link this war room to every nerve center of American power around the globe—to the bomber bases in continental America and overseas, to foreign capitals, to the seats of our alliances. And when the President calls, no matter how important or urgent any other call on the "red line," the line is yanked in midconversation and the President speaks.

It is this second, or military, web that follows him personally, wherever he may be. If Washington must, in emergency, be immediately evacuated, the President will depart instantly for a secret command post—and there the web is already installed with direct lines to all the prepared emergency evacuation offices of all critical agencies and of his military command. If the President leaves for vacation, if he journeys overseas on a diplomatic or ceremonial visit—the web will precede him and the United States Army will have ready for him the wires and the relays to tie his voice of command to any resolution of American decision.

It takes time for any man to adjust to this sense of power; yet no President in recent memory has used his telephone more constantly, more directly, more intrusively in all the affairs of all his executive departments and bureaus than John F. Kennedy—nor has any President more insistently, or more sincerely, urged his staff, his generals, his Cabinet secretaries, foreign ambassadors and foreign chiefs of state to call him directly, personally, at the White House when there is a problem he must quickly resolve.

Yet except for a handful of men on his personal staff, few dare avail themselves of the privilege. They approach him, when they need to see him, through his secretariat; they await his call and wait for his direction to move them; and, in the Oval Office, the telephone is silent—it rings with few or no incoming messages, it quivers, generally, only as he exerts his will through it.

The President's day—on any day—is as crowded with the world as the front page of a daily newspaper. For to him, news is not simply news but a report of his triumphs, his defeats and the stretch of his inescapable problems. The mind of the man must shift and wheel over the entire range of the American experience.

Thus, for example, in early winter of 1961, when John F. Kennedy was only a few weeks installed in his Presidency, a typical Thursday ran thus:

Early-morning reports by his personal staff on his appointments and the parade of daily visitors; the CIA's report on the doings and restlessness of friendly and hostile states around the world.

Then, to start the formal day, half an hour with former President Harry S. Truman, a pleasant breezy personal meeting; then a serious session of an hour and ten minutes with Atomic Energy Commissioner Glenn Seaborg, personal science adviser Jerome Wiesner, Budget Director David Bell, to review the science budget of the Atomic Energy Commission.

Then the twenty-five-minute courtesy call of American Ambassador Thomas Finletter, departing to take up his embassy to NATO in Paris; another brief discussion of France, DeGaulle and the problems in Paris with the new Ambassador to France, General James Gavin. A session then with the Cotton Growers Committee on Textiles, eight Southerners with whom the new President must review the whole interlocked problem of necessary American exports to Japan of cotton and the perplexing problem of imports of finished Japanese fabrics made of this cotton.

Then to the private quarters of the White House and a brief film-take to explain his views on the Peace Corps. An entirely private lunch with personal friends; after which the President returned to the White House for two ceremonial appointments—with the National Commander of the Veterans of World War I, and with the new and charming Treasurer of the United States, Elizabeth Smith of California.

Then the supreme and somber problem of war and peace: a long meeting of one and one quarter hours in the cabinet room with Secretary of State Dean Rusk; Secretary of Na-

tional Defense Robert S. McNamara; Chairman of the Joint
Chiefs of Staff, General Lyman Lemnitzer; Admiral Harry
D. Felt, Commander-in-Chief, Pacific theater; two personal
advisers, McGeorge Bundy and Walter Rostow; and Vice-
President of the United States Lyndon B. Johnson. Here at
this meeting he considered, not for the first time but for
the *decisive* time, American response to the newest thrust
of Communist pressure on the changing world—the movement of Communist guerillas over the jungles and ridges of
Southeast Asia into the formless Kingdom of Laos. Could
anything be done there, and if it could, should anything be
done there? This was the ugliest of problems; and if his
decisions were right the meeting would fade into history as
unimportant; but if the decisions brought war, then this,
indeed, was where the Americans chose war.

Then, from this meeting, freighted with ultimate dangers,
to another ceremony—the swearing in of the new Director of
the Office of Civil and Defense Mobilization. And, all the
while, all day long, in the background, the incoming reports of his staff—on the morning testing of Presidential
strength and purpose in the House Committee on Education,
the first trial of his massive Education bill; the reports on the
progress of his feed-grain bill through the House of Representatives; the reports on the first response that day to his
new program of housing and urban renewal; a quick glance
through the ceremonial album of photographs prepared for
an African Chief of State who had visited him in the White
House only the day before. Then another conference, with
Budget Director David Bell; his national security adviser,
McGeorge Bundy; his science adviser, Jerome Wiesner; his
personal personal adviser, Ted Sorensen, on the budget for
science—and coffee was hastily served to all of them from a
silver service before the President went on to the late
evening's work and ceremonies.

At the end of such a day, when I saw him last, one wonders
whether any man can be coherent. One lets him relax in
conversation. And perhaps because it is easier to reminisce
about the solid past at the end of such a day, he began by
reflecting on the election itself. He called it a "miracle," the
way it had turned out. He recalled the vote of individual
cities (whose citizens relaxed that evening all unaware of
the menace of Laos), and analyzed the vote and compared his
1960 totals with those of Alfred E. Smith in 1928; he commented on how the country had changed. From that to the
personality of Richard M. Nixon, which puzzled him—why
had Nixon, whom he knew as a forthright, cogent speaker

in private, talked that way to the American people in the
election? He said he had been browsing recently through
a collection of Nixon's campaign speeches and the style ap-
palled him. Why had Nixon talked *down* to the people? A man
running for the Presidency must talk up, way up there. From
that to the problem of Congress and the kind of Congress
that had been elected—and how narrowly a few hours before, by only seven votes, his bill on feed grains had passed
the House. But all of that—the housing program, the feed-
grain bill, even the education bill—that was not the real
problem. The real problem was out there (with a wave of
his hand)—out there in Laos, in the Congo, in Africa. Thus,
then, to one of his favorite themes, leadership and the kinds
of leaders you had to find around the world who could lead
their people—and now he began to rattle off names of
Laotians and Congolese, styling them in personality as, six
months before, he had been able to rattle off the names and
style the leaders of the delegations to the Democratic Convention in Los Angeles. Then to China, feeling his way and
musing on the apparently adamant, rigid Chinese state of
mind on Formosa and how that mind could be reached. Then
back to Africa, this time with a burst of confidence—think
of all the new states that had come into being there in the
last year or so, and not one of them, not even Guinea, could
be considered a Communist gain yet. It was a matter of
pressures; and our pressure on them was as constant as
their pressure on us; and he talked briefly, briskly about the
shape of strategy around the globe as it seemed to be coming
clear.

After a while, when it came time for me to go, he rose
from his desk where he had been sitting in shirt sleeves, knee
hooked over his wastebasket, and seemed to want to press
one more point as we stood by the door. It was as if there
were an echo, here on another level, in the quiet Oval Office,
of all the speeches he had made in all the squares and supermarkets of the country. The problem, he insisted, was in-
ertia. How could you get things moving? For years a Democratic Congress had sat with a Republican President and, as
an opposition Congress, had become unused to thinking in
national terms. Each Congressman had been free to think
in terms of his own district, of his own seat. They could vie
with the President in deflationary orthodoxy, and freeze
their thinking on keeping the country as is. Now this Democratic Congress had to learn to think again in national terms
—in national goals, in national movement, new things. You
had to move it forward.

He had won this office and this power by promising such movement to the American people. Now he had to keep the promise. He seemed very little changed in movement or in gracefulness from the candidate; only his eyes had changed —very dark now, very grave, markedly more sunken and lined at the corners than those of the candidate. The candidate had yearned for this office; now all the problems were his; now he must resolve them; and for John F. Kennedy in the sixties, the problems would be particularly difficult.

It was the atmospherics of 1960, more than anything else, that made it possible for John F. Kennedy's political exertions to triumph over the many divided pasts of the American people. And these atmospherics, as much as anything else, define the unique nature of his problem.

For 1960 was a year of national concern—but vague, shapeless, unsettling, undefinable national concern. It was a year in which the Congress of the United States saw fit for the first time to hold formal hearings on the National Purpose; it was a year in which the outgoing President of the United States saw fit to leave as his legacy to the incoming President and the people an official paper that, for the first time in American history, self-consciously attempted to define the National Goals. It was a political year ushered in, symbolically, by the greatest newspaper in the country, *The New York Times,* finding fit to print on its front page a dispatch from Moscow that reported that the *Russians* had now taken to referring to *themselves* as "the greatest power on earth"—a proud vulgarity hitherto reserved for Americans alone. It was a year in which Americans sensed the world about them changing as the politics of entire continents overseas changed; and they knew their own world to be changing too.

It was a year, above all, in which Americans were concerned with their identity. For Britons and Frenchmen, Russians and Germans, Arabs and Chinese, can pass through the uncadenced measure of time and history, swinging from greatness to nothingness and back again—yet still remain Britons, Frenchmen, Russians, Germans, Arabs or Chinese. But America is a nation created by all the hopeful wanderers of Europe, not out of geography and genetics, but out of purpose—by what men sought in fair government and equal opportunity. If other nations falter in greatness, their people remain still what they were. But if America falters in greatness and purpose, then Americans are nothing but the offscourings and hungry of other lands.

This was the central problem of the campaign of 1960—and yet it was a problem that could show itself in no visible, tangible crisis.

This lack of crisis was Kennedy's political campaign problem—and remains his Presidential problem. In his election, John F. Kennedy was able to persuade enough Americans that their vague concerns were justified enough to require a change in leadership that might arrest those trends carrying America irresistibly to less noble ends than those for which men believed their fathers had come to this country. He could not define, nor did he try to define, what measures he would take to arrest the disturbing drift that might make other nations greater than America; nor did he define those sacrifices that his cheering crowds offered to accept. Dwight D. Eisenhower can be seen historically as the man elected to end the Korean War, which he did. Franklin D. Roosevelt can be seen historically as a man elected to reorganize and refresh the American economy in the year of its worst collapse. These were vivid tangible crises, in which the American people required and received direct action of their elected leaders.

But John F. Kennedy was inaugurated in 1961, to preside over a nation to which no crisis was clear. The nation recognized, or at least it so indicated by its voting for him, that it sensed crisis—but crisis locked in the womb of time, swelling uncomfortably in embryo, crisis whose countenance was still unclear. If there were any mandate in the election of 1960, it was that the new President prepare for such obscure crises.

Yet he must first make them recognizable. The essential problems that lay on the desk of the new President in 1961 at his inauguration were none of them the kind that permitted him yes-or-no answers or a choice between sharply defined alternatives.

For the questions, as much as the answers, had to be invented first—and it would require not only all his astonishing political creativity to make Americans see the questions as he posed them, but even more, an act of historic intellectual perception to define the questions first.

At any point where one chose to look at the problems of America as a President must look at them, it was apparent that an entirely new order of thinking had to be brought to bear.

§ There were the unbelievable problems of education and knowledge, for it was American education, as much as America's resources or American courage or American enterprise, that had made this country great. Yet knowledge, increasing at its own impossible acceleration, could not provide the wisdom either for its own dissemination or for its own control.

At one level, in its dissemination, the spread of learning was the most acute of narrow political problems. All Americans agreed that the country needed more education, both in quantity and quality. Yet in the teaching of our children, the most intense forces of narrow politics clashed: Catholics of the extreme would have federal action conditioned only on state aid to church schools; Negroes of the extreme would suspend aid to any community that did not meet their interpretation of the doctrine of integration.

At another level, the use of knowledge and science in a democracy was a problem of civilization itself. During World War II, no nation managed its scientific brain power better or more brilliantly absorbed it in its national purpose than did America in the Office of Scientific Research and Development. Yet that brilliant improvisation was discarded in the postwar years and, instead, the most extravagant and generous policy of support for science degenerated into a system now unmanageable. Mere federal generosity to science would not solve the problem—the lavish federal appropriation for science in 1960 ($750,000,000 for pure, or basic research; $8,000,000,000 for all research and development) was, according to most scientists, more than adequate for all their needs. But it did not solve their problem of responsibility and direction. Who would judge the scientists? How were scientists and wise men to deal with political authority? How could they be freed of administrative entanglements to do their best? Who would decide which, and in what priority, of the many frontiers that they defined the nation would explore first?

§ What of the problems of the common wealth, both short-term and long-range? Could the disturbing cycles of the American economy in the 1960s be cured by the liberal nostrums that worked so well in the 1930s? Or had technology and a generation's development since 1933 so changed the nature of the American economy that the liberal answers of the thirties were, in the sixties, as constricting as the conservative orthodoxy of the twenties? And over the long-range—was it wise or foolish to match the growth rates of the Soviet Union, the United States and Western Europe in the mythological percentages of gross national product? Should American growth rates be stimulated to overtake the growth rates of other nations, growth rates peculiar to the needs of those specific societies—or should growth be stimulated to other forms of achievement, best fitting America's own unique needs?

§ In area after area of American life, the very questions posed by government code and regulation were entirely obsolete, and the answers to these obsolete questions would provide only obsolete answers. Nothing, for example, could be achieved of a large or revolutionary order in the chaotic confusion of American domestic transportation with the tools of regulations-and-rates inherited from the past. The competitive rivalries of trucks with railroads with airlines with private automobiles could be solved by no adjustment of taxes, by no system of road building, by no rate adjustments or abatements, by no appropriations for electronic separation of hurtling planes in the crowded sky. None of these rivalries could be reasonably governed by the traditional machinery of federal and state regulations, but only by entirely new concepts of national need; yet this could happen only after the first questions had been properly posed.

So too with the whole ramshackle structure of federal taxes, a tangled growth of imposts tacked on to the last clear thought on taxation back in Woodrow Wilson's time. No adjustment for tax grievance in any one sector of American life, no denial of established tax privilege to any other sector of American life could correct the federal tax system without creating new injustices. Taxes required thinking through all over again.

§ There were Constitutional problems swelling in the American system. So much of the old Constitution still had the quality of living genius—but so much else was obsolete. How, for example, under the federal Constitution could the federal government intervene in local government? And yet unless someone did intervene, the great sprawling belts of suburban-metropolitan growth, described by the census of 1960 as flopping across all municipal, township and state lines, would become increasingly ungovernable. How could the central cities be saved for their great cultural purposes and the suburbs be financed against their inevitable future needs, when township, municipal and state governments alike were powerless, legally, to act? And how about a Constitution that admitted an Alaska (with 224,000 inhabitants) to Senatorial equality with New York (16,500,000 inhabitants), that admitted a Hawaii (620,000 inhabitants) to equality with a California (15,500,000 inhabitants)?

§ And what of the problem of race, where the nation seemed paralyzed in search of a living, fair solution by an extreme white, an extreme Negro, and an extreme center dogma?

Here, in the problems of race relations, the most passionate and personal of all domestic problems, all thinking seemed manacled by dogma. It was obvious that the nation could not any longer live as two communities bearing two separate cultures, white and Negro, in its bosom. It was obvious that only education could bring the two cultures together in common standards. It was further obvious that this must be done in orderly fashion, by judgment on individuals as individuals, and on children as children. Yet the clashing dogmas demanded, on the one hand, that each child be irrevocably committed to a particular segregated sort of schooling by the color of his skin, and, on the other hand, that all children must mingle, at once, ready or not, whether their backgrounds and fitness were ready for harmony or not—as if all must sit at the table at once or none at all.

Race was only one of the problems obscured by dogma. For both the Republican and Democratic parties seemed frozen in dogma; and paradoxically, the most intellectual and idea-seeking President since Woodrow Wilson had arrived in office at a moment when American political invention seemed at its most sterile.

It was the problem of the President to cut through all these dogmas and pose the questions clearly—then give the answers to be judged. Yet of all the perilous families of dogma, the one that was certainly the most dangerous was that which froze the greater world that locked America round. For in facing out over the seas, the President faced a world whose inflexible thinking dates back not merely thirty or forty years (as did the chief current American political thinking) but back to sixty and seventy years ago, when the dogmas of communism and anti-communism were then, for the first time, fresh.

Here, in dealing with the outer world, the President had to contend with minds that had fossilized about ideas that were old before he was born. And on his dealing with such minds and ideas depended life and death not only for Americans—but for all humankind. He must deal abroad with schizophrenics—European, Asian and African—who believed, on the one hand, as an article of faith that the directionless technical mind of man creates its own faceless logic, its own irresistible dialectic that puts decision more and more in the hands of masses who are "engines of history." Yet on the other hand, these same schizophrenic leaders must certainly know that technology more and more removes decision from the hands of masses and puts it in their own moral or immoral hands.

So the President must play a three-dimensional chess game of war and peace—deploying missiles and warheads and submarines and airborne troops on a map that, to him, is clear, with weights that, to him, are measurable. Yet while reading the known map, the known weights and known speeds, he must fathom the mind of adversaries reading the same map, weights and speeds, and guess how they will read it. For if they miscalculate, then all his reason will be miscalculation too.

In the sixties, the office of the Presidency, which John F. Kennedy held, was above all an intellectual exercise. For the courage and skill required in the sixties in war and peace was no longer the simple manly courage and skill that dominated war from the days of the caveman to the last screaming combat of American P-51 and Japanese Zero over Okinawa. Of this old courage and skill, this new President of the United States had much. He was the first President of the United States to be born in the twentieth century; yet he was an authentic hero in one of the last wars that permitted any man to test his nerve and will against enemy fire in distant country and, by nerve and will, save both himself and his men with honor. But such courage and nerve is, in modern war, all but obsolete. This old kind of courage may possibly be reflected in an ultimate decision over the telephone console to trade the death of New York for the death of Moscow, the death of Los Angeles for the death of Leningrad, the death of Washington for the death of Peking. But it would require greater courage and exertion of mind to decide to change the rules of the new chess game, and greater skill to persuade his adversaries and friends, at home and abroad, to abandon dogma and meet him on the plains of reality.

It could be certain only, at the beginning of the incumbency of the thirty-fifth President of the United States, that he would try.

One could only imagine what he had learned from the exercise in politics that was 1960, what he might bring from a testing of will and power at one level to the testing of will and power at a higher level; one could only reflect again on the long year from the first glimpse of the preposterous young man in the snows of Wisconsin to the shirt-sleeved man, twelve months but many years older, in the Oval Office of the White House.

Above all it seemed, as one reflected on the exercise of 1960, that he had been able to recognize and distinguish between those great faceless forces that were changing his country and the individuals who influenced those forces. For if it is true that history is moved on by remorseless forces greater than any man, it is nonetheless true that individual men by individual decision can channel, or deftly guide, those impersonal forces either for the good or to disastrous collision. He had set out on his course in 1960 believing that if he understood the forces shaping America and could know, influence, and compel the partnership of the men who spoke for those forces, then he might come to command America's power. All the way, throughout the exercise, he alone had had to define the forces pressing on the leaders he must conscript, punish, defeat or win over—and, at every turn, make solitary judgment on himself and on how his own will and desire would affect such leaders.

Never, at any moment, even the most grotesque, in the exercise of 1960, had he believed that men were powerless to ask new questions or define new rules, or that individuals were helpless as the "engines of history" rolled toward them. He had always acted as if men were masters of forces, as if all things were possible for men determined in purpose and clear in thought—even the Presidency.

This perhaps is what he had best learned in 1960—even though he called his own victory a "miracle." This was what he would have to cherish alone in the White House, on which an impatient world waited for miracles.

APPENDIXES

AND

INDEX

APPENDIX A
Final Presidential Vote

STATE	TOTAL VOTE	REPUB.	%	DEMO.	%	OTHER	%
Ala.	564,242	237,981	42.2	318,303	56.4	7,958	1.4
Alaska	60,762	30,953	50.9	29,809	49.1	—	—
Ariz.	398,491	221,241	55.5	176,781	44.4	469	0.1
Ark.	428,509	184,508	43.1	215,049	50.2	28,952	6.7
Calif.	6,507,082	3,259,722	50.1	3,224,099	49.5	23,261	0.4
Colo.	736,246	402,242	54.6	330,629	44.9	3,375	0.5
Conn.	1,222,883	565,813	46.3	657,055	53.7	15	—
Del.	196,683	96,373	49.0	99,590	50.6	720	0.4
Fla.	1,544,180	795,476	51.5	748,700	48.5	4	—
Ga.	733,349	274,472	37.4	458,638	62.6	239	—
Hawaii	184,745	92,403	50.0	92,342	50.0	—	—
Idaho	300,451	161,597	53.8	138,853	46.2	1	—
Ill.	4,757,394	2,368,988	49.8	2,377,846	50.0	10,560	0.2
Ind.	2,135,360	1,175,120	55.0	952,358	44.6	7,882	0.4
Iowa	1,273,820	722,381	56.7	550,565	43.2	874	0.1
Kan.	928,825	561,474	60.4	363,213	39.1	4,138	0.5
Ky.	1,124,462	602,607	53.6	521,855	46.4	—	—
La.	807,891	230,980	28.6	407,339	50.4	169,572	21.0
Me.	421,767	240,608	57.0	181,159	43.0	—	—
Md.	1,055,349	489,538	46.4	565,808	53.6	3	—
Mass.	2,469,480	976,750	39.6	1,487,174	60.2	5,556	0.2
Mich.	3,318,097	1,620,428	48.8	1,687,269	50.9	10,400	0.3
Minn.	1,541,887	757,915	49.1	779,933	50.6	4,039	0.3
Miss.	298,171	73,561	24.7	108,362	36.3	116,248	39.0
Mo.	1,934,422	962,221	49.7	972,201	50.3	—	—
Mont.	277,579	141,841	51.1	134,891	48.6	847	0.3
Neb.	613,095	380,553	62.1	232,542	37.9	—	—
Nev.	107,267	52,387	48.8	54,880	51.2	—	—
N.H.	295,761	157,989	53.4	137,772	46.6	—	—
N.J.	2,773,111	1,363,324	49.2	1,385,415	49.9	24,372	0.9
N.M.	311,118	153,733	49.4	156,027	50.2	1,358	0.4
N.Y.	7,291,079	3,446,419	47.3	3,830,085	52.5	14,575	0.2
N.C.	1,368,966	655,648	47.9	713,318	52.1	—	—
N.D.	278,431	154,310	55.4	123,963	44.5	158	0.1
Ohio	4,161,859	2,217,611	53.3	1,944,248	46.7	—	—
Okla.	903,150	533,039	59.0	370,111	41.0	—	—
Ore.	775,462	408,060	52.6	367,402	47.4	—	—
Pa.	5,006,541	2,439,956	48.7	2,556,282	51.1	10,303	0.2
R.I.	405,534	147,502	36.4	258,032	63.6	—	—
S.C.	386,687	188,558	48.8	198,129	51.2	—	—
S.D.	306,087	178,017	58.3	128,070	41.7	—	—
Tenn.	1,051,792	556,577	52.9	481,453	45.8	13,762	1.3
Texas	2,311,670	1,121,699	48.5	1,167,932	50.5	22,039	1.0
Utah	374,981	205,733	54.8	169,248	45.2	100	—
Vt.	167,324	98,131	58.7	69,186	41.3	7	—
Va.	771,449	404,521	52.4	362,327	47.0	4,601	0.6
Wash.	1,241,572	629,273	50.7	599,298	48.3	13,001	1.0
W.Va.	837,781	395,995	47.3	441,786	52.7	—	—
Wis.	1,729,082	895,175	51.8	830,805	48.0	3,102	0.2
Wyo.	140,892	77,551	55.0	63,331	45.0	10	—
TOTAL	68,832,818	34,108,582	49.6	34,221,463	49.7	502,773	0.7

The foregoing page reproduces a final "official" tabulation of votes for the Presidency as reported by the Associated Press on December 17, 1960.

The "official" tabulation of Presidential votes in the United States is always something of a mystery, and the mystery becomes particularly puzzling in an election as close as this. Since the individual states, rather than the federal government, collect the votes and report them, the first national tabulations are always made by unofficial reporting groups. These unofficial "official" totals normally agree down to the tiniest percentiles—but in the last few digits of the grand totals they diverge.

I have used throughout this book the above tabulation of the Associated Press of December 17th, 1960.

For the record, however, it should be pointed out that the recount of the Hawaii vote was still in progress during the period of the AP tabulation and the final recount in Hawaii changed the balance in that state from a Nixon lead of 92,403 over Kennedy's 92,342 (as shown above) to a Kennedy lead of 92,410 over Nixon's 92,295. The table given above might therefore be altered to read that a total of 68,832,778 Americans voted for the Presidency; that Kennedy won 34,221,531 of these votes and Nixon 34,108,474; and that the Kennedy margin was 113,057 votes.

Since much of this book had already been sent to press by the time final, final "official" figures were available, I have for conformity used the December 17th Associated Press figures throughout. No amount of research yet gives an agreed-on final total for 1960. The highly reliable *Congressional Quarterly* set Kennedy's margin at 111,803 votes. The equally reliable official summary of the Republican National Committee sets Kennedy's margin at 112,801 votes. My adjusted figures above would indicate that Kennedy won by 113,057 votes. And, even as this final section of the book was being locked on press in early May another total was published—this time a "semiofficial-official" tabulation released by the Clerk of the House of Representatives—which puts Kennedy's margin at 119,450 votes out of a new grand total of 68,-836,385 ballots cast. Until the federal government sets up an official vote-counting agency these discrepancies will continue to baffle and annoy scholars and citizens alike. Most scholars in the field of American voting use as standard the voting compilations of the Governmental Affairs Institute prepared under the direction of Richard M. Scammon. These Scammon studies (*America Votes*) are superb, but they are not yet available for the election of 1960. Now that Mr. Scammon has been appointed Director of the Census by the Kennedy administration, one may hope that the census will, either officially or unofficially, interest itself in accurate reporting of the national vote.

This writer should commend to the reader also the researches of the Republican National Committee and their summary of the 1960 election called *The 1960 Elections*. Over the years I have found the research staff of the Republican National Committee the finest source of quick accurate tabulation and analysis of returns in Washington. It is remarkable that the high command of the Republican Party, which supports the finest research staff in Washington, should pay so little attention to their researches, while the Democratic National Committee, full of men who love politics, should have so primitive a research staff and resources.

Further oddities in the voting as noted by the AP were:

ALABAMA—Ballot splitting for electors who ran as individuals rather than as a slate made it impossible to determine the exact total vote. The 318,303 in the Kennedy column for Alabama represents the total polled by the top Kennedy-pledged elector. Top unpledged Democratic elector received 324,050. Six of the state's eleven Democratic electors ran unpledged, but later agreed to support Senator Harry F. Byrd, D., Va., in Electoral College.

MISSISSIPPI—Entire electoral vote of eight went to unpledged Democratic electors who later agreed to support Senator Byrd. They polled 116,248. Kennedy electors ran second and Nixon's third.

NEW YORK—Kennedy total includes 406,176 Liberal Party votes.

APPENDIX B

*FOLLOWING IS THE TEXT OF A STATEMENT
RELEASED BY GOVERNOR ROCKEFELLER
IN NEW YORK
SATURDAY, JULY 23, 1960*

The Vice President and I met today at my home in New York City. The meeting took place at the Vice-President's request.

The purpose of the meeting was to discuss the platform of the Republican Party. During the course of the meeting we discussed our views with Chairman Percy and other members of the Platform Committee by telephone. The Vice-President and I reached agreement on the following specific and basic positions on foreign policy and national defense:

1. The growing vigor and aggressiveness of communism demands new and profound effort and action in all areas of American life.
2. The vital need of our foreign policy is new political creativity—leading and inspiring the formation, in all great regions of the free world, of confederations, large enough and strong enough to meet modern problems and challenges. We should promptly lead toward the formation of such confederations in the North Atlantic Community and in the Western Hemisphere.
3. In the field of disarmament, we shall:
   a. Intensify the quest for better detection methods;
   b. Discontinue nuclear weapon tests in the atmosphere;
   c. Discontinue other tests as detection methods make possible; and
   d. Resume immediately underground nuclear testing for purposes of improving methods of detection.
4. In national defense, the swiftness of the technological revolution—and the warning signs of Soviet aggressiveness—makes clear that new efforts are necessary, for the facts of our survival in the 1950s give no assurance of such survival, in the same military posture, in the 1960s.
5. The two imperatives of national security in the 1960s are:
   a. A powerful second-strike capacity—a nuclear retaliatory power capable of surviving surprise attack to inflict devastating punishment on any aggressor, and
   b. A modern, flexible and balanced military establishment with forces capable of deterring or meeting any local aggression.
6. These imperatives require: more and improved bombers, airborne alert, speeded production of missiles and Polaris submarines, accelerated dispersal and hardening of bases, full modernization of the equipment of our ground forces, and an intensified program for civil defense.
7. The United States can afford and must provide the increased expenditures to implement fully this necessary program for

strengthening our defense posture. There must be no price ceiling on America's security.

The Vice-President and I also reached agreement on the following specific positions on domestic affairs:

1. Our government must be reorganized—especially in supporting the President in the crucial decision-making process—to cope effectively with modern problems and challenges. Specifically this calls for:
   a. Creation of a post to assist the President in the whole area of national security and international affairs;
   b. Creation of a post to assist in planning and management of domestic affairs; and
   c. Reorganization of defense planning and command to achieve, under the President, unified doctrine and unified direction of forces.
2. The rate of our economic growth must, as promptly as possible, be accelerated by policies and programs stimulating our free enterprise system—to allow us to meet the demands of national defense and the growing social needs and a higher standard of living for our growing population. As the Vice-President pointed out in a speech in 1958, the achievement of a five per cent rate of growth would produce an additional $10 billion of tax revenue in 1962.
3. Our farm programs must be realistically reoriented by:
   a. Finding and encouraging ways for our low-income farmers to become more productive members of our growing economy;
   b. At least doubling of the conservation reserve;
   c. Use of price supports at levels best-fitted to specific commodities in order to widen markets, ease production controls, and help achieve equitable farm income;
   d. Faster disposal of surpluses through an expanded "Food for Peace" program and allocation of some surplus to a stockpile for civil defense.
4. Our program for civil rights must assure aggressive action to remove the remaining vestiges of segregation or discrimination in all areas of national life—voting and housing, schools and jobs. It will express support for the objectives of the sit-in demonstrators and will command the action of those businessmen who have abandoned the practice of refusing to serve food at their lunch counters to their Negro customers and will urge all others to follow their example.
5. Our program for health insurance for the aged shall provide insurance on a sound fiscal basis through a contributory system under which beneficiaries have the option of purchasing private health insurance.
6. Our program for labor, while reaffirming our efforts to support and strengthen the processes of free collective bargaining, shall provide for improved procedures for the resolution of disputes endangering the national welfare.
7. Our program for education will meet our urgent educational needs by calling for prompt and substantial grant aid for school construction primarily on the basis of financial needs, under an equalization formula, and with matching funds by the states—including these further measures for higher education: grants-in-aid for such buildings as classrooms and laboratories, an expanded loan program for dormitories, expanded student-loan and

graduate fellowship programs and inauguration of a program of federal scholarships for the most able undergraduates.

These constitute the basic positions for which I have been fighting. If they are embodied in the Republican Party platform, as adopted by the Convention, they will constitute a platform that I can support with pride and vigor.

APPENDIX C

I am grateful for your generous invitation to state my views.

While the so-called religious issue is necessarily and properly the chief topic here tonight, I want to emphasize from the outset that I believe that we have far more critical issues in the 1960 election: the spread of Communist influence, until it now festers only ninety miles off the coast of Florida—the humiliating treatment of our President and Vice-President by those who no longer respect our power—the hungry children I saw in West Virginia, the old people who cannot pay their doctor's bills, the families forced to give up their farms—an America with too many slums, with too few schools, and too late to the moon and outer space.

These are the real issues which should decide this campaign. And they are not religious issues—for war and hunger and ignorance and despair know no religious barrier.

But because I am a Catholic, and no Catholic has ever been elected President, the real issues in this campaign have been obscured—perhaps deliberately in some quarters less responsible than this. So it is apparently necessary for me to state once again—not what kind of church I believe in, for that should be important only to me, but what kind of America I believe in.

I believe in an America where the separation of church and state is absolute—where no Catholic prelate would tell the President (should he be a Catholic) how to act and no Protestant minister would tell his parishioners for whom to vote—where no church or church school is granted any public funds or political preference—and where no man is denied public office merely because his religion differs from the President who might appoint him or the people who might elect him.

I believe in an America that is officially neither Catholic, Protestant nor Jewish—where no public official either requests or accepts instructions on public policy from the Pope, the National Council of Churches or any other ecclesiastical source—where no religious body seeks to impose its will directly or indirectly upon the general populace or the public acts of its officials—and where religious liberty is so indivisible that an act against one church is treated as an act against all.

For while this year it may be a Catholic against whom the finger of suspicion is pointed, in other years it has been, and may someday be again, a Jew—or a Quaker—or a Unitarian—or a Baptist. It was Virginia's harassment of Baptist preachers, for example, that led to Jefferson's statutes of religious freedom. Today, I may be the victim—but tomorrow it may be you—until the whole fabric of our harmonious society is ripped apart at a time of great national peril.

Finally, I believe in an America where religious intolerance will someday end—where all men and all churches are treated as equal—where every man has the same right to attend or not to attend the church of his choice—where there is no Catholic vote, no antiCatholic vote, no bloc voting of any kind—and where Catholics, Protestants and Jews, both the lay and the pastoral level, will refrain from those attitudes of disdain and division which have so often marred their works in the past, and promote instead the American ideal of brotherhood.

That is the kind of America in which I believe. And it represents the kind of Presidency in which I believe—a great office that must be neither humbled by making it the instrument of any religious group, nor tarnished by arbitrarily withholding it, its occupancy, from the members of any religious group. I believe in a President whose views on religion are his own private affair, neither imposed upon him by the nation or imposed by the nation upon him as a condition to holding that office.

I would not look with favor upon a President working to subvert the First Amendment's guarantees of religious liberty (nor would our system of checks and balances permit him to do so). And neither do I look with favor upon those who would work to subvert Article VI of the Constitution by requiring a religious test—even by indirection—for if they disagree with that safeguard, they should be openly working to repeal it.

I want a Chief Executive whose public acts are responsible to all and obligated to none—who can attend any ceremony, service or dinner his office may appropriately require him to fulfill—and whose fulfillment of his Presidential office is not limited or conditioned by any religious oath, ritual or obligation.

This is the kind of America I believe in—and this is the kind of America I fought for in the South Pacific and the kind my brother died for in Europe. No one suggested then that we might have a "divided loyalty," that we did "not believe in liberty" or that we belonged to a disloyal group that threatened "the freedoms for which our forefathers died."

And in fact this is the kind of America for which our forefathers did die when they fled here to escape religious test oaths, that denied office to members of less favored churches, when they fought for the Constitution, the Bill of Rights, the Virginia Statute of Religious Freedom —and when they fought at the shrine I visited today—the Alamo. For side by side with Bowie and Crockett died Fuentes and McCafferty and Bailey and Bedillio and Carey—but no one knows whether they were Catholics or not. For there was no religious test there.

I ask you tonight to follow in that tradition, to judge me on the basis of fourteen years in the Congress—on my declared stands against an ambassador to the Vatican, against unconstitutional aid to parochial schools, and against any boycott of the public schools (which I attended myself)—instead of judging me on the basis of these pamphlets and publications we have all seen that carefully select quotations out of context from the statements of Catholic Church leaders, usually in other countries, frequently in other centuries, and rarely relevant to any situation here—and always omitting, of course, that statement of the American bishops in 1948 which strongly endorsed church-state separation.

I do not consider these other quotations binding upon my public acts—why should you, But let me say, with respect to other countries, that I am wholly opposed to the state being used by any religious group, Catholic or Protestant, to compel, prohibit or persecute the free exercise of any other religion. And that goes for any persecution at any time, by anyone, in any country.

And I hope that you and I condemn with equal fervor those nations which deny their Presidency to Protestants and those which deny it to Catholics. And rather than cite the misdeeds of those who differ, I would also cite the record of the Catholic Church in such nations as France and Ireland—and the independence of such statemen as de Gaulle and Adenauer.

But let me stress again that these are my views—for, contrary to common newspaper usage, I am not the Catholic candidate for President. I am the Democratic Party's candidate for President, who happens also to be a Catholic.

I do not speak for my church on public matters—and the church does not speak for me.

Whatever issue may come before me as President, if I should be elected—on birth control, divorce, censorship, gambling, or any other subject—I will make my decision in accordance with these views, in accordance with what my conscience tells me to be in the national interest, and without regard to outside religious pressure or dictate. And no power or threat of punishment could cause me to decide otherwise.

But if the time should ever come—and I do not concede any conflict to be remotely possible—when my office would require me to either violate my conscience, or violate the national interest, then I would resign the office, and I hope any other conscientious public servant would do likewise.

But I do not intend to apologize for these views to my critics of either Catholic or Protestant faith, nor do I intend to disavow either my views or my church in order to win this election. If I should lose on the real issues, I shall return to my seat in the Senate, satisfied that I tried my best and was fairly judged.

But if this election is decided on the basis that 40,000,000 Americans lost their chance of being President on the day they were baptized, then it is the whole nation that will be the loser in the eyes of Catholics and non-Catholics around the world, in the eyes of history, and in the eyes of our own people.

But if, on the other hand, I should win this election, I shall devote every effort of mind and spirit to fulfilling the oath of the Presidency—practically identical, I might add, with the oath I have taken for fourteen years in the Congress. For, without reservation, I can, and I quote, "solemnly swear that I will faithfully execute the office of President of the United States and will to the best of my ability preserve, protect and defend the Constitution, so help me God."

INDEX

INDEX

Other SIGNET and MENTOR Books
You'll Want to Read

MEMOIRS *by Harry S. Truman:* Vol. I, Year of Decisions
Truman's own story of the crucial first year of the Presidency—the year that marked the end of World War II and the beginning of the Atomic Age.
(#Y2596—$1.25)

MEMOIRS *by Harry S. Truman:* Vol. II, Years of Trial and Hope
Truman discusses his most controversial decisions in this volume covering his administration during the first critical years of the cold war. (#Y2597—$1.25)

MANDATE FOR CHANGE—Volume I of The White House Years 1953-1956 *by Dwight D. Eisenhower*
Eisenhower's personal memoirs of his first term as President—crucial years that witnessed outbreaks in Indochina, the Suez, and Formosa; the era of McCarthyism; and the end of the Korean conflict.
(#Y2599—$1.25)

THE GREAT TREASURY RAID *by Philip M. Stern*
A blasting report on the abuses of America's laws with constructive proposals for revamping them on a more equitable structure. (#T2609—75¢)

THE COLD WAR AND THE INCOME TAX *by Edmund Wilson*
A world-famous critic brings to light some startling facts about the way our tax money is being spent.
(#P2475—60¢)

PARTIES AND POLITICS IN AMERICA *by Clinton Rossiter*
A colorful analysis of the major American political parties, which reveals the strengths and abuses at work upon the American political scene. (#MT741—75¢)

PRESIDENTIAL POWER *by Richard E. Neustadt*
A penetrating analysis of the function and authority of the Presidency and the politics of executive leadership. "The most brilliant and searching essay on the Presidency that we have had for a long time."—Arthur M. Schlesinger, Jr. (#MT708—75¢)

TO OUR READERS: If your dealer does not have the SIGNET and MENTOR books you want, you may order them by mail enclosing the list price plus 10¢ a copy to cover mailing. (New York City residents add 5% Sales Tax. Other New York State residents add 2% plus any local sales or use taxes.) If you would like our free catalog, please request it by postcard. The New American Library, Inc., P. O. ox 2310, Grand Central Station, New York, N. Y. 10017.